Landmark Trademark Cases in China

Landmark Trademark Cases in China

An In-depth Analysis

Wang Ze
Zhou Yunchuan
Zhou Bo
Rui Songyan
Xu Lin

Translator
Hui-Wen (Amy) Hsiao

Wolters Kluwer

Published by:
Kluwer Law International B.V.
PO Box 316
2400 AH Alphen aan den Rijn
The Netherlands
Website: www.wolterskluwerlr.com

Sold and distributed in North, Central and South America by:
Wolters Kluwer Legal & Regulatory U.S.
7201 McKinney Circle
Frederick, MD 21704
United States of America
Email: customer.service@wolterskluwer.com

Sold and distributed in all other countries by:
Quadrant
Rockwood House
Haywards Heath
West Sussex
RH16 3DH
United Kingdom
Email: international-customerservice@wolterskluwer.com

The title of Landmark Trademark Cases in China: An In-depth Analysis by Wang Ze, Zhou Yunchuan, Zhou Bo, Rui Songyan & Xu Lin is published and sold by Kluwer Law International, by permission of The Commercial Press, Ltd., 36 Wangfujing Street, Beijing, China, the owner of all rights to publish and sell same.

ISBN 978-90-411-6836-8

e-Book: ISBN 978-90-411-6842-9
web-PDF: ISBN 978-90-411-8950-9

About the Chief Editor

Dr. Wang Ze, Doctor of Law, is the Director of Beijing Justra Intellectual Property Center. He joined the Chinese Trademark Office under the State Administration for Industry and Commerce in 1997 and has been involved in reviewing and deciding trademark opposition cases. Dr. Wang subsequently held the following positions in China: Deputy Director of the Legal Affairs Division of the Trademark Review and Adjudication Board, Director of the General Affairs Division of the Trademark Review and Adjudication Board, and Deputy Secretary-General of the China Trademark Association. Dr. Wang was also appointed to serve as a committee member of the Expert Consultative Committee of the Beijing High People's Court and the managing director of the Association of the Copyright Society of China.

Dr. Wang has been chosen to serve as one of the national intellectual property experts in China by the State Intellectual Property Office. He was also a member of the drafting committee that was involved in the legislation of the third amendment to the Chinese Trademark Law. Dr. Wang has published monographs *The Modernization of China's Trademark Law: Theory, Institution and Practice*, and more than fifty articles in professional journals, such as *What Are the Differences Between Trademark Cancellation and Invalidation*, *Civil Reliefs and Limitations Available to Owners of Unregistered Trademarks in China*, *Trademark Infringement Discussion and Fair Use Defense*, and *Analysis on Trademark Concepts from the Perspective of a Mark and a Symbol*. Dr. Wang has also co-authored and published *Understanding and the Appropriate Application of the Trademark Law*.

About the Authors

Zhou Bo is a judge of Intellectual Property Division, Beijing High People's Court. He first worked as a judge of the People's Court of Shizhong District of Jinan, Shandong Province, and then as a judge of the No. 1 Intermediate People's Court of Beijing. Since 2010, Zhou Bo has handled more than 600 intellectual property cases in Beijing High People's Court, most of which are trademark cases. Some of the cases he handled have been selected as Yearly Top 10 Intellectual Property Cases of China by the Supreme People's Court of China. Judge Zhou is also an expert of Geography Indications in China.

Xu Lin, Doctor of Judicial Science, is Deputy Director of the General Offices of the National Committee of the Chinese People's Political Consultative Conference (CPPCC). Prior to joining CPPCC, Dr. Xu was the Deputy Director of General Affairs Division of Trademark Review and Adjudication Board (TRAB) of State Administration for Industry and Commerce. Working in TRAB for more than ten years, Xu Lin has rich experience in the review of trademark cases and has published many articles on trademarks in judicial journals, taking part in the third revision of *Trademark Law of the P.R.C.* and *Implementing Regulations of the Trademark Law of the P.R.C.*, the chief drafter of the *Trademark Review and Adjudication Rules* (2014), taking part in the revision of *Standards for Trademark Examination and Trial* (2016). Dr. Xu has been chosen to serve as one of the national intellectual property experts in China by the State Intellectual Property Office.

Rui Songyan is a judge of Beijing Intellectual Property Court. She received her LLB and LLM (Private International Law) from China University of Political Science and Law and her Ph.D. (Intellectual Property Law) from Chinese Academy of Social Science. She has heard intellectual property cases since 2002, and issued over 1,500 judgments, nine of which were selected as *Top Ten Typical Intellectual Property Cases of the Year* by Beijing High Court. She was awarded the honor of *Ten Beijing Outstanding Young Jurist* and *Beijing Elite Judge*.

Zhou Yunchuan, Of Counsel of Jones Day Hong Kong office, focuses primarily on intellectual property litigation and adversarial matters in China. Prior to joining Jones Day, Yunchuan was an IP Judge at the Supreme Court of China where he handled 300 cases involving patent, trademark, copyright, unfair competition, technical contracts, and antitrust. He also participated to draft judicial interpretations. Before that, Yunchuan was a Judge at Beijing No. 1 Intermediate Court where he adjudicated more than 700 IP cases. Special experiences have enabled him gain a deep and unique understanding of IP law and litigation in China. Yunchuan has authored and co-authored dozens of books and articles in the field of intellectual property law in China. He recently graduated from UC Berkeley Law School.

About the Translator

Hui-Wen (Amy) Hsiao is a Partner and Head of Asia Pacific Practice of The Sladkus Law Group. She focuses on helping Western brands to grow and protect their trademarks in China, and countries across Asia.

Amy is a US-educated trademark attorney with large private law firm and in-house experience. She is one of the few Western attorneys who truly specializes in trademark prosecution and enforcement in China and Asia. She has over 100 trademark opposition wins in China and has been successful in obtaining rare preliminary injunctive relief from the Chinese courts on behalf of well-known US brands. She has experience managing high-stake litigation and multi-million-dollar advertising campaign across Asia. She has advised clients on issues relating to Alibaba, Taobao, JD, Weibo, and WeChat.

Amy has ten years of large US law firm experience and has pursued cases through all levels of the Chinese judicial system, including the China Supreme Court. She has practiced in New York and Atlanta, worked in Shanghai, Beijing, Hong Kong, and Taipei. She travels frequently to Greater China and the Western world to provide strategy insight to businesses and training for legal/marketing teams. Amy has worked side by side with business teams from start-ups to Fortune 500 companies.

Amy is not only proficient in the US Law and the English language; she is also fluent in speaking/writing Mandarin Chinese, and experienced with the trademark system in Asia and the Western world. Amy publishes frequently in both English and Mandarin Chinese, in publications on both sides of the world.

Amy grew up in Taiwan and enjoys nature, travel, and any outdoor activity not involving heights.

Introduction

The Trademark Law promulgated in 1982 was the first intellectual property law of New China. With China's economic and social development and accession to relevant international treaties, the Trademark Law of China underwent three amendments, respectively, in 1993, 2001, and 2013. Now, China has established a modern trademark legal system that is both tailored to China's markets and aligned with the international practices. In China, the dual-track system of administrative enforcement and judicial protection has been established so as to offer a thorough and complete protection of the trademark rights.

This book, while giving a general introduction to the trademark protection system in China, selects twenty-six key cases in line with acquisition, maintenance, cancellation, invalidation, and protection of trademark rights in China. Through these selected cases, the authors of this book wish to provide a thorough and in-depth exploration on the scope and nature of China's trademark law to the readers, using experienced judges' and examiners' interpretations and opinions on issues such as the absolute grounds and relative grounds of nonregistrability of a trademark; determination of similarity between marks and goods; well-known trademark protection schemes; cancellation and invalidation of a registered trademark; types, constitutive components, defenses and protection measures of trademark infringement.

Table of Contents

Preface

On a hot summer night in August 2015, while I was watching *World News Tonight* in my tiny apartment in New York, the phone rang. It was my buddy Christopher calling from Beijing, China. Christopher, one of the top trial attorneys in China, and someone with whom I had worked for many years, had a challenge for me. The best legal minds in China – including judges from the intellectual property (IP) tribunals of the Intermediate Court, High Court, Supreme People's Court, deputy secretary-general of China Trademark Association, seasoned examiners from China's Trademark Appeal Board, and people serving as expert consultants to trademark litigation cases – had written a book. The book, which is partly a response to Western criticism about IP issues in China, identifies twenty-six landmark trademark cases in modern Chinese history. Rather than providing a two-sentence decision about each case, the authors delve into the relevant law in detail, review the relevant law, discuss how the specific facts were addressed by the Trademark Office/Appeal Board/Courts, and provide the rationale supporting each decision. In addition, the authors offer guiding "best practices" for each case. The book is, thus, a practice guide showing brand owners how to survive and prosper in China, a country long perceived as the Wild West in today's trademark world.

Since its publication, classes, seminars, and training sessions have been offered in big cities such as Shanghai and Beijing to study and discuss the book. Participants span the gamut from in-house counsel, to attorneys at private law firms, academics, researchers, examiners, and officials at different levels within trademark offices across China. The summarized cases involve well-known brands such as CHANEL, BMW, and LOUIS VUITTON, as well as the personal name rights of Kate Moss. While the book has stirred up a tremendous amount of conversation in China, the authors are also eager to share these discussions with people in the Western world. The people in China want to be understood; they want the world to understand why their courts rule A rather than B, decide to protect C instead of D.

There was just one problem – the book was written in Mandarin and thus inaccessible to most of the world.

Translating this work to ensure its accessibility was the challenge Christopher put to me during that call. After a six-month search, the publisher had been unable to find a suitable translator because the process requires a command of Chinese legalese as well as sufficient experience with Western versus Eastern legal concepts to be able to translate the underlying ideas in a persuasive and thoughtful way; so that the insights shared by a Chinese judge sipping tea in his office in Beijing can be understood or even appreciated by millions of American executives drinking their coffee across the Pacific Ocean wondering how to how to make money and also protect their companies' brands in China.

I was given a test case – it took me twenty hours to complete the first draft. I am grateful that the publisher was satisfied with my work and decided to engage me. In the last twelve months, I have spent most weekends in the library chewing, digesting, and translating these concepts so as to peel away the mystery surrounding trademark practice in China.

From this book, you will get answers to "hot" trademark issues in China. For example:

(1) Can one invalidate a registered trademark because it was obtained in bad faith?
(2) What are the criteria for recognizing a mark as a "well-known" trademark in China?
(3) Can one invalidate a trademark registration relying on a **well-known unregistered** trademark in China?
(4) Can one invalidate a trademark registration relying on a **well-known registered** trademark in China where the two marks cover different goods or services?
(5) Can a registered trademark be cancelled if it has become a **generic term**?
(6) Can one successfully oppose a trademark application based on **copyright**?
(7) Can one successfully invalidate a registered trademark if it is similar to a **trade name**?
(8) Can one successfully invalidate a registered trademark if it is similar to a **personal name**?
(9) Can one use a **design patent registration** as defense against a senior trademark registration?
(10) How are damage amounts calculated in trademark infringement lawsuits?

Each case is divided into three parts: (1) the facts; (2) the judgment; and (3) analysis and insight. Prior to diving into these cases, the chief editor provides a brief history of China's trademark system going back to the first recorded trademark more than 100 years ago, as well as the three amendments to the Trademark Law and the impact made by each.

The experience has been both humbling and educational. It has further clarified in my mind why a pair of glasses that fit me perfectly may not be a good fit for others. China needs a different pair of glasses tailored to its prescription.

For fifteen consecutive years, China has been the world's No. 1 country for receiving and processing the most trademark filings. The number of trademark filings in China in 2015 alone was one-third the trademark filings made around the globe. To put that in perspective, the number of trademarks filed in China in 2015 alone was three times more than the *combined* trademark filings made in the United States (second place) and the European Union (third place) over that same year. It is about time we understand how the trademark system works in China. What better way to gain insight into that system than to learn directly from the people who are making those decisions in China?

The Commentary Committee

Chief Editor:

Wang Ze Director of Beijing Justra Intellectual Property Center

Authors:

Wang Ze → Director of Beijing Justra Intellectual Property Center

Zhou Yunchuan → Judge at the Intellectual Property Tribunal of the Supreme People's Court

Xu Lin → Deputy Director of the General Offices of the National Committee of the Chinese People's Political Consultative Conference

Rui Songyan → Judge of Beijing Intellectual Property Court

Zhou Bo → Judge at the Intellectual Property Tribunal of Beijing High People's Court

Acknowledgments

CBI Financial Aid for Publication

CHAPTER 1
Outline of China Trademark Progress

I. Development of China's Trademark System.

A. Trademark System in the Late Qing Dynasty (From the End of the 19th Century to 1911).

China's use of trademarks can be traced back to the time around the Tang and Song dynasties. The earliest and most thorough use of a trademark (when the use is sufficient to represent a full grasp of the trademark concept) is the "White Rabbit" trademark. The White Rabbit trademark was used by the LIU family who had a needle shop in Jinan, Shandong Province. The White Rabbit trademark was used by the LIU family around the Song Dynasty (North Song). The White Rabbit Trademark was presented to the consumers along with stylized Chinese characters and colorful designs. In fact, the LIU family also came up with an advertisement tagline to go with the White Rabbit trademark. Underneath the White Rabbit mark, the LIU family inserted the following phrase: "Please recognize the white rabbit logo in the front of the shop; the white rabbit is a logo of our shop." The LIU family also came up with an advertisement tagline to accompany the White Rabbit mark: "The needles made by the LIU family were made of superior steel and with premium quality. The LIU family purchased superior steel specifically for this purpose only. The needles are convenient for household use. There is an additional discount if anyone would like to order the needles for wholesale, rather than personal use." Despite the above, China's formal trademark system incorporating modern concepts did not start until almost the end of the Qing Dynasty. The earliest record of China's modern trademark system was recorded in the unfair treaties between the Qing government and the Western countries after the Opium War. Specifically, the modern trademark concept was reflected in the Sino-British Mackay Treaty, which was signed on September 5, 1902 (the "***Treaty***") between the Qing Dynasty and the United Kingdom ("UK"). Section 7 of the Treaty stated that "the British government has the duty to protect the brands which are used by the Chinese merchants. It is important to protect the Chinese brands so as to prevent the British people from infringing or copying the Chinese merchants' brands. Similarly, the Qing government should also protect the brands of the British merchants so as to prevent infringement or copying of such brands by the Chinese people." In addition to the protection clause specified above, the Treaty stipulates that the Trademark Commissioners for the Southern and Northern ports of China should establish brand registration bureau in their respective jurisdictions; the bureau was to be charged with the responsibility to register commercial brands. Similar clauses can be found in the 1903 Sino-US Treaty and the 1904 Sino-Japan Treaty of Commerce and Navigation. In 1904, the Qing Dynasty government promulgated the "Trademark Registration Pilot Regulation" and the "Guidelines of the Trademark Registration Pilot Regulation" (collectively, the "***Regulations***"). The Regulations required registrations for any brands that the Chinese or foreign merchants would like to use and claim exclusive rights. The Regulations include detailed provisions with respect to trademark application process – such as whether or not priority should be claimed and the absolute grounds to refuse a trademark, trademark examination criteria, and specific situations that would constitute trademark infringement. Further, the Regulations include specific chapters to deal with trademark infringements where criminal prosecutions are possible. The Trademark Registration Pilot Regulation is therefore the first trademark statute in China's history; it marks the beginning of China's trademark legal system in modern times.

B. Trademark System During the Period of the Republic of China (1911–1949).

After the 1911 Revolution, China went through three separate governments: the National Government led by Sun Yat-Sen (1912–1914), the Northern Warlord Government (1914–1927), and the Nanjing National Government led by Chiang Kai-shek (1927–1949). The Northern Warlord Government published "Trademark Law" on May 4, 1923. On May 8, 1923, the Northern Warlord Government published the "Detailed Guidelines to Implement the Trademark Law." The Trademark Office, then under the Agriculture and Commerce Ministry, published the first Trademark Gazette on September 25, 1923. In 1927, the Nanjing National Government established the National Trademark Registration Bureau to handle trademark registration and related matters. On December 21, 1928, the Nanjing National Government separated the division that was in charge of trademark registration from the National Registration Bureau; an independent trademark office was established to handle trademark registration matters and this office belonged to the Industry and Commerce Ministry. On May 6, 1930, the Nanjing National Government published its version of the Trademark Law; it subsequently published the "Detailed Guidelines to Implement the Trademark Law" on December 30, 1930. The Trademark Law and the Guideline went into effect on January 1, 1931. In this version of the Trademark Law (published by the Nanjing National Government), it establishes the principle of voluntary trademark filing, the principle concerning good-faith senior use of a trademark and the fair use defense. The Trademark Law also establishes more thorough legal proceedings to handle trademark oppositions, trademark cancellations, and invalidations. After the civil war in 1949, this version of the Trademark Law was implemented in Taiwan; it was later amended in 2012.

C. Trademark System after the Founding of New China (1949-Present).

1. The Trademark System Before China's Reform and Opening-Up.

In 1949, the People's Republic of China ("PRC") was established ("***New China***"). New China abolished all rules and regulations that were established by the Nanjing National Government. New China therefore marked a new chapter in China's history because its legal systems were established based on the principles of socialism. The State Council of New China published "Trademark Registration Interim Regulations" on August 28, 1950, to protect the exclusive rights associated with a trademark for the industrial and commerce industry ("***Interim Regulation***"). This Interim Regulation is therefore the first trademark regulation established by New China that is specifically related to trademarks. The Interim Regulation includes thirty-four articles, and formally establishes the principle of voluntary trademark filing, and offers protection to the exclusive rights of one's trademarks. The Interim Regulation also stipulates the primary elements for a mark to be considered a trademark, texts and designs that are *not* allowed to be registered as a trademark, and establishes a system for trademark application, examination, registration, and trademark opposition. In the same year, the Financial, Political and Economic Committee under the State Council published the Detailed Guidelines to Implement the Interim Trademark Regulations. On January 17, 1957, the State Council issued an opinion titled "the Opinion of the Central Administration of Industry and Commerce Concerning the Comprehensive Trademark Registration System" (the "***Opinion***"). The Opinion confirmed the trademark registration principle – i.e., all marks used on the products that are manufactured or produced by any enterprise and credit union must be registered; any trademark that has not been approved for registration should not be used. On April 10, 1963, the State Council published the "Trademark Management Regulations" (the "***1963 Management Regulations***") and simultaneously abolished the Interim Regulation. The Trademark Management Regulations highlighted the importance of a proper trademark management system; it was written with the goal to enhance corporate promise and the quality guarantee of the underlying products. The Trademark Management Regulations reaffirmed the compulsory trademark registration system; the regulations in fact only comprised of fourteen articles after extensive deletion and revision of the original articles. On April 25, 1963, the Central Administration of Industry and Commerce published the "Detailed Guidelines to Implement the Trademark Management Regulations" (the "***Guidelines***"). The Guidelines set up the review process before a trademark is approved for registration; in other words, any trademark application documents should first be examined and approved by the respective company's management department. Furthermore, the trademark application paperwork must be accompanied by detailed specifications relating to the quantity and quality of the underlying products, and such specifications must be filled out in accordance with the industry standards. Furthermore, the specification chart must be reviewed and certified by the company's management department. With respect to the system governing the assignment of a trademark (which covers the registration, change, transfer, revocation, cancellation, and reissuance of a trademark registration certificate), the paperwork should be filed to the local administration of industry and commerce at the city or county level where the company is located. Once the paperwork has been examined and approved by the local authorities, it can then be transferred to the Central Administration of Industry and Commerce's further review and approval.

2. The Development of Trademark System after China's Reform and Opening-Up.

a. The Legislation of the Current Trademark Law.

Before the enactment of the current Trademark Law, China had been using the Trademark Management Regulations that were published in 1963. During China's cultural revolution (an extremely tumultuous time for roughly ten years in China's history), the political and social movement also took a great toll on the trademark system. During this time, there was no central governing system to manage the trademark registrations and to govern trademark use in China. In September 1978, the State Administration of Industry and Commerce was established; each trademark office was then tasked with the responsibility to conduct an audit and review of its respective trademarks in its jurisdiction. All trademarks in China then underwent the registration process at the end of 1978. In November 1979, China finally reestablished its national trademark registration system. Despite the fact that the country finally resumed and unified its registration system, the Management Regulations promulgated in 1963 were no longer adept at meeting the social and economic demands. The 1963 Management Regulations were especially inadequate in the following areas:

(1) The 1963 Regulations did not contain any provisions to protect the trademark owners' exclusive rights.
(2) The compulsory registration system was not able to meet the economic demands at that time.
(3) The 1963 Regulations did not have a thorough system to review and approve a trademark application.
(4) The 1963 Regulations did not have specific legal guidance in respect to foreign trademarks that were seeking registration in China.

In light of the above, and for the purposes of developing the socialist commodity economy and bettering the socialist legal system, the State Administration of Industry and Commerce conducted extensive research and drafted the "Trademark Law of the People's Republic of China" ("***Draft***"). The Draft was written by considering and giving deference to both the domestic and international legal customs. On August 23, 1982, the Trademark Law was adopted at the 24th Session of the Standing Committee of the Fifth National People's Congress ("NPC") and the Law went into effect on March 1, 1983. The 1983 version of the Trademark Law was the first intellectual property ("IP") law after the birth of New China. It even predates the China's Patent Law (1984), Copyright Law (1990), and the Anti-unfair Competition Law (1993).

The 1982 Trademark Law establishes and reaffirms some basic principles of the China's trademark system; most of these principles are still in use and followed today. Some primary examples include:

(a) China's trademark system seeks to strike a balance between protecting the exclusive rights of a trademark owner and consumers' interests.
Article 1 of the 1982 Trademark Law explicitly stipulates that "*this Law is enacted for the purposes to improve the administration of trademarks, to protect the exclusive rights associated with a trademark, to encourage manufacturers (or producers) to ensure the quality and quantity of their products so as to protect their business reputation, to protect consumer interests, and thereby, to promote the economic development of a socialist market economy.*" The trademark system is designed based on the trademark rights and the protection thereof; the system also seeks to protect consumer interests. The above principle is not only reflected in the fact that the Law requires the product manufacturers or service providers to ensure the quality and quantity of the underlying products and services, but is also reflected in the trademark examination system where an examiner must conduct a trademark clearance prior to approving a trademark. The system is in place so as to ensure a junior mark shall not be approved for registration if it is identical or closely similar to a senior mark; the step is to prevent a coexistence of similar marks in the marketplace. In other words, China's trademark system has mechanisms in place to prevent or minimize the possibility of consumer confusion.

(b) The first-to-file system and trademark registration principle.
The trademark registration principle refers to the acquisition of the trademark rights which must be based on the fact that the mark at issue has been approved for registration. Under the trademark registration principle, China's Trademark Law applies and strictly enforces the first-to-file principle. This principle determines the ownership of a trademark and awards the ownership to the party that first files for the trademark at issue.

(c) The principle of voluntary registration.
The modern Trademark Law applies the principle of voluntary registration, instead of the compulsory registration principle promulgated in the 1963 Management Regulations. Following the voluntary principle, it is up to each trademark user to determine whether or not it should also file for a registration for the mark it is using. Despite the above, the Law also outlines some exceptions to the voluntary registration principle. For example, Article 5 of the Trademark Law states that "for goods that can only be used in connection with a registered trademark as required by the government, the

owner must register the respective trademark. Such products are not allowed for sale in the marketplace unless a trademark registration has been granted."

(d) The principle of a unified trademark registration system and the principle that the management of trademarks is handled by different departments within a state government.

The principle of a unified trademark registration system refers to the fact that the registration process concerning all trademarks in China must be handled by one office only: the Trademark Office of the State Administration for Industry and Commerce ("SAIC") under the State Council. Any individual or company that is seeking to obtain the exclusive rights associated with a trademark must file relevant paperwork with the Trademark Office. The management of trademarks (including both pending and registered marks), however, is primarily delegated to different departments under each local administration of industry and commerce. In other words, each local government is responsible for the management and imposing administrative penalties concerning trademark violations such as infringing acts that occur within its jurisdiction.

b. Key Points in the Three Amendments to the Trademark Law.

There have been three amendments to the Trademark Law since its inception in 1982; each amendment took place in 1993, 2001, and 2013 respectively. The Law had undergone major changes during these amendments, not only in terms of quantity (from 43 articles to 73 articles in the third Amendment), but also in terms of substantive updates to the content of the Law.

First Amendment:

The main reason driving the First Amendment was because China had reaffirmed the socialist market economy system (with the continued "opening-up" and reform of the New China) and the society needed an updated law so as to keep abreast with the international legal system. The need became particularly acute when China joined the Paris Convention for the Protection of Industrial Property in 1985 and the Madrid Agreement Concerning the International Registration of Marks in 1989. Changes were called for so as to continue the progress of China's socialist market economy and to improve the ever-changing trademark legal system. After more than three years of extensive research and analysis (as well as countless drafting and revisions), the State Administration of Industry and Commerce completed an Amendment to the Trademark Law in 1993. The draft was approved during the executive meeting of the State Council and then delivered to the Standing Committee of the NPC for approval. On February 22, 1993, the 30th Session of the Standing Committee of the Seventh National

People's Congress approved the "Decision to Amend the Trademark Law of the People's Republic of China" ("***1993 Amendment***"). Major revisions to the Law in the 1993 Amendments are as follows:

(1) Service marks were formally recognized and protected as trademarks.
With the rapid development of the Chinese economy, especially with the rise of the third industry, the society had seen a tremendous growth of service marks; accordingly, more companies were demanding protection of such marks in China. The government also took notice that the Paris Convention for the Protection of Industrial Property required its Member States to recognize and protect service marks. In light of the above, the 1993 Trademark Law explicitly states that "any provision discussed in this Law shall also apply to service marks."

(2) Geographical references should not be approved as a trademark.
This provision was added in the 1993 Amendment because the Law then took into consideration that geographic reference lacked distinctiveness and should not be approved as a trademark. Such marks were likely to cause consumer confusion because they were not able to enable consumers to clearly identify the source of the underlying products or services. For example, there were situations where different companies in the same region were engaged in manufacturing the same types of products. However, if one of the companies was allowed to use the geographic reference that was shared among all the similarly situated companies as its trademark, it would put the other companies at a disadvantage and cause a monopoly.

(3) Unregistered trademarks were offered limited protection; additional provisions were added to address bad-faith registrations.
The trademark office was aware of the fact that some companies obtained trademark registrations through fraud or other improper means; the office was also aware of the fact that there were trademark squatters in the marketplace which secured trademark registrations of marks that were first put to use by a third party, and the marks had obtained a certain level of fame through such use. Despite the general awareness and understanding of the market reality, there were no specific provisions in the 1982 Trademark Law that could be utilized to discourage such bad-faith registrations. The 1993 Trademark Law addressed this issue by adding a specific provision – "the trademark office can cancel a trademark registration if the registration is obtained by fraud or other improper means; a third party (either a company or an individual) can also file a cancellation action with the Trademark Review and Adjudication Board ("TRAB") to have the registration cancelled."

(4) Broadening trademark infringement categories.
The 1993 Trademark Law further categorized and detailed acts that would constitute a trademark infringement as follows:

(i) using the same or similar trademark as a third party's registered trademark without prior authorization and the use involves the same or similar products;
(ii) selling products with the knowledge that such products were counterfeits of a registered trademark;
(iii) manufacturing or selling a registered trademark without authorization;
(iv) causing other damages to a third party's exclusive rights of its registered trademark.

Second Amendment:

The primary reason driving the Second Amendment to the Trademark Law was due to China's formal participation in the WTO (World Trade Organization); despite the WTO membership, China's legal system had a great discrepancy with the system articulated in the "Agreement on Trade-Related Aspects of Intellectual Property Rights" (**TRIPs**). Furthermore, the Trademark Law at that time was no longer adept to address and keep up with the rapidly growing market economy. The government was aware of the changes in the society and the urgent need to improve China's trademark legal system so as to better protect the exclusive rights associated with a trademark. In order to assist China and the society to get used to becoming a WTO member country and to meet the requirements articulated in TRIPs, a consensus was formed to push for the Second Amendment to the Trademark Law. In 2001, the SAIC considered feedback and input from experts, practitioners, and academia, summarized market experience to date, and took into account the TRIPs provision and drafted an amendment to the Trademark Law. The draft was approved during the State Council's executive meeting and was later submitted to the Standing Committee of the NPC for review. On October 27, 2001, the 24th session of the 9th NPC Standing Committee approved the "Decision to Amend China's Trademark Law." This amendment was driven primarily by the government's promise to update its trademark law as a condition for China to join the WTO; it had promised to update China's Trademark Law so that it was kept up to date with the framework set forth in TRIPs. The amendment was therefore "reactive" in nature. Key revisions in the Second Amendments are summarized as follows:

(1) Broadening the scope of trademark components.
The 1993 Trademark Law limited the elements of a trademark to words, devices, and the combination of word and devices only. The Second Amendment formally recognized a three-dimensional mark and a color combination mark as trademarks.
(2) Incorporating specific provisions to protect a well-known trademark.
The 1993 Trademark Law did not include specific provisions to protect a well-known trademark. The Detailed Guideline to Implement the Trademark Law only included some limited protections to trademarks that were "familiar to the public." Up until then, the protection of a well-known trademark was

mainly relied on the Provisional Measures on the Recognition and Administrative Control of Well-known Trademarks issued by SAIC in 1996. In this amendment, it specifically offered special protection to well-known trademarks. For example, an unregistered yet well-known trademark is afforded protection so that a third party could not use such a mark on the same or similar goods; similarly, a well-known registered trademark is protected not only with similar goods but also on different or dissimilar goods. In other words, a third party is not allowed to use a registered well-known mark on products that are dissimilar or different from the designed goods without authorization.

(3) Incorporating specific provisions concerning collective marks, certification marks, and geographical indications.

This Amendment specifically provided that registered trademarks not only included the traditional trademarks, but also included product trademarks, service marks, collective marks, and certification marks. The Amendment also offered definitions to help consumers understand the concept related to a collective mark and a certification mark. The Amendment also incorporated definitions and specific protection provisions to geographical indications, and thereby provided legal basis to protect such marks in China.

(4) Incorporating provisions relating to priority.

This Amendment incorporated two priority concepts: "priority based on the initial trademark application" and "exhibition priority." The time limit to claim priority is six month.

(5) Incorporating provisions for judicial review.

The 1993 Trademark Law adopted the administrative adjudication principle. In other words, the administrative office's review of trademark refusals, cancellations, and invalidation actions should be final. This Amendment introduced the judicial review concept. In other words, anyone that is dissatisfied with the decision made by the TRAB is able to institute an administrative litigation with the court (by listing the TRAB as a defendant). The appeal will then be reviewed by the people's court.

(6) Incorporating provisions for statutory damages.

It is clearly stipulated in the Trademark Law that "the amount of damages for a trademark infringement case should either be the actual losses suffered by the right holder as a result of the infringement or the profits the infringer has generated as a result of the infringement; the amount of damages should also include reasonable expenses that the trademark owner has incurred to stop the infringement." Meanwhile, the amended Trademark Law offers clear provisions concerning the statutory damages. Such statutory damages are defined as follows: "when it is difficult to determine the actual losses suffered by the trademark owner, or the profits obtained by the infringer, the court shall award damages up to RMB 500,000 (about USD 73,000) depending on the specifics of the case."

Third Amendment:

With the development of the socialist market economy in China, trademarks are playing a more and more important role in the today's society. However, the provisions stated in the 2001 Trademark Law were no longer able to meet the needs of the society. Due to the urgent need to update the Trademark Law so as to keep pace with the progression of the society, a further amendment of the Trademark Law was demanded by the society. The key issues relating to the 2001 Trademark Law were primarily reflected in the following areas:

(1) The procedures to register a trademark was overly complicated.
(2) The timeline for the Trademark Office or the Appeal Board to approve and determine a trademark registration was overly long.
(3) Bad-faith registrations and unfair competitions had evolved to be serious concerns to China's trademark system.
(4) The Trademark Law was inadequate to effectively address infringing applications and registrations.
(5) The Trademark Law did not offer adequate protection to the exclusive rights associated with a trademark.

After considering the above-listed inadequacies in the 2001 Trademark Law as well as practical experience and feedback from the practitioners and the academia, the SAIC drafted the Trademark Law of People's Republic of China ("***Examination Draft***").

The Examination Draft was submitted to the State Council for approval on November 18, 2009; it was approved by the 223rd executive meeting of the State Council on October 31, 2012. After the approval, the Examination Draft was approved by The 4th session of the 12th Standing Committee of NPC on August 30, 2013. There were two primary distinctive features of the Examination Draft:

(1) The Amendment was proactive in nature rather than reactive. The Amendment was prompted by China's desire to conform with the international treaties in which China had been a party and further tailored to China's specific social and economic realities.
(2) This Amendment focused on some specific key issues that had been threatening the integrity of China's trademark system. These key issues included: the overly complicated procedural requirements to obtain a trademark registration; standardizing trademark application and use requirements; maintaining a fair and competitive market; enhancing the protection to the exclusive rights associated with a trademark; ensuring and efficiently protecting the legitimate interests of the trademark holders.

The key issues in this Amendment included the following:

(1) Sound mark is recognized. The Trademark Law now formally recognizes sound/voice as a sufficient component for a trademark.
(2) Specific provisions have been incorporated to discourage trademark squatting. The Amendment seeks to discourage trademark squatting in China by incorporating the following provision: "*the registration and use of a trademark should follow the principle of good faith.*" This provision is now the fundamental principle in China's Trademark Law. In addition, the Amendment incorporated some provisions to discourage trademark squatting by listing some specific relationship between the parties. For example, Article 15 Section 2 states that "where an applicant is seeking to register a mark that is identical or similar to an unregistered trademark which has been put to use in connection with the same or similar products, such a trademark shall not be approved for registration if the following criteria are met: (1) an opposition is raised by the party which first put the unregistered mark to use; (2) there is sufficient evidence to prove that the two parties are in a contractual, business or other relationship and the trademark applicant either knows or should have known about the prior unregistered mark through such relationship; (3) agency or representative relationship is an exception to (2)."
(3) Specific types of infringement have been incorporated into the Trademark Law.
The amended Trademark Law clearly states that the following action also constitutes trademark infringement: an action that is "internationally designed to either assist a third party to infringe the exclusive rights associated with a registered trademark or help a third party to execute the infringement."
(4) Punitive damages are incorporated. The 2013 Trademark Law states that "the ultimate damage amount in an infringement lawsuit can be increased to more than one time (but no more than three times) of the statutory damage."
(5) The maximum statutory damage is raised. The statutory damage ceiling is raised from RMB 500,000 (about USD 73,000) to RMB 3,000,000 (about USD 437,400).
(6) Burden of proof on the trademark owner is reduced.
The Amendment now states that "for the purpose of determining the amount of damages, where the account books and information related to the infringement are controlled by the infringer, and where the trademark owner has presented as much evidence as practically possible, the court may order the infringer to submit such account books and information. If the infringer refuses to submit such account books and information, or submit false documents relating to such information, the court may determine the amount of damages based on the claims and evidence submitted by the trademark owner."
(7) Unfair competition recognized in the tradename situation.
In situations where a company is using a third party's trademark as its trade name without authorization (i.e., either using a registered trademark or an

unregistered but well-known mark), the court is allowed to recognize unfair competition if such use is capable to cause consumer confusion. Anti-unfair Competition Law of PRC is now applicable to such a situation.

(8) A trademark that has become a generic term can be cancelled.
The Amendment now incorporates a provision which states that a registered trademark can be cancelled so long as the trademark has become a generic term.
Any organization or individual can petition to have a registered trademark cancelled if such a mark has become a generic term through the trademark registrant's improper use or that the registrant fails to properly police and enforce its rights in connection with its products once the mark is registered. The cancellation stands even though the mark may have sufficient distinctiveness when it was first filed. This provision is aimed to prevent monopoly from the trademark owner whose mark has already become a generic term; allowing anybody to claim exclusive rights over a generic term will certainly disrupt the market order.

(9) Trademark owner's nonuse of the mark at issue is now recognized as a valid defense against trademark infringement.
Prior use has been formally established in the Amendment as one of the conditions for the trademark owner to recover damages. Specifically, Article 64 of the 2013 Trademark Law states that "when the trademark right holder is seeking infringement damages and the alleged infringer points out that the trademark holder has not put the mark to use, the court can then require the trademark holder to provide actual use evidence relating to the mark at issue. The use evidence can be anywhere in the last three years from the time the alleged infringer raises this argument. If the trademark holder is not able to provide actual use in connection with the mark in the last three years, or that it is not able to prove actual losses as a result of the alleged infringement, the alleged infringer shall not be liable for any damages."

(10) Protection to prior use recognized.
The Amendment includes a provision to protect prior use. Specifically, when an applicant is seeking to register a mark that is identical or closely similar to a third party's unregistered trademark, and both marks cover the same or similar products, the registrant's rights are limited. In other words, the registrant does not have the right to prevent the third party from continuing using its senior unregistered mark in connection with the original products so long as the unregistered mark has obtained a certain level of fame prior to the application date of the registered trademark. This provision is seeking to strike a balance between a senior user and trademark registrant's rights; it grants a senior user the right to continue using the mark so long as the use conforms with the original scope of use. A strict prohibition on any use once a third party has obtained trademark registration would not be fair to the senior user of the mark.

c. Administrative Rules.

On March 10, 1983, the State Council promulgated the Detailed Implementation Guidelines to the Trademark Law of the People's Republic of China ("***Detailed Guideline***") to facilitate the implementation of the Trademark Law. The Detailed Guideline had been amended four times in 1988, 1993, 2002, and 2014 respectively; it also later changed its name to Regulations to Implement the Trademark Law. In addition to the above, in order to resolve various practical issues to implement the Trademark Law, the SAIC had issued and subsequently revised a series of administrative rules throughout the years. These administrative rules included the following:

(1) Provisions on the Determination and Protection of Well-Known Trademarks (2014). These provisions aimed to provide consistency to the recognition of well-known trademarks in China and the scope of protection.
(2) Administrative Measures Concerning the Registration of Collective Marks and Certification Marks (2003). These provisions provided clear guidance on how to apply for collective marks and certification mark; they also discussed management details.
(3) Measures for the Implementation of Madrid International Registration of Marks (2003). These provisions discussed details relating to applications of international registrations where China was designated as the country of origin and applications for territorial extension to China.
(4) Rules relating to the Review and Examination of Trademarks (2014). They provided consistencies to the trademark review and examination process.
(5) Rules relating to the Administration of Trademark Agency (2010). These rules focused on maintaining a good order among the trademark agency industry and ensuring legitimate interests of clients and trademark agencies.

d. Judicial Interpretations Issued by the Supreme People's Court of China.

Following the amendments to the 2001 Trademark Law, the Supreme Court issued a series of judicial interpretations related to the trademarks in China; these interpretations were based on judicial practice on cases relating to the review, examination, and determination of trademark rights and infringements. The key points in the judicial interpretations are outlined below:

(1) Interpretation of the Supreme People's Court Concerning the Application of Laws in Trial Cases Relating to Civil Trademark Disputes (2002). This judicial interpretation is meant to ensure that trademark disputes will be correctly reviewed and examined by the lower courts in China.
(2) Interpretation of the Supreme People's Court on the Application of Laws for Preliminary Injunctions and Evidence Preservation Before the Filing of a

Lawsuit (2002). This interpretation aims to provide guidance relating to injunction and evidence preservation for trademark dispute cases.

(3) Provision of the Supreme People's Court Relating to the Civil Trademark Disputes to Resolve Conflicts between Registered Trademarks, Company Trade Names, and Prior Rights (2008). This provision is to provide guidance on civil trademark cases concerning the conflicting rights among the registered trademarks, enterprise names, and prior rights.

(4) Interpretation of the Supreme People's Court on Several Issues Concerning the Application of Law to the Civil Disputes Trial Cases Over the Protection of Well-Known Trademarks (2009). This interpretation is to protect well-known trademarks in trademark infringement cases.

(5) Interpretation of the Supreme People's Court concerning the Jurisdiction Issues over Trademark Cases and the Applicants of the Law After the Amendments to the Trademark Law (2014). This interpretation aims to resolve jurisdiction issue and the application of law issues on trademark dispute cases.

Apart from the judicial interpretations discussed above, the Supreme Court had published a series of judicial policies that were aimed to provide guidance on the review and examination of trademarks. The primary ones are outlined below:

(1) Opinion of the Supreme People's Court on Several Issues concerning Intellectual Property Trials and How Such Trials Could Serve the Overall Social Objectives Under the Current Economic Situation (2009). This Opinion aims to provide guidance to the lower courts so as to review intellectual property cases in a way that would allow the society to effectively respond to the international financial crisis. The goal is to promote a stable and rapid economic development.

(2) Opinion of the Supreme People's Court on Several Issues Concerning the Trial of Administrative Cases Involving the Authorization and Determination of Trademark Rights (2010). This Opinion considers trial experience and aims to bring consistencies to the review and examination of administrative cases in China involving the determination of trademark rights.

With decades of hard work and tireless efforts, China has already established a modern trademark legal system that conforms with the international rules, but in the meantime also preserves the unique and specific features that are appropriate to China's culture and society. We have also witnessed the change in overall society in that the public are now paying more attention to the protection to trademarks and brands. There were only 84,047 validly registered trademarks in China at the end of 1982 – this includes 70,899 domestic registered trademarks. When the Trademark Law became effective on March 1, 1983, there had only been 19,000 trademark applications. The trademark application number quickly rose to 1,881,500 in 2013. The total number of trademark as 14,257,000 at the end of June 2014; the number of accumulative trademark registrations was 9,075,000, and the number of validly registered trademarks was 7,611,000. Given that China has been the number one country in the world in terms of the number of trademark filings for many years, China is therefore *the* top country for trademarks in the world.

II. Characteristics/Key Features of China's Trademark System.

A. Comprehensive Review Principle.

China conducts substantive examination of any trademark application filed with the China Trademark Office. Following the rules in the Trademark Law and the Regulations to Implement the Trademark Law, the Trademark Office will first examine each application to see if it has complied with the formality requirements. The Trademark Office will then review each application based on its application date to conduct further search, analysis, comparison, and investigations if necessary. The Trademark Office will then issue a decision on the preliminary examination results either to approve or reject the trademark application.

The substantive examination contains two parts: (1) examination on the absolute grounds; and (2) examination on the relative grounds. The examination on the absolute grounds includes the following: (a) whether or not the application would disrupt the public order and negatively impact the public's interests once it is registered; (b) whether or not the application has sufficient distinctiveness; (c) whether or not the three-dimensional mark is functional. The examination on the relative grounds is to determine whether or not the application at issue is similar to prior registrations or pending applications. Since the review process in China is comprised of substantive examinations on the absolute grounds as well as on the relative grounds, China therefore follows the comprehensive review principle.

During the review process of the Third Amendment to the Trademark Law, the SAIC once decided to cancel the examination based on the relative grounds. In the 2007 draft titled "Draft: Seeking Opinion and Input to the Trademark Amendments," the council expressed the following views to support the cancellation of such review:

(1) Trademark right is a civil right which is in essence a form of a private right. The protection of a private right should be separately asserted by the relevant parties through valid legal proceedings, such as oppositions, cancellations, invalidations, and trademark infringement lawsuits. The dispute involving whether or not a junior application is similar to a senior trademark and therefore the registration should be denied is essentially a dispute involving two parties' private rights. The review process involving the relative ground means that the administrative authorities are inevitably involved, and in fact, taking a proactive role, in resolving the dispute concerning private rights. This process essentially transforms the administrative authorities to babysit the senior right holder and allow the

government to intervene and protect private rights. In other words, the process compels the authorities to get involved and interfere with the private rights.

(2) The relative ground review inevitably prolongs the overall review time of a trademark application. This process also imposes and adds a tremendous workload on the examiners. Over the years, the Trademark Office in China has experienced an extreme shortage on the number of qualified examiners due to the rapid increase in trademark applications in this country. The relative ground review process is rather time consuming, which results in the extreme backlog and the overly long period of time for a mark to mature to registration.

Despite the above, which advocated for the cancellation of relative ground review process, there was of course a different view supporting the continuation of this process. Supporters pointed out that through the relative ground review process, the administrative authorities not only protected the private rights but also ensured the overall public's rights to prevent consumer confusion. This process was therefore helpful and significant in maintaining a fair market. If the examination on the relative ground is cancelled, it is likely to cause disruption in the marketplace and unfair competition. The authorities decided to maintain the review on relative grounds, which thereby preserved the comprehensive review nature of China's system.

In accordance with the Trademark Law, a trademark application will be reviewed on its compliance with the absolute grounds and the relative grounds. The examination on the absolute grounds involves the following aspects:

(1) whether the trademark application violates some restrictions discussed in Article 10 of the Trademark Law;
(2) whether the trademark application is sufficiently distinctive as discussed in Article 11 of the Trademark Law;
(3) whether a three-dimensional mark consists symbols that are functional as discussed in Article 12 of the Trademark Law.

Examination on the relative grounds refers to the examination whether or not an application conflicts with senior trademarks that are either registered or have already been approved for registration (Article 30 of the Trademark Law). In addition, according to Article 31 of the Trademark Law and Article 19 of the Regulations to Implement the Trademark Law, where two or more applicants apply for the identical or similar trademarks, and such trademarks cover the same or similar goods, the application that is filed first should be approved for publication. If, however, the two marks are filed on the same day, each applicant shall submit evidence of prior use. Specifically, both applicants will have thirty days to provide use evidence upon receipt of a notification from the Trademark Office; the party that uses the mark first will have its mark approved for publication. The other party's application will be refused. If, however, neither applicant has ever used the mark, or if that use started on the same day, the Trademark Office will request that the parties negotiate among themselves.

The parties may negotiate and provide a written report to the Trademark Office within thirty days of receipt of the notification. For parties that refuse to negotiate or fail to reach a common ground through negotiation, the Trademark Office will simply determine the prior rights by drawing lots. If one party fails to participate in the lot drawing after being notified by the Trademark Office, it should be deemed to have voluntarily abandoned its application. The Trademark Office shall notify the party regarding its abandonment in writing.

B. Legal Framework Is in Place to Prevent Bad-Faith Filings.

China's Trademark Law adopts the first-to-file principle and the registration principle. In fact, under China's system, the applicant is not required to provide use evidence or declare its intent to use the mark upon filing. The fact that the system does not require use evidence therefore creates a backdoor for bad-faith filings. Trademark squatting is a classic form of unfair competition seeking to obtain the exclusive rights associated with a trademark; such trademarks are likely to have a serious impact on the market order. After three amendments, China's Trademark Law has established a legal framework to address bad-faith filings.

First, in the general rules of the Trademark Law, it states that the application or use of a trademark should follow the principle of good faith. This means all applications in China must observe the good-faith principle; any application filed in bad faith shall be refused.

Second, the amended Trademark Law affords protection to well-known trademarks. Protection also extends to unregistered yet well-known trademarks; however, such protection is limited to the same or similar products. Article 13 Section 2 of the Trademark Law forbids the use and registration of a trademark application which copies, reproduces, or translates a third party's registered well-known trademark in China. Article 13 Section 3 states that *"junior mark should be refused for registration or be prevented from being used if it covers different or unrelated products so long as the junior mark is a copy, imitation or translation of third party's mark that is already a registered well-known trademark in China, and the use/registration of the junior mark would lead to consumer confusion, and could potentially damage the legitimate rights of the owner of the well-known mark."*

The protection scope in respect to dissimilar or different products of a well-known trademark that has been registered in China should correspond to its level of fame. For a well-known trademark which is widely known to the general public and has been registered in China, the court shall give it a broader protection when deciding whether or not the protection should extend to dissimilar or different products.[1] In other words, the scope of protection should match its fame level rather than being restricted to the similarity analysis of the products involved. The above Law should be

1. Article 11 of Opinions of the Supreme People's Court on Several Issues Concerning the Trial of Administrative Cases Involving the Authorization and Determination of Trademark Rights.

helpful to discourage any bad-faith filings that are seeking to trade on the good will or commercial reputation of the senior well-known mark.

Third, the amended Trademark Law incorporated explicit provisions to discourage bad-faith filings. Specifically, the provisions are in place to refuse applications where the reason the applicant knows or should have known about the mark is through its relationship with the senior right holder - such a relationship includes contractual relationship or business partnership. Article 15 of the Trademark Law states that "*where an agent or a representative applies for registration of its principal's trademark (or the mark of the party being represented) without authorization, the trademark shall not be registered and shall be prohibited from use upon when the principal or the represented party raises an opposition. When an applicant is seeking to register a mark that is identical or similar to an unregistered trademark that has been put to use by a third party in connection with the identical or similar products, the application shall be denied once the senior right holder raises an opposition – it should be regarded as a bad faith application so long as the relationship between the parties is such that the only reason the applicant knows or should have known about the mark is through its special relationship with the principal or the represented party. The relationship described herein should include any other situations not discussed in the preceding paragraph relating to the contractual or business relationship.*"

The "opposition" term mentioned in the above two provisions should be broadly interpreted. In other words, it should be restricted only to the trademark oppositions; but rather, any actions that challenge a trademark application or registration such as invalidation actions. In some cases, the principal-agent relationship is not established until the mark at issue is filed. In other words, the agent is seeking a trademark application during the negotiation stage while the parties are still working out the details to form a principal-agent relationship. Despite the fact that the principal-agent relationship is not established prior to the application of the disputed mark, the mark should still be deemed a bad-faith application by the trademark agent or representative. Anyone who conspires with the trademark agent or trademark representative to seek registration of the principle's mark can also be regarded, by law, as the "trademark agent" or "trademark representative." The determination involving the "accomplice," whether or not it should also be considered as the "trademark agent" or "trademark representative," can be inferred based on the exact relationship between the trademark agent/representative and the accomplice.[2]

Fourth, the amended Trademark Law incorporated explicit provisions to prevent a third party from registering a trademark that has been put to use by a third party and has obtained a certain level of influence. According to Article 32 of the Trademark Law, "an applicant shall not register a mark that has already been put to use and has obtained a certain level of influence among the relevant public." The phrase "certain

2. Article 12 of Opinions of the Supreme People's Court on Several Issues Concerning the Trial of Administrative Cases Involving the Authorization and Determination of Trademark Rights.

level of influence" refers to a senior party's use of the mark in China, and the use is extensive enough that the mark is known to the relevant public.[3]

Fifth, the amended Trademark Law incorporated provisions to prevent a party from obtaining the trademark registration through other improper means. Article 44 Section 1 of the Trademark Law states that "a trademark registration shall be invalidated by the Trademark Office if it is obtained through fraud, deception, or other improper means; any other organization or individuals may also invalidate such a mark by filing an invalidation action with the Trademark Review and Adjudication Board." To determine whether a trademark is registered by "other improper means" as discussed in the Law, the factors to consider should not be limited to fraud or deception. The phrase should be broadly interpreted to include any means that might also threaten the integrity of the trademark registration system, have the possibility to negatively impact public interest, monopolize the public resources, or the fact that a trademark registrant obtains the trademark registration solely for the purpose to obtain illegitimate interests for the applicant.[4] In practice, the "improper means" prong is usually satisfied so long as the petitioner can provide evidence showing that the trademark applicant has sought to register third parties' unique or famous marks (either in a large quantity or for multiple times) and the evidence shows that the applicant is seeking trademark registrations not for legitimate use but for its own illegitimate interests. The above is likely to be seen a gesture to disrupt the order in the trademark system and has therefore satisfied the "other improper means" prong.

C. Different Resolution Mechanisms Are Established Based on the Underlying Conflicting Rights so as to Resolve Trademark Conflicts and Disputes.

Conflicts of rights include conflicts between registered trademarks, as well as conflicts between registered trademarks and other prior rights. Article 30 of the Trademark Law states that "if a trademark registration does not comply with relevant provisions of this Law, is identical or similar to another party's registered or published trademark and covers the same or similar goods, the Trademark Office shall reject the application and shall not publish the trademark." Article 32 of the Trademark Law states that "a trademark application shall not negatively impact a third party's existing rights." Article 45 of the Trademark Law further states that *"if a registered trademark violates Article 30 or Article 32 of the Trademark Law, a senior right holder or an interested party can petition to the Trademark Review and Adjudication Board to invalidate the registered trademark; the invalidation action must be filed within the first five years from the registration date of the disputed mark. Any party that is dissatisfied with the Appeal Board's decision can institute an action with the people's court. The court action must be filed within the first thirty days upon receipt of the notice. The people's court shall notify the opposing party in the prior proceeding with the Appeal Board to*

3. Article 18 of Opinions of the Supreme People's Court on Several Issues Concerning the Trial of Administrative Cases Involving the Authorization and Determination of Trademark Rights.
4. Article 19 of Opinions of the Supreme People's Court on Several Issues Concerning the Trial of Administrative Cases Involving the Authorization and Determination of Trademark Rights.

participate in the lawsuit as a third party." The above articles establish the invalidation proceeding in China's trademark system. The system is set up in a way that the TRAB can review and examine the validity of the registered trademark, which can be further reviewed by the people's courts.

Despite the above, the Law does not provide any clear, specific guidance regarding the following: (a) how to resolve the conflicting interests that arise from commercial use of a registered trademark; (b) how to structure the examination process concerning the validity of a trademark; and (c) how to set up the civil dispute procedures to effectively review infringement cases. There are primarily two approaches to addressing the above issues.

The **first approach** focuses on the administrative procedures. In other words, one must go through the administrative procedure and the following judicial procedures first to determine the validity of rights. Once the above procedures have been concluded, the action can then be reviewed through the civil infringement dispute procedures to resolve the dispute. In the Summary of Symposium of Certain Courts' Handling Intellectual Property Trials Across the Country (No. 65; 1998), the Supreme People's Court ("SPC") once pointed out that "*in cases involving intellectual property disputes or other civil disputes, the people's courts should hold off reviewing any issues relating to conflict of rights. Disputes relating to conflict of rights should first be resolved by the parties by filing an application with the relevant authorities in accordance with the relevant procedures (for example, such conflict can be resolved through invalidation or cancellation procedures). Once the relevant departments have resolved the conflict of rights between the parties, the people's courts can then review the intellectual property infringement dispute or other civil disputes. In situations where the parties' conflicting rights cannot be determined or resolved via cancellation or invalidation proceedings, or that the relevant authorities have failed to make a timely decision (without justification) within three months after the filing of the petition, the court shall continue to protect the parties' legitimate civil interests which are granted by law or based on the parties' prior use of the mark at issue. The courts can rely on the good faith principle as stated in the General Principles of Civil Law, and the principle of honesty and integrity to continue protecting the parties' legitimate civil rights as stated above.*"

The **second approach** does not put the administrative procedures as the priority. Supporters of this view hold that the essence of a dispute involving conflicting rights is basically a civil dispute; it is therefore part of the scope involving the civil infringement dispute and can be reviewed directly by the courts (i.e., there is no need for the court to hold off reviewing the case until the relevant authorities have first made a ruling to resolve the conflicting rights). For example, in the 2002 Beijing High People's Court's Answers to the Conflicting Interests Involving the Use of Trademarks and Company's Tradenames, the High Court pointed out the following: "*the People's Courts are entitled to review cases involving the dispute between the use of a trademark and a company's trade name in accordance with Article 108 of the Civil Procedure Law.*" The Supreme Court finally offered its opinion in 2008. In the regulations issued by the Supreme Court concerning "Certain Issues relating to the Court's Review of Civil Disputes Involving Registered Trademarks, Company's tradenames, and Other Prior Rights," the Court provided different rules in respect to each situation:

(1) If the conflict is between two registered trademarks, such dispute should first be reviewed by the relevant administrative procedures. Article 1 Section 2 of the Provision Law states "*if the plaintiff files a lawsuit on the ground that the defendant's registered trademark in connection with its approved goods is identical or similar to that of plaintiff's trademark, the court shall notify the plaintiff to file the complaint first with the relevant administrative authorities to resolve the dispute. The court can rely on Article 111(3) of the Civil Procedure Law to handle the process as listed above.*" However, the people's court should hear the following cases: the plaintiff files a lawsuit on the ground that the defendant has used its registered trademark beyond the original approved scope of goods or services; or the lawsuit involves the complaint that the defendant has altered the prominent characteristics of its trademark and thereby infringes upon the plaintiff's trademark rights. Article 1 Section 2 of the Provision Law allows the people's court to handle such cases as discussed above. Article 1 Section 2 states: "*if a lawsuit is filed on the ground that a registered trademark used by other party has exceeded the original scope of approved goods, or the other party has altered the prominent feature of its trademark (by splitting or combining the mark with other elements) and is therefore confusingly similar with the plaintiff's mark, the people's court shall accept the case.*"

(2) If the conflict is between a registered trademark and other existing prior rights, the adjudication of such a conflict does not need to be first resolved through the administrative proceedings. According to Article 1 Section 1 of the Provision Law, "*the people's court shall accept and hear the cases if the plaintiff files the lawsuit on the ground that the other party's use of words or designs has infringed upon the plaintiff's copyright, design patent, its tradename rights or the plaintiff's other senior rights and if the lawsuit satisfies the criteria as outlined in Article 108 of the Civil Procedure Law.*" The "prior rights" discussed in the above includes not only the numerated rights such as copyright, design patent, and trade name right; the following rights should also be included in the definition of prior rights: the plaintiff's senior rights in terms of its specific product name, packaging design, and decoration of the plaintiff's famous products, as well as the plaintiff's domain name rights and any other senior rights. If the defendant has already put the disputed mark to commercial use, the people's court can still hear such a case involving the disputed mark even though the disputed mark has not yet been approved for registration by the Trademark Office. On the other hand, the people's court should refuse to hear cases if the defendant's mark has not been approved for registration or put to any commercial use. The SPC pointed out the following in its 2005 No. 2 letter: "*when a trademark application remains pending, if the plaintiff is challenging the defendant's pending trademark on the ground that the defendant's use of paperwork during the application process has infringed upon the plaintiff's copyright, the action should first be resolved through procedures*

discussed in the Trademark Law such as oppositions. When a party has already filed an opposition and the opposition remains pending, and the plaintiff raises a civil lawsuit on the ground that the art work used in the defendant's paperwork in seeking a trademark application and the application has been preliminarily approved for publication, the people's court shall not accept such a case."

D. Emphasize on the Management in Connection with Trademark Use and Trademark Registration.

China has always put a lot of emphasis on the management of trademark use and trademark registration; the system is designed to promote trademark registration and thereby have the party using the trademark to offer certain guarantee for the quality and quantity of the underlying products. Article 1 of the 1982 Trademark Law states that: "this Law is designed with the following purposes in mind: improve trademark management, ensure consumers' interests, encourage manufacturers to ensure the quality of their products for the purpose of their commercial reputation, protect consumer interests, and to promote the development of China's socialist commodity economy." Article 1 therefore sets the objective of the Trademark Law as follows: "improve trademark management." Subsequent amendments throughout the years have always maintained the same objective. Article 1 of the 2013 Trademark Law states: "*this Law is designed with the following objectives: strengthen trademark management, protect the exclusive rights associated with a registered trademark, encourage manufacturers and business operators to ensure the quality and quantity of their products for the purpose of their commercial reputations, protect the interests of consumers, manufacturers and business operators, and to promote the development of the socialist market economy.*" The Trademark Law's objective to "improve/ strengthen trademark management" is reflected in the following:

(1) The Trademark Law requires the trademark user to take responsibility for the quantity and quality of the underlying products. Article 7 of the Trademark Law states: "*the user of a trademark shall be responsible for the quality and quantity of the underlying goods associated with such a mark. The administrative departments for industry and commerce at all levels shall, through proper management and administrative of trademarks, discourage and prevent fraud designed to target consumers.*"

(2) The Trademark Law has a specific chapter, Chapter VI, designed for the management of trademarks. This Chapter states "*if a trademark registrant alters its registered trademark while it is in use, changes the name or address of the registrant, or any other information associated with the registration of such a trademark, the local administrative department for industry and commerce shall order the registrant to make correction within a prescribed*

time limit; the Trademark Office shall cancel the registered trademark if the registrant fails to comply with the requests within the prescribed time limit."[5]

(3) The Trademark Law has designated any disputes related to cancellation that occur during the prosecution stage of a trademark as part of trademark management; the Trademark Office is tasked to handle such disputes. If the parties are not satisfied with the decision made by the Trademark Office, the parties can pursue an appeal with the TRAB. This process therefore leads to a unique feature in China's trademark law system where a trademark cancellation action will be reviewed by two administrative levels. Article 49 Section 2 of the Trademark Law states "when a registered trademark has become a generic name of a product or the trademark registrant has failed to use its mark for three consecutive years without justification, any entity or individual may petition to the Trademark Office to cancel such trademark registration. The Trademark Office shall make a decision within nine months after receiving the application to cancel a trademark." Article 54 of the Trademark Law states: *"if a party is not satisfied with the cancellation decision made by the Trademark Office (either to cancel or to maintain a registered trademark), the party can pursue an appeal with the Trademark Review & Adjudication Board within 15 days after receiving the decision. The Trademark Review and Adjudication Board shall make a decision within nine months after receiving the appeal and shall notify the parties its decision in writing. If, for some reasons, the Appeal Board needs to extend the timeline to review the case, the extension needs to be first approved by the administrative department for industry and commerce under the State Council and the extension shall not exceed three months. If the parties are not satisfied with the decision made by the Trademark Review and Adjudication Board, the parties may institute an action with the people's court within 30 days after receiving the decision."*

(4) The Trademark Law seeks to strengthen the management of trademarks by empowering the Trademark Office with the authority to invalidate a registered trademark by itself. If a party is not satisfied with the invalidation decision made by the Trademark Office, it can pursue an appeal with the TRAB. This has led to the same two level administrative review of a trademark invalidation case even though the Trademark Office has the full authorities to cancel a trademark registration by law. Article 44 of the Trademark Law states: "The Trademark Office can cancel a trademark registration if the mark violates Articles 10, 11, or 12 of this Law, or its registration is obtained by fraud or any other improper means." Article 44 goes on to say "The Trademark Office shall notify the interested parties regarding its cancellation decision in writing. If the interested parties are

5. Article 49 Section 1 of the Trademark Law.

> not satisfied with the cancellation decision made by the Trademark Office, the parties may pursue an appeal with the Trademark Review and Adjudication Board within fifteen days after receiving the cancellation notice. The Trademark Review and Adjudication Board shall make a decision within nine months after receiving the review application and shall notify the parties in writing. If, for any reason that the review period needs to be extended, the request to extend shall first be approved by the administrative department for industry and commerce under the State Council and can be extended up to three months. If any interested parties are not satisfied with the decision made by the Trademark Review and Adjudication Board, the parties can institute an action with the people's court within thirty days upon receipt of the notice."

E. "Dual-Track System" Offers Administrative and Judicial Protections to Safeguard the Exclusive Rights Associated with a Trademark.

A dual-track approach is in place to protect the exclusive rights of a registered trademark. The "dual-track" approach refers to the coexistence of an administrative law enforcement body and judicial protection. The dual-track protection system was already acknowledged and confirmed by the 1982 Trademark Law so as to improve trademark managements, protect the exclusive rights associated with a trademark, fully empower the industrial and commercial administrative office to execute the law, and to address the inadequacies from trademark trials alone. Article 39 of the 1982 Trademark Law states that a party can request the administrative department for industry and commerce at or above the county level where the infringement takes place to handle its infringement dispute; such a party can also ask people's court directly to address the trademark infringement matter. The relevant administrative department for industry and commerce not only has the right to order the alleged infringer to immediately stop the infringing act, but also the right to request the alleged infringing party to compensate the party for the loss due to the infringement. The administrative department for industry and commerce can also impose a monetary fine if it deems the underlying infringement as particularly egregious. If any party disagrees with the decision made by the administrative department, it can institute a lawsuit with the people's court within fifteen days upon receipt of the notification from the administrative department. The administrative department for industry and commerce can ask the people's court to enforce its decision if the interested party fails to seek a timely appeal and refuses to comply with the department's decision. The above was modified during the second amendment to the Trademark Law. Specifically, the 2001 Trademark Law modified the authorities originally reserved for the administrative authorities where it was used to be able to determine the compensation amount and compel enforcement. The department's authority in this regard was taken away because trademark infringement dispute was a form of civil dispute; empowering the administrative department for industry and commerce to decide the compensation amount and to enforce its decision was contradictory to the international customs. The 2001

Trademark Law therefore modified the authorities granted to the departments; the relevant articles were modified and stated as follows: "*upon request from an interested party, the administrative department for industry and commerce may conduct a mediation to discuss the compensation amount among the parties. If the parties fail to reach an agreed amount for infringement, the parties may institute a lawsuit with the people's court based on the Civil Procedure Law of the People's Republic of China.*" The 2013 Trademark Law kept the dual-track approach to protect the exclusive rights associated with a trademark by offering protection from the administrative departments and judicial courts. Article 60 of the 2013 Trademark Law states that "for any disputes involving infringement against the exclusive rights associated with a registered trademark, the parties may resolve the dispute through negotiation. If the parties are not willing to negotiate or the negotiation has failed to yield a satisfactory result for the parties, the trademark registrant or an interested party may institute an action with the people's court or request assistance from the administrative department for industry and commerce." Article 60 of the 2013 Trademark Law therefore offers three approaches for a party seeking relief in a trademark infringement case:

- Negotiation – the interested parties can negotiate among themselves to resolve the dispute. This approach is neither compulsory nor is it a necessary step in order to resolve the dispute. Rather, it is a voluntary and advisory provision; the negotiation should be carried out in a way where both parties are equal and interested in seeking to resolve the dispute this way.
- Court Action – the right holder can institute an infringement action with people's court, seeking judicial intervention and protection. This is also a common approach in the world to resolve trademark infringement disputes.
- Administrative Department – the right holder can also request assistance from the administrative authorities for industry and commerce for administrative protection and enforcement. In addition, Article 61 of the Trademark Law states that the administrative authorities for industry and commerce shall have the authority to investigate trademark infringement disputes and impose penalties. Accordingly, the administrative authorities for industry and commerce is entitled to take proactive actions in addressing any infringements during its daily routine market inspection; the administrative authorities do not need to hold off its action against infringements until the incident is first raised by the interested parties.

The dual approach offering protection from both administrative and judicial departments has played a positive role in strengthening the protection of trademark rights and maintaining fair competition and order in the marketplace in China. Addressing an infringement through the administrative channel has its advantages; for example, the administrative department is equipped with the enforcement team, has a full enforcement network, and its procedures are more straightforward and the complainant usually has a lesser burden of proof than that in a court proceeding. In fact, due to the efficiency and the relatively short time frame of an administrative proceeding, it has become the main force in China to address trademark infringements. For example, in 2013, the administrative authorities for industry and commerce in China investigated and handled a total of 81,300 cases involving counterfeit and infringement complaints. The value of these cases was around RMB 1.121 billion (roughly USD 162 million). The administrative authorities in 2013 raided 1,786 factories and stores involving the manufacturing or retailing of counterfeits. In the same year, the administrative authorities transferred 477 suspected criminal cases to the judicial authorities as required by Law which totaled around RMB 280 million (roughly USD 40 million). Addressing a trademark infringement dispute through the judicial channel has a number of drawbacks; for example, the complainant is required to navigate through much more complicated procedural requirements, and the complainant has to bear a higher burden of proof than that of an administrative proceeding. It usually takes the court a longer period to time to issue a decision and the cost is much higher than an administrative proceeding. Despite the above, the advantage of a judicial proceeding lies in its finality - decisions made by the courts are final and the courts have the authorities to award damages. In 2013, the local people's courts in China received a total of 23,272 new cases involving trademark dispute; this is a 17.45% increase compared to the same period in 2012.

F. Specialized IP Court Jurisdictions in Beijing, Shanghai, and Guangzhou to Offer Judicial Protection to Trademark Rights.

To further strengthen the judicial protection of intellectual property rights ("IPR"), to effectively protect the legitimate interests of the right holders and to maintain public interests, the Standing Committee of the Twelfth National People's Congress approved the Decision of the Standing Committee of the National People's Congress to Establish Intellectual Property Courts in Beijing, Shanghai, and Guangzhou (the "***Decision***"). The Standing Committee's approval of the Decision was made in accordance with the Constitution Law and the Organization Law of People's Courts. The Decision was adopted at the 10th session on August 31, 2014. The Decision outlines the specific requirements in respect to each court's jurisdiction and the review process. The key points include:

(1) IP court is the Court of First Instance; they shall have the jurisdiction over a civil or administrative IP case involving patents, new species of plants, integrated electronic circuit layout designs, technical know-how, or other cases that are more technical in nature. The Beijing IP Court should be the first instance court hearing any administrative appeal cases involving the granting or confirmation of any IPR. An IP court shall exercise inter-regional jurisdiction over cases specified in the first paragraph hereof. Inter-regional jurisdiction in the province (or municipality directly under the Central Government) where an IP court is located may be first implemented within three years from the establishment of the IP court.

(2) An IP court should hear any appeals concerning local court's civil or administrative judgments involving copyright, trademark, or any other IPR.
(3) The high courts where the IP courts are located should hear any appeals concerning decisions made by such IP court.

The Decision of the Standing Committee of the National People's Congress on Establishing Intellectual Property Courts in Beijing, Shanghai, and Guangzhou was published on October 31, 2014; it became effective on November 3, 2014. On November 6, 2014, Beijing took the lead and established the first IP court in China, the Beijing IP Court. Since then, Beijing IP Court has begun reviewing intellectual civil and administrative cases which would have been originally reviewed and decided by the Beijing Intermediate People's Courts.

III. Administrative Enforcement and Judicial System under China's Trademark System.

A. Law Enforcement System under SAIC of the PRC

With respect to trademark management and administrative law enforcement, the administrative departments for industry and commerce adopt the principle of unified registration and delegate the responsibilities among various management departments. The administrative department has a two-tier review system to handle trademark disputes.

Unified registration means that the Trademark Office under the SAIC shall be responsible for all the trademark registration work within the country. Anyone who is interested in registering a trademark shall file an application with the Trademark Office. Article 2 Section 1 of the Trademark Law states "the Trademark Office under the State Administration for Industry and Commerce is in charge of trademark registration and administration across the country." Article 4 Section 1 of the Trademark Law states that "any natural person, legal entity, or organization that is interested in obtaining exclusive rights associated with a trademark in connection with its goods or services during its course of business operations shall file an application with the Trademark Office." According to the Notice by the General Office of the State Council for the Issuance of the Interior Institutions of the Main Functions of the State Administration for Industry and Commerce and the Staffing Requirements (No. 88; 2008) (issued on July 11, 2008) and the Notice on Divisions (Departments, Bureaus, Offices) of the Interior Institutions of the Main Functions and the Staffing Requirements issued by the SAIC on September 8, 2008 (No. 195; 2008), the Trademark Office is tasked with the administrative responsibilities in connection with registration and management of a trademark. Specifically, the Trademark Office is responsible for handling the following: registration and management of all trademarks; protecting the registrant's exclusive rights associated with its registered trademark; reviewing trademark infringements; strengthening the recognition and protection of a well-known trademark; being responsible for the registration, recordal, and protection of special symbols and official marks; studying, researching, and publishing trademark information according to the relevant law; providing information services to the public as well as the government for the purpose of determining proper policies; and implementing trademark strategies across China.

Management by different departments means the local administrative departments of industry and commerce should be responsible for the following: (a) the supervision and management of trademark use within their respective jurisdiction; (b) reviewing and imposing punishments to trademark infringements ex officio or pursuant to the requests filed by the trademark owner; and (c) protecting the legitimate rights and interests of trademark owners and consumers. Each local administrative department for industry and commerce is further divided in three levels: the provincial level, the city level, and the county/district level. Each level is equipped with the trademark management department. Accordingly, the trademark administrative law enforcement system in China is divided to four levels: three levels within the local administrative department, and the Trademark Office under the SAIC. The local administrative departments for industry and commerce are mainly responsible for the following:

- trademark management in connection with the registrant's altering of the registered trademark, registrant information, address, or any other registration information without authorization during the registrant's use of the trademark;
- management in connection with actions in respect to any use of an unregistered trademark or a registered trademark that is in violation of the Trademark Law;
- investigating and imposing punishment to trademark infringement either ex officio, pursuant to a complaint filed by the right holder, or a report from the general public.

There are two levels of administrative reviews in handling trademark registration disputes. The first level of administrative review refers to the Trademark Office's decision for the underlying alleged trademark infringement. If the interested parties are not satisfied with the Trademark Office decision, the parties can pursue an appeal with the TRAB. The review by the Appeal Board is the second level of administrative review. Article 2 Section 2 of the Trademark Law states that "The Industrial and Commercial Administrative Department of the State Council establishes the Trademark Review and Adjudication Board to review trademark dispute matters." Accordingly to the Notice on Divisions (Departments, Bureaus, Offices) of the Interior Institutions of the Main Functions and the Staffing Requirements issued by the SAIC's on September 8, 2008 (No. 195; 2008) and the 2013 Trademark Law, the TRAB is primarily responsible for the handling of trademark dispute matters and making proper decisions in accordance with the law. The Appeal Board's specific responsibilities include the following:

- Reviewing trademark examination appeals when a respective trademark application is refused by the Trademark Office and the applicant decides to challenge the decision.
- Reviewing trademark opposition, cancellation, and invalidation appeals when the interested parties decide to challenge the decision made by the Trademark Office.
- Reviewing trademark invalidation requests filed by any interested parties.
- Reviewing administrative proceedings when the interested parties decide to challenge the decision made by the Trademark Office.
- Reviewing and determine a trademark as a well-known trademark in China pursuant to the relevant Law.
- Participating in the administrative litigations with respect to trademark review cases pursuant to the relevant Law.

B. Customs Administrative Law Enforcement System.

Customs protection for the trademark rights refers to the protection afforded to the exclusive rights associated with a trademark for the imported and exported goods offered by customs in accordance with the relevant laws and regulations in China. China's customs is a government agency that is charged with supervision and management of all goods going in and out of the PRC. Customs are set up with vertical management structure. Customs' basic responsibilities include: customs control, revenue collection, prevention against smuggling, collecting, and compiling import-export statistics, tax collection, IPR protection, and port managements. Customs in China are further divided to three different levels: General Administration of Customs ("***GACC***"), directly affiliated customs, and subordinate customs. The GACC is a ministry-level institution that is directly under the supervision of the State Council of the PRC. GACC manages and directly supervises all customs in China; GACC has also set up overseas offices in the European Union ("EU"), the Russian Federation, the United States of America ("USA" or "US"), etc. There are presently 46 directly affiliated customs (Guangdong Sub-Administration, GACC Supervising Offices in Tianjin and Shanghai, 41 customs that are directly affiliated under GACC and two customs academic schools), 600 subordinate customs and branch offices, and close to 4,000 customs clearance supervision spots. There are around 50,000 customs officers (including antismuggling customs police officers) across China.

According to the Regulation of the People's Republic of China On Customs Protection of Intellectual Property Rights, there are two ways that a trademark registrant can seek protection from customs. The first is an ex-officio protection; the second is protection by application. "Ex-officio protection," also known as "the proactive protection by customs," refers to the fact that customs and customs officials are authorized by Law to actively investigate and seize any infringing goods (imported or exported) without having to rely on any specific applications by the individuals or organizations. "Protection by application," also known as "passive protection," refers to the situations where customs only initiates its investigation and the enforcement procedures upon its receipt of specific applications by the trademark holders.

Any trademark owner that is interested in seeking customs protection should first file and record its application with the GACC. In other words, pursuant to the relevant provisions stated in the Regulation of the People's Republic of China on the Customs Protection of Intellectual Property Rights, any trademark owners interested in seeking protection from customs must file an application with the GACC for recordal. The application should include the following information: its imported/exported products, the infringing imported/exported products, its trademark rights, the status of its trademark(s). Once the above information has been properly recorded with customs, customs officials can then take an active role in protecting the relevant products and its IPR in their daily supervision and inspection duties.

According to Article 10 of the Regulation on Customs Protection of Intellectual Property Rights, once an application has been approved by the GACC, the application remains valid for ten years. Any trademark registrant can renew its recordal with customs by filing an application six months prior to the expiry of the ten-year period. Each renewal recordal is valid for yet another ten years. Any recordal with customs will become immediately invalid if the trademark owner fails to timely renew the trademark recordal, or the underlying trademark is no longer protected by the relevant laws or administrative regulations. Customs recordal is definitely not a precondition for the trademark owner to enjoy protection from customs; a recordal with customs, however, will definitely facilitate the protection process so that the officials will have an easier time to inspecting the imported and exported goods that might directly impact the registered trademark.

When it comes to the trademark owner's attention that some counterfeit products will soon be exported to or imported from China, the trademark owner can file an application with customs to detain such products. Upon the filing of the application, the trademark owner should also be prepared to provide a security bond with customs within the prescribed period of time; the value of the bond should be equal to the value of the seized products. Such a bond will then serve as a compensation for the loss suffered by the shipping party or the recipient party due to the trademark registrant's improper application, along with the storage, maintenance, and disposal fees associated with the seized products. Article 24 of the Measures of the General Administration of Customs for the Implementation of the Regulation of the People's Republic of China on the Customs Protection of Intellectual Property Rights states that any trademark owner that has filed and recorded its application with customs can provide letters of guarantee issued by banks or other financial institutions upon GACC's approval. The letter of guarantee will then serve as a general security when it seeks protection of its IPR with customs. If a trademark owner has already provided a general security with customs, and the security has been approved by the GACC, the trademark owner does not need to provide any additional security or bond until December 31 of the same year when it requests customs to seize suspected infringing imported or exported products in connection with its recorded IPR. The above is stated in Article 16 of the Regulation on the Customs Protection of Intellectual Property Rights.

A trademark owner is entitled to report and proactively request customs to seize any suspected imported/exported products so long as such products bear the trademark that has already been recorded with the GACC. The customs officials can then investigate the suspected shipment. On the other hand, when customs discover some imported/exported products that are suspected of trademark infringement and the underlying trademark has already been recorded with the GACC, the officials should notify the trademark owner of such suspected shipment in writing.

Once customs investigates the seized products and confirms infringement, customs can confiscate such products. Customs shall follow up with a written notification to the interested parties providing details related to the confiscated products. If the confiscated products can be used for public interests, customs will transfer such products to the relevant authorities or organization. If the trademark owner is interested in purchasing such products, customs may sell them to the trademark owner along with some monetary compensation. As for the confiscated products that cannot be used for public interests or the trademark owner is not interested in purchasing, customs may auction such products after removing their infringing features. Customs will destroy the confiscated products if the infringing features cannot be removed.

The trademark owner should bear all responsibilities if customs officials are not able to identify the infringing products, effectively and efficiently protect the underlying IPR due to the trademark owner's failure to timely provide accurate information. The trademark owner should also bear all responsibilities (including the responsibility to compensate for any losses) if upon request from the trademark owner, customs has detailed some products but are unable to confirm infringement, or that the people's courts have determined that the seized products do not constitute infringement of the trademark owner's rights.

C. Judicial System.

In China, the people's courts are tasked with the responsibility to execute the court's judgment. China's court system consists of four levels of courts: (1) the SPC; (2) the High People's Courts; (3) the Intermediate People's Courts; and (4) Local Courts. China also has specialized IP courts in Beijing, Shanghai, and Guangzhou; these IP courts are the equivalents of the Intermediate People's Courts. In accordance with the relevant laws and regulations in China, the courts should hear three types of cases: civil litigations, criminal litigations, and administrative litigations; all cases will be heard and reviewed by two-tier court system; all three types of litigations involve trademark disputes.

1. Civil Litigations in Connection with Trademarks.

In principle, any equal civil parties, such as citizens, legal entities, and other organizations, are entitled to pursue a civil litigation with the people's courts if the underlying dispute involves trademark matters. For trademark civil lawsuits, the people's courts should hear such cases and render decisions in accordance with China's Civil Procedural Law and other relevant laws and regulations. In 2002, the SPC issued the Interpretation on the Relevant Issues concerning the Jurisdiction Scope and the Application of Laws for Trademark Cases (No. 1; 2002; ***2002 Judicial Interpretation***). Section 1 of the 2002 Judicial Interpretation provides a summary of the types of trademark civil litigation cases that fall under the jurisdictions of the people's courts. China made amendments to the Trademark Law in 2013. In response to the 2013 amendments, the SPC also made some corresponding judicial interpretations in early 2014 – the Interpretation on Issues concerning the Jurisdiction over Trademark Cases and Application of Law after the Amendments to the Trademark Law (No. 4; 2014; ***2014 Judicial Interpretation***). Article 1 of the 2014 Judicial Interpretation includes a "catch-all and detailed listing" clause outlining the types of civil trademark litigation cases that fall under the jurisdiction of people's courts in China. Such cases include:

- trademark ownership dispute;
- trademark infringement;
- trademark noninfringement confirmatory petition;
- contract disputes involving trademark assignments;
- contract disputes involving trademark licensing issues;
- contract disputes involving trademark representation issues;
- preliminary injunction in trademark infringement cases;
- asset preservation cases concerning a preliminary injunction in trademark infringement disputes;
- evidence preservation cases prior to a trademark infringement lawsuit;
- any other trademark cases.

Article 3 of the 2014 Judicial Interpretation states that among the above trademark civil cases, except for cases involving protection of well-known trademarks, cases of the first instance in connection with civil trademark disputes are under the jurisdiction of the people's courts at the intermediate level or courts above the intermediate level, as well as the local courts that are designated by the SPC. Up until May 2014, there were a total of 140 local people's courts that were designated by the SPC to hear civil cases concerning trademark disputes. As for trademark dispute cases that involve protection of well-known trademarks, since there were no special rules concerning jurisdiction of such cases at that time, they fell under jurisdiction of all intermediate people's courts and the local people's courts designated by the SPC. However, around 2007, China had witnessed a severe "alienation phenomenon" in relation to well-known trademark protection. Considering the unique nature associated with well-known trademarks, and in an effort to standardize the applicable laws to protect such marks, the SPC issued the Notice Concerning Jurisdiction Over Civil Trademark Cases Involving the Recognition and Determination of Well-Known Trademarks (No. 1; 2009; the "***Notice***"); the Notice was issued on January 5, 2009. In this judicial interpretation, it adopts the principle of "centralized jurisdiction" for civil disputes involving the determination of well-known trademarks. The principle of centralized jurisdiction means that all such cases fall under the jurisdiction of intermediate courts that are located in the capital cities of either a province, an autonomous region, a city that is specifically designated in the state plan, or a municipality that is directly under the control of the Central Government; such cases can also be heard by other intermediate courts designated by the SPC. The above-mentioned Article 3 Section 2 of the 2014 Judicial Interpretation continues to follow the jurisdiction principle stated in the Notice. Pursuant to the Provisions on the Jurisdiction of the Intellectual Property Courts of Beijing, Shanghai, and Guangzhou over cases issued by the SPC on October 31, 2014, civil cases involving the determination of well-known trademarks in Beijing, Shanghai, and Guangdong provinces are under the jurisdiction of Beijing IP Court, Shanghai IP Court, and Guangzhou IP Court respectively. Up until now, except for the intermediate courts that are located in the capital cities of a province, an autonomous region, a city that is specifically designated in the state plan, and a municipality directly under the Central Government's control, the SPC has designated eight intermediate courts to hear civil cases involving the determination of well-known trademarks. These eight intermediate courts are: Xiamen City Intermediate Court, Dalian City Intermediate Court, Qingdao City Intermediate Court, Dongying City Intermediate Court, Weifang City Intermediate Court, Ningbo City Intermediate Court, Wenzhou City Intermediate Court, and the Eighth Agricultural Division Intermediate Court of Xinjiang Production and Construction Corps.

2. Administrative Litigations in Connection with Trademarks.

According to China Administrative Litigation Procedural Law, a party is entitled to raise an administrative litigation with the people's courts if the party is not satisfied with the specific administrative act made by the administrative authorities. Generally speaking, there are two primary types of administrative litigations that involve trademarks.

The first type of administrative litigation is raised by a party when it is not satisfied with the appeal decision rendered by the TRAB with respect to the determination of trademark rights. These types of cases fall under Beijing IP Court's jurisdiction. The second type of administrative litigation case is raised by a party when it is not satisfied with the specific administrative trademark decisions made by the administrative departments for industry and commence. In practice, the second type of administrative litigation is primarily brought against decisions made by the administrative law enforcement. If a party involved is dissatisfied with the decisions made by administrative departments for industry and commerce, it is entitled to file an administrative litigation with the people's court within three months from the date the party learns about the decision concerning the specific administrative act; the legal ground to support the administrative lawsuit is Article 39 of China Administrative Litigation Procedural Law. In addition to the above and pursuant to relevant rules in China Administrative Litigation Procedural Law, the people's court where the defendant is domiciled has the jurisdiction to hear such cases in the first instance. In other words, the people's court where the administrative agency is located and has made the initial decision is the court that has the jurisdiction to hear the subsequent administrative litigation. The people's courts should, according to the relevant provisions in China Administrative Litigation Procedural Law, conduct an investigation and carry out a comprehensive review regarding the specific administrative acts made by the administrative agency; the court can render its decision after the review has been completed. The people's court, in its judgment, can affirm, cancel, or amend the prior administrative decision.

3. Criminal Litigations in Connection with Trademarks.

The Criminal Law of the PRC includes three types of crimes in connection with trademarks: (1) counterfeiting a registered trademark;[6] (2) selling products bearing counterfeited registered trademarks;[7] and (3) manufacturing, or selling manufactured registered trademarks, without legitimate reasons.[8] Any victim of the above-listed crimes can file a report with the local Public Security Bureau ("***PSB***"). The PSB will then conduct a criminal investigation of the alleged trademark infringing acts. Once the investigation is completed, PSB will then transfer the cases to the prosecuting authority. The prosecutor will then decide whether or not to raise a criminal public prosecution with the people's court. In situations where there are solid evidence to support the trademark criminal infringements, the victims can also institute an action (criminal private prosecution) directly with the people's courts in order to hold the relevant parties criminally liable.

The people's courts will review the above cases (whether in the form of a public criminal prosecution or private criminal prosecution) in accordance with China's Criminal Procedural Law. The court will then render decisions in respect to the alleged crime, and the subsequent criminal liabilities. Primary forms of criminal liabilities, under China's Criminal Law, include: imprisonment, criminal detention and/or a monetary fine.

6. Article 213 of the Criminal Law stipulates that "whoever, without permission from the owner of a registered trademark, uses a trademark which is identical with the registered trademark on the same kind of commodities shall, if the circumstances are serious, be sentenced to fixed-term imprisonment of not more than three years or criminal detention and shall also, or shall only, be fined; if the circumstances are especially serious, he shall be sentenced to fixed-term imprisonment of not less than three years but not more than seven years and shall also be fined."
7. Article 214 of the Criminal Law stipulates that "whoever knowingly sells commodities bearing counterfeit registered trademarks shall, if the amount of sales is relatively large, be sentenced to fixed-term imprisonment of not more than three years or criminal detention and shall also, or shall only, be fined; if the amount of sales is huge, he shall be sentenced to fixed-term imprisonment of not less than three years but not more than seven years and shall also be fined."
8. Article 215 of the Criminal Law stipulates that "whoever forges or without authorization of another makes representations of the person's registered trademarks or sells such representations shall, if the circumstances are serious, be sentenced to fixed-term imprisonment of not more than three years, criminal detention or public surveillance and shall also, or shall only, be fined; if the circumstances are especially serious, he shall be sentenced to fixed- term imprisonment of not less than three years but not more than seven years and shall also be fined."

IV. Administrative and Judicial Procedures to Affirm the Trademark Rights.

A. Administrative Procedures.

Administrative procedures to confirm trademark rights include the following steps:

- trademark application;
- formality examination of a trademark application;
- substantive examination of a trademark application;
- refusal of a trademark application and the preliminary approval;
- trademark oppositions;
- approval for trademark registration;
- trademark review;
- renewal of a registered trademark.

(Figure 1.1 outlines the trademark registration process in China).

Figure 1.1 Flowchart of Trademark Registration

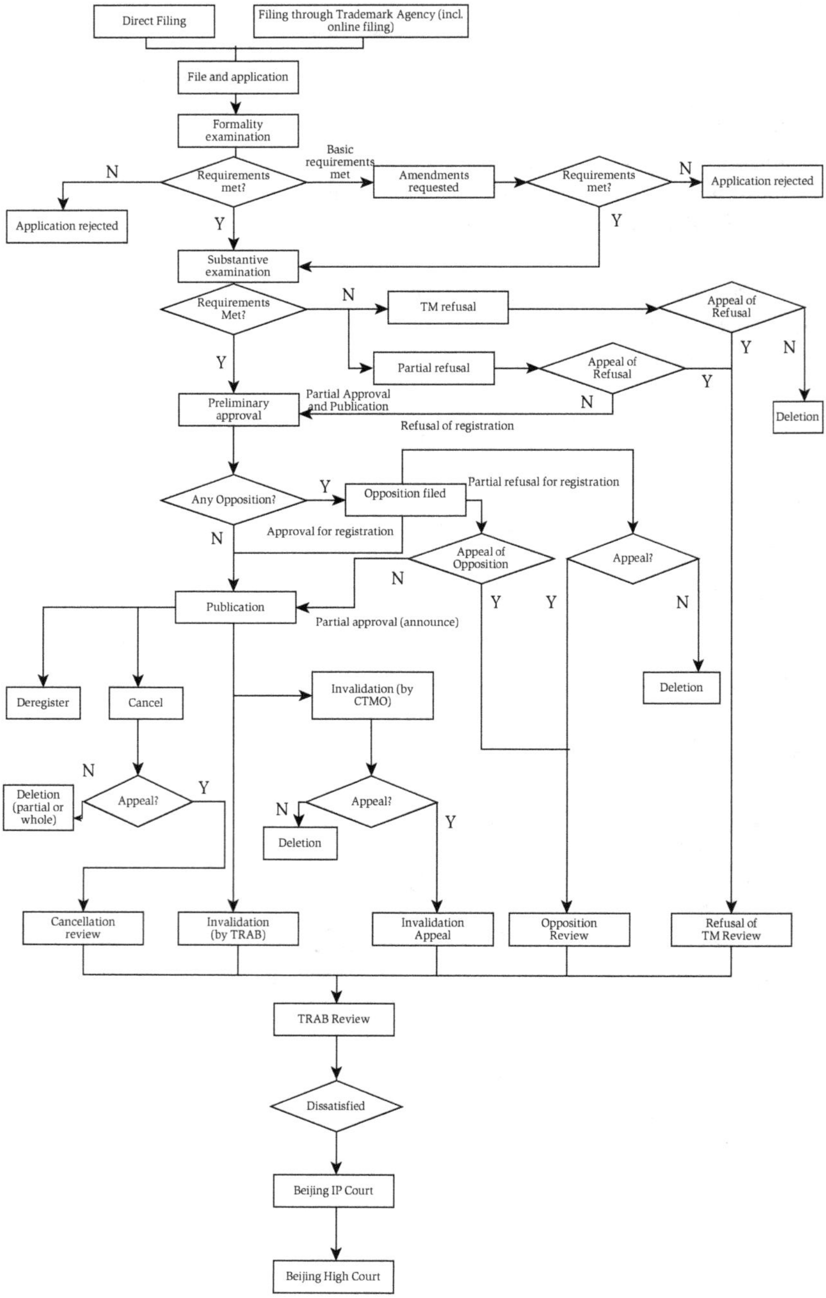

The 2013 amendments to the Trademark Law made improvements to the administrative procedure process when affirming or rejecting trademark rights. The primary changes introduced by the 2013 amendments to the process are outlined below.

1. Multi-class Trademark Application Is Allowed.

Before the amendment in 2013, China adopted the single class system ("one application for one class only"). In other words, if an applicant intends to use the same trademark on products or services in different classes, it shall submit a trademark application in each of the interested classes based on the classification of goods/services. The 2013 amendment introduced the "multi-class application" system which is also referred to as the "one trademark application form covering multiple classes." Under this system, one can file one trademark application covering products or services in different classes. Article 22 Section 2 of the 2013 Trademark Law states that "the applicant can file one application to apply for the same mark covering products or services in different classes."

2. Electronic Filings Are Allowed.

Article 15 Section 2 of the 2002 Implementation Guidelines to the Trademark Law of the People's Republic of China states that "all documents in connection with an application to register a trademark shall either by typewritten or printed." In 2006, the Trademark Office started the online application; the online application process, however, was only available to trademark agencies. The trademark agency's representation scope had also started to broaden after 2006. In the 2013 amendment, it explicitly allows for electronic filings and outlines the exact procedures to proceed with such a filing in China. Article 22 Section 3 of the 2013 Trademark Law states: "all documents in connection with an application to register a trademark can be filed either in writing or by other electronic means of data transmission." After the implementation of the new Trademark Law, electronic filings have also become available to all trademark applicants, not just limited to trademark agencies.

3. Communication Channel Is Included in the Substantive Examination Review Process.

Under the prior law, there were a large number of trademark applications that remained pending for a long time due to "unnecessary" refusals from the Trademark Office. Some of the refusals related to minor details which could be quickly addressed or explained by the trademark applicants if they were afforded the opportunities; in other words, many issues related to the trademark applications could be quickly rectified or corrected without having the Trademark Office issuing whole or partial rejections. The prior Trademark Law, however, did not give Trademark Office the authority to proactively reach out to applicants concerning these quick issues; there was no clear procedures showing the proper process that the examiners could reach out to the applicants either. This explained why there was a tremendous backlog in examining the pending applications; the trademark applicants were also frustrated and inconvenienced because they were compelled to deal with each minor detail in a formal way. This also caused delay in the overall process in granting trademark rights as well as imposing unnecessary heavy workload on the examiners.

To address this issue, the new Trademark Law formally incorporates a communication process. Article 29 of the 2013 Trademark Law states that "*examiners at the trademark office can request the applicant to explain or revise its application during the examination process; the lack of the explanation or revision from the trademark application, when requested, does not affect the examiner's decision.*"

4. Opposition Proceeding Has Been Redesigned.

Trademark opposition proceeding refers to the process where a third party can challenge registration of a trademark. Specifically, this third party can raise an opposition against any trademark applications so long as such applications have been preliminarily approved for registration and have been published by in the Trademark Gazette. Any individuals, legal entities, or organizations are entitled to raise an opposition with the China Trademark Office within the time frame provided by the law. The Trademark Office will then review the opposition and render a decision to approve or refuse the registration.

The 2013 Trademark Law "redesigned" the opposition proceeding in the following two ways.

First, the specific standing requirement. Under the 2013 Trademark Law, any party can file an opposition based on the absolute grounds (Article 10, Article 11, and Article 12). However, only the prior right holders and interested parties are allowed to raise an opposition based on the relative grounds (Article 13, Article 15, Article 16.1, Article 30, Article 31, and Article 32).

Second, the 2013 Trademark Law affords different relief to the parties in an opposition proceeding. The 2001 Trademark Law adopted a four-tiered review system to examine trademark opposition cases - two levels of review at the administrative level and two levels of review at the judicial level. Two levels of administrative review refer to the fact that any party dissatisfied with the opposition decision rendered by the Trademark Office can pursue an appeal with the TRAB. Two levels of judicial review refer to the fact that the parties can institute an administrative litigation with the people's courts if they are not satisfied with the decision made by the TRAB; the second level of court review, however, will be the final review of the opposition case. Although the four-tier review system definitely had its advantages, it prolonged the overall time frame to complete an opposition proceeding (and for the applicant to obtain its trademark rights). The 2013 Trademark Law addressed this issue in Article 35 Section 2: "*if the opponent is not satisfied with the decision made by the Trademark Office, it is no longer allowed to raise an appeal either with the Trademark Review and Adjudication Board or the people's courts. Instead, the only recourse the opposing party has is to wait until the underlying mark has become registered, then raise an invalidation action against it with the Trademark Review and Adjudication Board.* Despite the above, Article 35 Section 3 states that if the opposed party (the trademark applicant) is dissatisfied with the Trademark Office decision, it can still pursue an appeal with the TRAB; if the opposed party is dissatisfied with the Appeal Board's decision, it can further pursue an appeal with the people's court. Following the above articles in the 2013 Trademark Law, this means only the opposed party (i.e., the trademark applicant) is entitled to pursue a court appeal when it is dissatisfied with the decision made by the Appeal Board; only the opposed party can appeal if the Trademark Office decides to refuse its registration. In the event the Appeal Board approves the trademark application (i.e., rejects the opposition), the opposing party is still not allowed to initiate a legal proceeding. The opposing party can only raise an invalidation action with the Appeal Board after the underlying mark has been approved for registration.

5. Trademark Cancellation and Trademark Invalidation Actions Are Distinguished.

Both trademark cancellation and trademark invalidation proceedings can result in the termination of one's trademark rights. Cancellation of a trademark means that one's trademark rights are cancelled for reasons that occur after registration; accordingly, the mark loses the fundamental reasons to continue being protected as a trademark and the exclusive rights associated with the mark are cancelled by the relevant administrative authorities. Invalidation of a trademark refers to the fact that one loses its trademark due to defects during the process it obtains the trademark rights; the trademark administrative authorities thereby declare the mark invalid, and there are no exclusive rights associated with the mark from the very beginning. The trademark laws in most countries and jurisdictions in the world distinguish the concepts and separate the cancellation and invalidation proceedings. The 2001 China Trademark Law, however, did not specify any "invalidation" proceedings; it merely referred any proceedings that would result in the loss of the trademark rights as "cancellation actions." The 2013 Trademark Law makes a distinction; it further provides the specific time points as to when the cancellation and invalidation decisions will become effective.[9]

6. There Is No Longer Time Limit for a Well-Known Trademark Owner to Invalidate a Bad-Faith Registration.

Article 45 of the 2013 Trademark Law provides that "*any prior right holder or interested party can raise an invalidation action with the Trademark Review and Adjudication Board to challenge the registration of a trademark within the first five years since its registration if such a registration violates provisions of Articles 10 Section 2 and Section 3, Article 15, Article 16 Section 1, Article 30, Article 31 or Article 32 of the Trademark Law. However, if the registered is obtained by bad faith, the owner of a well-known*

9. Article 46 and Article 55.1 of the Trademark Law.

trademark is not subject to the five-year time frame and can raise an invalidation action any time." Article 13 Section 2 protects unregistered well-known trademarks with respect to the same or similar goods. Article 13 Section 3 protects registered well-known trademarks with respect to different or dissimilar products. Article 30 protects prior registered trademarks with respect to the same or similar goods. Article 45 states: "*if the junior registration is obtained in bad faith, the owner of a well-known trademark shall not be bound by the five-year time limit to raise an invalidation action if such an action is relying on Article 13 Section 2, Article 13 Section 3 and Article 30.*"

7. Specific Time Frame To Review and Examine Pending Applications and Actions Are Incorporated.

In order to ensure each applicant can obtain its trademark rights in a timely manner, the 2013 Trademark Law provides a specific time frame that the examiners and administrative authorities must complete its review of either the pending applications or dispute cases. Article 28 of the Trademark Law states that "*the Trademark Office shall complete the examination of a trademark application in nine months from its receipt of the application. A mark should be preliminarily approved and published on the Trademark Gazette if the application complies with relevant provisions of this Law.*" In addition to the time frame in reviewing pending applications, the 2013 Trademark Law also stipulates a specific time frame for the relevant authorities to complete its review for the opposition, cancellation, and invalidation cases.[10] These procedures are in place to ensure any trademark disputes can be resolved swiftly.

B. Judicial Procedures.

1. Types of Cases and the Scope of Judicial Review.

Before the amendment to the Trademark Law in 2001, any decisions made by the TRAB with respect to the determination of trademark rights were final; in other words, the Appeal Board's decisions were not subject to any judicial review. In the 2001 amendments, the Law was changed so that any cases decided by the Appeal Board were subject to the subsequent judicial review. Specifically, Article 32, Article 33, Article 43, and Article 49 of the 2001 Trademark Law stated that "*In respect to any refusal reviews, opposition reviews, invalidation, and cancellation decisions rendered by the Trademark Review and Adjudication Board, any party that is dissatisfied with the decision can initiate an administrative litigation with the people's courts within thirty days upon receipt of the decision.*" The 2013 Trademark Law maintained the above judicial review system. Pursuant to Article 34, Article 44, Article 45, and Article 54 of the 2013 Trademark Law, parties can pursue an administrative lawsuit with the people's courts within thirty days upon its receipt of the Appeal Board's decision in a trademark refusal review, invalidation, and cancellation action. The 2013

10. Article 34, Article 35, Article 44, and Article 54 of the Trademark Law.

Amendments made changes to the opposition procedures in that the opposed party (the trademark applicant) is not entitled to any appeals unless its application is refused by the Appeal Board. If the Appeal Board approves its trademark application (i.e., rejects the opposition), the opposing party can no longer appeal the decision to the people's court. Rather, the opposing party can only rely on the invalidation action with the Appeal Board pursuant to Article 44 and Article 45 of the Trademark Law. The cases referenced above are generally categorized as trademark recognition and determination of cases.

2. Jurisdiction.

With respect to the jurisdiction for the "trademark recognition and determination" cases, Article 2 of the 2001 Judicial Interpretation stipulates that the review of the Appeal Board's decisions should be handled by the intermediate courts. To decide the appropriate intermediate courts to review the Appeal Board's decisions, the Beijing High People's Court shall, upon authorization of the SPC, determine the jurisdiction of the relevant intermediate courts within its own jurisdiction.

On May 21, 2002, the SPC issued the Response on Issues of Jurisdiction over Cases Related to Patents and Trademarks after the Amendments to the Patent and Trademark Laws (No. 117; 2002; the "***Response***"). In the Response, the SPC clearly pointed out that such cases fell under the jurisdiction of the Beijing High People's Court and the Beijing Intermediate People's Courts (based on the relevant provisions of the Administrative Procedural Law). The Response also outlines division of work and respective responsibilities among the Intellectual Property Tribunals and Administrative Tribunals that are within the jurisdiction of each court. Following the Response issued by the SPC, the Beijing High People's Court published an Opinion on August 13, 2003 ("*An Opinion on Implementing the Supreme People's Court's Response on Jurisdiction Issues over Patent and Trademark Cases after the Amendments to Patent Law and Trademark Law and the Opinion in respect to the division of work concerning international trade administrative cases*"). In this Opinion, the Beijing High Court clearly pointed out Beijing No. 1 Intermediate People's Court has jurisdictions over appeal cases concerning decisions made by the Appeal Board. These appeals will be further assigned to either the civil tribunals or the administrative tribunals based on the nature of the cases.

On June 22, 2009, the SPC published "Regulations on the Division of Work in the Trial of Administrative Intellectual Property Cases Involving Recognition and Determination of Rights over Patent, Trademark, etc." (the "***Regulations***"). In the Regulations, the SPC stated that starting on July 1, 2009, Intellectual Property Tribunals at the Beijing Intermediate Courts, the Beijing High Court, and the SPC have jurisdictions over cases involving the recognition and determination of trademark rights for the first instance, second instance, and the review proceedings respectively.

On October 31, 2014, the SPC issued "*Regulations relating to the Jurisdiction of the Intellectual Property Courts in Beijing, Shanghai, and Guangzhou.*" On November 6, 2014, the Beijing High People's Court published "An Announcement Relating to the

Opening of Beijing Intellectual Property Court." In the Announcement, the High Court stipulates that the Beijing IP Court should have jurisdiction over any cases of the first instance that involve the recognition and determination of trademark rights. From this point forward, the Beijing IP Court handles such cases for the first instance, IP tribunals at the Beijing High Court handle such cases for the second instance, and IP tribunals for the SPC handle the appeal of decisions.

3. Parties.

If a party is dissatisfied with the decisions made by the Appeal Board with respect to the type of cases involving recognition and determination of trademark rights, it can institute a legal proceeding with the Beijing No. 1 Intermediate Court within thirty days upon receipt of the Appeal Board's decision. According to the provisions of the Administrative Procedural Law, the defendant in this type of appeal case should always be the TRAB. After the court's acceptance of cases, it will notify the Appeal Board to attend the lawsuit as a defendant. As for the administrative litigations involving review of a trademark refusal, there are only two parties: the trademark applicant as the plaintiff and the TRAB as the defendant. As for the administrative litigations involving trademark cancellation actions ex officio, there are also two parties, i.e., trademark registrant as the plaintiff and the TRAB as the defendant. In an administrative litigation involving an appeal of a trademark opposition decision, the court will also notify the opposing party to attend the hearing as a third party. As for an administrative litigation involving trademark invalidation, the court will inform the other party in the administrative proceeding to attend the lawsuit as a third party. As for trademark cancellation proceedings, if a party is dissatisfied with the Appeal Board's decision, the court shall inform the other party in the administrative proceeding to attend the hearing as a third party.

4. Scope of Examination.

Although there are different views about the proper litigation review process with respect to cases involving the recognition and determination of trademark rights, this particular issue was not addressed in the 2013 Amendments. Accordingly, the litigation review process involving the use of IP cases still follows the same rules and regulations (as outlined in China Administrative Procedural Law) and proceeds as an administrative litigation. In most instances, the court only reviews the specific points raised by the plaintiff; the court rarely conducts a comprehensive review of the underlying dispute. As for the arguments that are not specifically raised during the appeal, the court typically will not take an initiative to review such information. Despite the above, if the court comes across some flaws in the proceeding that are not raised by the parties, the court will still examine and address these flaws. Article 32 of the Administrative Procedural Law states that the TRAB, as a defendant in an administrative litigation, shall bear the burden of proof to provide evidence and legal basis upon which it relies to render its administrative decision. Except in cases involving review of trademark refusals and ex officio cancellation cases where there are two parties to a decision, all other cases involve three parties. The TRAB simply plays the role of an arbitrator; it does not (and should not) take an active part in collecting evidence. The Appeal Board shall participate in the subsequent administrative litigations as a third party. Therefore, in practice, the Appeal Board not only bears the burden of proof to provide evidence as a defendant, but is often involved in providing supporting documents even as a third party to a litigation. A plaintiff in a litigation can also submit evidence to the court proving that the prior decision is made in violation of the law. Generally speaking, the court adheres to the dossier doctrine and is mainly focused on examination of facts, evidence, and legal grounds raised in the review. Despite this, the court is open to accept and consider new evidence and new facts under certain circumstances.

According to Article 5 of the Administrative Procedural Law, the court will examine the legality in respect of the specific administrative acts. In other words, courts will examine the administrative acts made by the Appeal Board with respect to procedural matters, fact-finding, and application of the law when the Appeal Board issues decisions affecting the recognition and determination of trademark rights. The court will then make an independent conclusion concerning the substantive conditions that allow the Appeal Board to reach its administrative decision and if the court should affirm or reject the decision. In April 2010, the SPC issued *An Opinion on Issues Relating to the Trial of Administrative Cases Involving Recognition and Determination of Trademark Rights (No. 122, 2010)*. In this Opinion, the SPC provides clear guidance to the lower people's courts in respect to some classic issues, as outlined below, that the lower courts often face in adjudicating trademark cases:

(1) Guidance to the overall judicial policy when reviewing and deciding trademark cases.
(2) Guidance to determine whether or not the underlying trademark is distinctive.
(3) Guidance in offering protection to well-known trademarks.
(4) Guidance in finding trademark squatting carried out by agents or representatives.
(5) Guidance in determining whether or not the trademarks or the underlying products are confusingly similar.
(6) Guidance in offering protection to senior rights.
(7) Guidance in the judicial review process to cancel a trademark based on nonuse for three consecutive years.

5. Examination Proceedings.

Once the court of the first instance accepts a case, the court will – pursuant to the provisions of the Administrative Procedural Law and relevant judicial interpretations – form a collegial panel to examine the dispute. The Court of First Instance shall render a decision within three months from the date it accepts the case. Any extension of time for the courts to issue a decision must first be approved by the Beijing High People's Court. The Court of the First Instance will affirm the Appeal Board's decision as long as the following is satisfied: the decision is supported by solid evidence, the Appeal Board has applied the correct law to review the case, and the Appeal Board has complied with the relevant procedures in rendering the decision. On the other hand, the Appeal Board's decision will be vacated (partially or in whole) if the court finds the decision is not supported by adequate evidence, the Appeal Board has applied an incorrect law to review the case, the decision is made in violation of the relevant legal procedures, or the decision is beyond the scope or simply an abuse of the Appeal Board's authority. The court will, if necessary, request the Appeal Board to make a new administrative decision. The 2013 statistics show that in respect to the trademark cases (involving the recognition and determination of trademark rights), the Intellectual Property Tribunal of Beijing No. 1 Intermediate Court vacated 352 Appeal Board's decisions. This includes 49 trademark refusal reviews, 251 appeals of trademark oppositions, 44 trademark invalidation actions, and 8 trademark cancellation actions. These vacated cases are around 16.7% of the entire trademark cases reviewed by the courts in 2013; the number of vacated cases dropped by roughly 2% compared to 2012.

If a party is not satisfied with the first instance decision, it can pursue an appeal to the Beijing High People's Court within ten days upon receipt of the decision, or within fifteen days upon receipt of the judgment. If the Beijing High People's Court holds that the underlying facts to the dispute are clear, the Court can simply conduct a written review of the case rather than hold a public hearing. If the parties are disputing some underlying facts (which may have been recognized by the first level of courts), or that the second level of court believes the facts recognized by the first courts are unclear, the second level of courts will conduct a public hearing. The High Court (the second level of court) will dismiss the appeal and affirm the original court's decision if, after review, the original decision has made a clear determination on the facts, applied the correct sets of law, and followed the appropriate legal procedures to adjudicate the dispute. If the High Court is of the view that the first court has a clear understanding of the facts but has applied some incorrect laws or followed the incorrect legal procedures to render its decision, the judgment shall be amended by the High Court. If the original court's decision does not demonstrate a clear understanding of the facts, it renders a decision based on inadequate evidence, or the decision is made in violation of the due process which may impact the accuracy of the decision, the High Court may vacate the first decision, send the case back for retrial, or directly amend the first decision after clarifying the relevant facts. The judgment of the second instance is final.

If the parties believe the Beijing High People's Court has made some error in its decision, they may appeal to the Beijing High People's Court or the SPC. The courts will then examine the appeal and if, after review, there is justification to support an appeal, the court will initiate the retrial proceeding to review the second instance judgment. However, if the court does not deem there is sufficient justification to support a retrial, it will simply dismiss the parties' retrial petition.

V. Administrative Law Enforcement Procedures and Judicial Procedures to Review Trademark Infringement Cases.

A. Administrative Law Enforcement Procedures.

1. Types of Trademark Infringement.

According to Article 57 of the Trademark Law, and Articles 75 and 76 of the Implementation Guidelines to the Trademark Law of the People's Republic of China, the primary types of trademark infringement in China are as follows:

(1) Without prior authorization, using a mark that is identical to a third party's registered trademark in connection with goods that are identical to those designated under the registered trademark when the use is likely to cause consumer confusion.
(2) Without prior authorization, using a mark that is similar to a third party's registered trademark in connection with the same registered goods, or using a mark that is identical or similar to a third party's registered trademark in connection with goods similar to those covered in the registered trademark when the use is likely to cause consumer confusion.
(3) Without prior authorization, using a mark as a product name or decoration/packaging of a product, the mark is either identical or similar to a third party's registered trademark, the use covers the same or similar products as those in the third party's registered trademark, and the use is likely to cause consumer confusion.
(4) Selling products that infringe upon the exclusive rights of a third party's registered trademark.
(5) Forging or manufacturing a third party's registered trademark without authorization, or selling a third party's registered trademark that is forged or manufactured without authorization.
(6) Replacing or altering a registered trademark without the trademark registrant's prior consent and redirecting the products bearing the altered trademark to the market.
(7) Intentionally infringing the exclusive rights of a third party's registered trademark so as to provide convenience for other purposes.
(8) Assisting others in carrying out trademark infringement acts (the "assistance" includes, but is not limited to, the following: providing storage, transportation, mailing, or printing services, concealment or a business place, or an online trading platform to facilitate the infringing acts).
(9) Any other acts that would cause harm to the exclusive rights of a third party's registered trademark.

2. Filing and Establishing a Trademark Infringement Case.

The administrative departments for industry and commerce may, on its own initiative, start an investigation and prosecute any actions that in its view are likely to infringe upon a third party's exclusive trademark rights. The trademark registrant or any interested parties can also file a lawsuit before the people's courts, or may petition the administrative department for industry and commerce to handle the infringement case. Article 77 of the Implementation Guidelines to the Trademark Law stipulates that any person may file a complaint or report concerning any actions that may infringe upon a third party's registered trademark rights with the administrative departments for industry and commerce that are above county levels. Complaints should generally be presented in writing, providing specifics relating to the suspected infringement, along with evidence, such as the name and address of the suspected infringer, the place where the suspected infringement takes place, details relating to the trademarks at issue, along with pictures, images, or printing materials relating to the trademark infringement, as well as proof or supporting documents providing ownership information concerning the trademark at issue. The administrative department for industry and commerce shall, upon receipt of a complaint or report, formally accept the case (provided that the complaints or reports have followed all the technical requirements). Generally speaking, a complaint or report must include the following for it to be formally accepted by the administrative department: solid facts relating to the infringement, the requested relief from the administrative department, evidence supporting the administrative department's jurisdiction over the trademark infringement at issue, and confirmation that the case has not been filed or accepted by the relevant people's courts.

3. Investigation.

The administrative departments for industry and commerce at or above the county level have the authority to take the following actions upon receipt of evidence or reports relating to an alleged infringement:

(1) Questioning the relevant parties and conducting an investigation to gather evidence relating to the alleged infringement.
(2) Reviewing and requesting photocopies of contracts, invoices, account information (including account books), and any other materials that are relevant to the alleged infringement.
(3) Conducting an on-site inspection of the place where the alleged infringement takes place.
(4) Examining items that are related to the infringement; seizing or detaining items when the administrative office has sufficient evidence to show that such items infringe upon a third party's registered trademark rights.

The parties shall assist and cooperate with the administrative departments' investigation, including cooperating with the actions detailed in the above that fall under the departments' authority to investigate an infringement. The parties may not refuse assistance or cooperation with the administrative department for exercising its authority to investigate the infringement. The parties shall not obstruct or impede the investigation process either.[11] In addition to the above, the administrative department for industry and commerce can request the trademark owner or its licensees to confirm whether or not the items at issue are genuine or fake.[12]

4. Suspension.

The administrative department for industry and commerce may suspend its investigation if: (1) there is a dispute relating to the ownership of the registered trademark, or (2) the parties have instituted an infringement lawsuit with the people's courts in China. Once the reason that causes the suspension has disappeared, the administrative department for industry and commence should either resume its investigation or terminate the case entirely.[13]

If the dispute relating to the ownership of the trademark at issue is a pending case with the Trademark Office, TRAB or in the people's court, the outcome of the above proceedings may have a substantial impact on the administrative department's investigation. Accordingly, if the trademark ownership is being disputed by the parties and is a pending case in China, the administrative department can suspend its investigation.[14]

5. Result.

a. Administrative Penalty.

If, after investigation, the administrative department for industry and commerce recognizes and concludes an infringement, it can impose the following administrative penalties:

(1) Immediate cessation of the infringement. The administrative office can also confiscate and destroy the infringing goods along with the primary manufacturing tools to produce the infringing goods and/or counterfeits of the registered trademark(s).

(2) Monetary fines.
For infringers with business revenue (from the sale/manufacturing of the infringing goods) that is around or above RMB 50,000 (about USD 7,300), the

11. Article 62.1 and Article 62.2 of the Trademark Law.
12. Article 82 of the Regulation for the Implementation of the Trademark Law.
13. Article 62.3 of the Trademark Law.
14. Article 81 of the Regulation for the Implementation of the Trademark Law.

administrative office can impose a monetary fine that is equal to or less than five times of the infringer's business revenue.

For infringers that have not yet carried out any sales, have no business revenue, or the revenue is less than RMB 50,000 (about USD 7,300), the administrative office can impose a monetary fine up to RMB 250,000 (about USD 36,500).[15]

The following factors can be taken into account in calculating the infringer's illegal business revenue:

- sales price of the infringing products;
- sales price of the infringing products that have not been sold or introduced to the market;
- the average actual sales price of the ceased infringing products;
- the median market price of the genuine goods;
- infringer's other business revenues resulting from the infringement;
- other factors that would allow the administrative office to calculate the reasonable value of infringing goods.[16]

(3) The administrative office also has the discretion to impose stricter or heavier penalties if the infringer has committed two infringements in the past five years or other relevant factors that would justify placing the subject as an egregious infringer.

(4) The administrative office can still request an immediate cessation of the infringement even though the retailer or manufacturer (i.e., the infringing party) does not have actual knowledge that its activities have constituted infringement to a third party's registered trademark rights. If the retailer or manufacturer is able to provide information showing that the products have been obtained through legitimate means, explain the origin of the products, or provide supplier information, the administrative office should, in addition to ordering an immediate cessation of the infringement, report the case to the local administrative department where the supplier is located.[17]

The following information should be sufficient to allow an administrative department for commerce and industry to deem the underlying products are obtained or sourced from a legal channel: (a) the "infringing" party is able to provide the supplier information, payment receipts affixed with supplier's seal, or shipment contracts duly executed by both parties; (b) the above information is either verifiable or has been confirmed by the administrative office; (c) the contracting terms between the "infringer" and supplier have been duly performed by both parties; (d) the "infringer" has provided valid invoices reflecting the purchased goods and such goods conform with the products ceased by the administrative office.[18]

15. Article 60.2 of the Trademark Law.
16. Article 78 of the Regulation for the Implementation of the Trademark Law.
17. Article 60.2 of the Trademark Law and Article 80 of the Regulation for the Implementation of the Trademark Law.
18. Article 79 of the Regulation for the Implementation of the Trademark Law.

b. Administrative Mediation.

If, after receiving the penalty notification from the administrative department, the parties do not agree on the infringement damage amount, the administrative department can conduct a mediation upon request. The parties can further bring the dispute by filing a litigation with the people's courts if the parties fail to reach an agreement during mediation or a party fails to perform its obligation in accordance with the mediation results; the parties should rely on Civil Procedure Law of the PRC to institute such a lawsuit. Despite the above, it is important to point out that one does not need to go through the administrative mediation first to bring a lawsuit with the people's court; in other words, the parties can institute an action directly with the people's courts regarding any dispute concerning the administrative penalties without having to go through a mediation first.[19]

c. Case Transfer.

Article 61 of the Trademark Law requires the administrative department to timely transfer the infringement case to the relevant judicial authorities if, during its investigation, it comes across information that is indicative of a crime. There are three situations that would compel a transfer of a trademark infringement case from civil to criminal:[20]

- using a mark that is identical to a third party's registered trademark in connection with the same registered products without the trademark owner's consent;
- forging or manufacturing of a third party's registered trademark without authorization, or selling a forged mark that is identical to a third party's registered trademark;
- knowingly selling products bearing a forged or counterfeit trademark.

B. Judicial Procedures.

The judicial procedures with respect to a trademark infringement include three types of proceedings: administrative litigation, civil action, and criminal action. Administrative and criminal actions are already discussed in detail in the above paragraphs and will not be repeated here. This section will focus on the civil action only. In practice and from observing China's legal system in recent years, it is apparent that the civil action is now a primary and efficient channel to protect the trademark rights.

19. Article 60.3 of the Trademark Law.
20. Article 213, Article 214 and Article 215 of the Criminal Law.

1. Different Types of Trademark Infringement Acts.

With respect to categorizing the different "types" of trademark infringement acts, China's Trademark Law has adopted the following approach: listing the specific types of infringing acts in the Law but also including a catch-all clause at the end of the relevant section of the Law. The catch-all clause is in place to meet the demands of the ever-changing society. In addition to the types of infringements outlined in the Trademark Law and the Implementation Guidelines to the Trademark Law, the SPC also provided a few more types of infringement in its "Interpretation Concerning the Application of Laws in Civil Trademark Cases in 2002" (No. 32; 2002; the "***2002 Judicial Interpretation***"). The infringements discussed in the 2002 Judicial Interpretation are listed below:

(1) Using words or texts that are identical or similar to a third party's registered trademark as a company name, the use is in connection with the goods or services that are the same or similar to those covered in the registered trademark, and the use is likely to cause confusion among the relevant public.
(2) Copying, imitating, or translating a third party's registered well-known trademark, or the primary distinctive element of a third party's registered trademark, and using the mark as a trademark in connection with products or services that are dissimilar to those covered in the registered trademark. The use is sufficient to cause consumer confusion and thereby results in a negative impact on the registrant's exclusive rights.
(3) Registering words, texts, or characters as a domain name and such words/texts/characters are identical or similar to a third party's registered trademark. Engaging in electronic commerce with the domain in connection with products or services that are similar to those covered in the registered trademark. The use of the domain name is likely to cause consumer confusion among the relevant public.

Meanwhile, the 2002 Judicial Interpretation also pointed out that a person or entity shall immediately stop the infringing acts and bear the corresponding civil responsibilities if it copies, imitates, or translates a foreign well-known trademark (that is not yet registered in China), uses such a mark in connection with products or services that are the same or similar to those covered in the foreign trademark, and the use is likely to cause consumer confusion among the relevant public in China.

Although the above-referenced 2002 Judicial Interpretation was written in response to the 2001 amendments to the Trademark Law, the Interpretation is not at all contradictory to or in conflict with the subsequent amendments, such as the 2013 Trademark Law. The types of infringements set out in the 2002 Judicial Interpretation are therefore still being recognized and effective to this date. In practice, the types of infringements that trigger the most civil trademark lawsuits are the first three types discussed in the Trademark Law (Article 57 of the 2013 Trademark Law). Despite the "common" types of infringements, the exact types of actions that would constitute an infringement also change as our society evolves. In order to keep the law as updated as possible with the progress of the society, the Trademark Law includes a catch-all clause so as to provide legal grounds for the courts and administrative bodies to go after the nontraditional types of trademark infringements. The flexibility in the judicial system is therefore one of the advantages that is not immediately present in the protection offered by the administrative system.

2. Institute A Civil Action.

In accordance with Article 119 of the Civil Procedure Law of the PRC, the following conditions must be met in order to institute a civil action:

(1) the plaintiff must be a citizen, legal person, or other organization with a direct interest in the case;
(2) a specific defendant;
(3) a claim with supporting facts, legal grounds with specific requests for relief; and
(4) the people's court receiving the complaint must have jurisdiction and competence to adjudicate the dispute.

In practice, the condition that triggers the most disputes is the first requirement, the plaintiff's standing requirement (Article 119 of the Civil Procedure Law). A trademark registrant will by all means satisfy the standing requirement and is able to serve as the plaintiff and bring a trademark infringement lawsuit. However, most trademarks these days are not directly used by the trademark owners. Rather, the rights to use these marks are licensed to a third party. It can therefore be expected that the licensee's interests will inevitably be impacted by the underlying infringing conducts. Despite the above, a licensee is not always able to satisfy the standing requirement and serves as a plaintiff to institute a trademark infringement lawsuit. Whether or not a licensee can serve as the sole plaintiff in a trademark infringement case depends on the nature of license agreement between the parties. According to the 2002 Judicial Interpretation, a licensee in an exclusive agreement is entitled to bring a civil infringement action with the people's court; a licensee in an exclusive agreement serves as the sole licensee to the trademark owner can bring the lawsuit either with the trademark owner or by itself; the licensee in a nonexclusive license may, upon explicit authorization from the trademark registrant, institute a civil trademark infringement action on its own.

Apart from the fact that a trademark registrant and a licensee are both entitled to initiate civil trademark litigations, the recipient of a cease and desist letter concerning an alleged infringement can also bring a lawsuit to request and confirm noninfringement from the court. Today, most of the requirements to bring a noninfringement trademark lawsuit mostly follow the same requirements as a noninfringement patent lawsuit. In order to bring a noninfringement action with the court, the following conditions must be met:

- the party must have received a demand letter from the trademark owner (or its authorized licensee);
- the recipient (or other interested parties to the lawsuit) that has received the letter has reached out, in writing (the "***Response Letter***"), to the trademark owner (or its authorized licensee) regarding the latter's rights to institute a lawsuit;
- the trademark owner (or its authorized licensee) neither withdraws its requests nor files a lawsuit within one month upon its receipt of the Response Letter or within two months after the Response Letter is sent;
- the recipient of the demand letter (or the interested parties) can request a noninfringement confirmation from the people's courts.

It is worth noting that any trademark infringement lawsuit should be brought within the statutory period. According to the 2002 Judicial Interpretation, the statute of limitations for pursuing a trademark infringement lawsuit is two years, starting from the day the trademark registrant or the interested party knows or should have known about the infringement. If a trademark registrant or the interested party institutes an action after the two-year time period but the infringing act is still present at the time the lawsuit is filed, the people's court should accept the case and request that the infringement be stopped. However, the damage amount for the infringement should be calculated two years from the day the lawsuit is filed.

3. Jurisdiction.

Article 28 of the Civil Procedure Law of the PRC states that "for any infringement litigations, the people's court where the infringement takes place or the domicile of the defendant should have jurisdiction over the case." The jurisdiction for trademark infringement cases should be governed by the above article, given that trademark infringement is a classic type of infringement litigation. Despite the clear language in Article 28, there are still jurisdiction disputes in a trademark case. This is because although it is generally accepted the people's courts where the infringing acts occur or infringing outcome takes place should have jurisdiction over the litigation, there is not yet a consensus whether or not the courts that the infringing products go through in the channel of commerce should also have jurisdiction to hear such cases. To address this, the 2002 Judicial Interpretation offers some guidance. Section 6 of the 2002 Judicial Interpretation states that *"In a civil trademark infringement litigation, the following people's courts should have jurisdiction: where the infringing acts take place, where the infringing products are stored or confiscated or ceased, the defendant's domicile location."* Specifically, the "storage place" discussed in the Interpretation refers the location where the defendant either stores a large quantity of the infringing products, or a place where the defendant either frequently stores or hides its infringing products. The "confiscated or ceased place" refers to the location where the administrative authorities – such as the administrative department for commence and industry, or Customs – cease and detain the infringing goods in accordance with the law. It is clear that the above Interpretation is trying to narrow the scope where the infringement takes place and thereby limits the jurisdiction to certain specific courts. In addition to the above, it should also be noted that there are multiple types of infringing acts that occur in today's society. Due to the variety types of infringements, it is very likely that a single infringement litigation may involve multiple defendants, and concern different types of infringements. To address this, the 2002 Judicial Interpretation states that "for infringement actions against multiple defendants, as well as infringement that has occurred in multiple different places, the plaintiff can simply choose one of the people's courts where one of the defendants carries out the infringing acts as the court with jurisdiction. For an infringement action that is targeted against one defendant only, the people's court where the defendant commits the act of infringement has jurisdiction over the litigation." Based on the above, it is clear that the plaintiff can forum shop and pick the court to litigate the case if the action is brought against both the manufacturer and the retailer of the infringing products. In other words, in such a case, the people's court where the underlying manufacturing takes place and the people's court where the subsequent sales take place can both serve as the court to hear and adjudicate the infringement. If the defendant's domicile in the above case is different from the manufacturing and retailing location, the plaintiff can also designate the people's court where the defendant lives as the court with jurisdiction.

4. Preservation Mechanism.

Preservation measures in an infringement litigation involve the following: (1) Preliminary injunction; (2) Evidence preservation; and (3) Property preservation.

There are two kinds of preliminary injunctions in China: (a) preliminary injunction prior to litigation; and (b) preliminary injunction during litigation. The system of preliminary injunction was not established in either the 1982 or the 1993 Trademark Law. The 2001 Trademark Law first incorporated the preliminary injunction concept. Article 57 of the 2001 Trademark Law specifically allows for a prelitigation preliminary injunction if a trademark registrant or any interested party provides evidence that is sufficient to prove that a third party has engaged or will soon be engaging in actions that will infringe upon its trademark rights; the parties will suffer irreparable harm if the court does not grant the injunction. The 2013 Trademark Law keeps the above article and maintains the preliminary injunction filing system in China. In addition to the above, the SPC offered further specific guidance for requesting and issuing preliminary injunction in "Interpretation on the Applicable Law to Stop Infringement and Preserve Evidence before the Filing of a Lawsuit" (No. 2; 2002). The 2012 Civil Procedural Law of China further improved the original preservative measures and systems stated in the Civil Procedural Law. Pursuant to the above provisions and up until 2002, the preliminary injunction should be filed by either the trademark owner or the interested parties with the people's court that has jurisdiction over the trademark infringement case, i.e., the court where the infringement takes place or where the defendant domiciles. In conjunction with the request for preliminary injunction, the plaintiff should submit sufficient evidence regarding: (1) the alleged infringing facts that the defendant is engaging in or is about to be engaged in that will infringe upon the plaintiff's exclusive rights over its registered trademark; and (2) the plaintiff will suffer irreparable harm if the court does not grant the injunction. In addition to evidence and information for (1) and (2), the plaintiff also needs to provide a financial bond prior to the court's granting of the injunction. The people's court will review the preliminary injunction request and shall issue a decision in forty-eight hours. If the injunction is granted, it shall be enforced immediately. The trademark owner or the interested parties shall file an infringement lawsuit with the court within thirty days upon the approval of the preliminary injunction. If the lawsuit is not timely filed, the court will remove the injunction. Conversely, if there are mistakes in the process (such as there is no infringement in the first place) and the injunction has caused damages to the respondent (either to its business revenue, reputation or both), the plaintiff will be required to compensate the corresponding loss. In addition to the prelitigation injunction, the trademark owner and interested parties can also request an injunction when filing the lawsuit or during the lawsuit.

Evidence preservation can take place prior to and during litigation. Evidence preservation during litigation has always been specifically recognized in the Civil Procedure Law and has already applied to trademark infringement lawsuits. Evidence preservation during litigation is justified when the relevant evidence may be destroyed, lost, or otherwise unavailable. The parties can request evidence preservation if the above situation is likely; in fact, the court can take initiative in preserving the evidence without awaiting an application from the parties if it deems the relevant evidence is likely to be lost or destroyed by either party.

The 2001 Trademark Law provides the mechanism allowing the parties to request preservation of evidence prior to litigation. In other words, in order to stop trademark infringing acts, if the evidence is likely to be destroyed or become unavailable during the trial, a trademark registrant or an interested party may can request the court to preserve the evidence prior to the filing of the lawsuit.

Property preservation can also take place either prior to the litigation or during the litigation. The primary purpose to preserve a party's property is for the purpose to execute the judgment (to ensure the enforcement of a judgment). According to the relevant law, the people's court can grant the motion to preserve properties if it would be difficult to enforce the judgment due to action or inaction of one party or other reasons, or the inability to execute the judgment may cause damages to the parties. The motion to preserve property can be filed either prior to a lawsuit or during the lawsuit.

5. Evidence.

Trademark infringement lawsuit is a type of civil action; accordingly, the general evidence rules in civil actions, such as a party shall bear the burden of proof for any claims it is asserting, are applicable to a trademark infringement case. Applying the above general rule to trademark infringement cases, the plaintiff shall bear the burden of proof regarding its ownership of the respective trademarks, and provide evidence establishing the infringing acts it is alleging in the lawsuit and the civil liabilities that the defendant shall bear. As for the defendant, it shall bear its burden of proof if it either argues that its action does not constitute an infringement or that it is exempt from the subsequent infringement liabilities. In an effort to reduce the trademark owner's burden of proof in a trademark infringement litigation, the 2013 Trademark Law incorporates an additional clause which is set forth below:

> *"In order to determine the monetary amount in an infringement lawsuit, when the plaintiff has presented as much information as practically possible, and the fact that the alleged infringer has full access and control to its account book and profit information, the court may order the infringer to submit such account books and information. In situations where the infringer refuses to submit the requested account books or information, or that it provides false documents and materials, the court may simply determine the amount of damages based on the claims and evidence submitted by the trademark owner."*

6. Legal Liability.

Since trademark infringement is a classic type of infringement, the legal liabilities discussed in China General Principles of Civil Law and the Tort Liability Law are applicable to trademark infringement litigations. Article 134 of China General Principles of Civil Law states that *"the primary ways to bear the civil liabilities in a lawsuit include: cease infringements, remove obstacles, eliminate dangers, compensate losses, eliminate negative effects, and extend apologies."* Article 118 of China General Principles of Civil Law also explicitly provides that *"the owner or the interested parties shall have the rights to request the infringement to be immediately ceased, the negative effects to be eliminated and its damages to be compensated for if its copyright, patent rights, exclusive rights in a registered trademarks, invention rights, discovery rights, rights in any scientific or technological research results are being plagiarized, altered, or forged without its prior authorization."* Section 21 of the SPC's Interpretation on the Applicable Law in Civil Trademark Cases further states that *"the people's court may order the infringer to bear the civil liabilities in a trademark infringement litigation to cease infringement, remove obstructions, eliminate dangers, compensate for financial losses and eliminate all negative effects due to its infringement in accordance with Article 134 of General Principle of the Civil Law and Article 53 of the Trademark Law. In addition to the above, the people's court has the discretion to impose a fine, detain infringing goods, confiscate manufacturing tools and equipment that are used to produce the infringing products in its judgment."* In practice, the infringing party is typically requested to bear the following civil liabilities: cease infringements, compensate for financial losses, and eliminate the negative effects. Cessation of infringements is actually a permanent injunction that requires the infringing party to stop infringement. In some cases, the courts will not only request the infringing party to stop infringement, but also request the party to destroy all infringing products as well as tools and equipment that are used to manufacture the infringing products. Compensation for losses is primarily a mechanism allowing the plaintiff to recover losses that it suffers as a result of the infringement. Generally speaking, courts typically adopt the "making the plaintiff whole" approach when determining the amount of compensation. The 2013

Trademark Law states that the amount of damages in a trademark infringement lawsuit can be based on the actual loss suffered by the plaintiff as a result of the infringing acts. In situations where the actual loss cannot be calculated or is difficult to determine, the damage amount can be calculated based on the profits obtained by the infringing party due to its infringement; in situations where it is difficult to determine the plaintiff's loss or the infringing party's revenue, the damage amount can be calculated based on several times of the reasonable licensing fee that a party would have paid had there been a license agreement between the parties. For egregious or malicious infringement, the court can request a compensation amount that is one to three times of the damage amount discussed above. The compensation should also take into account the reasonable expenses that the trademark owner has incurred in order to stop the infringement. In situations where it is difficult to determine the actual loss suffered by the plaintiff, the infringer's profits or the reasonable licensing fees, a court can consider the specific facts to the case and award damages up to RMB 3,000,000 (around USD 437,000). Elimination of negative effects means that the infringing party should eliminate any adverse effects on the plaintiff's reputation or business goodwill as a result of the defendant's infringement.

CHAPTER 2

Acquisition of Trademark Rights

1. Analysis of "Other Negative Impact" as a Ground to Refuse a Trademark Application

Appeal of administrative litigation regarding the trademark refusal for "FOBAO in English and Chinese characters and design" filed by Guangdong Province Guangmei Fobao Mineral Water Co., Ltd.

- First Instance: Beijing No. 1 Intermediate People's Court (No. 1388; 2012) - Decided on May 17, 2012
- Second Instance: Beijing High People's Court (No. 1224; 2012) - Decided on August 17, 2012

BACKGROUND

Guangdong Province Guangmei Fobao Mineral Water Co., Ltd. (the "***Applicant***") applied for a trademark "FOBAO in English and Chinese character and design" (Application Number 7268691; *see* Image One below; the "***Application***" or the "***Mark***") on March 20, 2009; the designated goods include beer, juice, and mineral water in Class 32 in China. The Chinese Trademark Office ("***Trademark Office***") was of the view that the registration of the Application would have a negative impact on the society and refused the Application on the basis of Article 10 Section 1(8) of the 2001 Trademark Law. The Applicant appealed the decision to TRAB under SAIC of PRC (the "***Appeal Board***").

Image One

The Applicant's primary appeal grounds are threefold:

(1) The character "FO"("佛") refers to the county "FOGANG"("佛冈") where the Applicant is located, and it does not meant to refer directly to any religion – the use of the Mark on products such as mineral water does not have any negative impact on the religions in China.
(2) The Applicant has used the Mark for twenty years; it is therefore a distinctive and famous trademark for the underlying products. The use of the Mark will not cause any consumer confusion in China.
(3) The Trademark Office has in the past approved applications of "FOBAO" on other applications with products and services similar to the subject Application. The examiner should apply a consistent examination standard and approve the Mark.

The primary evidences provided by the Applicant include:

(1) The business license of the Applicant.
(2) Various awards and certificates dating back in the 1990s – including sports events designating the mineral water bearing the subject mark as the official mineral water for the events.
(3) A copy of the certificate showing the subject Application was recognized as one of China's famous brands in 2005.

The Appeal Board maintained the refusal on the ground that the "FO" character is likely to have a negative impact on the society. The Application is therefore refused based on Article 10 Section 1(8) of the 2001 Trademark Law. The Applicant did not agree with the decision and raised a timely administrative court action to Beijing No. 1 Intermediate People's Court (the "***Court***").

COURT DECISION

The key issue to the Court is whether or not the registration of the Mark violates Article 10 Section 1(8) of the 2001 Trademark Law.

The phrase "Other Negative Impact" refers to components in a mark that is likely to cause a negative impact on the public interests and social order in the politics, economics, culture, religion, and ethnicity in China. The "FO" character in the Application is generally understood by members of the Chinese society to refer to Buddha in the Buddhism religion. This is therefore a character with special meaning among the Buddhist society in China. Accordingly, the incorporation and use of the character in a trademark is likely to trigger unpleasant feelings or cause a negative impact on the religions and the religious systems in China. Although the Applicant maintained the position that the "FO" character is originated from the county name (namely, the inclusion of the FO character is "innocent" and that it does not mean to invoke any religious connection), the general public is not likely to have such an association. Indeed, they are more likely to regard the "FO" character as a character with religious meaning. The situation described in Article 10 Section 1(8) of the Trademark Law is a legal restriction – it forbids a registration of the mark regardless whether or not the mark has become a famous mark through use. Furthermore, the analysis in the Application is different from other FOBAO formative marks that were approved for registration. As a result, the registration status of other "FOBAO" marks is not directly relevant to the subject case. The Applicant disagreed with the Court's decision and filed an appeal to the Beijing High People's Court (the "***High Court***").

The High Court agreed with the Court that the "FO" character has a different meaning in Buddhism and is generally understood as the characters for Buddha that Buddhists pay respect to. Furthermore, the character is commonly used in Buddhist phrases such as "FO FA SENG"("佛"; "法" & "僧") – i.e., three treasures in Buddhism. The Application combines two characters – "FO"("佛") and "BAO"("宝") (typically understood by the Chinese public and can be roughly translated to: "Buddha" and "treasure") in connection with beer products when in fact drinking behavior is not accepted in the Buddhism religion – the use of the FO character, a character deeply ingrained and connected with Buddhism – is therefore contrary to the Buddhist discipline and would have a negative impact on the Chinese Buddhist society. The Application therefore violates Article 10 Section 1(8) of the Trademark Law and should not be allowed. The use situation and fame status of the Application cannot overcome this refusal. According to the case-by-case review principle, the fact that other marks have been approved for registrations do not have direct bearing in the subject case. In light of the above, the High Court maintained the refusal of the Application.

ANALYSIS & INSIGHT

Article 10 Section 1(8) of the Trademark Law states that "*A symbol/word/design cannot serve as a trademark if it damages the general morality and customs of the society or has* ***other negative impact*** *on the society.*" This case is a classic example when a trademark application is refused because its registration would lead to "other negative impact on the society" as discussed in Article 10 Section 1(8) of the 2001 Trademark Law.

I. Definition of "Other Negative Impact" as Discussed in Article 10 Section 1(8) of the 2001 Trademark Law.

Since its inception in 1982 and despite three subsequent amendments, the Trademark Law has maintained a consistent position by not allowing registration of any mark that would "*damage the general morality and customs or have other negative impact on the society.*" The consistency has amply demonstrated the importance of this clause in the trademark system.

Similar restrictions can be found in the trademark law in most modern countries and jurisdictions in the world. For example, the trademark laws in the UK, Germany, Japan, and Taiwan clearly state that any trademark application shall be refused if the registration of such mark will "negatively affect public morality and society order." Article 6(5) of Paris Convention for the Protection of Industrial Property states that "any applications that are contrary to the public morality and society order – especially those that are of deceptive nature - shall be refused for registration." European Community Trade Mark Regulation also include this as an absolute ground to refuse a trademark application.

The idea of "public morality and social order" is one of the basic principles for civil law; it serves as a catch-all phrase to avoid abuse of the legal rights. The application of this principle requires flexibility. This principle has been widely applied in civil and commercial cases. The premises remains the same in respect to the "morality principle" clause discussed in the trademark law in the above countries/ jurisdictions and Article 10 Section 1(8) of the Chinese Trademark Law. The difference is that the Chinese Trademark Law takes it one step further so that it is not only a ground to refuse registration of a mark, but also in respect to use of the mark. The idea of "public morality" is similar to the phrase in Article 10 Section 1(8) of the Chinese Trademark Law: "general good morality and customs of the society;" the remaining phrase "other negative impact" in Article 10 Section 1(8) should therefore be understood to reference "social order."

Based on the structure of Article 10 Section 1, it lists eight situations where a word/symbol/design cannot serve as a trademark. The first five situations specify limitations in respect to the mark itself while the last three involve analysis in respect to the nature of the mark. The "other negative impact" clause is placed at the end of this section and is generally perceived to be a fallback catch-all provision; it is meant to describe situations outside those described in the first seven provisions where a trademark application shall nevertheless be refused.

Section 3 of the Opinions on Several Issues Concerning the Trial of Administrative Cases Involving the Authorization and Determination of Trademark Rights issued by the SPC states that "*when considering a mark for registration in respect to its 'other negative impact,' a civil court should evaluate the mark itself or its components to see if the registration causes a negative effect on the politics, economics, culture, religion, ethnicity and other public interests or public orders of the Chinese society. If the registration of a mark would detriment a third party's civil rights, this situation - however - should not be regarded as a ground to refuse the mark's registration because the Chinese Trademark Law already discusses this situation and provides appropriate reliefs."*

To summarize, the "other negative impact" clause governs situations where a registration of a mark would have had a detrimental impact on the public interest and social order which is not specified in the first seven provisions of Article 10 Section 1 and does not fall under the definition of "damaging the general good morality and customs of the society."

II. Analysis of "Other Negative Impact."

The analysis of "Other Negative Impact" should consider the perception of a certain group (either the "relevant" or the "certain" public in a society); the analysis should include the components of the mark as well as its designated goods and services. The analysis should also consider the following factors to determine if the registration of the mark would lead to any negative impact on the public interests and public order: social background, political background, historic background, culture and traditions, customs, and religious policies.

A. Must Concrete Examples Be Presented to Satisfy This Clause?

We have seen cases where the applicants would seek to defend the registrability of their marks by pointing out that there is no evidence demonstrating the negative impact following use of their marks; these applicants sometimes counter the refusals of their marks by asking the authorities to provide negative impact evidence. The determination of "Other Native Impact" does not require any actual occurrence of the event; the authorities only need to prove the correlation between the mark itself and the possibility that "Other Negative Impact" could occur. This is because the purpose of law is not only to punish, but also to prevent, deter, and provide guidance. It is therefore a good law if it could provide guidance to the general public, and prevent violations (as opposed to punish and evaluate violations); it is in fact a "better" law in terms of the social capital savings (because the violation has not yet happened) and is more efficient to promote social harmony. In addition, the goal of Article 10 Section 1(8) of the Trademark Law is to forbid use - if the application of this law requires an example of actually "using" the law, it would be contradictory to the reason why this clause is in existence in the first place.

In this case, the Appeal Board and Courts considered the meaning of the Chinese character "FO" and its role in the Buddhism religion in China. They decided that the use and registration of the Application would lead to a negative impact on the Buddhist society and the overall religious systems in China.

B. The "General" Public Versus the "Relevant" Public Analysis.

The registrability of a trademark involves both the "general" public and the "relevant" public. In accordance with Section 8 of the Judicial Interpretation of the SPC Concerning the Application of Laws in the Trial of Cases of Civil Disputes Arising from Trademarks, "*the relevant public in the Trademark Law refers to the relevant consumers who view the subject mark as the source identifier in connection with its* designated goods/services as well as the other operators who are closely connected with the channel of trade with the said goods/services." Accordingly, under the Trademark Law, the "relevant public" emphasizes the close connection between the manufacturers, service suppliers, operators, and personnel the mark touches on as it moves through the channel of trademark and relevant public) and the designated goods/services that have become closely associated with the mark. The distinctiveness and the fame status of a mark also hinge on the perception of the "relevant" public.

With respect to the "general" public, it refers to the average consumers with no specific criteria. The "general" public should be the "relevant" public in this case to determine the issue relating to "Other Native Impact" because it involves evaluation of public interests and public order. In other words, it is based on the general public's perception whether or not the use/registration of the mark would have a negative impact on the politics, economics, and culture of the Chinese society.

For example, in the review of trademark application of "GANGSTER RABBIT in Chinese" (Application Number 3237636)[21] the Appeal Board refused the registration of the mark on the ground of Article 10 Section 1(8). The decision demonstrates that a trademark serves not only as a source identifier for the underlying products, but also serves as a medium carrying message to the public in general. GANGSTER RABBIT clearly sends a message different from its usual cartoon image because the word "gangster" describes some rough and rude behavior. Considering the general public's perception towards the word "gangster" and the general unacceptance of a trademark inclusive of the "gangster" word, the courts have decided to support the Appeal Board's refusal decision.

The scope of the "general" public sometimes needs to be defined when one is considering the negative impact on religion and ethnicity, or impact on certain gender/vocational groups. If a "certain" group would have a negative reaction towards the mark at issue, then their interests should be considered. The scope of a "certain" group within the affected religion, ethnicity, gender and vocation differs from the scope for the "relevant" public. The former emphasizes the relationship between the group itself and the mark while the latter emphasizes the relationship between the designated goods/services of a mark and the group itself. In the subject case, the Appeal Board and the courts analyzed the refusal of the Application from the perspective of the "certain" public – the Buddhist society in China. The Application is refused because the "FO" character (which suggests connection with Buddhist) in connection with beer products

21. Case Index: Trademark Review & Adjudication Board [2005] No. 2493; Beijing No. 1 Intermediate People's Court, Yi Zhong Xing Chu Zi [2006] No. 765; Beijing High People's Court, Gao Xing Zhong Zi [2006] No. 571.

is contrary to Buddhist principles; the use and registration of the Mark will therefore have a negative impact on the Buddhist society so it should be rejected.

In the case involving "CHENG HUANG in Chinese (城隍)" under Application Number 1218394,[22] the mark was registered on October 28, 1998 covering precious stones, pearls, and emerald; it was recognized as a well-known trademark by the Trademark Office in May 2011. The Appeal Board and courts failed to take into consideration that although the phrase could be regarded as a famous mark by the "relevant" public for the underlying pearls and precious stone products, the phrase nevertheless has a special meaning to the "general" public (i.e., a special "Taoism" term meaning "city moat"). In respect to the "certain" public in the Taoism society where the people in fact associate the term with the someone to whom they pay respect, the use and registration of the term as a trademark would therefore cause a negative impact to this certain group in the Chinese society as described in Article 10 Section 1(8) of the Trademark Law.

In the case involving the appeal of trademark refusal of "泼妇鱼庄" (English phonetics: "PO FU YU ZHUANG; the phrase can be roughly translated to mean "Shrew's Fish Restaurant") (Application Number 8724085),[23] the "POFU" term is understood to describe overly aggressive and unreasonable women – a demeaning term for women. The female group (i.e., the "certain" public) in the society would therefore be opposed to the use and registration of this mark which would inevitably and negatively affect their interests. The mark is therefore refused for registration in respect to restaurants and cafeteria services.

C. Should the Underlying Products/Services Be Considered?

There's still no consensus as to whether or not the "Other Negative Impact" analysis should involve the underlying products/services. The first school of thought considers this level of analysis necessary; for example, this is listed as one of the required factors to analyze "Other Negative Impact" in the 2005 Standard for Examination and Review of Trademarks. Another school of thought does not believe the analysis should involve the underlying products/services – the analysis should strictly focus on the trademark itself or the components of the mark, as opposed to any negative impacts when the mark is used in connection with its designated products. For example, both courts followed this school of thought in deciding the administrative litigation on review of refusal in respect to the trademark application for "华夏第一井" (Hua Xia Di Yi Jing in English phonetics; the phrase can be roughly translated to mean "China's No. 1 Well)" (Application Number 5697580).[24] Specifically, the courts overturned the Appeal

22. Case Index: Trademark Review & Adjudication Board [2013] No. 07311; Beijing No. 1 Intermediate People's Court, Yi Zhong Zhi Xing Chu Zi [2013] No. 1860; Beijing High People's Court, Gao Xing Zhong Zi [2014] No. 485.
23. Case Index: Trademark Review & Adjudication Board [2013] No. 18684; Beijing No. 1 Intermediate People's Court, Yi Zhong Zhi Xing Chu Zi [2013] No. 2538.
24. Case Index: Trademark Review & Adjudication Board [2012] No. 11601; Beijing No. 1 Intermediate People's Court, Yi Zhong Zhi Xing Chu Zi [2012] No. 1905; Beijing High People's Court, Gao Xing Zhong Zi [2012] No. 1923.

Board's decision which refused the application. The trademark itself - as well as its components - does not have any negative impact on the Chinese society in respect to public interest and social order in politics, economics, culture, religion, and ethnicity. However, the Appeal Board held the view that the application was likely to mislead consumers into believing the underlying products - i.e., "alcohol (drinks)" - are extracted from the best well (or, the No. 1 well) in China. The courts rejected the Appeal Board's view in that there is no substantial evidence to support this Negative Impact analysis. The courts therefore overturned the Appeal Board's decision and approved the registration of the mark.

Although the emphasis should be focused on the correlation between the mark itself and the possible negative impact, the underlying products/services will inevitably play a part in the analysis - a trademark is, after all, a source identifier for its products/services. Even in a hypothesis, one should pay attention to the perception in respect to the mark at issue from the "general" or "certain" public perspective - the mark's designated goods and services should also be taken into account in the analysis of "Other Negative Impact." This level of analysis is often overlooked because the disputed marks are typically rejected when the use and registration of the underlying products *will* lead to negative effects on the society. For example, all the products have been refused even if for mineral water in the subject case, jewelry in "CHENG HUANG in Chinese (城隍)," and the goods/services in Classes 3, 9, 10, 16, 21, 25, 28, 29, 30, and 41 for "GANGSTER RABBIT in Chinese." This is why most people only focus on the trademark itself or its components when analyzing the "Other Negative Impact" prong and overlook the possible negative effects when the mark at issue is applied in connection with the designated goods. Indeed, one may reach a different conclusion if the mark at issue involves different goods/services. For example, the "BLACKMAN in Chinese" brand is allowed for registration for toothpaste; however, it is likely to be refused for registration due to its potential negative impact on race and ethnicity if the mark were to be used in connection with sanitary products.

D. The Applicant's Subjective View and Actual Use of the Mark.

The analysis of "Other Negative Impact" should be concerned about the perception and view of the "general" or "certain" public towards the mark at issue and determine if the use and registration of the mark would result in any negative impact on the public interest and social order. This analysis, therefore, does not need to take into account the application's subjective view and its use situation of the mark at issue. In other words, the fact that the applicant does not have any bad faith in adopting and using the mark, or the mark has accumulated a substantial amount of fame through extensive use in the "relevant" public does not serve as a valid ground to support its registration.

In the subject case, the application should nevertheless be refused even though the applicant insists the "FO" character refers to the county where it is located and does not have any connection with the Buddhist religion, the applicant does not have any intent to offend the Buddhist society in China, and the mark has been put into use for over twenty years and indeed, the FO BAO branded mineral water has received various awards in the 1990s and was recognized as a famous brand in China in 2005. This is because the use and registration of the "FO" character, as a trademark, is likely to negatively impact the Chinese religion and accordingly, none of the above fame and use information would serve as valid counter arguments to support its registration.

III. Application of the "Other Negative Impact" Clause.

A. Common Scenarios.

Common scenarios where the "Other Native Impact" clause is applicable include the following:

(1) Negative impact on politics: This type of marks include: (1) marks that are identical or closely similar to country names, regional names or names of political figures of international organizations; (2) marks that have a negative implication or connotation of a country's regime, sovereignty, and its overall image; (3) marks that are composed of numbers which have political meanings; and (4) marks that are identical or closely similar to the names of terrorism groups, cults, gangster groups or of their leaders.
(2) Negative impact on ethnicity: This type of marks include applications that are either disrespectful or are likely to offend different ethnic groups in a society.
(3) Negative impact on religions or folk beliefs: This type of marks include applications that are identical or similar to idols, symbols, a combination of distinctive elements of a religion or folk belief, common gathering place references, their particular denominations and disciplines, popular usages in a particular religion or folk belief, rituals, customs, and religious appellations and figures or people with whom the common public have become associated a particular religion or folk belief.
(4) Negative impact on social political groups including names and symbols that are identical or closely similar to social political parties in China, its governmental organizations and social groups.
(5) Negative impact on military including names and symbols that are identical to the specific titles, administrative duties and title references in a political organization or the military of PRC.
(6) Negative impact on currency references including references and logos that are identical or closely similar to currency of each country.
(7) Negative impact on the Chinese culture including names and symbols that are contrary to China's traditions and cultures.

B. Default Use and Possible Abuse of the Clause.

In addition to the scenarios described above, the "Other Negative Impact" clause is commonly used as a default clause in the Trademark Law so as to forbid situations where there are no directly applicable laws but the use and registration of the trademark at issue are likely to mislead consumers, cause unfair competition or result in unjustifiable profits to certain groups in a society. This clause is therefore particularly important to maintain a good balance in today's society, the integrity of the trademark system and to make sure a regulation is in place despite the lack of specific black-and-white laws. The "default" use of this clause can be seen in the refusal of the following trademark applications. In the application for "九朝贡胶"(Jiu Chao Gong Jiao in English phonetics; the phrase can be roughly translated to mean "Tributary Gelatin for Nine Dynasties") under Application Number 6403947,[25] for example, the mark was refused because the public were likely to be misled and have a preconceived notion of the underlying products (health supplements) because the mark literally described the product as a political tribute in nine dynasties in China. In other words, the description of the product suggested the product as being rare and extremely valuable – something only the emperors and royalties could enjoy – the use and registration would therefore have an impact on the public interests and the mark was refused. Another example relates to the appeal of trademark refusal for "HARRY POTTER in Chinese and in English phonetics (Ha Li Bo Te)" (Application Number 1674835).[26] This application was refused because, prior to its filing date, there was already a high level of fame and influence in the relevant public in respect to the Harry Potter book and its story figures, the HARRY POTTER character combination in Chinese is not a fixed dictionary phrase (i.e., it is a coined phrase), and the applicant was not able to offer a reasonable explanation as to how it came up with the HARRY POTTER combination in English and Chinese. Accordingly, the mark was not an application in good faith because the applicant was aware of the fame associated with the real Harry Potter book, its storyline and figures prior to its trademark application – the mark therefore fell under the category of "Other Negative Impact" and was refused. In the appeal of trademark refusal for "THE HARRIS PRODUCTS GROUP" (Application Number 6081872),[27] the mark itself was about "The Harris Group" while the applicant for the mark was another group: "the Lincoln Global, Inc." The discrepancy would result in consumer confusion and was refused under the "Other Negative Impact" clause. In the trademark applications for "LI XIAO LONG (Bruce Lee's name in Chinese)"[28] and "LIU DE HUA (Andy Lau's name in Chinese),"[29] the examiner was not able to refuse either application on the basis of prior name rights for public figures under Article 31 of the 2001 Trademark Law. Nevertheless, these applications were

25. Case Index: Trademark Review & Adjudication Board [2011] No. 1830; Beijing No. 1 Intermediate People's Court, Yi Zhong Zhi Xing Chu Zi [2011] No. 1636.
26. Case Index: Trademark Review & Adjudication Board [2009] No. 30606; Beijing No. 1 Intermediate People's Court, Yi Zhong Zhi Xing Chu Zi [2010] No. 401; Beijing High People's Court, Gao Xing Zhong Zi [2011] No. 669.
27. Case Index: Trademark Review & Adjudication Board [2010] No. 24137; Beijing No. 1 Intermediate People's Court, Yi Zhong Zhi Xing Chu Zi [2011] No. 1462; Beijing High People's Court, Gao Xing Zhong Zi [2012] No. 1085.
28. Case Index: Trademark Review & Adjudication Board [2012] No. 35443; Beijing No. 1 Intermediate People's Court, Yi Zhong Zhi Xing Chu Zi [2013] No. 2100.
29. Case Index: Trademark Review & Adjudication Board [2012] No. 09341; Beijing No. 1 Intermediate People's Court, Yi Zhong Zhi Xing Chu Zi [2011] No. 2272.

rejected under the "Other Negative Impact" clause because the applicants were seeking to trade off the goodwill associated with the respective passed public figures and other's name when there's a namesake and the applications were therefore not filed in good faith. In the trademark application for "中国劲酒" ("Zhong Guo Jing Jiu" in English phonetics; the phrase can be roughly translated to mean "China's Excellent Liquor")" under Application Number 4953206,"[30] the mark was not refused on the basis of Article 10(1)(1) of the 2001 Trademark Law because the mark, as a whole, was not identical or similar to the country name of PRC. However, a country's name should not be abused by allowing it to be included as a component of any trademark. It would otherwise lead to negative impact on the social order and public interests as well as a country's overall image. Accordingly, although the mark was not a literal violation of Article 10(1)(1) of the 2001 Trademark Law, it was nevertheless refused because the use and registration are likely to cause "Other Negative Impacts."

Despite the above, simply allowing the clause to serve as a default rule for any situation might constitute an overuse of the law – the over application of this clause might be contrary to the spirits of the law and disrupts the balance between this clause and others in the Trademark Law. This tricky balance explains why it has been difficult to apply the "Other Negative Impact" clause as a default rule. One needs to be particularly sensitive in applying this clause in situations where a mark is likely to mislead the public either in respect to the quality features of the underlying products or as a source identifier, a mark that is likely to contribute to a negative effect on others' civil rights, or a mark that was not applied for in good faith. In situations where there are no directly relevant laws, it has been established that the applicant did not apply for the mark at issue for justifiable commercial purposes, and there is sufficient evidence to prove that the applicant has exhibited a bad-faith filing pattern – there still exits different interpretations of the "Other Negative Impacts" clause and whether or not the clause applies in the situations such as squatting trademarks for a big amount or many times with a bad faith. Accordingly, there have been some inconsistent applications and decisions in respect to this clause. We will try to reconcile the inconsistencies below.

First, in respect to the issue whether or not the "possibility to lead to consumer confusion" falls under the category of "Other Negative Impact" under Article 10(1)(8), it would soon be resolved by the amendment to Article 10(1)(7) of the Trademark Law. The third amendments to the Trademark Law revised Article 10(1)(7) from "exaggerated and deceptive promotion" to "deceptive, likely to lead to consumer confusion with respect to **quality and quantity** features of the underlying products or its **source.**" However, the New Law will still need to define the specific features besides "quality" and "quantity" of a product. The New Law also needs to address how to interpret the word "source" (such as the place from which the product is originated, compared to the "origin") so as to offer a uniform interpretation and application of the law. The New Law will therefore be helpful to better define the application of the "Other Negative

30. Case Index: The Supreme People's Court, Xing Ti Zi [2010] No. 4.

Effect" clause, and the interaction between the two clauses in order to maintain the market order and integrity of the trademark system.

Second, in respect to the issue where the "Other Negative Impact" clause is applicable to the situation where a mark was not applied for in good faith, and/or the use and registration of the mark will negatively impact civil rights of others, it has been addressed in Section 3 of the Opinions on Several Issues Concerning the Trial of Administrative Cases Involving the Authorization and Determination of Trademark Rights issued by the SPC. The Opinions on Several Issues Concerning the Trial of Administrative Cases Involving the Authorization and Determination of Trademark Rights reads: *"if a registration of a mark is likely to impact a certain group's civil rights, and its impact is limited to such civil rights, the "other negative impact" clause is not applicable. This is because the trademark law already discusses the appropriate relief and procedures to address situations where a certain group's civil rights are impacted in other clauses."* The "Other Negative Impact" clause is an absolute refusal ground which is different and distinguishable in respect to the nature, legal origin and protection terms from other clauses discussed in the Trademark Law. Simply applying the "Other Negative Impact" as a default clause for any situation will disrupt the balance between different trademark rules and regulations; accordingly, it is preferable to refuse this type of trademark applications on the basis of specific rules in the Trademark Law rather than relying on the "Other Negative Impact" clause. The 2013 Trademark Law first incorporated the good-faith principle in regulating trademark applications. Although it would be difficult to apply this as a ground to refuse a trademark application (since it functions more like a legal principle), the interpretation and application of the law should still embody this principle. Guided by the principle of good faith and integrity, once the New Law goes into effect, we believe bad-faith applications can be refused on the basis of one's prior rights or other specific legal regulations rather than resorting to the "Other Negative Impact" as a default rule.

Lastly, in respect to the issue where the "Other Negative Impact" clause is applicable to the situation where one squatting a third party's famous or distinctive trademarks for profit instead of use for a big amount or many times, it is commonly viewed as a disruption to the trademark system. The situation therefore falls under Article 44(1) of the 2013 Trademark Law "obtain trademark registration illegitimately." Since there is already a consensus in respect to the specific rule to govern this situation; the "Other Negative Impact" clause should be less applied.

2. Analysis of "Publicly Well-Known Foreign Toponyms or References" as Grounds to Refuse a Trademark Application

Administrative litigation regarding the review of trademark refusal for "OLYMPIA 66" filed by Hang Lung Properties (Trade Marks) Limited

– First Instance: Beijing No. 1 Intermediate People's Court (No. 1206; 2012) – Decided on August 21, 2012

BACKGROUND

Hang Lung Properties (Trade Mark) Limited (the "***Applicant***") applied for a trademark "OLYMPIA 66" (Application Number 7473333; *see* Image One below; the "***Application***" or the "***Mark***") on June 16, 2009; the designated goods include posters, instruction manuals, pictures and photos, etc. The Applicant has also sought to register a number of "OLYMPIA 66" and "HENG LONG PLAZA in Chinese characters and OLYMPIA 66" marks in Classes 19, 35, 36, 39, 41, and 42 covering a wide range of goods and services in China. The Chinese Trademark Office ("***Trademark Office***") refused the Application and most of the Applicant's other similar trademark applications on the grounds that they included "a publicly well-known foreign toponym" as discussed under Article 10 Section 2 of the 2001 Trademark Law. The Applicant appealed the decision to the TRAB under SAIC of the PRC (the "***Appeal Board***").

Image One
Olympia 66

The Applicant's primary appeal grounds are as follows.

The Application as a whole will not be understood conceptually as a location (toponym); it has meaning other than merely being a foreign location reference. The "OLYMPIA" word in the Mark is not a protected trademark in the Regulations on the Protection of Olympic Symbols (the "***Olympic Regulation***"); the use of Mark therefore will not have any negative effect on the society. The Trademark Office in China, along with trademark authorities and offices in other countries, have approved applications inclusive of the OLYMPIA word in prior occasions. The Applicant's trademark applications – similar to the subject mark – have also been approved for registration in other countries and jurisdictions.

The primary evidence provided by the Applicant includes:

(1) copies of the Applicant's company introduction, financial information and websites;

(2) award information as well as partial annual reports of the Applicant and its affiliated companies;
(3) a copy of the Olympic Regulation that went into effect in 2002;
(4) prior trademark applications inclusive of the OLYMPIA word that were approved by the Trademark Office;
(5) information showing Greece and other European countries approved the "OLYMPIA" trademark applications; and
(6) trademark registrations that belong to the International Olympic Committee (IOC).

The Appeal Board maintained the refusal on the ground that the "OLYMPIA" word in the Application is one of the protected OLYMPIC formative trademarks as promulgated by Olympic Regulation. The Application was not authorized by the relevant authorities owning the OLYMPIC trademarks and its use and registration would therefore have a negative impact on the society, which violates Article 10 Section 1(8) of the Trademark Law. The Application also violates Article 10 Section 2 of the Trademark Law because "Olympia" is a city in ancient Greece and the place from which Olympic sports are originated – it is therefore a well-known reference and plays an important role in the history of the world's sports. The fact that other similar trademarks have been approved for registration cannot serve as a basis to justify the approval of the subject Application. The information and evidence provided by the Applicant cannot prove the registrability of the Mark. Accordingly, the Appeal Board agrees with the refusal decision based on Article 10 Section 1(8), and Article 10 Section (2) of the 2001 Trademark Law. The Applicant did not agree with the decision and raised a timely administrative court action to Beijing No. 1 Intermediate People's Court (the "***Court***").

COURT DECISION

The key issues to the Court are threefold:

(1) whether or not the registration of the Mark would result in "other negative impact" on the society as defined by Article 10 Section 1(8) of the Trademark Law;
(2) whether or not the Application falls within the definition as a "well-known foreign toponym/reference" as defined by Article 10 Section 2 of the Trademark Law; and
(3) whether or not the fact that other OLYMPIC formative word marks have been approved for registration, both domestically in China and internationally, can serve as the registrability basis for the subject Application.

With respect to the first issue: Olympic Regulation is the administrative regulation developed by the PRC; its goal is to increase the overall protection of the Olympic Trademarks (defined below), guarantee the legal rights of the respective trademark holders, and to safeguard the dignity of the Olympic sports and the spirit the event embodies. Article 2, Section 2 of the Olympic Regulation defines the Olympic Trademarks to include OLYMPIC in Chinese, OLYMPIA in Chinese, OLYMPIC SPORTS COMMITTEE in Chinese and its abbreviations as well as any established exclusive terms associated with any of the above references (collectively, the "***Olympic Trademarks***"). The subject Application is composed of the English word "OLYMPIA" and the number "66" – the English word "Olympia" already has an established corresponding set of Chinese characters which is composed of four individual characters: AO LIN PI YA. These four characters represent OLYMPIA and together, they form one of the protected trademarks as defined in Olympic Regulation. To the relevant public in China, there is already an exclusive connection between the English word "OLYMPIA" and the corresponding four characters in Chinese - they represent the same thing. The use and registration of the Application which includes the English word "Olympia" will not be beneficial to the overall protection of the Olympic Trademarks. The use of the Application as a trademark would in fact have a detrimental effect to the Olympic Sports and the spirit the event embodies and have a negative impact on the social order and public interests of the Chinese society.

With respect to the second issue: Article 10 Section 2 of the Trademark Law states that "publicly/commonly known foreign toponyms/references" should not be approved as a trademark. The exception to this rule is when the mark has already acquired "other meaning" in addition to serving as a location reference. "Other Meaning" (as opposed to "secondary meaning" where a mark acquires additional meaning through use) in this context should be taken to mean that the foreign location reference has acquired a fixed dictionary meaning, and the meaning associated with the term is stronger (or more well-known) than the term serving as a location indicator. "Olympia" refers to an ancient city in Greece and is the origin of the Olympic sports. Given the long-standing history of the Olympic sports, and the support of such events from the Chinese government and the popularity associated with these sports among the Chinese consumers, the term is a well-known reference in China; it is commonly understood as the city where the Olympic sports originated. Accordingly, it is reasonable to refuse the Application on the ground that it includes a well-known foreign toponym, Olympia. The Applicant argued that the "foreign location references/names" as defined in Article 10 Section 2 of the Trademark Law should be limited to current references only which are still in use; it should not be interpreted to include any ancient location references. Furthermore, the Trademark Law does not include any specific limitation in respect to the application of Article 10 Section 2 nor is there any judicial interpretation offering any similar restrictions when interpreting this clause. We therefore do not support this argument.

The Applicant also argued that the mark as a whole has a definite "other" meaning and the meaning is stronger and more well-known than its original meaning which is a reference to an ancient city in Greece. However, in reality, the Mark is composed of two parts: the English word "Olympia" and the number "66" – the mark as a whole has not yet accumulated any known definite meaning. Considering the fact that the Mark as a whole has not yet acquired any meaning, and Olympia – being one of the distinctive elements of the Application – will inevitably trigger some connection between the ancient city in Greece and the designed goods covered by the Mark, the Mark is therefore not registrable under the Chinese Trademark Law.

With respect to the third issue: a trademark application in China is reviewed based on the case-by-case principle. Following this principle, it is not inappropriate for the Appeal Board to refuse the Application even though the Applicant has provided evidence noting that other OLYMPIA formative marks were approved for registration in the past. Furthermore, some of the OLYMPIA formative word marks were approved prior to the effective date of Olympic Regulation – these registrations are therefore not bound by the Olympic Regulation; they should not be viewed as a justifiable ground to evidence the registrability of the subject Application either. Lastly, the trademark law is a territorial law by nature. Accordingly, the fact that some OLYMPIA formative word marks are approved for registrations in jurisdictions outside China does not itself serve as a ground that a similar application should also be approved in China.

In sum, the court maintained the decision of the Appeal Board and the plaintiff did not appeal.

ANALYSIS & INSIGHT

The case is a classic application of the clause: "publicly well-known foreign toponyms/ references" as defined in Article 10 Section 2 of the Trademark Law which serves as a ground to refuse a trademark application.

I. Legislative Goal for the "Well-Known Foreign Name/References" Clause.

The 1982 Trademark Law did not include any restriction in respect to the use and registration of a trademark that is composed of location references. In the 1993 amendments, Article 8 Section 2 was added which states: "*administrative divisions that are at or above county level or publicly well-known foreign toponyms or references shall not serve as a trademark; location references that have acquired additional meanings or marks that include location references but have already been approved for registrations are an exception to this rule.*" The 2001 Trademark Law maintained the clause as stated in the 1993 amendments. In addition, Article 10 Section 2 expanded the above exceptions as one of the situations where marks "as part of the registered certification marks and collective marks" can be approved for trademark registrations. The third amendment of the 2013 Trademark Law retained Article 10 Section 2 of the 2001 Trademark Law.

The fundamental function of a trademark is a source identifier. The so-called source allows the consumers to identify the service provider or product manufacturer with respect to the services/products that bear the mark, rather than the locational origin. If one registers a location as a trademark, it is likely to mislead consumers to believe that the mark refers to the geographic supply origin of the underlying goods/services. The mark will then be regarded as a descriptive term for the location because it would not and could not describe or identify a specific manufacturer/ supplier; the mark is therefore not distinctive. Furthermore, a toponym or reference is part of the public resource and should not be converted to private property just because a third party has registered the name/reference as a trademark; the use and registration of such a mark would also prevent others in the same geographic location from using the name as a location reference. This is why most countries in the world have restrictive clause preventing a location reference from becoming or being used as a trademark. Similarly, in China, we take the same restrictive approach. The Trademark Law forbids the use and registration of a mark that is composed of administrative division names at or above the county level or well-known foreign toponyms/ references. The restriction, however, does not apply to administrative division names that are below county level or foreign names/references that are not publicly well known. Furthermore, registration is allowed (or continues to be allowed) with respect to foreign names/ references that have already acquired additional meanings, or are simply components to a part of the registered certification marks and collective marks, and the registered marks remain valid.

II. Determination of a "Publicly Well-Known Foreign Toponym or Reference."

The application of this clause involves the analysis of the following issues.

A. Determination of "Publicly Well-Known."

Trademark law is territorial by nature. Accordingly, the determination of the "publicly well-known" phrase should be based on the perception of the Chinese public with respect to the foreign toponym at issue. Specifically, the concept of "public" in the subject clause is different from the "relevant public" concept as generally discussed under the Trademark Law. The "relevant public" concept under the Trademark Law refers to the product manufacturers or service providers, the relevant consumers, and the operators and associated personnel with whom the mark comes into contact as its products/services move through the channel of trade. This concept pays attention to the close connection between these "subjects" - namely, suppliers, manufacturers, consumers, and operators - and the goods/services identified by the mark. With respect to the analysis of Article 10 Section 2 of the Trademark Law, it emphasizes that regarding the general public's recognition toward the toponym at issue, the focus is not on the public's recognition in respect to the toponym as a trademark. Accordingly, the relevant scope of "the public" to analyze Article 10 Section 2 should refer to the average, common consumers in China in general, rather than limited to any specific groups in the society.

Turning to the present case, "Olympia" is the corresponding English term for the four Chinese characters "奥林匹亚" that – as a combined phrase – has been established to refer to Olympia in English. Given the long-standing history of the Olympic sports events, their popularity and fame around the world (as well as in China), we have concluded that the English term "Olympia" is a "publicly well-known" location reference in China.

Although the determination regarding a "publicly well-known" toponym involves an objective fact, the process nevertheless involves some subjective analysis. The analysis must take into account the average Chinese consumers' recognition towards the toponym and reference at issue – it is not a straightforward rigid process such as simply recognizing a toponym because it has been listed in the popular dictionaries in China. A location reference can be determined as "publicly well-known" because it is a developed country's capital or an internationally influential city in some countries, it is known for its rare natural resources or products, it has a special historic connection with China, it has become a sister city with some cities in China, it includes a famous tourist spot, or it owns a famous sports team which is generally known to the average public in China. Generally speaking, a location can be recognized as a "publicly well-known" foreign toponym under Article 10 Section 2 of the Trademark Law if the average public in China can be easily exposed to the name through education, books and publications, media, and the internet, etc. In fact, one may sometimes reach a different conclusion in respect to the "publicly well-known" toponym depending on the "form" in which the name has been presented to the Chinese public – in its Chinese translation form versus its original form in a language that is not familiar to consumers in China. It is not uncommon that the public is sometimes more familiar with the Chinese version for the location and are not familiar at all with the name in its original language. Under such circumstances, the name as it appears in its original (foreign) language should not be regarded as "publicly well-known."

In the administrative litigation on review of refusal of a trademark "SHIMIZU & Design" (Application Number 5645357),[31] the Appeal Board rejected the application because "Shimizu" is referenced in the English-Chinese Dictionary as a city name in Japan. However, the courts held a different view and did not consider the SHIMIZU term as a "publicly well-known foreign toponym" due to the language differences and the vast distance between Japan and China; in other words, the general public in China would not instinctively and immediately associate the SHIMIZU term with a city name in Japan and there was insufficient evidence to prove that that the average consumers are aware of the term as a toponym in Japan.

In the administrative litigation on the review of trademark refusal of the "MILWAUKEE & Design" (Application Number 6819548),[32] both level of courts overturned the Appeal Board's decision and approved the registration of the mark even though the 2007 English-Chinese Dictionary and the internet search results have revealed a corresponding four-character term representing "Milwaukee" in English as the city name in the state of Wisconsin in the USA. This is because there is insufficient evidence to support the term "Milwaukee" – in its original English form – to be highly

31. Case Index: Trademark Review & Adjudication Board [2010] No. 27457; Beijing No. 1 Intermediate People's Court, Yi Zhong Zhi Xing Chu Zi [2013] No. 2409; Beijing High People's Court, Gao Xing Zhong Zi [2011] No. 1376.
32. Case Index: Trademark Review & Adjudication Board [2011] No. 22731; Beijing No. 1 Intermediate People's Court, Yi Zhong Zhi Xing Chu Zi [2012] No. 1715; Beijing High People's Court, Gao Xing Zhong Zi [2012] No. 1922.

recognizable by the average consumers in China. The use of the English term "Milwaukee" in a trademark therefore does not violate Article 10 Section 2 of the Trademark Law.

B. Determination of "Foreign Toponyms/References."

The subject clause has a different criterion in respect to restricting toponyms in China versus toponyms outside China. The restriction for the toponyms in China only applies to those that are at or above county level; there's no such restriction for foreign toponyms even though it might be a remote small town's name or ancient toponym. The use of the name in a trademark would not be allowed so long as it was generally known and recognizable by the average consumers in China.

In the subject case, the Applicant argued that "foreign toponyms" in Article 10 Section 2 should only apply to current active toponyms; it should not also apply to "ancient" city names such as "Olympia" in the present case. This view, however, was not supported by either the Appeal Board or the first level of the court. There is no specific restriction in the language of Article 10 Section 2 to limit the scope of "foreign toponyms" to current names only. Accordingly, even though Olympia is an ancient city name in Greece, it is a publicly well known and widely recognizable "foreign toponym" as defined by Article 10 Section 2 of the Trademark Law - the average consumers can easily recognize it as the place of origin for the Olympic sports.

If an application resembles a publicly well-known foreign toponym as a whole and the mark itself does not have any other dictionary meaning, the mark can also be refused on the ground that it is a commonly recognizable "foreign toponym." In the administrative litigation on review of refusal of a trademark "HAVANNA" (Application Number 5782202),[33] the Appeal Board refused the application on the ground that the mark as a whole is visually and phonetically similar to the capital city of Cuba: Havana (where the two words are only different by one letter); the Appeal Board held that the application did not comply with Article 10 Section 2 of the Trademark Law and the application should therefore be refused. Both courts agreed and maintained the Appeal Board's refusal decision.

C. Components of a "Publicly Well-Known Foreign Toponym."

In practice, an application typically includes additional components other than the toponyms alone. Take the subject case for example, it is composed of both the English term "Olympia" and the number "66." The issue would then become whether or not

33. Case Index: Trademark Review & Adjudication Board [2009] No. 25615; Beijing No. 1 Intermediate People's Court, Yi Zhong Zhi Xing Chu Zi [2010] No. 1506; Beijing High People's Court, Gao Xing Zhong Zi [2010] No. 1066.

the scopes of Article 10 Section 2 of the Trademark Law also cover such composite marks where additional non-toponyms are incorporated?

According to China's Standard for Examination and Review of Trademarks, Article 10 Section 2 covers not only marks that are composed strictly of foreign names, but also marks that *include* a publicly well-known foreign name simply as a component of the entire mark. The subject case therefore falls under the adjusted scope of Article 10 Section 2. In the administrative litigation on review of refusal of a trademark "ZURICH HELPPOINT" under Application Number G980884,[34] the Appeal Board rejected the application because the mark includes ZURICH that already has a set Chinese translation referring to a city in Switzerland. The city name is widely recognizable and publicly well known among average consumers in China and the mark therefore was refused based on Article 10 Section 2 of the Trademark Law. The first level of the court, however, overturned the refusal decision because the language in the clause includes the word "only" and should be applicable strictly to trademark applications that are composed *only* of foreign toponyms. The subject mark includes one additional element that renders the entire mark outside the adjusted scope of the law; the Appeal Board's decision therefore should be overturned because it involves an incorrect application of the law. The Appeal Board challenged the decision and filed an appeal to the Beijing High People's Court. The second level of the court reviewed the clause of Article 10 Section 2 and held that the law is applicable not only to trademark applications composed of domestic toponyms in China that are at or above the county level or publicly well-known foreign toponyms, but also marks that *include* the above-referenced domestic Chinese location as well as foreign toponyms.

III. Determination of a Toponym that Has Other Meaning.

Article 10 Section 2 of the Trademark Law carves out an exception where a toponym can still serve as a trademark so long as it has "other meaning" even though the name itself may be categorized either as a domestic toponym at or above the county level or a publicly well-known foreign toponym. "Other meaning" in this clause refers to meanings other than the mark serving merely as a location reference; in addition, such "other meaning" must be more recognizable to the general public than being a location reference. Since Article 10 of the Trademark Law is a restriction clause - this means applications composed of "administrative division toponyms in China that are at or above the county level or publicly well-known foreign names" shall not be approved for trademark registration or used as a trademark. Accordingly, the "other meaning" clause shall not be read to include the secondary meaning where a mark acquires additional meaning through use.

34. Case Index: Trademark Review & Adjudication Board [2011] No. 02276; Beijing No. 1 Intermediate People's Court, Yi Zhong Zhi Xing Chu Zi [2011] No. 2708; Beijing High People's Court, Gao Xing Zhong Zi [2012] No. 1001.

A. The Toponym Itself Has Other Meaning.

One of the difficulties in applying Article 10 Section 2 of the Trademark Law is that a toponym may sometimes have other meaning and if so, would the mark then become registrable? The key to this issue is to determine whether or not this "other meaning" has become more recognizable than itself being a location reference; the determination should still be based on the general public's perception in China. In the administrative litigation on review of refusal of a trademark "DETROIT" (Application Number 5705649),[35] the applicant argued that DETROIT is not only a city name, but also a river name in the USA; the mark therefore has "other meaning" and should be approved for registration. The Appeal Board refused the registration on the ground that the general public's understanding and perception of the Chinese translation for "DETROIT" - De Te Lv - is that it represents the capital of the Michigan State in the USA. The public is therefore more aware of the DETROIT word being the "city of automobiles," rather than a river name. The applicant's appeal grounds are rejected because the "other meaning" of DETROIT is not more publicly recognizable than itself being a location indicator. The application is refused on the ground of Article 10 Section 2 of the Trademark Law. The case was reviewed by two levels of courts; and both courts agreed and maintained the Appeal Board's refusal decision.

In some occasions, marks that are composed of foreign languages can be understood both as a location reference, as well as a common surname in some countries. It is then a case-by-case determination to see if the name is more widely recognized as a surname or as a location reference; the determination will need to take into account several other factors which also involve a subjective analysis. In the administrative litigation on review of refusal of a trademark "WASHINGTON in Chinese characters and Design" (Application Number 3330317),[36] the mark covers Class 31 products such as fresh fruit, flowers, and trees. In the applicant's appeal, it pointed out that WASHINGTON in Chinese characters refers not only to the capital in the USA, but also a common surname - it is for example the last name for George Washington, the first president of the US. The mark therefore should be approved for registration because it has "other meaning" than being a location reference and this "other meaning" is generally known to the public in China. The Appeal Board refused the registration of the mark pointing out that to the general public in China, the characters for WASHINGTON are more widely recognized as the capital for the US, rather than as a surname; the mark is therefore refused under Article 10 Section 2 of the Trademark Law. The case was reviewed by two levels of courts and both courts maintained the Appeal Board's refusal decision. On the other hand, in the administrative litigation on review of refusal of a trademark "HAMPTON MANOR" (Application

35. Case Index: Trademark Review & Adjudication Board [2009] No. 25080; Beijing No. 1 Intermediate People's Court, Yi Zhong Zhi Xing Chu Zi [2010] No. 901; Beijing High People's Court, Gao Xing Zhong Zi [2010] No. 882.
36. Case Index: Trademark Review & Adjudication Board [2006] No. 0048; Beijing No. 1 Intermediate People's Court, Yi Zhong Zhi Xing Chu Zi [2006] No. 1161; Beijing High People's Court, Gao Xing Zhong Zi [2007] No. 107.

Number 6565593),[37] the Appeal Board refused the mark on the ground that the general public tended to associate the Chinese translation for HAMPTON more as a city in South Eastern Virginia in the US; the public is less likely to view it as a surname and the mark should therefore be refused under Article 10 Section 2 of the Trademark Law. However, the first level of court viewed it differently in that HAMPTON in Chinese is more widely perceived and recognized as a surname, rather than a location indicator. Article 10 Section 2 of the Trademark Law is therefore inapplicable and the Appeal Board's decision was overturned.

B. The Mark Is Composed of a Publicly Well-Known Foreign Toponym as well as Other Elements; the Mark as a Whole Has Other Meaning(s).

According to the Opinions on Several Issues Concerning the Trial of Administrative Cases Involving the Authorization and Determination of Trademark Rights issued by the SPC (April 20, 2010), Section 4 states that *"if a mark includes other distinctive elements and the mark is therefore distinctive as a whole (i.e., it no longer has location reference as the only or primary meaning), the mark should not be refused simply because it includes administrative division location names at or above the county level in China or publicly well-known foreign location references."*

From the way the clause is written and viewing the enforcement of the law in practicality, the criteria are lenient for the mark which is composed of a publicly well-known foreign toponym as well as other elements; if the additional components in a mark are separate and distinct, then generally speaking, the mark should be approved for registration because the mark – taken as a whole – no longer means or can be primarily referred to simply as a location indicator. In the present case, although the Application includes "OLYMPIA" and "66," the combination of these two components does not have any new meaning. The OLYMPIA term is still the primary distinctive element of the Application. It is therefore refused for registration under Article 10 Section 2 of the Trademark Law.

In the above-mentioned appeal of trademark refusal for "ZURICH HELPPOINT," although the second level of the court regarded the first level of the court's interpretation of Article 10 Section 2 as too narrow, it also recognized the first level of the court's view in that the mark, taken as a whole, was distinctive and should not be held as a violation of Article 10 Section 2 of the Trademark Law. In addition to the inclusion of foreign toponym "ZURICH," the mark also includes an additional element "HELPPOINT" which is represented in the same or similar font and size as the ZURICH word. Furthermore, each word takes up roughly the same or similar portion of the entire mark. In light of the above, the relevant public will not understand the mark simply as a location indicator for ZURICH. The mark - as a whole - is therefore registrable and the court rejected the appeal and maintained the decision.

37. Case Index: Trademark Review & Adjudication Board [2011] No. 29188; Beijing No. 1 Intermediate People's Court, Yi Zhong Zhi Xing Chu Zi [2012] No. 1508.

In the administrative litigation on review of refusal of a trademark "MUNICH RE & Design" (International Registration Number G1024730),[38] the second level of the court overturned the decisions of the first level of the court and the Appeal Board and approved the registration of the mark. This is because even though the mark includes a location reference, it also includes other elements that allow the entire mark to have meanings different from being simply a location indicator. The mark should not be refused simply because it includes a publicly well-known foreign toponym. In the administrative litigation on review of refusal of a trademark "THE VENETIAN & Design" (Application Number 4815053; *see* Image Two below);[39] and the other two series applications for "THE VENETIAN & Design," the first level of the court was of the view that the applications - as a whole - are distinctive and have meaning other than just being a location indicator because the marks include a distinctive design. The court overturned the Appeal Board's refusal decision and approved the registration of these applications.

C. The Mark Includes a Toponym as well as Other Separate Distinctive Elements; the Role of the Toponym is Merely to Reference the Location of the Applicant.

According to China's Standard for Examination and Review of Trademarks, Article 10 Section 2 of the Trademark Law does not apply to marks that include a toponym as well as other separate and distinctive elements and the role of the location reference is simply to indicate the applicant's origin. For example, Article 10 Section 2 does not apply to the below "GENEVE" application (*see* Image Three below) because the applicant - QUINTING S.A. - is located in Geneva, Switzerland.

<table>
<tr><th>Image Two</th><th>Image Three</th></tr>
<tr><td>
</td><td>
</td></tr>
</table>

38. Case Index: Trademark Review & Adjudication Board [2012] No. 20021; Beijing No. 1 Intermediate People's Court, Yi Zhong Zhi Xing Chu Zi [2012] No. 3335; Beijing High People's Court, Gao Xing Zhong Zi [2013] No. 884.
39. Case Index: Trademark Review & Adjudication Board [2011] No. 15982; Beijing No. 1 Intermediate People's Court, Yi Zhong Zhi Xing Chu Zi [2012] No. 353.

3. Distinctiveness Analysis of a "Position Trademark"

Appeal of administrative litigation regarding the trademark refusal for an international registration of "Device" filed by SATA GmbH & Co. KG

- First Instance: Beijing No. 1 Intermediate People's Court (No. 1716; 2009) - Decided on November 11, 2009
- Second Instance: Beijing High People's Court (No. 188; 2010) - Decided on March 26, 2010

BACKGROUND

SATA GmbH & Co. KG ("***SATA***") filed an international trademark registration seeking to claim exclusive rights over a specific part of its spray gun products. SATA describes the trademark as follows: "the trademark consists of a blue marking (the "***Marking***") at the bottom of the grip of a paint spray gun; the Marking has the form of a platelet and can be seen from below and from three sides of the grip; the Marking is around 3–5 mm thick, and its length and width is around 10–20 mm; other features associated with the spray gun products are not part of the trademark (i.e., SATA does not claim exclusive ownership of other features except for the specific position of the blue marking). " (*see* Image One below; the position mark is referred to herein as the "***Application***" or the "***Mark***"):

Image One

The Chinese Trademark Office ("***Trademark Office***") refused the Application on the ground that the Application does not comply with Article 11 of the 2001 Trademark Law. SATA appealed the decision to TRAB under SAIC of PRC (the "***Appeal Board***"). The Appeal Board was of the view that "the Application was composed of a common design in respect to the designated goods (i.e., gun) and accordingly, it is not likely consumers would associate or recognize the Mark as a distinctive trademark. The Application therefore lacks the necessary distinctiveness to operate as a source identifier." The Mark failed to fulfill the distinctiveness requirement as specified under

Article 11 Section 1(3) of the 2001 Trademark Law. The Appeal Board maintained the refusal of the international registration and rejected SATA's designation to China in connection with Class 7 goods – i.e., paint spray gun.[40]

SATA filed an appeal with the Beijing No. 1 Intermediate People's Court (the "***Court***"). Its primary appeal grounds were summarized below:

(1) The Mark consisted of a colorful dish-shape design that is unique and distinctive; it is therefore capable to function as a source identifier.
(2) The Application and other similar device marks were approved for registration in numerous other countries; their registration status demonstrate that that the Mark was sufficiently distinctive to function as a trademark; the Mark's distinctiveness has been recognized by the trademark offices in other countries and should be approved for registration in China as well.
(3) The Mark has been put to use in China and is available to consumers in China. The Mark has therefore acquired sufficient distinctiveness through market use and is capable to function as a source identifier.

In summary, SATA pointed out that its Mark was distinctive and capable to function as a trademark. To show that the Mark has acquired distinctiveness through use in China, SATA submitted some internal documents that included promotional brochures as well as sales information statistics showing evidence of the sales and popularity of the Mark in China.

COURT DECISION

The Court maintained the Appeal Board's refusal decision. Specifically, the Court pointed out that the Application consists of a device which occupies only a tiny part of the overall spray gun design. Furthermore, the design in the Application cannot be used independently; it must be used in connection with the rest of the spray-gun device. In light of the above, the overall impact to consumers concerning the Application is not the Marking itself, but the Marking along with the rest of the spray gun device. Accordingly, the Mark lacks the inherent distinctiveness required of a trademark and it is not capable to function as a source identifier. The Court denied SATA's arguments noting the distinctiveness associated with SATA's Application.

According to Article 11 Section 2 of the 2001 Trademark Law, a trademark application can still be approved for registration even though it lacks inherent distinctiveness so long as it has acquired distinctiveness through use in the marketplace. Despite the above, the Trademark Law does not offer clear guidance regarding the specific situations where an inherently indistinctive trademark can be approved for registration given its acquired distinctiveness. The Court pointed out two situations where a mark would be considered lacking inherent distinctiveness as discussed under Article 11 Section 1 of the 2001 Trademark Law: (1) the mark has some fixed meaning

40. Case Index: Trademark Review & Adjudication Board [2008] No. 30558.

and accordingly, consumers may associate the mark as certain characteristics of the underlying goods or services; or (2) consumers will not inherently regard the mark as a trademark; in other words, the mark is not capable to function as a source identifier for the underlying products or services. In light of either situation described, the only way such a mark can be approved as a trademark is when it has acquired sufficient distinctiveness through use so that consumers would associate the mark more with its acquired distinctiveness rather than with its original meaning. Since consumers are much more familiar with the original meaning of the mark, the required level of acquired distinctiveness of the mark at issue must be stronger and more readily available to consumers than the mark's original meaning so as to allow the mark to become registrable as a trademark.

In the subject case, the evidence submitted by SATA was in fact "internal" documents (as opposed to documents prepared and produced by independent third parties); it was therefore difficult to ascertain the authenticity of such evidence. Accordingly, the submitted evidence was not able to prove that the consumers were familiar with the acquired distinctiveness of the Mark and that the Mark had acquired distinctiveness through use in the marketplace. In light of the above, the Court did not support SATA's claim that the Mark had acquired sufficient distinctiveness to become registered as a trademark.

In summary, the Court decided to uphold the Appeal Board's decision based on Article 54, Section 1 of the Administrative Procedure Law of China.

SATA appealed the decision to the Beijing High People's Court (the "***High Court***"). The High Court rejected the appeal and upheld the verdict.

ANALYSIS & INSIGHT

The subject case concerns a nontraditional trademark: the registration of a position trademark. Neither the 2001 nor 2013 Trademark Laws include "position trademark" as one type of trademark and neither Trademark Law mentions the phrase "position mark;" therefore, there is not yet a clear definition concerning a position mark. Based simply on the cases available to date, "position mark" generally refers to a particular feature of the trademark appearance. In other words, any application that encompasses certain specific part (or parts) of the products - as opposed to the entire visual feature of the products - is a position trademark.

Given the unique nature of a position mark, it typically encounters the following registrability issues:

A. Should a "Position Mark" Be Approved for Registration as One of the "Acceptable Trademarks" under the Trademark Law?

Article 8 of the 2001 Trademark Law discusses different types of the acceptable trademarks under the Chinese trademark system. Article 8 states: "*Any visible marks / signs – including words, designs, letters, numbers, 3D (three-dimension) marks, color components or any combination of the above-referenced elements – can be approved for registration as a trademark so long as it distinguishes the products provided by an individual, a legal entity or an organization from those provided by others."*

Based on Article 8 of the Trademark Law, it appears that there are three types of trademarks: two-dimensional trademarks, three-dimensional trademarks, and color trademarks. Position mark, however, is not included in the above literal language. It is therefore unclear whether or not a position mark can be approved as a trademark based simply on the definition provided by Article 8 of the Trademark Law. Given the unclear status of a position mark, there is not yet a uniform procedure in place to handle a position mark application. In fact, the China Trademark Office and the Appeal Board, as well as the courts have since adopted different approaches in examining and reviewing a position mark application. These different and often inconsistent approaches have impacted individual as well as corporate applicants. Given the law now requires a trademark applicant to specify the "type" of trademark applications on the application form, and since there is not yet a specific category where one could check off the box for a "position mark," the applicant is often compelled to pick a category based on its own interpretation of the law. Generally speaking, a position mark application has been categorized as one of the following three "types" of trademarks.

1. Filing the Position Mark as a Three-Dimensional Trademark.

Most of the time an applicant would describe a position mark as a "Three-Dimensional trademark;" however, the applicant would include more descriptions in the note section either explaining the specific parts in the mark that need protection or using the dotted and solid-line approach to highlight the parts that it is requesting a trademark registration. Below are some notable examples.

Gibson Guitar Corporation sought to register a position mark on its electronic guitar products. As shown below in Image Two, the parts for which Gibson was seeking trademark protection were the solid lines that were actually part of the main body of the guitar itself.[41] Hermes has also sought trademark registration of a position mark consisting of the switch/lock section on top of its handbag - as illustrated by the solid lines in Image Three below.[42] The Application in the subject case sought by SATA in connection with the spray gun and gun parts also included the following explanation in the publication material: "the protection is only limited to the red ring portion on the upper end of a paint cup of a spray gun, going around the ring and roughly arranged around the circumference, in particular directly below the lid of the paint cup and in particular having a width of 5-20 mm" (*see* Image Four below).[43]

41. Case Index: Beijing No. 1 Intermediate People's Court, Yi Zhong Zhi Xing Chu Zi [2010] No. 1173.
42. Case Index: Beijing No. 1 Intermediate People's Court, Yi Zhong Zhi Xing Chu Zi [2008] No. 323.
43. Case Index: Beijing No. 1 Intermediate People's Court, Yi Zhong Zhi Xing Chu Zi [2010] No. 1272.

Image Two	Image Three	Image Four

2. The Position Mark Is Not Filed as a Three-Dimensional Trademark but the Applicant Includes Specific Descriptions Pointing out the Part (or parts) that It Requests a Trademark Protection.

The subject application (filed by SATA) was carried out this way in China. SATA did not categorize the Mark as a Three-dimensional trademark application; instead, it includes the following explanation: "*the trademark consists of a blue marking at the bottom of the grip of a paint spray gun; the marking has the form of a platelet and can be seen from below and from three sides of the grip; the marking has a thickness of about 3-5 mm and a length and width of about 10-20 mm; further features which can be seen on the picture do not form a part of the mark.*"

Another example is the Adidas' trademark registration. Adidas AG sought to register a trademark consisting of three lines - these distinct three lines appear on the side of shorts, pants and trousers. In the description, Adidas provided the following explanation: "the mark consists of three parallel stripes with a background of pants; the outline of the trousers only serves to show how the trademark appears on trousers/shorts/pants; the outline of the trousers, however, is not part of the mark." (*see* Image Five below)[44]

44. Case Index: Beijing High People's Court, Gao Xing Zhong Zi [2011] No. 387.

Image Five

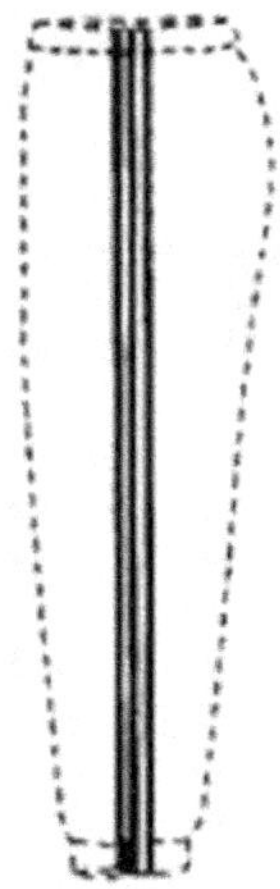

One of the primary reasons the Courts have adopted various different approaches to a position mark is due to the unclear status of the position mark afforded by Article 8 of the Trademark Law. Another factor that contributes to the inconsistent approaches to a position trademark is the different selection each applicant has chosen for its "label" regarding its position mark application. In practice, Courts have adopted the following three approaches in examining and reviewing a position mark:

(1) The Court regards the position mark application as a three-dimensional trademark; however, the Court considers the mark *as a whole* rather than focusing on certain specific parts (i.e., positions) of the mark.
As mentioned above, Hermes' position trademark application was filed as a three-dimensional trademark; however, it requested protection on the solid-line portion only (i.e., the switch/lock section on top of its handbag design). The court, however, did not support this approach on the ground that there was "no specific protection on a partial 3D trademark based on the current Trademark Law and Regulation for the Implementation of the Trademark Law;" accordingly, the Court examined the registrability of the application as a whole to decide whether or not trademark registration should be granted. In the Hermes case, the Court did not consider the "position" of the lock design on top of the handbag as a trademark; instead, it considered the handbag as a whole as a trademark application (which was then rejected for lacking distinctiveness).
(2) The Court regards the position mark as a two-dimensional trademark; however, the Court considers the mark *as a whole* rather than focusing on certain specific parts (i.e., positions) of the mark.

As discussed above, in Adidas' trademark application consisting of three lines, Adidas included the following explanation:

> *"the mark consists of three parallel stripes with a background of pants; the outline of the trousers only serves to show how the trademark appears on trousers/shorts/pants; the outline of the trousers, however, is not part of the mark."*

Despite Adidas' inclusion of the above statement in the "Trademark Design Note Section" on the "Trademark Application Form," the Court decided *not* to consider the Adidas application as a three-dimensional application because it did not specify or declare the application should be considered as a three-dimensional trademark application. Accordingly, based on Article 13 of the Regulation for the Implementation of the Trademark Law, the Adidas application would be treated as a two-dimensional trademark in light of its lack of three-dimensional declaration. Furthermore, the Court pointed out that the way to determine the type of a specific trademark application should be based strictly on the specimen submitted to the Trademark Office; any special or additional explanation included in the Trademark Design Note Section should not replace or limit the mark itself as represented in the specimen. In the Adidas case, the Court rejected the application given the application includes the pants design and the mark was therefore lacking sufficient distinctiveness to operate as a trademark.

(3) The Court is open to a position mark although the Court never specifically refers to the mark at issue as a "position mark."
The Court in the subject case followed this approach. In the decision issued by the Court, the Court referred to the mark as: "the subject application is part of the spray gun device; the subject application does not include the entire spray gun device." In other words, although the opinion itself did not use the phrase "position mark," the Court accepted the Mark as a specific position on the device that indirectly recognized that position mark should be one of the trademarks protected by the Trademark Law. Another example is the above-referenced electronic guitar design application. Although the Court in that case never directly referred to the mark at issue as a "position mark," it pointed out that "the subject application is a three-dimensional design on the main body of the electronic guitar" – this once again shows the Court's position in substantively supporting the protectability of a position mark.

The above analysis shows that although the courts have adopted different approaches in analyzing a position mark, each approach is in fact reasonable based on the specific facts in each case. Also, in light of the current unclear status of a position mark under China's trademark system, it is in fact reasonable to expect different approaches adopted by the Courts and trademark office. Despite the above, we applaud the approach adopted by the Court in the subject case – we agree with the Court's general approach in approving the position mark as one of the acceptable trademarks in China.

There are three primary reasons to support this approach.

First, although Article 8 of the Trademark Law includes three specific types of trademarks only (two-dimensional, three-dimensional, and color marks), the literal language in Article 8 actually refers to "any *visible* marks/signs." A position mark is certainly a "visible" mark. The list in Article 8 should not be regarded as an exhaustive all-inclusive summary of marks allowed under the China Trademark Law. Given a position mark is certainly one type of "visible" marks, its status - whether or not it should be specifically afforded protection under the Chinese Trademark System - should be open to discussion. Moreover, under the Interpretation Guideline of China's Trademark Law, it is reasonable to infer that a position mark is one of the visible marks that should be allowed for registration and protection under the China Trademark System. In light of the literal language of Article 8, it appears that the lawmakers actually accept all visible marks as trademarks and such marks should be approved for registration under the Trademark Law.

Second, even in the event that a position mark should not be regarded as an independent type of trademark, it is reasonable to simply categorize it as a three-dimensional trademark. As one of the recognizable trademarks under China's Trademark Law, a three-dimensional trademark includes the following three primary forms: (a) appearance of a product; (b) product packaging; and (c) decorations of certain products or services. Type (a) - product appearance - is actually the most important category of a three-dimensional trademark. A position trademark refers to a certain position of the product appearance. Under the current law, it is in fact unclear whether or not a three-dimensional trademark can only include the entire appearance of the products (in other words, there is no clear restriction in limiting only a certain appearance of a visual product appearance in the three-dimensional trademark). In light of the above and given the law does not clearly restrict the partial versus entire product appearance in a three-dimensional trademark, a partial three-dimensional trademark should not be regarded as a violation of the Law. This explains why most applicants of a position mark choose to categorize their applications as a three-dimensional trademark. A word of caution: for this approach to work, one must specifically circle the three-dimensional trademark application category in the application form; otherwise, the application would be similarly rejected as the Adidas case.

B. What Are the Relevant Criteria to Determine the Distinctiveness of a Position Trademark.

Although the Court in the subject case approves the general registrability and protection of a position mark, this cannot be taken to mean that any position mark application should be approved for registration. Any position mark application should also meet the absolute and relative requirements specified under the Trademark Law before it can be approved for registration. In the subject case, the specific issue involves the distinctiveness of the position trademark.

Article 11 of the 2001 Trademark Law governs the determination of distinctiveness associated with a trademark. Specifically, Article 11 states that the following marks shall not be approved for registration as a trademark: *1) marks that only encompass generic names, designs and models /serial numbers of the products at issue; 2) marks that simply include or represent the quality, quantity, raw materials, functionality, purpose, weight, or other characteristics of the products or services at issue; and 3) marks that lack distinctiveness. Despite the above, the above marks can nevertheless be approved for registration once they have acquired distinctiveness through use and are easily distinguishable."*

Section 1 of Article 11 governs inherent distinctiveness; Section 2 of Article 11 governs acquired distinctiveness of a trademark. The application of Section 2 is independent and it can be used to support a registration of a mark even when Section 1 is not yet satisfied. In other words, if an application lacks inherent distinctiveness (Section 1 of Article 11), it can still be approved for registration as a trademark so long as it has fulfilled the acquired distinctiveness prong set forth under Section 2 of Article 11.

The rules concerning inherent distinctiveness apply to position marks just as they apply to regular trademarks. Generally speaking, a mark must fulfill the following two requirements for it to be recognized as "inherently distinctive:"

- whether or not the relative public would consider the mark as a trademark;
- whether or not the mark is a direct description of the characteristics of the underlying goods or services.

In practice, both the academia and the real-world legal practice pay more attention to the second level of requirement; we often pay less attention to the first requirement when making a determination concerning the distinctiveness of a mark. It is therefore important to point out that the 1st requirement is in fact an important and fundamental precondition and it must be satisfied first before one can move on to the next level of distinctiveness examination. This is especially important when it comes to the distinctiveness examination of nontraditional marks.

The key to the first level of distinctiveness examination process is the relevant public's perception and awareness of the mark at issue. A mark will not be recognized as a trademark possessing the required level of inherent distinctiveness under the Trademark Law unless it is possible for the relevant public to first perceive it as a trademark. In this level of analysis, the way a mark is being categorized would have a substantive impact on the distinctiveness examination process.

In the 2001 Trademark Law, two-dimensional marks, three-dimensional marks as well as color marks were regarded as "visible" marks that were capable to be approved for registration as a trademark. The 2013 Trademark Law expanded the scope of registrable trademarks to include sound marks that are not the traditional "visible" marks. The 2013 Trademark Law therefore included sound and smell marks that were capable of being registered and protected as trademarks. In light of the progress of the modern trademark law, it is clear that the Trademark Law maintains an open approach to all types of marks and embraces the possibility that any marks can be approved for registration as long as they meet the specific requirements under the Trademark Law.

Despite the open approach, it is worth pointing out that the required level of distinctiveness does vary depending on the type of marks at issue.

In general, different marks would have to meet different levels of distinctiveness requirements (except, of course, the two-dimensional marks which do have a relatively straightforward distinctiveness requirement). There are varying degrees of distinctiveness requirements to nontraditional trademarks including the position marks discussed hereto. The above observation is based on each mark's use situation on the everyday marketplace and the corresponding impact on the relevant public. The types of trademarks that are most familiar to the average public are the two-dimensional trademarks; this is also the most popular type of trademarks in the everyday marketplace. This market reality therefore has a decisive impact on the public's perception of what constitutes a trademark – i.e., the specific elements that constitute the "external manifestation" of a trademark. In other words, due to this market reality, most consumers would automatically assume a two-dimensional mark in connection with certain products or services as a trademark when they counter such a mark in the marketplace. On the other hand, the public is less likely to instinctively assume the visual appearance of a product, the product packaging, the product color, the sound of the product or the smell of a product as a trademark when they are confronted with such an external manifestation of a trademark. Before such a "trademark" has been widely promoted or has generally become available to average consumers, consumers are likely to simply regard such a "mark" as the appearance, packaging design, color feature, sound or scent characteristic of the underlying producer – in other words, the average consumers would not instinctively assume such a manifestation as a source identifier for the underlying products or services.[45] This explains why the nontraditional trademarks typically would not be able to satisfy this level of distinctiveness requirement; this is exactly why the 2001 Trademark Law limited the scope of registrable trademarks to two-dimensional marks only and excluded the three-dimensional marks and other nontraditional marks.

With the above in mind, it is therefore understandable why the Court made the following statement concerning the subject Application: "the Marking in the subject Application only occupies a tiny portion of the spry gun design; the Marking in fact has always to be used in connection with the rest of the spray gun device and it can never appear or be used by consumers independently by itself. Accordingly, the overall impact to consumers concerning the Application is in fact the entire spray gun device as a whole rather than on the Marking itself as shown in the Application. In light of the above, the Application does not have the required inherent distinctiveness and its trademark application is therefore denied." Based on the above, it can conclude that the Court rejected the Application for lacking inherent distinctiveness because the relevant public would not consider the Application as a trademark.

The above point of view has also been supported by other courts in similar cases. For example, in the Gibson Guitar case, the Court rejected the trademark application

45. If the relevant public is able to connect the above-mentioned trademark with the specific source provider, the trademark then has acquired distinctiveness through extensive use, rather than the inherent distinctiveness.

because the mark at issue was only part of the electronic guitar components and the relevant public would not automatically associate such a component as a trademark. In yet another trademark application case filed by SATA, the court also rejected SATA's application on the ground that the relevant public would regard the application simply as a direct description of the underlying products; the application therefore should not be approved as a trademark because it would not be able to function as a source identifier for the underlying products.[46]

The above view (i.e., not supporting the trademark registration of position marks) is in fact quite common when it comes to the determination of other nontraditional trademarks involving the three-dimensional marks (most cases) and the color combination marks (fewer cases). Generally speaking, the court's approach to nontraditional trademark cases in fact does not have too many substantive differences. Take the ice-cream three-dimensional trademark application case as an example, the application as shown in Image Six was refused for lacking distinctiveness.[47] Specifically, the Court pointed out that the application was likely to be regarded by consumers merely as the shape of the underlying products (i.e., ice-cream) so the application was not capable to function as a source identifier. In the case involving a trademark application consisting of different colors of a saw blade (*see* Image Seven), the court also rejected the application for lacking distinctiveness.[48] Under the current judicial practice and system, only a very small proportion of nonconventional trademarks have ever been approved for trademark registration in China.

Image Six	Image Seven
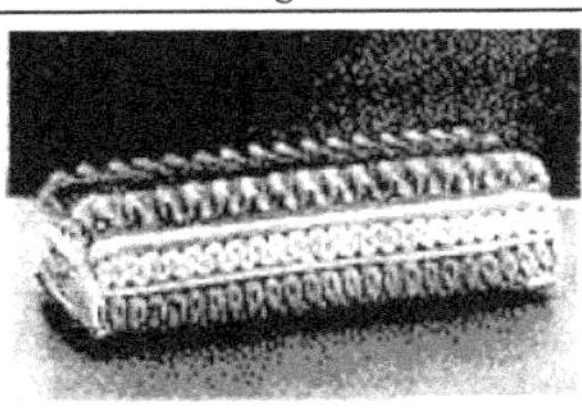	

It is worth pointing out that no matter how "novel" the nontraditional marks are, or whether or not such a mark has been created solely by the owner does not have any direct connection on whether or not the relevant public would intuitively perceive the mark as a trademark; it does not matter either whether or not the mark has ever appeared in front of the public before its application date. The distinctiveness determination process is drastically different from that of a two-dimensional trademark. In

46. Case Index: Beijing No. 1 Intermediate People's Court, Yi Zhong Zhi Xing Chu Zi [2010] No. 1272.
47. Case Index: Beijing No. 1 Intermediate People's Court, Yi Zhong Zhi Xing Chu Zi [2007] No. 1350.
48. Case Index: Beijing No. 1 Intermediate People's Court, Yi Zhong Zhi Xing Chu Zi [2005] No. 1084.

the latter case, the more novel the mark is, the more likely the mark would be considered as having sufficient distinctiveness. In the case involving nontraditional trademarks, however, the novelty value of a mark at issue does not have any direct impact on its distinctiveness. In the case involving Nestle's application of a three-dimensional trademark involving a square bottle design, the court expressly discussed the above point of view. In the Nestle decision, the Court pointed out that 'there is no direct relationship between the inherent distinctiveness of a three-dimensional mark and the fact that it was the original design created by the owner … ." In other words, the general public would still assume the underlying three-dimensional mark simply as a packaging design, the shape or decoration of the underlying product. The relevant public may consider such a packaging, shape or decoration feature creative or novel; however, no matter how novel or creative the shape of the product may be, it still does not impact the public's perception that the shape should be in fact regarded as a trademark."[49] This also explains why the Court in the subject case did not support SATA's appeal arguments pointing out the originality and novelty of the underlying Application.

Despite the above, a nontraditional mark can still be recognized and approved as a trademark so long as the mark has been put to use for a sustained period of time and has acquired a certain level of fame among the relevant public in China. In the subject case, the Court also pointed out that SATA's use of the Application was sufficient to prove that the relevant public already regarded the Application as a trademark; the Application therefore fulfilled Article 11 of the Trademark Law. However, the evidence submitted by SATA was internal evidence as opposed to evidence prepared and produced by independent third parties – it was therefore difficult to ascertain the authenticity of such evidence. This explains why the Court ultimately decided to uphold the refusal decision because the submitted evidence did not prove that the consumers were familiar with the Application and the Application had acquired sufficient distinctiveness to become a registered trademark.

49. Case Index: Beijing No. 1 Intermediate People's Court, Yi Zhong Zhi Xing Chu Zi [2012] No. 269.

4. Analysis Regarding the Distinctiveness of a Three-Dimensional Trademark and Its Aesthetics Functionality

Administrative litigation filed by Kaiping Weishida Seasoning Co., Ltd. regarding the trademark invalidation action of a three-dimensional international trademark registration owned by SOCIETE DES PRODUCTS NESTLE S.A.

- First Instance: Beijing No. 1 Intermediate People's Court (No. 269; 2012) - Decided on August 2, 2012
- Second Instance: Beijing High People's Court (No. 1750; 2012 - Decided on September 13, 2013

BACKGROUND

The disputed trademark (the "***Subject Registration***" or the "***Disputed Mark***") is a square bottle design with color claim as shown below in Image One; the designated product is seasoning. The registrant is SOCIETE DES PRODUCTS NESTLE S.A. ("***Nestle***"). The application date is March 14, 2002; and the registration date is July 27, 2005.

Image One

Kaiping Weishida Seasoning Co., Ltd. (the "***Company***") filed an action to the TRAB under SAIC of PRC (the "***Appeal Board***") to invalidate the Subject Registration based on the following grounds. First, the Subject Registration lacks distinctiveness. The Company was of the view that the square bottle design lacks distinctiveness because it has been a common and popular design widely used by many companies in China for their sauce (especially soy sauce) products. Based on the evidence submitted to the Appeal Board, it was not sufficient to prove any one-on-one connection between the design in the Subject Registration and Nestle has been established among the relevant public through Nestle's extensive use; the Subject Registration therefore lacks distinctiveness and was in violation of Section 11 of the Trademark Law. Second, the Subject Registration is of aesthetics functionality. The Company pointed out that due to the long-standing use and promotion of the design in the Subject Registration by the Chinese companies and the sauce industry, a brown square bottle design and packaging have an sufficient impact on consumers in their purchasing decision - the aesthetics functionality of the bottle design is therefore an important factor for the design to be successful commercially. The design therefore has a substantive impact on its designed products; it is therefore of aesthetics functionality. The Subject Registration is in violation of Section 12 of the Trademark Law. To prove its point, the Company has provided sufficient evidence to prove the following two points:

(1) Prior to the filing date of the Subject Registration, the Company and its predecessors have started using a bottle similar to that of the Disputed Mark on soy sauce products (*see* Image Two below).

Image Two

(2) Many manufacturers in the sauce industry in China have also used a design similar to that in the Disputed Mark for their soy sauce products (*see* Image Three below).

Image Three

Nestle believed that the Subject Registration was not only inherently distinctive, but was also a mark which has acquired a high level of fame as well as distinctiveness through its long period of use in the Chinese market. The evidence submitted by Nestle to prove the actual use of the Subject Registration, however, was provided by Nestle itself or its affiliated companies – the only independent third party evidence were six advertisements in magazines such as *East Eat* and *Chinese Cuisine* – all of which were published after 2002. In addition, Nestle claimed that the Disputed Mark did not have any aesthetics function.

The Appeal Board refused the Company's invalidation action and decided to maintain the registration of the Disputed Mark.[50] The Company appealed by filing an administrative litigation to the Beijing No. 1 Intermediate People's Court (the "***Court***"). The Company raised the same arguments as those presented to the Appeal Board.

COURT DECISION

The Court was of the view that the Disputed Mark was likely to be believed as the mere packaging of the designed products by the relevant public. In other words, the Mark lacks the inherent distinctiveness required for a trademark because it was not able to function as a source identifier for the underlying products. The submitted evidence was insufficient to prove the mark had acquired a high level of distinctiveness through use so the Disputed Mark did not have acquired distinctiveness either. The Dispute Mark was therefore in violation of Section 11 of the Trademark Law. On the other hand, the Court ruled that the public was not likely to make a purchase decision simply based on the bottle design of the Disputed Mark - the Subject Registration therefore did not have aesthetics function; the Registration was not in violation of Section 12 of the Trademark Law. The Court concluded that the Appeal Board had an incorrect understanding of Section 11 of the Trademark Law. The Court vacated the Appeal Board's decision based on Section 54(2) of the Administrative Litigation Law of the People' s Republic of China and asked the Appeal Board to make a new decision.

Nestle appealed the decision to Beijing High People's Court (the "***High Court***"). The High Court rejected the appeal and maintained the decision.

ANALYSIS & INSIGHT

One of the most important changes in the 2001 amendments to the Trademark Law was the recognition of the registrability of the three-dimensional trademark. After the amendments, we have seen a dramatic increase of three-dimensional trademark applications. The registrability in respect to such marks has been a key focus to the academia and trademark practitioners in China due to the increase of such applications since 2001.

Unlike the two-dimensional marks, three-dimensional marks have a number of inherent differences. This explains why the Trademark Law requires such trademarks to not only have distinctiveness (as similarly required for a two-dimensional trademark), but also the requirements with respect to technical and aesthetic functionality. In other words, a three-dimensional mark can only be registered as a trademark if it does not have any technical or aesthetic functionality. Despite the above rules and regulations, most three-dimensional trademarks only involve the analysis and determination associated with the distinctiveness of the trademark. The subject case is

50. Case Index: Trademark Review & Adjudication Board, [2010] No. 15921; the adjudication of reexamination for Case No. 00789 regarding the trademark dispute of the international registration No. G640537 "three-dimensional mark."

therefore a classic example to demonstrate not only the distinctiveness analysis, but also the aesthetics functionality analysis concerning a three-dimensional trademark.

A. Distinctiveness Determination of the Disputed Trademark.

Section 11 of the Trademark Law states that the following marks cannot be registered as a trademark: (1) generic names, references, designs and serial numbers of the underlying products; (2) marks that are merely descriptive of the quality, quantity, primary raw materials, function, purpose, weight, and other characteristics of the products; (3) marks that are not distinctive. Marks that have acquired distinctiveness through use, and are capable to function as a source identifier, can become registered as a trademark. The above regulation actually touches on two kinds of distinctiveness associated with a trademark: the "inherent" distinctiveness and the "acquired" distinctiveness. Any mark cannot be registered as a trademark if it does not have "inherent distinctiveness" as described in Section 11(1) of the Trademark Law. However, the exception of Section 11(1) is Section 11(2) where an inherently indistinctive mark can still become registered as a trademark so long as it has acquired fame, through use, and is therefore capable to function as a source identifier for the underlying goods or services. The mark therefore can be recognized as having "acquired" distinctiveness and can become registered as a trademark.

1. The Disputed Mark Does Not Have Inherent Distinctiveness.

The key factor to determine if a mark has inherent distinctiveness is to see if the relevant public would recognize the mark as a trademark. If the relevant public would not consider the mark as a trademark to identify the underlying goods or services, the mark then – in principle – does not have inherent distinctiveness; conversely, simply because the relevant public would perceive a mark as a trademark does not automatically mean the mark should be legally approved as such. Generally speaking, if a mark is directly descriptive of the characteristics of the goods or services (such as the quality, functionality, packaging and color, etc.) and such a descriptive term would convince the relevant public to associate the term merely as a description of the underlying products or services rather than as a source identifier for such products or services, the mark is not inherently distinctive.

Section 8 of the 2001 Trademark Law states that "any visual marks, such as words, designs, letters, numbers, three-dimensional marks, a combination of colors, and the combination of the above-mentioned elements, can be registered as a trademark so long as they are capable to function as a source identifier that allow the public to distinguish the products or services of an individual, a corporate entity, or other organizations from those of others." In other words, any two-dimensional, three-dimensional and color combination marks can be registered as a trademark. However, this does not mean these marks enjoy the same level of inherent distinctiveness. Similarly, even though the 2013 Trademark Law has broadened the scope of trademark registrations to include nonvisual marks such as sound marks, this does not mean these "nontraditional" trademarks enjoy the same level of distinctiveness as that of the traditional two-dimensional trademarks. The inherent distinctiveness of the above nontraditional marks should still serve as the basis allowing the relevant public to consider them as a trademark.

Given most of the trademarks in the Chinese market have long been presented in the two-dimensional forms, the relevant public therefore have a preconceived notion and would instinctively regard such a visual representation as a trademark. In other words, the relevant public is likely to and would have an easier time to associate a two-dimensional mark as a trademark for the associated goods or services as opposed to trademarks that are not represented in a two-dimensional form. This means two-dimensional trademark enjoys a higher level of inherent distinctiveness than other types of visual or nontraditional representations of a trademark. This explains why the Chinese Trademark Law prior to 2001 only recognizes two-dimensional marks as the only forms capable of becoming registered as a trademark and did not include three-dimensional marks and other types of representations.

Unlike the two-dimensional mark, a three-dimensional mark, taken as a whole, does not typically fit into the relevant public's general perception about the "visual form" of a trademark. Accordingly, the relevant public would not instinctively consider or recognize a three-dimensional mark as a trademark. This of course is a generalization and there are certainly exceptions where the relevant public would instinctively consider a three-dimensional form mark as a trademark; most of these "exceptions" occur depending on the particular way the mark is being used and the generally accepted norms within that particular industry. A three-dimensional mark is usually represented in one of the following three forms: (1) a visual representation of the product itself (*see* Image Four below); (2) a visual representation of the product packaging (as shown in the Subject Registration); or (3) as a decoration for the underlying goods or services (*see* Image Five below).

Image Four (The designated goods are ice-cream, etc.)	Image Five (The designated goods are clothes and luggage, etc.)
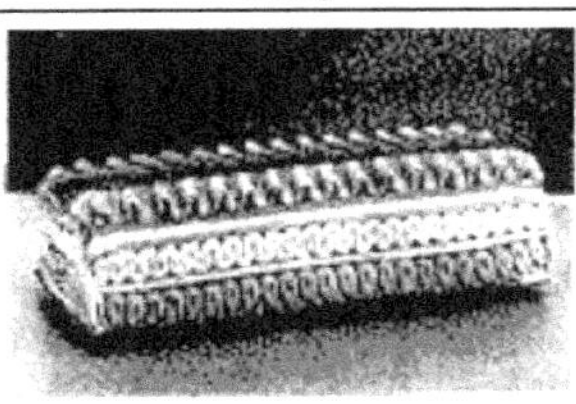	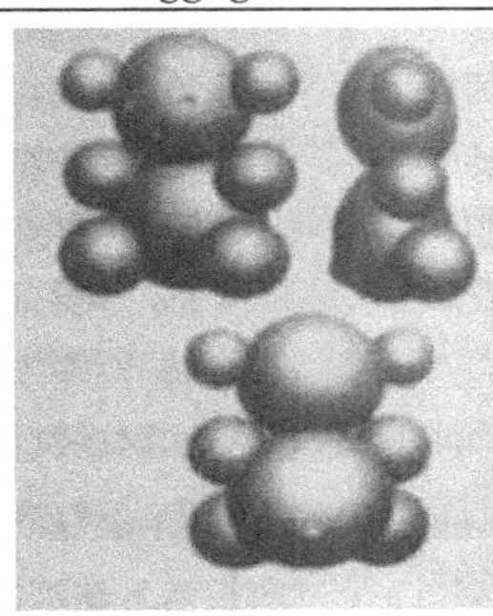

Among these three forms of representation, other than being a "decoration" of the underlying goods or services which typically does not bear any connection with the designed goods or services, the relevant public would not immediately recognize a three-dimensional mark (which represents either the packaging or the shape of the underlying product) as a trademark. This is because the public is likely to associate the mark simply as a feature of the underlying products rather than as a source identifier. This explains why a three-dimensional mark typically does not have the inherent distinctiveness when it is either in the form of packaging or the overall shape of the product because the public would associate it simply as a feature of the underlying product.[51] When deciding whether or not the underlying three-dimensional marks should be regarded as a trademark, most examiners take a balanced approach and consider not only the inherent distinctiveness associated with the decorative three-dimensional marks, but also the industry norms and accepted practices within that industry – if the industry has an established practice in using and accepting a three-dimensional mark as a trademark, then the mark is more likely to be recognized as such because it is easier to recognize the inherent distinctiveness of the mark under that circumstances. Take the automobile industry as an example, the industry already has an established practice in adopting and accepting a three-dimensional mark as a trademark. Accordingly, if the underlying three-dimensional mark is seeking registration in connection with automobile products, the mark is more likely to be regarded as having inherent distinctiveness. For industries that do not have an established norm in adopting or accepting a three-dimensional mark as a trademark, the underlying mark is likely to be accepted merely as a decoration for the goods and services; the mark is therefore lacking the inherent distinctiveness and is less likely to be accepted and recognized as a trademark. Take the three-dimensional bear trademark case as an example (shown above in Image Five), the court has decided not to recognize it as a trademark on the ground of lacking distinctiveness in connection with clothing and luggage products – "the relevant public is likely to consider the mark merely as a decoration of the underlying product and will not associate the mark as a source identifier."[52]

Applying the above principle to the subject case, the Disputed Mark is seeking registration for seasoning products. When the Disputed Mark is applied on the seasoning products, the relevant public is more likely to recognize the mark merely as

51. As to the aforesaid "Ice Cream" case, the court held that the trademark application lacked distinctiveness because it was likely to be identified as the shape of the ice-cream by the relevant public. Case Index: Beijing No. 1 Intermediate People's Court, Yi Zhong Xing Chu Zi [2007] No. 01348.

As for the "BIC pen" case, the court held that the trademark application lacked distinctiveness because it was the common shape of a pen holder. Case Index: Beijing No. 1 Intermediate People's Court, Yi Zhong Xing Chu Zi [2008] No. 328.

As for the "Adidas Originals" case, the court held that the trademark application lacked distinctiveness, because it would convince the relevant public to associate the design merely as a shape of the underlying product (the mark would be regarded simply as the sealing terminal of the machine). Case Index: Beijing No. 1 Intermediate People's Court, Yi Zhong Xing Chu Zi [2009] No. 71.

52. Case Index: Beijing No. 1 Intermediate People's Court, Yi Zhong Zhi Xing Chu Zi [2005] No. 2205.

a packaging of the seasoning products, rather than a source identifier. This shows that the Disputed Mark does not have inherent distinctiveness required for a trademark so as to allow the public to distinguish the subject products from those provided by other suppliers.

In addition, for some specific three-dimensional marks, their inherent distinctiveness does not have any direct connection as to whether or not these marks are coined marks or have indeed been created by the owners. This is one of the key features distinguishing a three-dimensional mark from a two-dimensional mark. For a two-dimensional mark, the fact that the term is a coined word or involves a unique design typically means the mark enjoys a high or a higher level of inherent distinctiveness as opposed to a mark which is composed of existing terms or common designs. This principle however does not apply to a three-dimensional mark. Even though a three-dimensional mark is composed of a novel design and has never been used in connection with the subject products, so long as the mark is represented in the form of packaging, shape or a form of decoration of the products, the relevant public is likely to simply regard the mark as such – namely, merely a feature in connection with the product itself, rather than as a source identifier for the products. The relevant public, at most, would consider the mark a "novel" representation of the product packaging, shape or decoration but still would not associate it as a source identifier for the underlying products or services. The inherent distinctiveness of a mark is tied to the perception of the relevant public. Public perception of a three-dimensional mark is heavily influenced by the way the mark is being used, rather than the mark itself. This explains why the inherent distinctiveness of a three-dimensional mark is less influenced by the fact whether or not the mark is a coined phrase or creation of the owner; rather, it is influenced by the way the mark is being used. The public would nevertheless consider the mark as a mere decoration as long as the way the mark is being used is likely to convince the public that the mark is part of the product packaging or shape, and if so, the public would not perceive it as a mark with inherent distinctiveness no matter how novel the mark is. Accordingly, in the subject case, even though Nestle might be the party first using the Disputed Mark in connection with seasoning or the mark was created by Nestle, it does not affect the determination with respect to the inherent distinctiveness of the Disputed Mark.

In fact, most types of marks that are not two-dimensional trademarks lack inherent distinctiveness, not just the three-dimensional marks. For example, the public usually consider a color combination mark a representation of the colors for the underlying products rather than a distinctive trademark.[53] Similarly, a sound mark is typically being perceived by the public as a mere sound representation even though such a sound is unique and created by the owner. The same lacking distinctiveness issue also applies to a mark composed of distinctive smells because the public would

53. With regard to the color combination trademark application composed of the colors blue and orange that was filed by Capman Company in the designated good of saw blades, both the Appeal Board and the court held that the trademark application lacked the inherent distinctiveness because it could not function as the source identifier. Case Index: Beijing No. 1 Intermediate People's Court, Yi Zhong Xing Chu Zi [2005] No. 1084.

simply associate it as a type of smell, rather than as a source identifier for the underlying products or services. This is because these forms of representations, either as sound, smell, color combination or a three-dimension shape, do not "fit" in the public's general understanding and perception of a trademark. This also explains why such marks are generally not approved for registration unless they have acquired distinctiveness through consistent and long-standing use.

2. The Disputed Mark Has Not Yet Acquired Distinctiveness.

According to Section 11(2) of the Trademark Law, a mark that lacks inherent distinctiveness can still be approved for registration so long as the applicant can prove that the mark has achieved a certain level of fame in connection with certain goods or services through the owner's consistent and long-standing use, and such fame and popularity are sufficient to allow the public to form the one-on-one association between the mark and the suppliers/manufacturers of such products or services so as to allow the distinctiveness recognition.

The key to recognize distinctiveness depends on the fame recognition. Put it more precisely, the central issue resolves on the "level" of fame so as to allow a mark to be recognized as having acquired distinctiveness and can be approved accordingly as a trademark. In the subject case, the court held that the mark can be recognized as having acquired distinctiveness so long as the applicant can prove the following: the mark has become a "popularly known" source indicator in China which is sufficient to allow the relevant public to identify certain goods or services and has established an one-on-one connection between itself and its suppliers or manufacturers. This fame recognition is similar in principle with the standards required to recognize a mark as a well-known trademark. Accordingly, the evidentiary requirement should also be similar to those required for a mark to be proven as well-known in China. It is also worth noting that the burden of proof would increase if the relevant public is more likely to associate the mark with certain fixed meanings.

The reason for the increasing burden of proof is because a mark is typically being recognized as lacking inherent distinctiveness since the relevant public would instinctively associate it with some "fixed" meanings which is different from the mark being functioning as a source identifier. Furthermore, the relevant public typically would have some basic understanding for such "fixed" meanings such as the mark would be seen as the color representation for the underlying products. For a three-dimensional mark, its fixed meaning is usually associated with the product packaging or shape so the relevant public is less likely to consider it as a trademark. For a directly descriptive two-dimensional mark, the relevant public would typically recognize the mark based on its fixed meaning so the mark is simply a description of the quality, quantity, raw material, or color of the underlying products or services. Under such circumstances, if the owner of the mark would like the mark to be perceived and recognized as a trademark, it must prove that through use the public is more likely to perceive the mark as a trademark, rather than a description with its original fixed meanings. This level of recognition is possible when the mark has acquired a certain level of fame through use.

Further, if there is already an established norm in the industry where operators in the same industry are using the same three-dimensional mark, this would further the public's perception of the mark with its fixed meaning. If so, the use of the mark must acquire an even higher level of fame so as to allow the public to recognize it as a trademark.

Applying the above principle to the subject case, based on the materials provided by both parties, the court cannot conclude that the Disputed Mark has acquired distinctiveness through use.

First, based on the evidence provided by the Company, the Company and its predecessors have started using similarly designed bottles on sauce products in China prior to 2002, the filing year of the Disputed Mark. The above conclusion is based on the evidence submitted by the Company which includes more than forty newspapers, such as *Kaiping Industry Developing History Since The Founding of The People's Republic of China (1949–1990)*, *Encyclopedia of China National Light Industry (1993–1994)*, the January 1988 edition of *Compilation on Kaiping Industrial Products*, the September 1997 edition of *Brand-name Products In Guangdong*. In addition, it is clear that not only the Company has prior use involving sauce bottles similar to the Disputed Mark, but also other operators have adopted and used similar design on the same products. The above background was confirmed in the civil litigation decision (No. 418; 2010)by the Guangdong High People's Court on November 17, 2010. This shows that the original fixed meaning in connection with the Disputed Mark has in fact been reinforced by other operators in the same industry. As discussed above, if Nestle wants to prove that the Disputed Mark has acquired distinctiveness through use, it must satisfy a higher burden of proof supporting the fame status in connection with the Disputed Mark.

Second, although Nestle claimed that the Disputed Mark was created and put to use since 1896, its submitted evidence only involves six advertisements published after 2002 showing use situation of the Disputed Mark. These advertisements were insufficient to prove that Nestle was the first party using the Disputed Mark nor were they sufficient to prove that the design was popularly known by the relevant public in China. Accordingly, the court did not support the acquired distinctiveness claim based on the evidence provided by Nestle.

B. Determination Relating to the Aesthetics Functionality of the Disputed Trademark.

Section 12 of the Trademark Law states that: "a three-dimensional trademark application shall not be approved for registration if the mark is composed merely of the basic features of the product itself, the product shape with some technical effect, or the substantive form of the product itself." The phrase "substantive form of the product itself" usually refers to the aesthetics functionality. In other words, Section 12 of the Trademark Law has two types of product functionality in mind: aesthetics and technical.

Even though the subject case does not fall under Section 11 of the Trademark Law, the Disputed Mark still should not be approved for registration under current situation regardless of conforming to Section 12 of the Trademark Law or not. The court nevertheless decides to comment on the differences between these two sections in the Trademark Law. Section 11 of the Trademark Law governs situations where a mark shall not be approved for registration. This means even though the Disputed Mark does not comply with Section 11(1) of the Trademark Law and is not allowed for registration at the present stage, it may still be approved for registration once it has acquired distinctiveness through use in the future. This is not the case for Section 12 of the Trademark Law because this section does not discuss situations where a three-dimensional mark can be approved for registration. In other words, once a mark is found not to be in compliance with Section 12 of the Trademark Law, it no longer has the possibility to be approved as a trademark. Put it differently, even though a mark with aesthetics functionality has acquired a high level of fame, it still cannot be registered as a trademark. Accordingly, the analysis concerning Section 12 of the Trademark Law would have a substantive impact on Nestle.

The court believes that the analysis and determination of the aesthetics functionality of a trademark should consider both aesthetics and substantive value of the mark. Although trademark owner would typically consider aesthetic value of its mark during the design stage, it does not necessarily mean that the mark should be recognized to have aesthetics functionality (otherwise, most trademarks would be recognized as such). Put it more precisely, only when a three-dimensional mark's aesthetic value allows the mark to have "substantive" value can it then be recognized to have aesthetics functionality as defined under Section 12 of the Trademark Law.

A three-dimensional mark with an aesthetic value should also be deemed to have a "substantive" value when the former is significant enough to impact the relevant public's purchase decision. Generally speaking, if consumers make the purchase decision based on the three-dimensional mark itself, rather than the product provider information the mark conveys, the mark should be deemed to have "substantive" values. Typical three-dimensional marks with substantive values are marks in connection with "visual" products such as stuff toys and art crafts. Such products share a common feature in that the visual appearance of the products is the key factor impacting the consumers' purchasing decision. For example, the primary reason a consumer decides to purchase a Mickey Mouse stuff toy rather than a Donald Duck one is primarily because he or she likes the Mickey Mouse visual appearance better, as opposed to his or her overwhelming trust for one supplier over another. Although consumers would certainly take into account the product provider information, this information does not usually come into play until and after the consumer has decided to purchase the product with specific visual features - for example, once a consumer has decided to purchase a Mickey Mouse stuff toy, he or she will then decide the most suitable supplier for such products rather than considering this information before deciding to purchase a Mickey Mouse versus a Donald Duck toy. Even in situations where a visual appearance of a product is functioning as a source identifier, the sequence of order the above information plays is roughly the same to impact a consumer's purchasing decision. Under such circumstances, the visual appearance of such products does have "substantive" values for the underlying products.

Three-dimensional marks that have the above characteristics should not be approved for registration as a trademark. This is because it would then face the following obstacles when one is seeking to protect the mark as a trademark under the Trademark Law:

First, there is no proper foundation to justify protection of such marks under the Trademark Law. Trademark Law is designed to protect trademark owners' rights and interests that come with the distinctiveness of their marks. If Trademark Law were to offer protection for marks with aesthetics functionality, the protection should be justified on the basis of a mark's distinctiveness feature rather than on other basis because it would then be contrary to the basic principle of the Trademark Law. With respect to this type of marks, however, although their aesthetics functionality also enables consumers to regard the marks as a source identifier, the primary reason impacting a consumer's purchasing decision is still the visual appearance of the mark itself. If the Trademark Law were to offer protection for such marks, this means protection has been extended beyond distinctiveness and has now included visual aesthetics feature of the mark. This clearly exceeds the protection scope of the Trademark Law.

Second, if protection were offered to this type of marks, it basically took away the term limitation system associated with the interests protected under the Copyright and Patent Law. In most circumstances, marks that have aesthetics functionality are protectable artwork under the Copyright Law, and are eligible for design patent registrations under the Patent Law. Accordingly, we must also consider the roles of different laws in respect to this type of marks and the time limitations offered by the respective systems. The protection term differs depending on the mark is being protected as a trademark, copyright or design patent. Copyright and Patent Law have specific time limits to protect the underlying rights. On the other hand, although Trademark Law does set a time limitation on the marks being protected as trademarks, the owners can nevertheless renew and continue renewing such marks. In other words, the exclusive rights in connection with a registered trademark can be extended without any time limits. Accordingly, if a three-dimensional mark with aesthetics functionality can also be protected under the Trademark Law, this not only exceeds the scope of Trademark Law (as discussed above), but also leads to situation where an owner's rights can be protected without complying with any specific term limits as set forth in the Copyright, and Patent Law. This essentially takes away the term limitation system governing different rights under both laws.

Third, if Trademark Law were to offer protection for such marks, it would put the operators in the same industry in a disadvantage and result in unfair competition. Operators in the same industry as the owner might be interested in using the same visual three-dimensional design (but with aesthetics functionality) to increase their competitive strength. Since visual aesthetics is not the subject of protection under the Trademark Law, other operators in the same industry should have the right to use the design once the term limitation under Copyright and Patent Law has both expired. If Trademark Law were to offer protection to such marks, it would exclude operators in the same industry from using the design because it would then constitute trademark infringement. This clearly would lead to monopoly of the public resources and would place other operators in an unfair disadvantage.

In the subject case, the Disputed Mark involves a square bottle design with color claims and the designated product is seasoning. Since the determination of a mark's aesthetics functionality should involve the purchasers, and the purchasers in the subject case would primarily consider the product packaging rather than product supplier information when deciding on the type of seasoning to purchase, the Disputed Mark should be deemed to have aesthetics functionality. However, based on the relevant public's perception, it is clear that consumers are more focused on the product quality and supplier information when purchasing seasoning; in other words, although product packaging does play a role, it does not play a key role in impacting consumers' purchasing decision. Consumers would not make a purchase decision solely because they like the packaging design when buying seasoning. The Disputed Mark therefore does not have aesthetics functionality and does not violate Section 12 of the Trademark Law.

5. Analysis of an Application in Conflict with Prior Registered or Preliminarily Approved Trademarks

Administrative litigation regarding the appeal of trademark opposition for "JIN LIN SHUI FU"

- First Instance: Beijing No. 1 Intermediate People's Court (No. 2434; 2010) - Decided on September 18, 2010
- Second Instance: Beijing High People's Court (No. 1352; 2010) - Decided on December 28, 2010
- Retrial: The SPC of the PRC (No. 47; 2011) - Decided on October 18, 2011

BACKGROUND

On February 24, 2004, a Chinese individual named "Tian Xiu Hua" (the "***Applicant***") applied for a trademark "金临水福" - English phonetics JIN LIN SHUI FU) (Application Number 3924167; *see* Image One below; the "***Subject Application***" or the "***Opposed Mark***"); the designated goods included wine (beverage), shochu, rice wine, and wine. During the opposition period, An Hui Lin Shui Distillery Co., Ltd. (the "***Company***") opposed the Application. The Trademark Office under SAIC of PRC (the "***Trademark Office***") rejected the opposition and approved the Opposed Mark for registration. The Company challenged the decision by raising a timely appeal to the TRAB under SAIC of PRC (the "***Appeal Board***"). Its primary appeal grounds include:

(1) The Company owns a registration for "LIN SHUI in Chinese characters & Design" under Registration Number 187252 (*see* Image Two below; the "***Cited Mark***"). The Cited Mark had been approved for registration in connection with Class 33 wine (alcohol) products since 1983. Through the Company's extensive use and promotion for many years, the Cited Mark has acquired a high level of fame in connection with wine products. The Subject Application fully includes the two characters in the Cited Mark (as the 2nd and 3rd character); the additional characters in the Opposed Mark - namely, the first character "JIN" and the last character "FU" – are merely decorative characters; the inclusion of these characters do not add any meaning to the mark overall. The Subject Application should therefore be regarded as confusingly similar to the Cited Mark.

(2) The Company and the Applicant are located in the same region of China; therefore, the Applicant presumably should have been aware of the fame associated with the Cited Mark. However, the Applicant still sought to register the Subject Application that is confusingly similar to the Cited Mark and covers the same or similar products. The Subject Application should be viewed as a bad-faith application and be refused under Section 28 of the 2001 Trademark Law.

The evidence provided by the Company includes: corporate documents to prove its Company legal status in China, promotional materials and award information for the Cited Mark, the Applicant's bad-faith use of product packaging images for the Subject Application, investigations carried out by the local authorities and copies of the civil decision by courts in China in respect to the Subject Application, and product packaging, etc.

Image One	Image Two
金临水福	

The Applicant responded to the appeal by pointing out that the Subject Application should be approved for registration because it should not be regarded as a confusingly similar mark as the Cited Mark in respect to the applied-for products.

The Appeal Board refused the Subject Application on the following grounds: the JIN and FU characters (the 1st and 4th characters) in the Opposed Mark are common descriptive characters in connection with wine products; they are therefore not the primary distinctive elements of the Opposed Mark. Rather, the 2nd and 3rd characters in the Opposed Mark – which are the same as the characters in the Cited Mark – are the primary distinctive element. Since the 2nd and 3rd characters of the Opposed Mark are the primary distinctive element of the Opposed Mark, and they are identical to the characters in the Cited Mark, the two marks are therefore conceptually similar in terms of the overall commercial impression. The products covered by the Opposed marks are similar to those covered by the Cited Mark. The Cited Mark enjoyed a high level of fame prior to the filing date of the Opposed Mark. Since the Company and the Applicant are from the same area in China, the latter should therefore be aware of the fame associated with the Company's Cited Mark. The coexistence of the Opposed Mark and the Cited Mark will therefore lead to consumer confusion. The Opposed Mark constitutes a confusingly similar mark in respect to similar products as discussed under Section 28 of the 2001 Trademark Law and should therefore be refused.

The Applicant did not agree with the decision and raised a timely administrative court action to the Beijing No. 1 Intermediate People's Court (the "***Court***").

COURT DECISION

Both the Court and the Beijing High People's Court held the view that the Opposed Mark is confusingly similar to the Cited Mark and covers similar products. The

Opposed Mark should therefore be refused under Section 28 of the 2001 Trademark Law; both courts maintained the Appeal Board's appeal decision.

The Applicant petitioned for a review of the decision to the SPC of the PRC (the "***Supreme Court***"). The Supreme Court was of the view that the LIN SHUI characters in the Opposed Mark are the primary distinctive visual and phonetic elements. This is the same LIN SHUI phrase that the Company refers to on its own white wine products as evidenced by its various award certificates. There is accordingly appropriate to hold that the LIN SHUI characters are the primary component in the Cited Mark. The Applicant argued that the well design in the Cited Mark should be viewed as the primary element; this, however, was not supported by any evidence. Both the Cited Mark and the Opposed Mark included the same LIN SHUI characters and therefore referred to the same thing. Considering the high level of fame associated with the Company's LIN SHUI brand on the white wine products, and the fact that both parties are manufacturing and selling white wine in the same area in China, and the Applicant's prominent use of the LIN SHUI characters on its white wine products, and the Applicant's subjective intent when seeking to register the Subject Application, for the purpose to avoid consumer confusion, the Supreme Court agrees with the Appeal Board and the courts' decision that the Subject Application should be refused under Section 28 of the 2001 Trademark Law. In light of the above, the Supreme Court refused the Applicant's appeal petition.

ANALYSIS & INSIGHT

Section 30 of the 2013 Trademark Law (i.e., Section 28 of the 2001 Trademark Law) states that "*an application shall be not be published if it violates the Trademark Law or is the same or confusingly similar to a registration or a preliminarily approved application and covers the same or similar products.*" The subject case is a classic application of the above law where a trademark application is refused due to its conflict with a third party's prior registration or a trademark application that has been preliminarily approved in China.

I. Legislative Purpose.

Section 30 of the Trademark Law states that a trademark application shall not be the same or confusingly similar to a registered trademark or an application that has been preliminarily approved and covers the same or similar products. Taking this section literally, the relevant trademark authorities must examine and make a determination prior to approving an application to see if it is confusingly similar to prior trademarks and covers similar goods/services. However, it is worth pointing out that this level of examination process is merely a way to carry out the law; this should not be taken to refer to the entire picture of the law nor the reason why the law is in existence in the first place. Section 30 should not be read in a way it is restricted to its literal meaning

- one must also understand the intent of the law that is to "avoid confusion." The primary function of a trademark is to identify the source of the products /services; the protection of the trademark rights is therefore aimed to avoid consumer confusion that would prevent a trademark from performing its basic function: enabling the consumers to identify the origin of the products/services. Based on the "avoid confusion" principle, the scope to prevent a mark from becoming registered is broader than that of one's exclusive rights to use a trademark. The exclusive rights of a registered trademark are limited to its approved form and goods/services. However, the scope to prevent a mark from becoming registered can be expanded to include the determination involving whether or not the underlying application is similar to prior marks and covers similar products. Accordingly, in making a determination in respect to the similarities of two marks and the respective underlying products, the goal should be the protection of a trademark so that it can fully function as a source identifier. The analysis process should not be focused simply on the literal comparison of the two marks; instead, it should focus on whether or not the coexistence of the marks would lead to consumer confusion.

In the third amendment to the Trademark Law, Section 57(2) expanded the "easily lead to confusion" concept to include the following situations as necessary conditions to prove trademark infringement: use of a mark similar to the registered trademark on the same products, or use of the trademark same or similar to the registered trademark on similar products. This is the first specific embodiment of the basic trademark protection principle: "avoid consumer confusion." This also helps to interpret the legislative goals for Section 30 of the 2013 Trademark Law.

The Supreme Court analyzed the subject case from the perspective to "possibly avoid consumer confusion" and concluded that the Opposed Mark and the Cited Mark constituted similar trademarks under Section 28 of the 2001 Trademark Law. The Supreme Court's decision fully demonstrates its understanding of the legislative goal for this law.

II. Determination of "Similar" Trademarks.

To determine if two trademarks are similar, one must take into account the following factors to see if the coexistence of the marks would lead to consumer confusion:

(A) The similarities between the components of each respective mark, as well as the trademarks as a whole.

(B) The distinctiveness and fame associated with the cited mark.

(C) The international class categorization of the underlying goods/services and their industry specific differences.

(D) The way the mark is being used in everyday life.

(E) The subject intent of the applicant.

A. Similarity Analysis.

The similarity analysis should compare the visual, phonetic, conceptual and overall impression of the marks at issue, from the perspective of the general attention of the relevant public; the analysis should view the respective marks in a vacuum, and focus on the comparison of the primary components of the marks, as well as the marks as a whole.

1. General Attention of the Relevant Public.

"Relevant public" is an important concept in the Trademark Law. This is because a trademark enters a market by "attaching" itself to the underlying goods/services; it serves as a source identifier for the various "social subjects" that come in contact with the mark. Accordingly, the similarity analysis involving a trademark as well as the determination of its distinctiveness and fame status should involve this group of "social subjects" – i.e., the perception of the "relevant public." The "relevant public" therefore involves the product manufacturers or service providers, the relevant consumers, and the operators and associated personnel with which the mark comes into contact as its products/services move through the channel of trade. When analyzing a mark and making a similarity decision, the trademark authorities, examiners and judges should not view the mark from the perspective of a trademark professional; instead, the analysis should be based on the general perception of the "relevant public."

With respect to "general attention," it refers to the relevant public's nonheightened attention when choosing a product in a market and if such attention would pick up the differences in the font, design, phonetics, letter or character sequence between two marks. For example, Image Three is a comparison of two marks composed of the same English letter and number; the only differences are the font and the design of the English letter. Image Four involves two designs with similar components and overall impression. Image Five involves two English words composed by the same letters but in a slightly different order; the two words do not differ in meaning. Image Six involves two English words with more than four letters; these words either do not have a meaning on their own or do not have any specific meaning for their individual components – there is only one letter spelling difference between the two words in Image Six. Generally speaking, a mark will be regarded as confusingly similar to a senior mark if they share visual, phonetic, and conceptual similarities.

Image Three

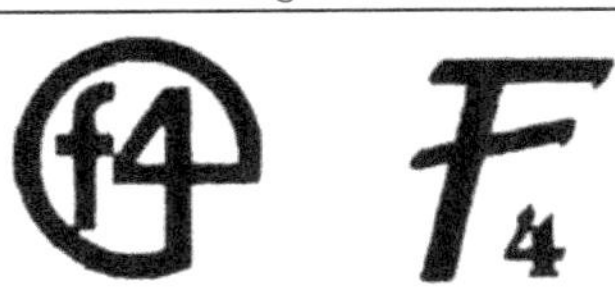

Image Four

Image Five

Wintech Techwin

Image Six

BILLDAN **BILLDANY**

2. Viewing the Marks in a Vacuum.

When consumers want to purchase a product the second time, a trademark reduces the overall search cost because the mark - acting as a source identifier - immediately allows consumers to identify the products they have already purchased and want to purchase again. Consumers typically rely on their memories and their overall impression about a mark in order to make the purchase decision; this is especially common when the purchase decision is in respect to inexpensive daily necessities. In other words, it is very rare that a consumer will compare two trademarks side by side prior to making a purchase. Accordingly, when making a similarity analysis regarding two marks, they should be compared in a vacuum; the determination should be on the subjective impression of the first mark and see if such an impression is similar to that of the second mark.

3. The Combined Approach to Compare Respective Trademarks as a Whole and to Compare Their Primary Components.

Comparing trademarks as a whole means analyzing their components, symbols, and combinations of these individual parts and viewing them as an inseparable and integral part to the overall trademarks. Comparing the primary components of the trademarks means focusing on the most prominent and noticeable elements of the mark – the very elements of the mark that are most likely to attract consumers' attention or trigger their memory prior to making a purchase decision. When making a similarity analysis, one must also consider the overall impression of the mark at issue. In addition, one must take into consideration the specific ways Chinese consumers approach a trademark such as any special interpretation, phonetic reference, visual recognition, memory association and cultural customs/habits. Sometimes it may be necessary to focus on some specific parts of a trademark such as its Chinese components (if any). It is difficult to have a black-and-white rule in respect to which comparison approach should play a more significant role in analyzing similarities of the marks: viewing the marks as a whole or paying attention to their primary elements. It would be more appropriate to take a case-by-case approach in making this determination by taking into account different factual scenario in each case.

The marks in Image Seven are determined to be similar.

Image Seven

The marks in Image Eight are determined to be distinguishable.

Image Eight

In the subject case, the Cited Mark is composed of the Chinese characters "LIN SHUI" and a well design. The LIN SHUI Chinese characters are therefore the primary visual and phonetic element to consumers in China. The Opposed Mark is a word mark that fully incorporates the LIN SHUI characters. Although the Opposed Mark incorporates two additional characters - namely the character JIN as the beginning of the Opposed Mark and the character FU at the end - these are common decorative characters in the Chinese language and do not contribute to any conceptual differences between the Cited Mark and the Opposed Mark. When the relevant public are confronted with these two marks without paying much focused attention to either mark, confusion can be expected. The two marks should therefore be held confusingly similar.

B. The Distinctiveness and Fame Associated with the Cited Mark.

1. Distinctiveness of the Cited Mark.

If the primary component of a cited mark belongs to some specific terms or images in the "public" area, then the determination should consider not only the senior trademark owner's rights and the mark's commercial reputation, but also the "public" nature of such terms and images and seek to strike a balance between the two rights. It is therefore advisable to take a more literal approach in making a similarity determination in such a situation so as to avoid "trademark monopoly."

For example, in the appeal of a trademark refusal concerning the below image in Image Nine (Application Number 6596007),[54] the Appeal Board refused the mark on the ground that it was confusingly similar to the cited mark No. 829594 as shown in Image Ten below. The appeal examiner held that the two images were similar because both were composed of the tree image and a circle design; the two marks were therefore held to be confusingly similar in terms of their individual components and overall visual impact. The court, however, reached a different conclusion. In the court's view, the two images represented the tree concept differently and "tree" is part of the public resources existing in everyday life. The cited mark represents the tree image in a way it is commonly represented in everyday life so the distinctiveness associated with the design is low. It would therefore be unreasonable to assume the cited mark enjoys monopoly and exclusive rights over the tree image in general and can prevent others from obtaining the trademark registration of a tree image that is represented in a way different from that in the cited mark. Accordingly, the two marks were not considered as legally similar.

54. Case Index: Trademark Review & Adjudication Board [2012] No. 12567; Beijing No. 1 Intermediate People's Court, Yi Zhong Zhi Xing Chu Zi [2012] No. 2785; Beijing High People's Court, Gao Xing Zhong Zi [2013] No. 161.

Image Nine	Image Ten

2. Fame Status of the Cited Mark.

As mentioned earlier, the relevant public usually makes a purchase decision by relying on their memory alone – it is sometimes simply a decision because the products bear a certain brand/trademark rather than the products are superior in any way based on solid market research. The more famous the senior marks are, the more the public would be able to recall such marks. Accordingly, this leads to a greater possibility of consumer confusion when the public encounters a junior mark that is similar to the famous mark and it involves the same or similar products. This explains why when the senior cited mark enjoys a certain level of fame, it is advisable to take a more stringent approach when evaluating the similarities between two marks. One should take a combined approach in evaluating the distinctiveness and fame status in connection with the cited mark and consider all relevant factors rather than taking a rigid approach. For example, if a cited mark is not a coined phrase, it is therefore less distinctive; however, it may still be considered as a "distinctive" trademark if, through use and promotion, the mark has acquired secondary meaning in connection with specific goods/services. For such trademarks, one should still take a more stringent approach in considering not only the distinctiveness associated with the cited mark, but also its fame level and public recognition.

In the subject case, the Cited Mark had been registered and put to use for a substantial period of time prior to the application of the Opposed Mark. Also, there was sufficient evidence – including award information – to support the famous status associated with the Cited Mark in connection with white wine products. The fame evidence of the Cited Mark carries a substantial amount of weight to the Appeal Board and the courts; and this explains and supports their position to take a more strict approach in evaluating the similarities between the two marks. It is in fact a common approach to consider the fame status associated with the cited mark when making a similarity determination. In the appeal of trademark opposition concerning "Zui Liang Ye" (a description for certain alcohol beverage products in China) (Application

Number 4063136),[55] the Appeal Board and the Beijing No. 1 Intermediate People's Court refused the opposition and approved the trademark application despite the fame associated with the senior cited mark: Wu Liang Ye" (it is a trademark for a famous Chinese wine/alcohol brand; the mark is suggestive of the underlying wine being brewed out of five different kinds of grains). Specifically, although the decisions recognized the fame status associated with the cited mark in the alcohol/wine industry, the cited mark was nevertheless not regarded as a strong distinctive trademark for such products. Balancing the public's and the industry's interest, the Appeal Board and the court therefore refused to give the cited mark broad protection and decided to hold the two parties' marks distinguishable in light of the phonetic, conceptual and visual differences. The Beijing High Court, however, had a different view and overturned the opposition decisions. The court held that the two parties' marks should be held confusingly similar given there was no substantive differences and the cited mark already enjoyed a high level of fame prior to the application of the subject application. Under such circumstances, given the two marks cover the same/similar products, consumer confusion was likely and the two marks should be held confusingly similar. In the trademark dispute involving "KAISABOSSR" (Application Number 3054811) (*See* Image Eleven),[56] the mark was considered confusingly similar to the cited mark (*See* Image Twelve). This is because the cited mark was proven to enjoy a high level of fame on the disputed products (clothing), the disputed mark fully incorporates the distinctive element in the cited mark (i.e., BOSS), and the disputed mark does not have any new dictionary meaning.

Image Eleven	Image Twelve
KAISABOSSR	**BOSS** BOSS HUGO BOSS

C. The International Class Categorization of the Underlying Goods/Services and Their Industry Specific Differences.

The similarity analysis should be based on the relevant public's perception and their average attention towards the products/services at issue. The scope of "relevant public" is closely tied to the designated products/services of the mark at issue. The underlying products/services therefore are the key; the public's perception and attention differ depending on the nature of the underlying products/services. The public typically has a limited attention or a lesser ability to distinguish the products/

55. Case Index: Trademark Review & Adjudication Board [2011] No. 20213; Beijing No. 1 Intermediate People's Court, Yi Zhong Zhi Xing Chu Zi [2012] No. 175; Beijing High People's Court, Gao Xing Zhong Zi [2012] No. 1245.
56. Case Index: Trademark Review & Adjudication Board [2010] No. 8420; Beijing No. 1 Intermediate People's Court, Yi Zhong Zhi Xing Chu Zi [2010] No. 2627.

services at issue when they involve general consumer products (such as clothing, leather goods, cosmetics, food, and medicine), agricultural products (such as seeds, pesticide,

fertilizer, farm implement), and general services that do not involve much science or technology (such as advertising and promotion for others). The above goods and services are closely connected with the public's health, safety and general wellbeing. Given these goods/services target the average consumers that have limited attention and lower discernment, and there are a vast number of (unregulated) manufacturers/service providers involved, it is advisable to take a more stringent approach when determining the similarities of marks involving the goods/services mentioned above.

For professional goods/services – such as industrial chemical products, medical devices or financial services as defined in Class 36 – it makes sense to take a more relaxed approach when conducting the similarity analysis for marks involving the above goods/services. This is because the manufacturers, service providers and consumers would or should have possessed a certain degree of "professional" knowledge, experience or background which enables them to have a better ability to recognize and distinguish the marks at issue. Similarly, when conducting a similarity analysis for marks involving luxury goods/services of a higher value – such as precious metal, jewelry, automobiles, aviation devices or plastic surgery services – it would be sensible to take a more relaxed approach because consumers would typically pay more attention when purchasing such products/services due to their high price.

In the appeal of trademark opposition, China FAW Group Corporation ("***FAW***") opposed Application Number 1479169 as shown in Image Thirteen below which was filed by Dongfeng Motor Corporation ("***Dongfeng***").[57] FAW believed the application was similar to its senior registration, Registration Number 1455143 as shown below in Image Fourteen ("***FAW Cited Mark***"); the application should therefore be held as a confusingly similar mark in respect to the same/similar products under the Chinese Trademark Law. The Appeal Board refused the opposition. It pointed out that the trademark similarity analysis should take into account the relevant public's perception and average attention, their purchase habit, the marks as a whole and their general impact on consumers as they appear in the marketplace and throughout the transaction process and determine if consumer confusion is likely. The application and the FAW Cited Mark both include distinctive elements; in fact, the FAW Cited Mark includes two Chinese characters, YI QI, as part of its distinctive feature that furthers the differences between the two marks. Although the two marks are used in connection with the same products (automobiles), such products typically involve a complicated decision process on the part of the consumers due to the expensive nature of the products and the specific types of cars for individual preference and purpose. Consumers therefore would pay a high (or higher) attention throughout the purchasing process as opposed to the average attention given to general consumer goods. Due to the differences between the two parties' marks and the public's high attention towards such products,

57. Case Index: Trademark Review & Adjudication Board [2008] No. 30193. FAW did not appeal and the TRAB ruling has come into effect.

the coexistence of two marks is not likely to lead to consumer confusion. The two parties' marks therefore are not confusingly similar even though they both cover the same automobile products.

Image Thirteen	Image Fourteen

D. The Way the Mark Is Being Used in Everyday Life.

1. Market Coexistence.

According to Section 1 of the Notice of the Supreme People's Court on Several Issues Concerning the Trial of Administrative Cases Involving the Authorization and Determination of Trademark Rights (the "***Opinion***"), *"in respect to the disputed marks that have been in use for a while, and have established a high level of market reputation among certain groups in the society, it would be important to maintain a balance between the need to maintain the market order and the need to protect the rights the disputed marks have already accumulated in the marketplace. It is therefore important to keep in mind the market reality that the relevant public is able to distinguish the disputed mark from other similar marks which is part of the market order that's already been established."*

Based on the legislative purpose of "avoid confusion" of Section 30 of the Trademark Law, the trademark similarity analysis should focus on consumer confusion. Even though the disputed mark is similar to the cited mark, if it can be established that the disputed mark has acquired a high level of fame through use and its fame and recognition are part of the **established stable market order**, and the relevant public is able to distinguish the marks, it should follow that the two parties' marks should be held distinguishable; coexistence should therefore be allowed. Despite the above, it is important to emphasize the determination standards and evidentiary requirement in order to prove and justify the registration of the disputed mark is part of the "established stable market order." The situation described in the Opinion should be considered as an exception which should be applied only on a case-by-case basis when determining the similarities between marks; it should not be abused in a way to reduce any level burden of proof on the part of the junior trademark owner or to expand the scope of protection on the disputed mark particularly during the trademark examination and opposition process. The reason to take a narrow and careful approach with respect to the above is twofold:

(1) The Chinese Trademark Law emphasizes the importance of registration; a company or individual should avoid conflict with any other marks that have obtained registration during the application process and are in everyday use. The publication of a trademark registration also provides a certain level of guarantee so that others have constructive notice of such senior marks. With respect to unregistered trademarks during the examination and opposition process, unless there is sufficient evidence to support an established stable market order in respect to the coexistence of two marks prior to the filing date of the cited mark, the registration of the junior mark should be presumed not acceptable even if the request for trademark coexistence is filed based on the use evidence after the filing date of the cited mark. This is because the junior mark owner fails to pay attention to the registration status of the senior marks and carry out its responsibility to avoid conflict with such a prior mark. Without such a presumption, the law would then preserve rights for the owner of the unregistered mark that is contrary to the basic premise of the Chinese Trademark Law where registrations are encouraged so as to avoid confusion.

(2) In practice, even assuming there is sufficient use evidence to support the coexistence of the disputed mark and the cited mark (which are confusingly similar) and the disputed mark has obtained a certain high level of reputation, it does not necessarily follow that there is no consumer confusion in the marketplace. It is likely that the market reputation of the disputed mark is built on the confusion where the relevant public believes the two marks are connected at some level or in fact originated from the same source. Accordingly, one should not reach a conclusion that the two marks are not likely to result in consumer confusion and there is an established stable market order to support the coexistence if the owner of the disputed mark simply provides use and fame evidence. The owner of the disputed mark must also provide supporting materials showing evidence that the relevant public can and have been able to distinguish the disputed mark from the cited mark.

2. Actual Use Evidence of the Disputed Mark.

In practice, it is sometimes necessary to also take into account the way the disputed mark has been put to use in order to determine the similarities between the disputed mark and the cited mark. Although there might be noticeable differences between the marks, it is still possible to conclude the two marks as confusingly similar if - for example - the owner of the disputed mark has made some changes to the way its mark is being represented to the public and such changes, however minor, are sufficient to cause consumer confusion or the way the disputed mark is presented is likely to convince the public it is seeking to trade off the goodwill associated with the cited mark. Under such circumstances, an examiner should still conclude the two parties' marks as confusingly similar because one should examine the marks from a more narrow approach so as to avoid consumer confusion and to prevent bad-faith filings. In the subject mark, based on the use evidence provided by the Company, the Applicant had made some changes to the Opposed Mark in the everyday market in a way that resulted in the prominent use of the two characters: LIN SHUI (the same characters as in the Cited Mark). *See* Image Fifteen regarding the prominent use of the LIN SHUI characters in the Subject Application. Anhui Province Luan City Industrial and Commercial Administration imposed an administrative penalty on the Applicant in respect to their illegal acts of altering the opposed mark in trademark use. The prominent use of these characters shows that the Applicant was fully aware of the fame associated with these characters in connection with white wine products in China but still chose to use the same characters in connection with the same products so as to trade off the Company's goodwill, market reputation and to profit from consumer confusion. Accordingly, it is reasonable to take a narrow and more stringent approach and conclude the Opposed Mark is confusingly similar to the Cited Mark.

Image Fifteen

E. Consideration in Respect to the Coexistence Agreement.

When the disputed mark has clearly constituted as a confusingly similar mark with the cited mark in respect to the same or similar products, the owner of the disputed mark would sometimes present a coexistence agreement between itself and the owner of the cited mark as a counter argument to seek the registration of its application. There are two schools of thoughts in respect to the coexistence agreement and the role it plays in determining the similarities between two marks.

First, as an active and reasonable player in the market place, the fact that the owner of the cited mark agrees to coexist with the disputed mark show that the former must have taken steps to evaluate the similarities between the two marks and conclude consumer confusion unlikely (or is not likely to cause a significant impact on its interests). From the perspective that the trademark law is to protect some private rights and self-governance, the coexistence agreement thus fully protects such private third party's rights and should be treated as such unless there is sufficient evidence showing that the coexistence of the two marks would be harmful to consumer interests, public interests or result in some level of monopoly of the public resources.[58] **Another school of thought** believes that the basic principle of the Trademark Law is to prevent confusion among the relevant public. With this in mind, so long as the disputed mark is held to be a confusingly similar trademark to the cited mark, it should be regarded as such regardless of the coexistence agreement between the parties. This is because the existence of such an agreement is not likely to change the confusion reality among the relevant public. Under this school of thought, the marks should nevertheless be regarded as confusingly similar despite the fact the parties have reached a coexistence agreement.[59]

Although trademark governs to some extent private parties' rights, it also serves to protect the public's interests in the society. For example, consumers can expect to greatly reduce their search costs so long as they can recognize the trademarks associated with the interested products and/or services. The "avoid confusion" principle thus protects not only the senior trademark owner's rights, but also consumers' interests in the society. Following the above, the fact that the two parties have reached a coexistence agreement does not negate the fact that the marks at issue are still confusingly similar; the agreement itself should not serve as the only ground that justifies the registration of the junior mark. The coexistence agreement, however, can still be considered as one of the relevant factors to exclude the likelihood of confusion between the two marks. The following factors should also be taken into account to determine the role of a coexistence agreement in the trademark similarity analysis:

(1) The level of similarities between the marks at issue and their respective goods/services. If the two marks constitute confusingly similar trademarks in respect to the same products/services, the junior mark should not be allowed for registration because the mere existence of the coexistence agreement does not diffuse confusion.

(2) The extent the parties have carved out market territories and specified limitations and restrictions in respect to use of their marks so as to avoid confusion. If a coexistence agreement merely acknowledges a third party's junior rights, and does not restrict in any way the use of the trademarks or other necessary measures in the marketplace so as to avoid confusion, the agreement itself should not be regarded as sufficient to diffuse consumer confusion.

    For example, in the appeal of a trademark refusal concerning "RAGE & Design" (Application Number 8533178),[60] the applicant provided a coexistence agreement between itself and the trademark owner for RAGE. The Appeal Board and two levels of courts, however, have decided to refuse the

58. Case Index: Beijing High People's Court, Yi Zhong Gao Xing Zhong Zi [2013] No. 281.
59. Case Index: Beijing No. 1 Intermediate People's Court, Yi Zhong Zhi Xing Chu Zi [2012] No. 1174.
60. Case Index: Trademark Review & Adjudication Board [2012] No. 27235; Beijing No. 1 Intermediate People's Court, Yi Zhong Zhi Xing Chu Zi [2013] No. 1477; Beijing High People's Court, Gao Xing Zhong Zi [2013] No. 1772.

application. This is because although the coexistence agreement acknowledges the fact that the disputed mark and the cited mark involve different sectors of consumer groups in the society, the applicant has not yet provided any evidence showing that the cited mark would not be used in connection with computer software products. Considering the similarities between the two marks and the fact that both involve computer software products, consumer confusion remains a possibility among the relevant public for the overlapping goods (recorded computer software). Accordingly, the application is refused because it is a confusingly similar mark in respect to the same or similar products.

Despite the above, a coexistence agreement will be considered and accepted even if two marks are regarded as confusingly similar in respect to the same/similar products so long as: (1) the marks do not involve actual overlapping products in the real marketplace; (2) the marks target different groups of consumers; (3) the marks involve different sectors of the marketplace – and the agreement has made reasonable efforts and/or arrangements to allow the two marks to coexist in the marketplace. For example, in the appeal of trademark refusal concerning GERBE (Application Number 10823556),[61] the application covers "stocking, tights and socks while the cited mark, GERBER, covers "baby clothing, underwear, diapers, and children's clothing." Based on the evidence provided by the applicant, the applied-for mark is only used in respect to adult stocking, socks and tights products and the mark in fact enjoys a certain level of fame in connection with female stocking products. The cited mark, on the other hand, belongs to the Nestle Group based in Switzerland and is a brand focused specifically on baby clothing products. Nestle has provided a coexistence agreement which evidences its acceptance of the applied-for mark; the agreement also acknowledges the fact that the cited mark is only used in respect to children's clothing. The Appeal Board has taken the above into consideration and reached the conclusion that since the applied-for mark only targets the female stocking and underwear market while the cited mark focuses on a different sector of the marketplace – i.e., the children's clothing products – the two marks should not be considered as confusingly similar. The two marks involve different products that clearly contrast in materials, functionalities, purposes, channels of trade, as well as targeted consumers; therefore, given these differences, the coexistence of the marks would not lead to consumer confusion. In light of the above differences and the fact that the owner of the cited mark has provided a coexistence agreement which acknowledges its

61. Case Index: Trademark Review & Adjudication Board [2013] No. 92769.

consent regarding the registration and use of the application in China, the Appeal Board has decided that the application and the cited mark do not constitute confusingly similar trademarks in respect to the same or similar products and approved the registration of the application.

(3) The coexistence agreement shall not have a clear detrimental impact on the public interests. In the appeal of trademark refusal concerning the design application (*See* Image Sixteen below) for Application Number 7358249,[62] both the Appeal Board and the Beijing No. 1 Intermediate People's Court reached the same conclusion deciding that the subject application was a confusingly similar mark to the cited mark (*See* Image Seventeen below) in respect to the same or similar products. In the appeal to the Beijing High People's Court, the applicant provided its coexistence agreement with the owner of the cited mark. Although the High Court took the agreement into consideration (and specifically expressed its interest in the agreement in the ruling), the court nevertheless decided to refuse the application. This is because the application involved a design of chemical molecular structure which is a publicly well-known design and is therefore part of the public resources (it should not become a private third party's property through a trademark registration). Despite the fact that the parties have reached a coexistence agreement, the use of a molecular structure design in connection with Class 5 raw materials for pharmaceutical/medicine products are likely to negatively impact the public interests and lead to a monopoly of public resources. Accordingly, the High Court rejected the appeal and refused the registration of the application despite the fact that the parties have reached a coexistence agreement.

Image Sixteen	Image Seventeen
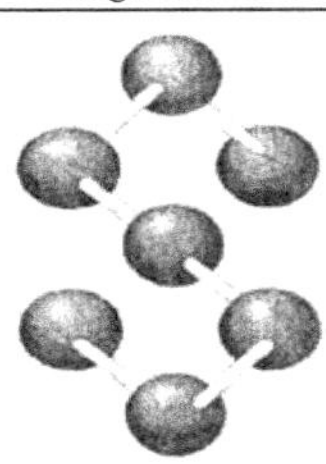	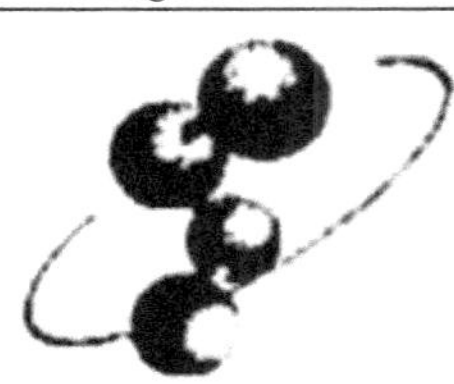

62. Case Index: Trademark Review & Adjudication Board [2011] No. 30383; Beijing No. 1 Intermediate People's Court, Yi Zhong Zhi Xing Chu Zi [2012] No. 2753; Beijing High People's Court, Gao Xing Zhong Zi [2013] No. 281.

III. Determination of "Similar" Products/Services.

Section 11 of the China Interpretation of the SPC Concerning the Application of Laws in the Trial of Cases of Civil Disputes Arising from Trademarks(the "***Interpretation***") explains that "similar products" (as defined in Section 52(1) of the 2001 Trademark Law) are about products that have the same functionalities, purposes, manufacturing process, channels of trademark, target consumers or that the relevant public would easily confuse such products due to the connection between them. "Similar services" are about services that share the same purposes, content, methods, target consumers or that the relevant public would easily confuse such services due to the connection between them. "Similarities between services and products" refer to the particular connection between such services and products that would easily lead to confusion among the relevant public.

Analyzing trademark civil disputes from the angle of trademark infringement, the SPC provides specifics in the Interpretation in respect to the so-called similar products, similar services, similar products and services as defined in Section 52(1) of the 2001 Trademark Law. Although Section 28 and Section 52(1) of the 2001 Trademark Law are regulations about different subjects, with different scope of applications, the concept about "similar products/services" in the Trademark Law should be uniform. Accordingly, the specifics discussed in Section 11 of the Interpretation concerning similar products, services and similar products/services are applicable as well to Section 28 of the 2001 Trademark Law (Section 30 of the 2013 Trademark Law).

In respect to the determination for similar products or services, Section 12 of the Interpretation states that: "*the civil courts should decide whether or not the underlying goods or services are similar in accordance with Section 52(1) of the Trademark Law by taking into account the relevant public's combined perception towards such products or services. The courts can also take into account the classifications as outlined in the following when making the determination: the International Classification of Goods and Services for the Purposes of the Registration of Marks; the Table for Differentiating Similar Goods and Services.*"

There are however two primary issues that need to be clarified when making a determination about the similarities for goods/services.[63]

1. The Role in Respect to the Guide Book – "The Summary Table to Differentiate Similar Goods and Services" – When Making the Similarity Determination for Goods/Services at Issue.

The Summary Table to Differentiate Similar Goods and Services (the "***Subclass Classification***") is based on *the International Classification of Goods and Services for the Purposes of the Registration of Marks* (the Nice Classification) provided by the World Intellectual Property Organization ("***WIPO***") and has taken into account the

63. Except for special clarification, "similarity of goods" includes similar goods and services hereinafter.

functionalities, purposes, production processes, channels of trade, and target consumers in respect to the underlying products as well as purposes, content, methods, and target consumers of the underlying services that are specific and special in the Chinese markets. The Subclass Classification has therefore considered the world's classification system and is tailored to the Chinese society – it is therefore an open, consistent and reliable classification system for trademark goods and services.

The role the Subclass Classification plays in determining the similarities for goods/services should be different with respect to the types of trademark procedures involved – typical procedures include an examination of a trademark application, an opposition proceeding, an invalidation procedure of a trademark and a trademark infringement dispute. During the examination process of a trademark application, the Subclass Classification should serve as the basic guidance in determining the classification and the similarities for the applied-for goods/services – administrative efficiency and fairness should be the key determining factors in this process. In 2013, the Trademark Office accepted around 1,881,500 trademark applications for registrations; among these, the Trademark Office reviewed 1,424,600 cases. Due to the vast number of trademark applications in China these years, the Subclass Classification offers great convenience, plays a vital role in increasing the overall review efficiency as well as maintaining the consistencies in the related administrative trademark decisions during the trademark application process.

Different from the reviewing process involving a trademark application, the procedures involving a trademark opposition, an invalidation action and an infringement dispute are different because they deal with disputes that have already occurred. The focus during these processes should be more about fairness, as opposed to the administrative efficiencies – specifically, the goal is to make a case-by-case determination regarding the similarities of goods/services so as to maximize the value of fairness within the confines of the law. Furthermore, the Subclass Classification is based on the Nice Classification that primarily provides classification of goods/services during the trademark registration process – the goal is to establish a system for classifying goods/services that can be utilized internationally. When the process is no longer about an application for registration of a trademark, but is about an opposition, invalidation and infringement dispute of a trademark, the role the Subclass Classification plays should be shifted from being a "basic guidance" to being merely an "important reference."

On balance, the role the Subclass Classification plays in determining the similarity of goods/services should be objective and flexible depending on the exact type of trademark procedure at issue. During the trademark examination for registration process, the focus is on increasing the administrative efficiency. Accordingly, one should follow the Subclass Classification as much as possible (i.e., a narrow approach) in designating, classifying and reviewing the international classes, subclasses and subgroups of the applied-for goods/services in the application at issue. In the trademark opposition proceeding, the trademark invalidation proceeding and the trademark infringement dispute proceeding, the focus is shifted from increasing the administrative efficiency to fairness. The goal during these proceedings is to prevent consumer confusion, bad-faith applications (and registrations), malicious trademark registrations that trade off the commercial goodwill of the senior mark, and to crack down trademark infringements. The determination should focus on the objective market realities of the goods/services, and factors specific to the case at issue so as to make a balanced approach in determining the similarities of goods/services. The Subject Classification serves as an important reference point, but it should not be taken as the only guidance and being applied rigidly in classifying and determining the similarities of goods/services at issue.

2. Factors to Consider when Making the Similarity Analysis Concerning Goods/Services.

As discussed earlier, taking into account the legislative purpose of Section 30 of the Trademark Law, the determination of goods/services (whether or not they are "legally similar") should focus on consumer confusion and if the relevant public would be confused in respect to the source of the products when the same products are being offered by the same or similar marks. In other words, the underlying goods/services should be determined "similar" if the relevant public is likely to be confused regarding the source offering the products or would inevitably assume there is some level of connection between the different manufacturers or suppliers of such products/services. The first level of analysis should involve the objective factors of the subject products and their specific industries. Take products for example, the analysis should take into account its raw materials, manufacturing process, craftsmanship, functionality, purpose, channel of trade, and targeted consumers. Take services for example, the analysis should involve the purposes, content, delivery method, channel of trade, target consumers, service suppliers and exact scope of services. The above analysis and comparison should be the first step in determining the similarities of good/services; and the Subclass Classification can serve as an important reference during this process. In addition, the determination should also take into account the specific situations in each case including the distinctiveness and the fame associated with the cited mark. This involves "subjective" analysis including the level of diversified business operation for the manufacturers or suppliers concerning the cited mark and the subjective intent of the owner of the disputed mark. Generally speaking, if the relevant public would assume the products are provided by the same source or there exists a certain level of connection between the service suppliers (or product manufacturers) even though such services/products are not exactly the same, the examiners would typically rule the underlying services/products are "legally similar."

In the trademark dispute case involving the application for "FU AN NA in Chinese characters" under Application Number 3493244,[64] the mark was registered in respect to Class 27 goods such as "carpet, mat, bath mat, non-textile wall hanging." The cited mark is also composed of the same three characters, FU AN NA, but it covers Class 24 products such as quilt, quilt cover, decoration, and blanket. The Appeal Board and the

64. Case Index: Trademark Review & Adjudication Board [2012] No. 41084; Beijing No. 1 Intermediate People's Court, Yi Zhong Zhi Xing Chu Zi [2013] No. 1084; Beijing High People's Court, Gao Xing Zhong Zi [2013] No. 1768.

two levels of courts have taken a balanced and combined approach and considered many factors including the identical or overlapping nature of the functionalities, purposes, target consumers, the ways and consumer places the products are being used involving both marks. The examiners and judges also took into account the high level of distinctiveness of the cited mark, its fame status (through use), and the fact that both marks are identical involving the exact three Chinese characters. The Appeal Board and the courts all recognized that consumer confusion is likely between the cited mark and the disputed mark and the products are therefore "legally similar" products even though they do not fall under the same classifications as defined by the Subclass Classification. Given the appeal, examiners and the judges have already ruled on the similar nature of the products at issue, the disputed mark was therefore requested to be cancelled based on Section 28 of the 2001 Trademark Law.

It is important to clarify the scope of protection between the regulations designed to protect a well-known trademark and those designed to protect a regular trademark by ruling the underlying goods/services as legally similar regardless of the classification in the Subclass Classification guidebook. The Trademark Law, by design, offers different levels of protection to regular trademarks and well-known trademarks that are widely known by the relevant public. For regular trademarks, a third party is only prevented from using the same or similar products (or services) that bear the same mark. For a well-known trademark, however, a third party can be restricted from using the mark even on dissimilar products (or services) so as to protect the distinctiveness and commercial reputation of such a senior well-known trademark. On one hand, in accordance with the well-known trademark recognized by the Trademark Law (recognized based on the case-by-case need basis), it is still possible to recognize different products as legally similar despite the classification in the Subclass Classification guidebook so long as there is a strong relationship between such products, the relevant public would conclude such products are offered by the same source or there is a certain level of connection between the different sources providing such products; if so, Section 30 of the Trademark Law is then applicable. On the other hand, one should also avoid an overzealous and overly broad application of this rule in determining different goods/services as similar regardless of the Subclass Classification guidebook because it would essentially diminish the effectiveness of the relevant regulations designed to protect a well-known trademark. Accordingly, it is more appropriate to apply the rules and regulations designed to protect a well-known trademark in situations where there is a clear distinct difference between the goods/services, the relevant public is less likely to be confused, but the use of such "different goods (or services") would nevertheless dilute or smear the strong connection between the well-known trademark and its designed goods/services.

6. Trademark Applications that Are Refused on the Grounds of Causing Cross-Class Confusion or Possible Dilution to Well-Known Trademarks in China

Appeal of administrative litigation regarding Chanel Company's petition to reject the trademark application for "CHANEL in English and Chinese characters and Design" by Foshan Huaxingli Building Material Co., Ltd.

- First Instance: Beijing No. 1 Intermediate People's Court (No. 2546; 2011) – Decided on January 10, 2012
- Second Instance: Beijing High People's Court (No. 567; 2012) – Decided on June 18, 2012

BACKGROUND

This is a review of a trademark opposition case. The opposed mark is "CHANEL in English and Chinese characters and Design" under No. 3221732 (*see* Image One; herein referred to simply as the "***Subject Mark***"). The designated goods are Class 19 products such as ceramic tiles, mosaics glasses. The applicant for the Subject Mark, which also serves as the plaintiff in the present court appeal, is Foshan Huaxingli Building Material Co., Ltd. (the "***Applicant***").

Chanel Company raised a timely opposition action against the Subject Mark to the Trademark Office under the SAIC of PRC (the "***Trademark Office***"). The Trademark Office decided to allow the registration of the Subject Mark.

Chanel Company challenged the decision by raising another timely appeal to the TRAB under the SAIC of PRC (the "***Appeal Board***"). Its primary appeal grounds were:

- The textual elements in the Subject Mark – namely "CHANEL" in English and "CHANEL" in Chinese characters – are closely similar to the Chanel Company's senior trademark registrations in China (*see* Image Two; collectively referred to herein as the "***Cited Mark***").
- The Subject Mark is a direct copy of Chanel Company's famous mark; it not only will diminish and dilute the distinctiveness of Chanel Company's senior famous trademark, but also will lead to consumer confusion.
- In light of the above, the registration of the Subject Mark violates Article 13, Section 2 of the 2001 Trademark Law and should therefore be refused for registration.

Image One	Image Two
Subject Mark	Cited Mark
CHANEL 香奈尔	CHANEL 香奈儿

The Appeal Board made a ruling and decided that the Subject Mark had violated Article 13, Section 2 of the 2001 Trademark Law and should not be allowed for registration.[65]

The Applicant did not agree with the decision and raised a timely court action to Beijing No. 1 Intermediate People's Court (the "***Court***"). The Applicant pointed out that even though the Cited Mark is a well-known trademark in China, the registration of the Subject Mark would not lead to consumer confusion. Accordingly, the registration of the Subject Mark would not violate Article 13, Section 2 of the Trademark Law; the Court should therefore revoke the Appeal Board's decision and allow the Subject Mark to be registered.

COURT DECISION

The Court noted that since the Cited Mark had become a well-known trademark in China, if the use of the Subject Mark would cause either "cross-class confusion" or "dilution" against the Cited Mark, the application should be refused on the basis of Article 13, Section 2 of the Trademark Law. The decision to allow the registration of the Subject Mark is not otherwise sustainable if it can be shown there is either "cross-class confusion" or "dilution" against the Cited Mark.

In respect to the "cross-class confusion" prong, the Court's view was that this condition was not met. This is because Chanel Company failed to provide supporting materials evidencing the fact - or a noticeable pattern - that the manufacturers for clothing or cosmetics (i.e., products covered by the Cited Mark) are or can also be involved in the manufacturing of glazed tiles (i.e., products covered by the Subject Mark). Chanel also failed to provide additional supporting evidence, noting the relevant public may connect the Subject Mark with the Cited Mark when the former is being advertised and put to use in connection with tiles and other Class 19 related

65. Case Index: Trademark Review & Adjudication Board, [2011] No. 10557.

products. Furthermore, Chanel Company had not yet put its mark to use on Class 19 or related products, such as glazed tiles. Accordingly, the submitted evidence could not prove that the use of the Subject Mark was likely to cause any cross-class confusion with the Subject Mark.

In respect to the "dilution" prong, the Court's view is that this condition can only be met if the following is satisfied:

> *The senior well-known trademark is not entitled to the anti-dilution protection unless the relevant public of the disputed mark can still make a connection of the two marks despite the fact that the goods/services they encounter are not related at all with those generally covered by the senior mark.*

In light of the above, the registration of the Subject Mark violated Article 13, Section 2 of the Trademark Law and was not registered. The Court maintained the decision in accordance of Article 54(1) of Administrative Procedure Law of the PRC. The Applicant challenged the Court's decision by filing an appeal to the Beijing High People's Court (the "***High Court***"). The High Court rejected the appeal and maintained the Court's initial decision.

ANALYSIS & INSIGHT

This case involves various issues associated with the application of Article 13, Section 2 of the Trademark Law. This opinion therefore provides a detailed analysis concerning the application of Article 13, Section 2.

I. The "Relevant Public" under Article 13, Section 2.

Although the Trademark Law generally uses the phrase "the relevant public" as a framework to define the scope and subject affected by the law, the application of Article 13, Section 2 would nevertheless involve "different" goods and services which means that the "relevant public" would change accordingly. Furthermore, "different" sectors of the public may have a different perception of the same subject matter. Accordingly, one of the key issues in discussing the application of Article 13, Section 2 is to determine the proper scope of the "relevant public." Key questions include: which sector(s) of the public should be deemed "relevant" so as to determine whether or not the cited mark is a well-known trademark? Which sector(s) of the public should be deemed relevant so as to determine if the registration of the disputed mark, along with its designated goods/services, would lead to consumer confusion?

The judgment offered a clear answer in respect to this question. It held that, since the well-known trademark is well known with respect to its designated goods/services, the "relevant" public should be limited to those consumers who are or likely to be affected by such designated goods/services. Despite this, the scope of "relevant" consumers is different when it comes to determining whether or not the use and registration of the disputed mark would lead to consumer confusion. In the consumer confusion determination analysis, the relevant public should be those affected or likely to be affected by the disputed mark's designated goods/services, rather than those of the well-known trademark.

From the above analysis, it is clear that the public "relevant" to determine whether or not the cited mark is well known are the consumers affected by the designated goods/services (i.e., clothing or cosmetics consumers in this case). Similarly, to determine whether or not the use and registration of the disputed mark will lead to consumer confusion, the "relevant" public should be those affected by the disputed mark's goods and services (i.e., consumers for glazed tiles).

In the present case, because the "relevant public" for the Cited Mark and the Subject Mark does not differ much, so the discussion in respect to which sector of the population shall be deemed "relevant" does not cause too much of a debate. However, this has been and can be a determining factor in various other cases when it comes to applying Article 13, Section 2.

For example, in the case involving the "De Li Xi" (DELIXI德力西) trademark,[66] the designated goods for the opposed mark cover "sausage casings" in Class 18 and the designated goods for the senior well-known trademark cover "AC contactor" in Class 9. The reason the court rules that the registration of the opposed mark does not violate Article 13, Section 2 of the Trademark Law is because "*the relevant public for the opposed mark does not overlap, or has very little overlap, with those of the cited mark. Under such circumstances, even though the cited mark is a well-known trademark in respect to Class 9 goods such as "AC contactor, thermal relay, airbreak circuit breaker, light distribution box," given the relevant public for the opposed mark is unaware of the fame associated with the senior mark, they would not associate the two marks together and accordingly, the use and registration of the opposed mark will not lead to consumer confusion.*"

Also in the case involving "TONGWEI in Chinese characters and Design" trademark,[67] the court held that even if the cited mark "TONGWEI in Chinese characters and Design" was recognized as a well-known trademark for *fodder*, the opposed mark's registration on *electric welding apparatus* would not cause consumers' confusion.

II. Analysis of the "Public Confusion" Phrase in Article 13, Section 2.

Article 13, Section 2 of the Trademark Law forbids the use and registration of a trademark application which copies, reproduces or translates a third party's registered well-known trademark in China despite the fact that such an application covers dissimilar or unrelated goods/services from those of the senior mark. Article 13, Section 2 applies so long as such an application is capable of causing **public confusion** and can negatively affect the registrant's rights in China.

66. Case Index: Beijing No. 1 Intermediate People's Court, Yi Zhong Xing Chu Zi [2009] No. 2029.
67. Case Index: Beijing No. 1 Intermediate People's Court, Yi Zhong Xing Chu Zi [2012] No. 2440.

From the literal interpretation of Article 13, Section 2, it appears that the "public confusion" phrase can be taken to mean "cross-class confusion" – in other words, confusion arises when the relevant public cannot differentiate the owner of the disputed mark and the owner of the senior well-known trademark (i.e., direct confusion), or is led to believe that the owners of the two marks are somehow connected (i.e., indirect confusion). However, after the implementation of *Interpretation of the Supreme People's Court on Several Issues Concerning the Application of Law to the Trial of Cases of Civil Disputes over the Protection of Famous Trademarks* (the "***Judicial Interpretation***"), the scope of "public confusion" has been expanded.

According to Article 9 of the Judicial Interpretation, acts that are sufficient to convince the relevant public that there is a certain connection between the disputed mark and the well-known trademark and such an association is capable of diminishing the distinctiveness of the senior well-known trademark, damage its reputation and cause others to unjustly profit from its fame should be governed by the following sentence in Article 13, Section 2 of the Trademark Law: *"[the application is] capable of causing public confusion and can negatively affect the [senior] registrant's rights in China."* The "public confusion" phrase in Article 13, Section 2 therefore covers two situations: (1) diminishing the distinctiveness associated with the well-known trademark (i.e., dilution); and (2) negatively damaging the commercial reputation of the well-known trademark (i.e., smearing).

Although the above Judicial Interpretation originally only had civil actions in mind, the guiding principles for administrative cases do not differ much from those in the civil cases. The above interpretation is therefore applicable to trademark administrative lawsuits as well. This means that the scope of the "public confusion" phrase in Article 13, Section 2 not only covers "cross-class" confusion situation, but also dilution and smearing.

In light of the above and with the understanding that the Court already recognizes the well-known status of the Cited Mark, in order to make a determination whether or not the registration of the Subject Mark violates Article 13, Section 2, one must consider both "cross-class confusion" as well as dilution situations. Note that smearing is not relevant to the subject case so it will not be separately analyzed.

III. Evidence Requirement for Proving "Cross-Class Confusion."

The standard to recognize confusion in a cross-class situation for a well-known trademark is similar to a regular mark involving the same or similar goods/services. In other words, if use of a disputed mark is likely to mislead the public into believing that the goods/services involved are provided by or connected with the owner of a senior famous mark, confusion will be recognized.

Despite the above, there are still some practical differences – primarily involving the burden of proof and the sufficiency of evidence – when it comes to recognizing confusion in a cross-class confusion situation versus a situation where related goods/services are involved. When it comes to recognizing confusion for similar or related goods/services, the owner of the senior mark only needs to prove that its goods/

services are *similar or related* to those provided by the junior disputed mark. In other words, the owner of the senior mark does NOT need to provide additional supporting evidence showing that confusion is likely when the disputed mark has been put to use. This is because in today's society, the business owner providing goods or services of Type X is also likely to provide similar goods or services related to Type X because such similar goods/services typically enjoy the same functionality, purpose, or channel of trade. Accordingly, the relevant public will naturally make the connection once the owner of the senior mark has proven the relatedness or similar nature of the goods/services offered by its senior mark and those by the junior disputed mark; no other supporting evidence is therefore required.

On the other hand, when it comes to recognizing confusion in a cross-class confusion situation, the owner of the famous mark must also provide additional "particular instances" so as to show that the *use* of disputed mark will nevertheless lead to confusion despite the goods/services offered by the disputed mark not being related at all (hence, cross-class) to those provided by the senior mark. This is because, without proving the "relatedness" of the goods/services at issue, the relevant public will not instinctively make the connection of the two marks, and additional evidence is therefore required so as to recognize confusion. This also explains why the burden of proof typically shifts to the owner of the famous mark in a cross-class confusion case. Additional evidence that is helpful to a senior trademark owner includes its use of the mark on the unrelated goods/services that are presently offered by the junior mark.

Based on the above, cross-class confusion is not present in this case unless Chanel Company can provide specific instances pointing out that the relevant public is likely to believe the goods offered by the Subject Mark are either offered by or connected with Chanel Company. Based on the evidence submitted by Chanel Company, Chanel did not establish any recognizable pattern evidencing clothing or cosmetics manufacturer is also likely to be involved in the manufacturing of tiles, or that the public has recognized the Cited Mark in connection with glazed tiles based on the prior use, nor any evidence showing the registration of the Subject Mark is likely to cause confusion with the Cited Mark in terms of unrelated cross-class goods. Accordingly, based on the evidence at hand, the Court was not able to recognize cross-class confusion in the Chanel case.

IV. "Dilution" Analysis and Determination.

Although there are some cases providing anti-dilution protection for well-known trademarks, these cases do not presently offer much guidance in terms of the specific instances where the use of the disputed mark will lead to dilution of the senior well-known trademark. Accordingly, in this case, the Court has fully considered this aspect and provided below some detailed analysis, along with three specific conceptual requirements so as to recognize dilution. We, of course, also understand more case studies are necessary in order to make sure these requirements stay as reasonable and objective as possible so as to embody the spirit of the Anti-Dilution Law.

A. The Objectives of Anti-Dilution Law.

The objective of the Anti-Dilution Law ("***Law***") is to ensure that the one-to-one connection between the well-known trademark and its owner (i.e., the distinctiveness of the mark) will not be negatively impacted by the use or registration of the junior mark. To put it more accurately, the purpose of the Law is to protect the owner's commercial and legitimate benefits stemming from this exclusive connection between itself and the mark.

The reason the Trademark Law needs to protect this exclusive relationship (i.e., the distinctiveness associated with a mark) is because although a trademark embodies itself with exterior forms such as a logo or a word mark, its essence is really about its distinctiveness, uniqueness, and its overall conceptual impression in the relevant public's mind from which the trademark owner derives commercial benefits. The uniqueness and distinctiveness associated with a trademark will be negatively impacted once a mark has been put to use in connection with goods/services unrelated to its original goods/services that the mark is famous for. In other words, dilution to a famous trademark ensues once its image is diminished or "decreased" in the minds of its relevant public.[68]

Although the two parallel tracks (anti-dilution and confusion protection) to protect a well-known trademark both seek to protect this exclusive connection, or rather, the distinctiveness feature of a mark, the focus is different.

"Confusion Protection" protects the public by forbidding any actions that are designed to take advantage of the exclusive relationship and preventing a third party from reaping unjustified profits from the market place. It is worth noting, however, that the exclusive relationship between a well-known trademark and its owner is not destroyed in situations where confusion is recognized because the public still believe that the goods/services provided by the disputed mark are offered by or connected with the owner of the famous mark. On the other hand, in situation where anti-dilution is recognized, the distinctiveness associated with the famous mark is destroyed. This is because the relevant public will not associate the disputed mark with the owner of senior famous mark (hence no confusion). As time goes by, the senior famous mark will gradually lose its distinctiveness because the public will become unable to identify the provider associated with the senior mark, and the senior mark will then fail to become a source identifier for its goods and services. Accordingly, the focus of "Anti-Dilution Protection" is on the distinctiveness feature of a trademark itself and to prevent others from diminishing this exclusive connection between a mark and its owner.

Based on the understanding of the Law, the opinion concludes the following:

> *When encountering the disputed mark, although its relevant public will instinctively think of the senior well-known trademark, the public will not assume any*

68. House Report on the Federal Trademark Dilution Act Of 1995, H.R. 104–374, p. 3; quoted from Huang Hui in his book, "LEGAL PROTECTION OF WELL-KNOWN TRADEMARK AND FAMOUS MARK," published by Law Press, p. 145 (2001).

relationship or connection between the owner of the disputed mark and the senior well-known trademark; if so, the use of the disputed mark will constitute dilution against the senior well-known trademark.

The above conclusion is the basic principle to recognize and apply the Anti-Dilution Law. If, however, the relevant public of the disputed mark will assume some connection between the owner of the disputed mark and the famous mark, it is then a "confusion" situation, not a "dilution" situation.

B. Three Levels of Awareness Required in order to Apply the Anti-Dilution Law.

In addition to the above analysis, we think it would be helpful to discuss the specific steps required in order for the Law to apply. In summary, if the relevant public has acquired the below three levels of awareness, we think the senior well-known trademark at issue is entitled to the protection of the Anti-Dilution Law.

1. First Level of Awareness.

The relevant public of the disputed mark is aware of the exclusive connection between the "well-known trademark," its respective "owner," and those "certain" goods/services that have become exclusively connected with the senior famous mark.

This level of understanding is the first requirement to recognize dilution. Otherwise, there would be no distinctiveness to be diluted to start with.

In respect to the specific situations that allow this level of awareness to arise, the opinion points out the following: upon encountering the famous mark, as long as the relevant public of the disputed mark will immediately think of the specific goods/services associated with the senior famous mark, the first level of understanding is satisfied. For example, the first level of understanding is met in the dilution claim for the Apple Logo case because most of the public will immediately think of cell phones when seeing the Apple Logo. It is worth pointing out that the focus to satisfy the first level of understanding is on the trademark itself, rather than its designated goods or services. The specific goods and services are of little relevance here because the dilution claim is focused on the similarities between the disputed mark and the famous mark, and the diminishing of the famous mark rather than on any specific products or services.

There are multiple factors to determine if the relevant public of the disputed mark does have this level of awareness for the senior mark; the primary factors are threefold: **(1)** the extent of **overlapping** in respect to the "relevant public" and the "goods/services" between the disputed mark and the famous mark; **(2)** the **inherent distinctiveness** associated with the senior famous trademark; and **(3)** the level of **fame** associated with the senior mark.

a. The "Overlapping" Requirement.

Generally speaking, the first level of awareness can only be recognized when all or the majority of the relevant public of the disputed mark overlaps those of the senior well-known trademark. The reason the exact scope of the relevant public is of importance here is because, as discussed previously, not all members in the public are relevant for a dilution claim - only those relevant to the goods/services concerning the disputed mark matter. Following this line of reasoning, only those members who are both "relevant" to the disputed mark *and* the famous mark would possess the first level of awareness; accordingly, it follows that the level of overlapping must involve either all or the majority of the relevant public of the disputed mark. *The overlapping public (majority or all) is therefore the first condition to be met in order to satisfy the first level of awareness for a dilution claim.*

Turning to the present case, the Cited Mark covers cosmetics and clothing products which belong to the category of "general consumer products;" its relevant public is therefore broad. The Subject Mark covers ceramic tiles which fall under the category of "decorative products;" its relevant public is therefore narrow. The relevant public of the Cited Mark therefore entirely overlaps those of the Subject Mark.

The discussion is quite different in respect to the earlier-discussed "De Li Xi" (DELIXI德力西) case in that the relevant public for the disputed mark is far larger than that of the senior mark. Accordingly, it is difficult to satisfy that the relevant public's "overall" awareness concerning the senior mark is present; the case therefore fails to satisfy the first level of awareness.

b. The Inherent Distinctiveness Requirement (Discussed under the Below Section 3).

c. The Fame Requirement.

In addition to the overlapping requirement for the relevant public, the distinctiveness and the fame status associated with the senior well-known trademark - as well as the interaction between these two factors - also play an important role in determining whether the first level of awareness is satisfied. If the well-known trademark has lower inherent distinctiveness (i.e., it is a descriptive or common phrase), it will then require a higher level of fame in order for the relevant public of the disputed mark to acquire the first level of awareness. Conversely, if the senior well-known trademark has a higher level of inherent distinctiveness (i.e., it is a coined phrase), its fame requirement in order to satisfy the first level of awareness will decrease accordingly.

If the well-known trademark is not an inherently distinctive phrase - for example, it is a descriptive or common existing phrase such as "Great Wall" or "Mount Taishan" - then the relevant public may not instinctively regard it as *the* senior well-known trademark when they first encounter the phrase. Rather, the public may simply regard the phrase as something that's already commonly known - namely, the Great Wall of China, and the mountain named "Taishan"- or any other existing trademarks that have been otherwise registered and put to use for goods and services similar to those of the disputed mark (e.g., clothing or wine for "Great Wall," and gypsum or installation for elevators services for "Mount Taishan"). Under such circumstances, the senior well-known trademark at issue must have a very high fame status so that the relevant public's understanding for the "phrase" at issue points *only* to the senior trademark, rather than the landmark it embodies or other existing trademarks (in other words, the fame level must be high enough so as to establish the one-to-one connection between the phrase and the senior trademark). Conversely, if the senior well-known trademark is composed of coined or fancy words with inherently high distinctiveness - such as Coca-Cola - the fame requirement is decreased accordingly. This is because there is no other corresponding image or impression about such a phrase; since it is a made-up word so it is highly unlikely (except for coincidence) to be used or applied for as another trademark. Similarly, because the mark is not an existing phrase in the language, it will not point to commonly known landmarks or structures. Such a mark therefore naturally enjoys the exclusive one-to-one connection between the wording itself and the senior famous mark and the requirement of fame is accordingly decreased.

Turning to the present case, although the word "CHANEL" in the Subject Mark can be understood and has been used as a name, it is not a phrase commonly known to the relevant public in China. The same wording in the Cited Mark "CHANEL" is in fact a coined word; it does not have any meaning - accordingly, the relevant public of the Subject Mark are not likely to have any fixed understanding or association with the word (other than for the senior trademark itself). Also, the word "CHANEL" in the Cited Mark is not an existing word in the Chinese language so it would be difficult to explain - except for, of course, pure innocent coincidence - why a third party has adopted the same or a similar phrase and applied for it as a trademark. Furthermore, there is insufficient evidence to support that the owner of the Subject Mark has been using the same or similar mark on the applied-for products for a certain period of time or has acquired some level of fame for such a mark. This means that it is unlikely that the relevant public would associate or misunderstand the Cited Mark as any other existing trademarks. Considering the above and the fact that the relevant public of the Cited Mark exceeds and overlaps that of the Subject Mark, the relevant public of the Subject Mark does possess the first level of awareness concerning the Cited Mark.

2. Second Level of Awareness.

Upon seeing the disputed mark, the relevant public of the disputed mark is capable of associating the mark with the senior well-known trademark.

Generally speaking, if the disputed mark is the same as or shares a close similarity with the senior well-known trademark, it is easier to satisfy the second level of awareness. This is because association is the basis for dilution; if the relevant public will not associate or connect the senior mark with the disputed mark, then the use and registration of the disputed mark will not negatively affect the distinctiveness of the senior famous mark since there is no association in the first place. The ability to associate, in this instance, focuses strictly on the mark itself and not on its designated goods or services because the products/services the relevant public encounters are not related at all to those covered by the senior famous trademark. In other words, when the ability to associate is based simply on the trademark itself, the closer the two marks are, the easier it is for the relevant public to form the association and it is therefore more likely to satisfy the second level of awareness. *To summarize, the disputed mark must either be the same or bear a close similarity to the senior famous mark so as to allow association and thereby allow the famous mark owner to establish a dilution claim.*

Turning to the subject case, the English and Chinese characters in the Subject Mark are the same as those in the Cited Mark. The additional design element is not the dominant distinctive element of the Subject Mark because the textual element is the primary impression of the entire mark, and it is the way the mark will be referred to – at least phonetically – by the public. In light of the identical nature of the two marks, the relevant public will immediately think of the Cited Mark when they encounter the Subject Mark (as opposed to any other marks) and accordingly, the second level of awareness is satisfied.

Unlike the present case, the second level of awareness is not satisfied in the Apple case. In the Apple case, although the cited mark is indeed a famous mark, the wording in the disputed mark ("APPLE" in Chinese characters "苹果") and the cited mark ( ) can be understood to refer to a commonly known object in real life – i.e., an apple. Further, the two parties' marks do not share a close visual similarities (one is a word mark while the other is a design mark). Accordingly, the cited mark ( ), in connection with Class 25 clothing products, will not be the only association when the relevant public sees the disputed mark. This explains why the second level of awareness is not satisfied in the Apple case.[69]

3. Third Level of Awareness.

The relevant public of the disputed mark realizes that the disputed mark is not connected at all with the senior well-known trademark.

Generally speaking, the distinctiveness associated with the senior well-known trademark is not "damaged" if the relevant public of the disputed mark confuses the two marks or thinks that there is still a one-to-one connection between the well-known trademark and its owner (i.e., the association is still present). In other words, dilution only occurs when the relevant public of the disputed mark does not immediately associate the disputed mark with a well-known trademark (i.e., the association is therefore "broken" or "diluted").

69. Case Index: Beijing No. 1 Intermediate People's Court, Yi Zhong Zhi Xing Chu Zi [2010] No. 2291.

This level of awareness can have many different contributing factors, such as the senior mark's price, its targeted consumers, and its commercial positioning in respect to its products and services. For example, the relevant public will *not* immediately associate the disputed mark with the senior well-known trademark (even assuming the two marks are identical) if the latter is positioned or being perceived as a luxury brand – such as "LV" and "Hermes" – and the two marks have a substantial price difference. Also, in situations where the senior trademark is not being positioned as a luxury brand or it is in fact targeting the same group of consumers as the junior disputed mark, dilution is still likely when the disputed goods/services have never been offered under the senior brand so the relevant public cannot immediately make an association of the two marks. For example, although the CHANGHONG （长虹） trademark is quite well known in terms of consumer electronics products, the relevant public will not immediately connect the mark with the owner of yet another CHANGHONG （长虹） mark if the latter is used in connection with, for example, clothing products. Under such circumstances, the criteria for the third level of awareness are met.

Applying the above principle to the present case, the relevant public is *not* likely to associate the Subject Mark with the Cited Mark because the latter is a luxury brand and its price range is generally out of reach for average consumers. There is also not enough evidence suggesting that the Cited Mark has been put to use in connection with the disputed goods such as high-end ceramic tiles. Even assuming that the Cited Mark has been put to use for high-end ceramic tiles, there is still insufficient evidence suggesting that the owner of the Cited Mark – Chanel Company – has used its mark for ceramic tiles to the point that it is famous enough to enable the relevant public to immediately associate the Subject Mark with the Cited Mark for tile products. This lack of association – due to the price reason, the commercial positioning of the Cited Mark and the lack of use of the CHANEL brand in connection with the tile products – give rise to the third level of awareness.

Considering the fact that the relevant public of the Subject Mark fully possesses the three levels of awareness, the registration of the Subject Mark will therefore cause dilution of the Cited Mark. This explains why the Subject Mark violates Article 13, Section 2 of the Trademark Law and is therefore refused for registration.

7. Refusal of a Trademark Application on the Ground that It Negatively Impacts a Third Party's Prior Rights

Administrative litigation regarding the appeal of the trademark opposition filed by REEBOK INTERNATIONAL LIMITED against a trademark application for "IVERSON AND DESIGN" – an application filed by Lin Zedong

– First Instance: Beijing No. 1 Intermediate People's Court (No. 1384; 2012) – Decided on August 17, 2012

BACKGROUND

The subject case involves the appeal of a trademark opposition action. The opposed mark is "IVERSON & DESIGN" (the "***Opposed Mark***"); its designated Class 18 products include leather cloaks, genuine cowhide, umbrellas, hides (animal skins). The applicant is an individual named Lin Zedong (the "***Applicant***").

Reebok International Limited ("***Reebok***") was authorized by Allen Iverson, a famous NBA basketball star, to file an opposition action to the China Trademark Office (the "***Trademark Office***") against the Opposed Mark. The Trademark Office reviewed the opposition and dismissed Reebok's action.

Reebok in a timely manner raised an appeal to the TRAB under the SAIC of PRC (the "***Appeal Board***"); its primary appeal ground was that the registration of the Opposed Mark would negatively impact Allen Iverson's personal name rights. The Opposed Mark therefore violated Article 31 of the Trademark Law, where it states that a trademark application "shall not negatively impact a third party's existing prior rights." In addition, the application of the Opposed Mark violated Article 10 Section 1(8), Article 13, Article 41 Section 1 of the Trademark Law; the Opposed Mark should therefore be denied for registration.

Reebok submitted relevant supporting evidence proving that Allen Iverson, as a famous NBA basketball star, enjoyed a high level of fame in China. Additionally, the submitted evidence also showed that the Applicant owns thirty other trademark applications and registrations including "ALLEN IVERSON," the English word "IVERSON," and Mr. Iverson's silhouette when playing basketball.

The Appeal Board reviewed the case and was of the view that "IVERSON" is a common last name in the US and it is not the full reference to Allen Iverson. Accordingly, the Appeal Board denied Reebok's claim that the Opposed Mark violated Mr. Iverson's personal name rights. The Opposed Mark was approved for registration because Reebok's other claims were not supported by the Appeal Board either.

Reebok filed a trademark administrative litigation to the Beijing No. 1 Intermediate People's Court (the "***Intermediate Court***"), insisting on the same appeal grounds that it submitted to the Appeal Board.

COURT DECISION

The Intermediate Court reviewed the case and was of the view that, given that Allen Iverson is an individual, Mr. Allen Iverson enjoyed personal name rights over the name, his name rights are entitled to protection in China, and he can prevent others from using his name for improper purposes. Based on the evidence submitted to the Court, a large number of the search results on Baidu and Google websites using "IVERSON" as the search term pointed to Allen Iverson the NBA basketball star. There were four magazines providing exclusive stories focusing on Allen Iverson; all were published prior to the filing date of the Opposed Mark. The above evidence was sufficient to prove that NBA star Allen Iverson enjoyed a high level of fame in China and was commonly referred to simply as IVERSON. The above was also supported by the 400+ pieces of evidence of news reports submitted by Reebok, all of which were published prior to the filing date of the Opposed Mark. The Court therefore acknowledged that Allen Iverson the NBA basketball star enjoyed a high level of fame among the relevant public in China and was typically referred to simply as IVERSON. With the above understanding, it was reasonable to impute the Applicant's awareness or knowledge of the IVERSON brand and basketballs, because the Applicant not only sought to register the Opposed Mark, but also 30+ others inclusive of IVERSON word marks as well as design marks where athletes play basketball. The Applicant's awareness or knowledge of the ALLEN IVERSON name could also be supported by the fact that the Applicant and its related companies manufacture basketball shoes, and its promotion from its corporate website also to some extent uses the reputation and goodwill associated with the ALLEN IVERSON name (the famous NBA basketball player). In light of the above, even though IVERSON was a common foreign last name, the Applicant should have been aware of the ALLEN IVERSON name and that Mr. Iverson was a star NBA basketball player. Accordingly, it can be inferred that the Applicant sought to register the Disputed Mark for improper business purposes, which would therefore negatively impact Mr. Allen Iverson's personal name rights.

Although Reebok and Allen Iverson the NBA basketball star are not the same party, there is no specific standing requirement, given that this is a review of a trademark opposition case. Furthermore, Reebok did have standing to bring the appeal, because it was already authorized by Mr. Allen Iverson via a written authorization. The Court therefore supported Reebok's claim that the Opposed Mark would negatively impact Mr. Iverson's personal name rights. The registration of the Opposed Mark violated Article 31 of the Trademark Law, where it states that a trademark application shall not negatively impact a third party's prior rights.

The Appeal Board misunderstood the law when it determined that the Opposed Mark did not violate the law. Based on Article 54 Section 2 of the Administrative Litigation Law of the PRC, the Court vacated the appeal decision and requested that the Appeal Board make a new decision concerning Reebok's appeal.[70]

70. Case Index: Beijing No. 1 Intermediate People's Court, Yi Zhong Zhi Xing Chu Zi [2012] No. 1384.

Neither party raised any further appeal after the Intermediate Court's decision; the decision is therefore final.

ANALYSIS & INSIGHT

Article 31 of the Trademark Law states that "an application shall not negatively impact a third party's prior existing rights." Although not many cases exist that involve prior personal name rights, these cases usually receive a lot of attention because they usually involve famous people.

A. Relevant Criteria to Consider if a Trademark Application Would Negatively Impact a Third Party's Prior-Existing Rights under Article 31 of the Trademark Law.

Article 31 of the Trademark Law states that "an application shall not negatively impact a third party's prior existing rights." Article 17 of the SPC on Issuing the Opinions on Several Issues Concerning the Trial of Administrative Cases Involving the Authorization and Determination of Trademark Rights states that the People's Court should grant special protection to rights that are specifically protected under the Chinese Trademark Law and protect such rights in accordance with the Trademark Law; for rights that are not specifically protected under the Trademark Law but fall under the category of legitimate rights based on the Civil Law General Rules or other relevant Laws, the People's Court should nevertheless give general protection to such rights. Generally speaking, the relevant date to determine "prior-existing rights" is the filing date of the disputed mark. If the prior-existing rights are no longer in existence by the time the disputed mark is registered, then such rights should not be the basis to refuse the registration of the disputed mark. The prior-existing rights in the subject case include general civil rights, such as personal name rights, trade name rights, design patent rights, and copyrights, as well as rights afforded under the unfair competition law - namely, the unique reference, packaging, decoration of famous products and domain name rights, as well as other existing rights under the law.

The Trademark Law does not specifically describe any particular situations where a registration of a trademark would negatively impact another party's prior rights. In practice, the general view is that the above Law is in existence to prevent conflicting legal rights among two or more parties so as to avoid the situation where the use of a registered trademark would infringe upon a third party's rights or constitute unfair competition. Considering the above legislative goal of the Law, when determining whether or not the registration of the disputed mark would have any "negative impact" on a third party's prior-existing rights, the determination should follow the same criteria for the civil infringement or unfair competition case. In other words, if the use of the disputed mark would have led to an infringement or is itself an unfair competition, then the Court can safely conclude that the registration of the mark would have a negative impact on prior-existing rights.

The courts in fact have already followed the criteria discussed above. In the design patent case involving "JING TAI LUN in Chinese characters," the court specifically pointed out that the infringement criteria against a design patent should be the relevant criteria in determining whether or not the registration in the subject design patent would have had a negative impact on a third party's prior-existing rights.[71] In the copyright case involving "LAORENCHENG in Chinese, English phonetics and Design," the court also pointed out that the relevant criteria in determining whether or not the registration of the disputed mark has a negative impact on the prior copyright should follow the same determination criteria in a copyright infringement case.

B. Different Approaches Regarding the Determination of Negative Impact on an Individual's Personal Name Right.

The existing cases, however, do not point to a consistent approach to deciding cases involving personal name rights. The primary reasons contributing to the present lack-of-consistent approach are twofold: the different views relating to: (1) the preconditions so as to protect an individual's personal name; and (2) the relevant criteria to determine when an individual's personal name rights have been negatively impacted.

1. The Preconditions to Protect an Individual's Personal Name Rights.

Based on the existing cases, there are two primary approaches to determine when the plaintiff in a civil case is entitled to personal name right protection:

(a) The name is automatically entitled to the personal name right protection so long as it is the name of an individual.
The subject case follows this approach. In the Intermediate Court's decision, it points out that "Allen Iverson is entitled to personal name right over his name 'ALLEN IVERSON' because he is an individual and such rights are protected in China." Following the above, it is clear that for a personal name to be entitled to protection, the name must belong to an individual. In other words, an individual is automatically entitled to protection of his or her personal name, and as long as this condition is satisfied, no further requirements exist to grant protection. In addition to the subject case, many other cases follow the same approach and make similar statements. For example, in the TOM FORD case, the court essentially made the same statement as the one discussed in the subject case.[72]

(b) The name of an individual is not automatically protected unless/until such an individual has fulfilled certain criteria.

71. Case Index: Beijing No. 1 Intermediate People's Court, Yi Zhong Zhi Xing Chu Zi [2008] No. 519.
72. Case Index: Beijing No. 1 Intermediate People's Court, Yi Zhong Zhi Xing Chu Zi [2013] No. 2409.

Yet, other cases exist where the courts and the Appeal Boards are of the view that an individual's personal name right is not automatically entitled to protection; such an individual must first fulfill certain criteria before his or her name is protected under the law. Following this view, the courts and the Appeal Board have adopted a number of different approaches that institute their "criteria" before the personal name right can be granted.

(1) An individual is not entitled to any personal name right protection unless he or she has obtained a "certain level" of fame in China. In the KATE MOSS case, the Appeal Board followed this view: it stated that, "based on the submitted evidence, it is sufficient to prove that "KATE MOSS" is the name of a model and the model has enjoyed a certain level of fame in the fashion industry. Accordingly, the use of the disputed mark on the designated products could possibly lead to a negative impact on Kate Moss's personal name rights."[73] In the "ELLE MACPHERSON," the court rejected the plaintiff's request for personal name right protection on the same principle discussed above. In the decision, the Court stated that the submitted evidence was "insufficient to prove that the name, ELLE MACPHERSON, has obtained a certain level of fame among the relevant public in China prior to the filing date of the opposed mark; the evidence has not proven that the use of the name is likely to cause consumer confusion among the relevant public in China - accordingly, the negative impact on the plaintiff's personal name right is not supported."[74]

(2) An individual is not entitled to any personal name right protection unless/until he or she has obtained a "certain level" of fame and such a name has formed an exclusive connection with the individual among the relevant public in China.

In the "Qiao Dan" case (QIAO DAN is Michael Jordan's last name, JORDAN, in Chinese), although the Appeal Board did not deny the high level of fame concerning Michael Jordan in China, the protection for Qiao Dan was nevertheless rejected because Qiao Dan (JORDAN in Chinese) is a common last name in the USA and UK and no exclusive connection exists between the name and the basketball player outside of the professional sports field. In the "BRITNEY" case, the court also followed the same approach. In the decision, although the Court recognized that Britney Spears, an American singer, has obtained a high level of fame among the relevant public, the name BRITNEY is in fact a common first name for a European or an American woman, and insufficient evidence exists to prove that the name BRITNEY has formed an exclusive connection with the pop culture singer Britney Spears. In light of

73. Case Index: Trademark Review & Adjudication Board, [2009] No. 27162.
74. Case Index: Beijing No. 1 Intermediate People's Court, Yi Zhong Zhi Xing Chu Zi [2013] No. 2435.

the above, the evidence was insufficient to prove that the use and registration of the opposed mark would have had a negative impact on Britney Spears's personal name rights."[75]

2. The Relevant Criteria to Consider Whether or Not an Individual's Personal Name Right Has Been Negatively Impacted.

In addition to the different approaches and criteria to consider prior to granting the personal name rights, there are also different approaches, as reflected in the existing cases showing that there is not yet a consistent approach in determining when a person's name rights have been negatively impacted by the use and registration of the disputed mark.

a. Subjective Approach: Subjective Review to Determine Whether or Not the Owner of the Disputed Mark Has Illegitimate Purposes.

The subject case followed this approach; in the Intermediate Court's decision, it pointed out that "any violation of an individual's personal name right should be for improper purposes – in other words, not all use of an individual's personal name right will constitute a violation; the so-called improper purposes include 'financial gains, third parties' private interests, bringing harm to others or avoiding the rule of law."

In the TOM FORD case, the Court pointed out that the plaintiff enjoyed personal name rights over "TOM FORD;" he has rights to prevent others from using the name for improper purposes under the rule of law. The applicant of the opposed mark should have known and been aware of the TOM FORD name and that he is a well-known designer in the fashion industry. Based on the above, it can be inferred that the owner is seeking to register the TOM FORD mark for the purpose of profiting from the reputation. The registration will therefore negatively impact Tom Ford's personal name rights.[76]

b. Objective Approach: Consider Whether or Not the Registration of the Disputed Mark Would Mislead the Relevant Public into Believing that the Disputed Mark Is Somehow Connected with the Individual Who Enjoys the Personal Name Right over the Disputed Mark.

In the "YI JIAN LIAN" case, the Court pointed out that "under normal circumstances, when the relevant public sees a trademark and they would inevitably connect the trademark or the supplier/provider of the trademark with an individual's name, an

75. Case Index: Beijing No. 1 Intermediate People's Court, Yi Zhong Zhi Xing Chu Zi [2013] No. 2208.
76. Case Index: Beijing No. 1 Intermediate People's Court, Yi Zhong Zhi Xing Chu Zi [2013] No. 2409.

individual's personal right should be considered being negatively impacted." The plaintiff registered a mark that is identical to the name, YI JIAN LIAN, in connection with sports footwear products; the disputed mark is likely to convince the relevant public that it or its manufacturing source has a certain connection with the third party, Yi Jian Lian – this connection negatively affects Yi Jian Lian's personal name rights and his other legitimate interests in connection with his famous name.[77]

In above-referenced BRITNEY case, the court adopted the same standard as that in the YI JIAN LIAN case; despite this, the Britney court reached a different conclusion. In the Britney decision, it states that "the evidence submitted by the plaintiff was sufficient to prove that Britney Spears has obtained a high level of fame in the music and entertainment industry." However, the designated products for the opposed mark include shrouds and nonwoven textile fabrics and they are far afield from the industry in which the plaintiff's name was well-known; these products also share very little connection with the music entertainment industry. No one-to-one connection exists between the industry in which the plaintiff's name is well-known and the products covered by the opposed mark; the registration of the opposed mark in connection with such products would not negatively impact Ms. Britney Spears's personal name rights.[78]

C. Necessary Criteria to Consider in order to Determine the Negative Impact on an Individual's Personal Name Rights.

Based on the above discussion, the personal name right analysis would necessarily involve the analysis of an action. In other words, if the use and registration of the disputed mark would have constituted a violation of a third party's personal name rights, the action would have been deemed a violation.

Under the existing Laws, the provisions that are related to personal name rights protection are discussed in the General Principles of the Civil Law and the Opinions on Several Issues Concerning the Implementation of the General Principles of the Civil Law (For Trial Implementation) issued by the SPC (the "***Opinions***"). Article 99 of the Opinions states that "An individual shall enjoy the rights of personal name and shall be entitled to determine, use or change his/her personal name in accordance with relevant laws. Any act that intervenes, copies or uses the individual's personal name without authorization shall be prohibited." Meanwhile, Article 141 of the Opinions states that an unauthorized acts of copying, using a third party's personal name or trademark, and the action has caused damages shall be deemed as infringement over personal name rights and trade name rights.

Based on the above, the rights involving an individual's personal name are not only offensive (the individual has rights to decide, use and change his own name in accordance with the relevant rules), but also defensive (an individual has the right to stop others from intervening, copying and using his/her name). The goal of Article 31

77. Case Index: Beijing No. 1 Intermediate People's Court, Yi Zhong Zhi Xing Chu Zi [2010] No. 707.
78. Case Index: Beijing No. 1 Intermediate People's Court, Yi Zhong Zhi Xing Chu Zi [2013] No. 2208.

of the Trademark Law is to protect an individual's personal name rights (for defensive purposes); specifically, Article 31 of the Trademark Law helps an individual to prevent others from registering his or her name as a trademark. On balance, it can be concluded that Article 31 of the Trademark Law requires the following conditions prior to granting protection of an individual's personal name right.

1. An Individual Is Automatically Entitled to His/Her Personal Name Rights; the Rights Are Given and the Individual Does Not Need to Fulfill any Other Requirements.

The existing law limits the protection of the personal name right to "natural person;" no further requirements are specified. Accordingly, a civil plaintiff only needs to prove that he or she is a natural person to satisfy this requirement – there is no further burden of proof regarding other requirements. In light of the above, an individual is entitled to the protection of his or her personal name rights regardless of whether or not it has obtained a high level of fame in China or if the name has already formed an exclusive connection with him or herself. In other words, anyone can assert personal name rights, and such a claim is and should not be limited to famous people, such as Yao Ming or Yi Jian Lian. This law does not mean that an individual's fame status carries no weight in the outcome of the case or the extent of protection being afforded by the courts and the trademark authorities. This conclusion merely points out that an individual's fame status should not be regarded as a precondition for one to assert protection for his or her personal name.

The Court in the subject case shared the above view and concluded that Allen Iverson enjoys personal name rights over his name, and that such rights are entitled to protection under China's legal system.

2. Any Unauthorized Attempt to Register a Third Party's Personal Name Should Be Deemed a Violation of an Individual's Existing Personal Name Rights.

An infringement determination concerning civil rights usually involves both subjective and objective factors and analysis. An objective analysis concerns the action at issue. This analysis refers to the specific types of actions that the right holder can prevent others from doing. A subjective analysis relates to the intent requirement on the action party, whether or not the action is intentional.

Multiple types of actions would involve the violation of an individual's personal name rights. However, one of the more serious types of violation involves "using or pretending to be the right holder without prior authorization." Registering a third party's personal name is clearly an action involving using other's names. In the administrative litigation involving trademarks, the defendant's action in (attempting to) register the plaintiff's name as a trademark should be deemed a satisfaction of the objective criteria unless, of course, the defendant has first obtained the plaintiff's authorization. In the subject case, the trademark applicant did not provide any evidence showing that its trademark application involving Allen Iverson's name had been first authorized by Mr. Iverson; its action to submit the trademark application has therefore satisfied the objective requirement involving the adjudication of personal name right.

Although the Law does not provide any specific requirements concerning the subject criteria, typically the court would require the party carrying out the action to have some "faults," such as improper purposes. From the literal language of the Law, it is clear that the subjective bad-faith intent is required; the academia also widely accepts this interpretation of the law; "the action to use the same name should be regarded a violation of an individual's personal name rights if such an action is carried out with the intent to cause confusion."[79] In the subject case, the Intermediate Court also shared this interpretation. In its decision, the Court stated "an improper purpose should be required in recognizing one's violation of a third party's personal name rights; it is therefore incorrect to believe that any use of a third party's name is a violation of the other party's personal name rights - such a violation must involve improper purposes or intent. An improper purpose includes seeking financial gains, seeking financial interests for itself, harming others or avoiding the law."

In the trademark administrative litigation cases, the subjective analysis primarily involves the determination concerning the applicant's awareness or knowledge regarding the third party's name. If the trademark application is aware of the third party's name and it is not able to provide any justification for its trademark, it can then be inferred that the registration of the mark is primarily for improper purposes. There are multiple ways to infer this bad-faith subjective intent; for example, this criteria can be satisfied when: the defendant is seeking to trade off the goodwill and reputation of a third party's name so as to cause consumer confusion (in that the products or services provided by the trademark registration are somehow related to the famous person); the defendant is trying to gain exposure of its products/services or trying to attract the media's attention by using a third party's famous name (but the use of the name may not necessarily cause confusion among the relevant public); or that the defendant is merely interested in seeking financial gains for itself through registration of a third party's famous name (so as to prevent the third party from obtaining trademark registration in China and later to compel the third party to pay for its registration).

The analysis involving the trademark applicant's subjective knowledge and improper purposes should consider specific facts in each case; primary factors to consider when making a determination on the bad-faith intent include the following factors:

- the fame status concerning the right holder of the personal name;
- the level of distinctiveness concerning the name;
- any past or current commercial connection between the trademark applicant and the right holder of the personal name, if both are involved in the same industry.

79. Wang Liming, CHINA CIVIL LAW CASE STUDY AND RESEARCH CHAPTER OF GENERAL PRINCIPLES, China Legal Publishing House 52 (2003).

Although the fame status of the natural person is not a precondition to assert personal name right, it is nevertheless relevant and helpful in the subjective bad-faith intent analysis. In the subject case, for example, the Intermediate Court's decision simply states "the fame status of the right-holder is one of the factors to consider in determining the trademark applicant's subjective intent."

In addition to considering the status or fame of the third party's name, it is important to take into account the distinctiveness of the name at issue. If the name is an existing (common) phrase, it cannot then infer that the trademark applicant has subjective bad-faith intent to register the mark even assuming that the name belongs to a famous person. Other relevant factors concerning the name should be similarly considered. In the trademark case involving the name "LI MING" (the name of a famous Hong Kong singer) in connection with Class 36 real estate services, the Hong Kong singer Li Ming raised a timely opposition action against this application. The Trademark Office rejected the opposition action; it pointed out that "LI MING" is a common phrase in modern Chinese language and not a unique coined phrase. Any products or services bearing the LI MING mark would not confuse the public or mislead them into believing that the products or services are somehow connected with the Hong Kong singer.[80] As the LI MING case points out, it would be fairly difficult to read any subjective bad-faith intent on the part of the trademark applicant when the third party's name is an existing common phrase.

Despite the above, most of the cases where the trademark applications are identical to a third party's name involve improper purposes (pure coincidence is rare). Different factors however have different weight in the determination of the subjective intent. In the subject case, the primary factors the Court considered include the fame status of Allen Iverson, the applicant's trademark filing history in China, and the way the ALLEN IVERSON mark was used in the everyday market.

In the subject case, ALLEN IVERSON is an NBA basketball star and enjoys a high level of fame among the relevant public in China; he is commonly referred to simply as IVERSON. Although IVERSON is a common last name in the USA, the applicant of the disputed mark has filed more than thirty trademarks involving the term IVERSON; some of these marks not only include texts, but also designs depicting an athlete playing basketball – in fact, even Mr. Iverson's tattoo was part of the subject of the applicant's trademarks. It can therefore be inferred that the applicant was aware of Mr. Iverson, his NBA star status, and his fame in the basketball industry. Furthermore, the evidence showed that the applicant of the disputed mark is involved in the manufacturing and retail of basketball footwear products; its company included Allen Iverson as an NBA star in its promotional materials on the website. On balance, it is clear that the applicant of the disputed mark was fully aware of the background that Allen Iverson was an NBA basketball star and its goal for registering the disputed mark was to trade on the goodwill and reputation of Allen Iverson and his star status. The

80. Case Index: Trademark Review & Adjudication Board, [1996] No. 008.

applicant therefore had an improper purpose to seek registration of the disputed mark, and the registration of the disputed mark would therefore have a negative impact on Allen Iverson's personal name rights.

It is important to point out that fame status is merely one of the factors in determining whether or not the applicant of the disputed mark has an improper purpose for seeking registration; it is, however, not the only factor for consideration. In some cases, even though the individual does not have any fame status in China, it can still be inferred that the application of the disputed mark was filed for improper purposes based on other factors, one of which is the distinctiveness associated with the name. In the "ZANG TOI" case, although there was no evidence to show that Zang Toi enjoyed much fame in China, the ZANG TOI combination was not part of the existing phrases; it was also not a common foreign name that was constantly exposed to consumers in China. In light of the unique combination of ZANG and TOI, it was very unlikely that the applicant created the mark out of pure coincidence. In other words, it can be safely inferred that the applicant of the disputed mark was aware of the Zang Toi name, unless it can provide a reasonable and logical explanation as to how it came up with the combination (it did not). In the "ZANG TOI" case, the Court also considered other relevant factors, such as the fame status of the Zang Toi name in countries and markets outside China and the fact that the applicant had a commercial relationship with the Zang Toi company at one point before the company formally introduced the ZANG TOI brand to China.[81]

Similarly, in the KATE MOSS case, although both letters in the name are common words in English, there was no evidence to prove that the combination was in fact a common name. Under such circumstances, and the fact that the applicant of the disputed mark was not able to provide a logical and reasonable explanation as to how it came up with the combination to register as a trademark, the Court can infer that the applicant was seeking to register the KATE MOSS trademark for improper purposes.[82]

D. Common Mistakes when Determining the Negative Impact Involving a Third Party's Personal Name Rights.

1. The Role the Public Confusion Plays in the Determination Involving Violation of a Third Party's Personal Name Rights.

There are yet some other views in practice pointing out that the protection of an individual's personal name rights should also consider whether or not there is likelihood that the relevant public can be confused. When applying this view to cases, the outcome of such cases is typically no violation of a third party's personal name right, especially when the disputed mark covers products or services that are not significantly related to the industry where the right holder is.

81. Case Index: Beijing No. 1 Intermediate People's Court, Yi Zhong Zhi Xing Chu Zi [2012] No. 1954.
82. Case Index: Beijing No. 1 Intermediate People's Court, Yi Zhong Zhi Xing Chu Zi [2010] No. 534.

Article 19 of the Guidelines of the Beijing High People's Court for Hearing Administrative Cases on Trademark Authorization and Determination (draft for comment) ("***Case Guidance***") shared the above view; it states "the specific products or services covered by the disputed mark would also influence the relevant public's assumption between the mark at issue and the third party's famous name; accordingly, the protection scope of the personal name right should be adjusted accordingly based on the specific products and services at issue in a particular case." However, Article 19 was later deleted and no longer included in the final version of Case Guidance.

The primary issue of the above approach is that it introduces the trademark determination criteria in cases involving personal name rights. Consumer confusion is one of the standard examination criteria to recognize trademark infringement; it should not be a necessary criterion involving the violation of personal name rights. The key criteria in deciding whether or not a trademark would violate a third party's personal name rights should be based strictly on whether or not the trademark application is filed for improper means (as opposed to whether or not the application is likely to cause consumer confusion). Although the fact that the relevant public's confusion can serve to some extent as a base to infer the trademark applicant's bad-faith subjective intent, the lack of consumer confusion does not mean that the trademark application is therefore filed for good faith or legitimate purposes. As discussed earlier, the applicant's improper purposes can manifest in multiple ways, such as causing consumer confusion, attracting the relevant public's attention (rather than causing confusion), or merely selling the mark at a high price after it is registered. In other words, despite the lack of public confusion, a trademark can still be deemed a violation of a third party's personal name rights as long as the applicant's subject bad-faith intent is present.

In the present case, Allen Iverson's primary involvement is basketball, which is an industry far afield from the products designated in the Opposed Mark – namely, leather cloaks, genuine cowhide, umbrellas, and hides (animal skins). However, given that the Applicant's main goal is clearly to attract the relevant public's attention so as to profit from the registration of the Opposed Mark, the Intermediate Court still concluded that the Applicant's application of the Opposed Mark was a violation of Mr. Iverson's personal name rights.

2. Proprietary Aspect of an Individual's Personal Name Rights.

The General Rules of Civil Law categorizes personal name rights as a right of personality; trademark rights, on the other hand, are property rights. In light of the above division, some individuals are of the view that given that an individual has no right to prevent others from using one's name as a property right; accordingly, the individual does not have the right to prevent others from registering his or her name as a trademark.

In respect to the proprietary right of an individual's personal right, the law already sets forth some regulations. Article 120 of the General Rules of Civil Law states that "a citizen enjoys personal name rights, image rights, reputation and honor rights; a citizen has rights to ask the third parties to stop any violation of the above rights, recover its reputation, remove any negative effects, ask for compensation, and demand apologies and any financial losses as long as any of his or her above rights have been negatively impacted." Given that an individual has rights to ask for financial compensation, it can therefore be concluded that the General Rules of Civil Law acknowledge the proprietary nature of an individual's personal rights. In addition to the above, some experts in China also share the view that there are indeed proprietary aspects for some of the personal rights, such as personal name rights, image rights, and trade name rights.[83] In light of the above, an individual has rights to prevent others from using its name without authorization, including registering the name as a trademark for financial gains.

83. Wang Liming, PERSONAL RIGHT LAW, China Renmin University Press 3 (2009).

CHAPTER 3

Maintenance of Trademark Registrations

8. Trademark Assignment and Good-Faith Acquisition of a Trademark

Administrative litigation regarding the trademark assignment concerning the "MT.WUTONG in English and Chinese characters" mark; the litigation was brought by Shenzhen Chinese Parasol Landscape Drink Limited Company against the China Trademark Office and a third party Shenzhen East River Source Industry Development Limited Company

- First Instance: Beijing No. 1 Intermediate People's Court (No. 1842; 2010) - Decided on September 19, 2010
- Second Instance: Beijing High People's Court (No. 7; 2011) - Decided on February 14, 2011

BACKGROUND

On October 6, 1998, Shenzhen East River Source Industry Development Limited Company ("***East River***") filed a trademark application, "MT.WUTONG in English and Chinese characters," in connection with Class 32 mineral water products with the China Trademark Office (the "***Trademark Office***"); the application was assigned application number 1359214 (the "***1359214 Trademark***" or the "***Mark***"). The Trademark Office preliminarily approved the 1359214 Trademark and published it on the trademark gazette on October 28, 1999. On January 18, 2000, Shenzhen Kang Li Mineral Spring Balneation Center filed an opposition action with the Trademark Office contesting the 1359214 Trademark. On August 2, 2001, the Trademark Office made a decision, referred to herein as the "***1447 Decision***", where the 1359214 Trademark was refused for registration. East River failed to request a timely appeal concerning the 1447

Decision to the TRAB under SAIC of the PRC (the "***Appeal Board***"). The 1447 Decision was later published on the Trademark Publication Gazette on November 28, 2002, (No. 857; page 1149) and became effective.

On November 7, 2008, Shenzhen Chinese Parasol Landscape Drink Limited Company (the "***Company***") filed a trademark assignment application to the Trademark Office, seeking to assign the ***1359214 Trademark*** from East River to itself; the Company also applied for a reissuance of the trademark registration certificate concerning the 1359214 Trademark. In connection with its assignment application, the Company included a trademark assignment agreement executed by and among East River and itself dated as of November 4, 2008 (the "***Agreement***"). The Trademark Office confirmed receipt of the Company's assignment application on December 4, 2008; it subsequently approved the assignment on August 6, 2009 – the approval of the assignment regarding 1359214 Trademark was also published on the Trademark Assignment Gazette. The Trademark Office reissued the registration certificate concerning the 1359214 Trademark on September 25, 2009; the certificate reflected that the Company was the owner of the mark.

In January 2010, the Trademark Office received a letter from Shenzhen Kang Li Mineral Spring Balneation Center titled, "Explanation concerning the 1359214 Trademark;" the letter pointed out that the mark was refused for registration based on the earlier opposition decision. Accordingly, the Trademark Office should not grant the Company's request to reissue the registration certificate.

On January 29, 2010, the Trademark Office issued a decision titled, "Notification regarding the Revocation on Trademark Assignment and Reissuance of Registration Certificate of the 1359214 Trademark" (the "***No. 33 Decision***"). In the No. 33 Decision, the Trademark Office decided to vacate its earlier assignment approval concerning the 1359214 Trademark, and vacated the registration certificate issued earlier to the Company (where the Company was listed as the owner of the mark). The No. 33 Decision also vacated all of the related materials including the assignment proof, registration certificate, and the public notice published in the Trademark Publication Gazette.

The Company filed a trademark administrative litigation to the Beijing No. 1 Intermediate People's Court (the "***Intermediate Court***"), requesting the Court to vacate the No. 33 Decision and to order the Trademark Office to make a new decision.

COURT DECISION

The Intermediate Court reviewed the case and pointed out that any trademark that is the subject of an assignment application should be a valid trademark approved for registration by the Trademark Office; additionally, the mark must still be valid within its term. When the Company applied for an assignment of the Mark on November 7, 2008, it was not a valid registration because it had been refused for registration based on the 1447 Decision (issued on August 2, 2001); and the Decision was already published in 2002 on the Trademark Publication Gazette (No. 857). The above facts were sufficient to support that the Mark was never approved for registration by the

Trademark Office; and accordingly, the Mark never fulfilled the legal requirements to become capable of being assigned. In light of the above, the Company's request to vacate the No. 33 Decision was not supported by the Intermediate Court. The facts that the Company had invested a large amount of financial capital to expand its manufacturing capacity, to promote the brand, and to purchase a vast number of drinking water buckets after it had obtained the Mark, and it had invested over RMB 3 million, were not within the scope of this case. The Intermediate Court maintained the No. 33 Decision.

The Company filed an appeal to the Beijing High People's Court ("***High Court***") to challenge the Intermediate Court's decision, and to ask the High Court to confirm its use rights over the 1359214 Trademark, and reactivate its renewal request that was terminated due to the Trademark Office's decision to vacate the assignment and registration certificate issuance for the Mark. Additionally, the Company requested a written apology from the Trademark Office. The Company's primary arguments are set out below:

The Company obtained the use rights in connection with the Mark through a legal and valid channel with the Trademark Office; meanwhile, the Company had obtained the reissued registration certificate and the assignment approval concerning the Mark. Once the Company had obtained use rights of the ***1359214 Trademark***, it had invested heavily to expand its manufacturing facilities and to promote the brand so as to develop the market. The Company is at risk of a significant financial loss once the Trademark Office issued its decision to vacate the assignment approval.

The High Court reviewed the case and pointed out that the Mark had been refused for registration based on the 1447 Decision. The 1447 Decision has since become effective when the owner of the Mark at that time, East River, failed to file a timely appeal to the Appeal Board. In light of the above, the 1359214 Trademark was never approved for registration; and it has never been a valid registered trademark. Although the Company was not a party to the 1447 Decision, it was imputed with the knowledge of the Decision (and the fact that the Mark was never a registered trademark in China) since the Decision was published by the Trademark Office through the required legal process. The fact that the Company obtained the Mark through a valid legal channel but it later suffered a significant financial loss due to the Trademark Office's omission was therefore not supported by law and facts. The regulations in the Trademark Law concerning the renewal and assignment of a mark are preconditioned on the fact that the mark is a valid registered trademark. In the subject case, the Mark was never approved for registration so it was not a valid registered trademark; it therefore did not fulfill the necessary conditions required by the Trademark Law to be assigned or renewed. The No. 33 Decision was made in accordance with the required administrative procedure so that the Trademark Office can timely correct its mistakes in its trademark registration and management work. The Company's appeal therefore lacks proper legal and factual support; the High Court maintained the Intermediate Court's decision.

ANALYSIS & INSIGHT

In the case, the first level of the court was of the view that "the trademark that is the subject of an assignment application must be a valid registration approved by the Trademark Office." In practice, however, the rights that can be assigned are not limited to the exclusive rights associated with a registered trademark – in fact, rights associated with a trademark application can also be assigned. This explains why the second level of the court did not accept the above viewpoint; rather, it simply responded to the appeal arguments submitted by the Company. The rights that can be assigned can be divided into two categories exclusive rights associated with a trademark; and rights associated with a pending trademark application.

1. Transfer Exclusive Rights Associated with a Registered Trademark.

According to the Trademark Law,[84] a registered trademark can be assigned. Under such circumstances, the subjects to be assigned are the exclusive rights of a registered trademark. In this situation, it is correct to point out that the subject mark to be assigned must first be a valid registration; otherwise, the trademark to be assigned does not exist and assignment application cannot be completed either. Additionally, each trademark registration is valid for ten years and the ten-year term starts from the registration date of the trademark.[85] This means the trademark that is the subject of an assignment application should still be a valid trademark registration within this ten-year term. For marks that have not yet been approved for registration, given they do not enjoy any exclusive rights, they do not yet have any exclusive rights to be assigned. For any trademark registration that has been registered for more than ten years but has not been duly renewed, it cannot be a subject of any assignment either because its exclusive rights have been extinguished. Accordingly, the first level court's perspective is correct in respect to the assignment concerning the exclusive rights of a registered trademark. The following are some noteworthy points during the transfer process to assign exclusive rights associated with a registered trademark.

a. The Necessity of an Assignment Agreement.

An assignment agreement is the foundation upon which the parties can start the process to transfer a registered trademark. This is the agreement between the assignor and the assignee in respect to the exclusive rights associated with the trademark registration that is the subject of the transfer. Article 42 Section 1 of the 2013 Trademark Law states that "The assignor and assignee should execute a trademark assignment agreement to start the transfer of a registered trademark; the parties should

84. Article 39 of the 2001 Trademark Law; Article 42 of the 2013 Trademark Law.
85. Article 39 of the 2013 Trademark Law.

also jointly file an application to the Trademark Office concerning the transfer. The assignee should also provide certain representations and warranties in respect to its use, and the quality of use, in respect to the trademark for the registered goods or services." Despite the above, following the spirit of Contract Law which respects the parties' free will, the meeting of the minds is achievable in various forms such as through writing or verbal agreement;[86] in fact, the parties can sign the agreement *after* they have performed their respective duties in accordance with their agreement.[87] Accordingly, a written assignment agreement is not a required document when parties are interested in transferring the exclusive rights associated with a registered trademark. In fact, a written document evidencing the parties' intent to carry out the assignment is only required when the examiner needs to verify parties' signatures or the authenticity of the company stamps. The above position in respect to the requirement to submit a written assignment agreement is also reflected in Article 31 Section 1 of the 2014 Implementation Regulation of the Trademark Law of the PRC where only a "trademark assignment application form bearing the assignor's and assignee's signatures" is required when the parties are seeking to transfer a registered trademark. The assignment process should be "jointly carried out by the assignor and assignee."

The above position in respect to the submission of a written assignment agreement is also supported by the courts. For example, in the administrative litigation concerning the trademark assignment of "LING MU" in Chinese characters (Registration Number 1406730), the court pointed out that "although Article 39 of the Trademark Law[88] requires the assignor and assignee to execute an assignment agreement if the parties are interested in transferring rights in connection with a registered trademark, the Law does not require the parties to submit such a written agreement when they are seeking approval from the Trademark Office. Accordingly, the fact that the Trademark Office did not require the parties to submit the assignment agreement concerning the LING MU registration does not violate the law."[89] The above view takes the position that the requirement related to the assignment agreement only applies to the assignor and assignee; it does not apply to the Trademark Office when it approves or rejects a trademark assignment application. This is why the Trademark Office only needs to request an assignment application and then it can be jointly executed by both the assignor and assignee. The Trademark Office does not need to (nor can it) request the parties to submit an assignment agreement. In fact, the Trademark Office cannot make it a necessary requirement prior to its approval of an assignment application.[90]

---

86. Article 10 Section 1 of the Contract Law stipulates that "The parties may use written, oral or other forms in entering into a contract."
87. Article 37 of the Contract Law stipulates that "Where a contract is to be concluded in written form, if one party has performed its principal obligation and the other party has accepted it before signing or sealing of the contract, the contract is established."
88. The 2001 Trademark Law was applied in this case, and Article 39 of the 2001 Trademark Law corresponds to Article 42 of the 2013 Trademark Law.
89. Case Index: Beijing No. 1 Intermediate People's Court, Yi Zhong Xing Chu Zi [2006] No. 787.
90. Zhang Dianqing, *In-depth Examination and Approaches Adopted by Court in Judging Trademark Assignment with respect to A Registered Trademark*, People's Judicature – Cases, Vol. 4, 2008 at 110.

b. The Restriction to Transfer a Trademark.

Given the assignment of a registered trademark would inevitably impact the source and origin of the underlying products or services, as well as the business reputation, countries and jurisdictions around the world have adopted different approaches in respect to the requirements to transfer the exclusive rights associated with a trademark. One approach is to assign everything at once – this means the trademark can only be assigned when it is assigned in connection with the operation of the original manufacturing company. In other words, it is not possible if one simply transfers the trademark but not the associated business. The second approach is to allow the owner of the mark to either assign the mark together with the operation or to assign it separately (i.e., only assign the trademark).[91] When the Trademark Law was amended in 2013, although the amendments did not require that a trademark must be assigned together with its original business operation, it did require that all similar or identical marks covering the same or similar products must be assigned together so as to avoid confusion among the public in connection with the source of the products. Article 42 Section 2 of the 2013 Trademark Law states that: "*when a registered trademark is to be assigned, the owner must also assign all similar marks that have been registered in connection with the same type of products, or the same or similar trademarks in connection with similar products.*" In addition to the above, to better safeguard a third party and the public's interests, the 2013 Trademark Law went one step further to specify situations where trademark assignment would be rejected – Article 42 Section 3 states that "The Trademark Office can refuse a trademark assignment that is likely to result in confusion or any negative impacts." If the assignment is rejected, the Trademark Office must "notify the applicant and detail the refusal reasons in writing."

c. The Timing when a Transfer Becomes Effective.

The assignment agreement is the contract between the assignor and the assignee in connection with the registered trademark; the agreement is therefore binding among the parties. Section 33 of Answers Provided by the Beijing High People's Court Regarding the Application of Laws in Trademark Civil Disputes Trial Cases expressly states that: "*The assignment agreement is effective once the parties have affixed the signatures or company stamp unless, of course, the agreement specifies other effective dates.*" However, the timing in respect to the transfer of the exclusive rights of a registered trademark is different from the timing the underlying assignment agreement becomes effective. The change in relation to the exclusive rights of a registered trademark is part of the necessary result once the parties carry out their obligation under the agreement. Given the rights of a trademark are exclusive (i.e., the owner can prevent others from enjoying rights associated with the trademark), the assignee's rights under an assignment agreement must also be "publicized" in a certain way in

91. The legislative affairs commission of the Standing Committee of the National People's Congress, ed., INTERPRETATION OF THE PEOPLE'S REPUBLIC OF CHINA TRADEMARK LAW, 82 Law Press (2013).

addition to the transfer being approved by the Trademark Office. Article 42 Section 4 of the 2013 Trademark Law states that *"once the assignment application has been approved, the assignment must also be published. The assignee will start enjoying the exclusive rights associated with such trademark since the publication date."* In other words, to complete the transfer of the exclusive rights concerning a registered trademark, the process not only needs to be solidified through an assignment agreement between the parties and be approved by the trademark authorities in China; it must also be published in accordance with the relevant law so that it becomes effective." The exclusive rights associated with a registered trademark still belong to the assignor prior to the publication date.

2. Transfer Rights in Connection with a Pending Trademark Application.

The right associated with a pending trademark application refers to a kind of civil rights and interests that arises from the application filed by the trademark applicant and lasts until it is eventually approved for registration by the trademark authorities after examination.[92]

a. Nature of a Pending Trademark Application.

Although neither the Trademark Law nor the Implementing Regulation of the Trademark Law has any direct regulations in respect to a pending trademark application, one can still reach the conclusion that one's right associated with a pending trademark application is recognized and deserves protection. The conclusion can be reached both in theory and in practice.

The right associated with a pending trademark application is the so-called expectancy right in Civil Law. "Expectancy right" refers to a type of conditional right – namely, the protection of one's right to expect certain possible rights in the future and such right has been recognized as a present existing right. Although this is quite different from the so-called future conditional right (a right that is recognized once conditions are met), they are generally interchangeable to a certain extent.[93] The right associated with a pending trademark application belongs to the former category – namely, it is a conditional right – this refers to the right that is being recognized at the present time because it is in existence to protect the expectancy towards certain future rights down the road. By nature, the right associated with a pending trademark application is a present existing right; it is not the type of right that occurs down the road. There is no guarantee that a trademark application will certainly mature to registration because the application is still pending on the Trademark Office's review and approval. Despite this, the right associated with a pending trademark application has already been protected by the existing law such as Article 29 of the 2001 Trademark

92. Zhou Bo, *Rights Associated with A Pending Trademark Application Shall Be Protected as Legitimate Rights and Interests*, People's Judicature – Cases, Vol. 16, 2012 at 100.
93. Liu Dekuan, GENERAL RULES OF CIVIL LAW (Revised fourth edition), China University of Political Science and Law Press, 260 (2006).

Law, Article 31 of the 2013 Trademark Law, Article 17 Section (2) of the 2002 and 2014 Implementing Regulation of the Trademark Law, and Article 8 of the 2005 and 2014 Rules for Trademark Review and Adjudication; accordingly, such right is a present existing and a legitimate right. The "possible future rights" in connection with a trademark application refers to the exclusive rights of a trademark registration. As for the "conditions"[94] (the conditionals attached to the rights of a conditional right), they refer to the fact that such an application must be first reviewed, approved and published by the relevant trademark authorities - an application does not guarantee that the applicant will eventually own a trademark registration. The conditions must be met before the applicant can own the exclusive rights associated with a registered trademark which then gives right to the application right. If the conditions are not met, the right associated with a pending trademark application is not in existence. In other words, once an applicant has obtained a trademark registration, it can refer back and obtain the protection for its rights associated with a pending trademark application; conversely, it does not enjoy any right associated with a pending trademark application.

b. Transfer Effect of a Pending Trademark Application.

A transfer of the rights associated with a pending trademark means any substantive rights associated with the trademark will then be transferred to the assignee. Such rights include the exclusive rights in connection with the trademark application once it matures to a registration.

In terms of the procedural rights in connection with a pending trademark, a successful transfer means that the assignee will then have the right to participate in all trademark review and administrative litigation procedures. In other words, the assignee can then participate in all procedures in connection with the pending trademark application in its own name. The courts have given ample guidance in this regard in a number of cases. The flip side of the assignee's procedural rights is that the assignor will then lose all its rights (i.e., its standing) to participate in the subsequent review and administrative litigations in connection with the pending application. For example, in the administrative litigation of appeal of a trademark opposition, the two levels of courts were of the view that Shanghai City Foods Import and Export Company no longer had the right to bring a litigation to challenge the appeal board's decision in respect to the trademark "Treasure in Chinese, JUMBO and Design" (Application Number 1165053). This is because the company already assigned its rights in connection with the application to a third party named "Shanghai Mao Ji Import Export

94. "Conditions are the additional articles to legal acts, which determine the establishment of infinite facts objectively in the future or not, to bring legal acts into effect or cause the legal effects to eliminate. Facts themselves can also be deemed as conditions." Liu Dekuan, *id.*, 247 (2006).

Limited Company" during the appeal proceeding of the opposition decision. The court therefore rejected the Shanghai City Foods Import and Export Company's appeal.[95]

3. Obtaining Exclusive Rights of a Registered Trademark in Good Faith.

In the subject case, the Company claimed that it obtained the use rights in connection with the 1359214 Trademark through legitimate channels and its rights were approved by the Trademark Office. Although the Company's claim was not eventually supported by the court (because the 1359214 Trademark was never approved for registration), this appeal argument did trigger yet another important question. Assuming the 1359214 Trademark had been indeed approved for registration, can the exclusive rights of a registered trademark be granted on the basis of "good faith"? In other words, does the good-faith principle in the Civil Law also apply to the trademark area?

Previously, there have been different interpretations and approaches in practice in respect to the good-faith acquisition system and whether or not the assignee could obtain the exclusive rights of a registered trademark in good faith. One school of thought believes that we should not deny the possibility that a trademark can be obtained in good faith; otherwise, people would lose confidence in the registration and publication system; the integrity of the system and safety of any transaction would be called into question.[96] The other school of thought believes that "an assignee cannot obtain the exclusive rights associated with a registered trademark if such an assignment is carried out without expressive consent of the original trademark owner. In fact, a third party, which subsequently obtains the exclusive rights of the trademark at issue from the assignee in the regular course of business, will still not be regarded as the owner of the trademark even if the transfer has been published."[97] The above different approaches were gradually consolidated and were effective when the Property Law was announced and became effective in 2007. The idea that the good-faith acquisition system is and should be implied in every transaction has expanded beyond the mere property transaction and extended to, for example, transactions involving real estate. More and more people hold the view that good faith should also be a requirement through the transaction involving the exclusive rights associated with a registered trademark.[98]

---

95. Case Index: Beijing No. 1 Intermediate People's Court, Yi Zhong Xing Chu Zi [2007] No. 841; Beijing High People's Court, Gao Xing Zhong Zi [2008] No. 18.
96. Both Shanghai No. 1 Intermediate People's Court and Shang High People's Court held this view in the trademark ownership dispute case (*Huangyan BeiCheng Woolen Sweater Factory v. Shang Shuting Fashion Co., Ltd.*). Case Index: Shanghai No. 1 Intermediate People's Court, Hu Yi Zhong Min Wu Zhi Chu Zi [2005] No. 45; Shanghai High People's Court, Hu Gao Min San (Zhi) Zhong Zi [2006] No. 75; Zhou Yongjian; Xu Chuncheng, *On the Legal Liability of Intellectual Property Infringement – Taking an Example of Illegally Transferring Other's Registered Trademark*, Journal of Shanghai Youth College of Management, Vol. 3, 2011, at 63.
97. Section 40 of Answers of the Beijing High People's Court Concerning the Application of Laws in the Trial of Cases of Civil Disputes Arising from Trademarks (No. 68 [2006]).
98. Liu Xiaojun, *Study on Several Issues in Trial in Relation to Disputes over Registered Trademark Assignment*, Journal of Law Application, Vol. 8, 2006, at 50–54; Chen Yong, *Some Thoughts on The Dispute of Illegal Transfer of Registered Trademark*, People's Judicature – Cases, Vol. 2, 2008

Whether or not good faith should be required during the assignment process concerning a registered trademark is in fact a value question where one seeks to strike a balance between the trademark owner's rights and public interests – it is a purposeful legislative choice. The question can be rephrased as follows: whether or not the law should seek to protect all dynamics involving the order and safety in a property transaction; or if the law can simply passively protect the ownership safety concerning the property at issue.[99] The importance to actively protect the dynamics in a property transaction has been recognized by the legislature (and reflected in the updated Property Law), we believe that the good-faith principle should also be required in every transaction involving IPR – this is especially so given the property rights involving IP are becoming increasingly important in today's society, and the line between tangible and intangible property is becoming less and less pronounced especially along with the securitization of tangible and intangible property rights. Despite the above, it is also important to note that strict requirements must be met so as to apply the good-faith principle. For example, the assignee must obtain the underlying property in good faith and pay sufficient compensation to obtain the rights.[100] As for the requirements to satisfy the good-faith principle, one must consider the exclusive rights associated with a registered trademark and also the fact that the rights to be transferred have been published by the relevant trademark authorities in China.

Article 106 of the Property Law[101] states that one must consider the following criteria when deciding whether or not the assignee has obtained the registered trademark in good faith:

(a) The assignee can provide a reasonable explanation regarding the transfer.
(b) The transfer of a trademark is based on a nonright disposition.
(c) The third-party assignee is willing to be assigned with the trademark in good faith.

---

at 60–63; Liu Qijia, *Study on Trademark Good-Faith Acquisition System – From the Perspective of Transfer of Registered Trademark*, Political Science and Law, Vol. 11, 2009 at 133–141; Yuan Bo, *Legal Basis in Acquisition of Registered Trademark in Good Faith*, People's Judicature – Cases, Vol. 22, 2011 at 44–45.

99. Liu Xiaojun, *id.*, at 54.

100. Tong Rou, ed., CIVIL LAW OF PEOPLE'S REPUBLIC OF CHINA, 244–245, Law Press(1990).

101. Article 106 of the Property Law stipulates that "In case a person who is unauthorized to dispose a realty or chattel transfers the realty or chattel to an assignee, the owner is entitled to recover the realty or chattel. The assignee shall obtain the ownership of the realty or chattel if meeting all of the following conditions, unless it is otherwise prescribed by law:

(1) To accept the realty or chattel in good faith;
(2) To purchase the realty or chattel at a reasonable price;
(3) In case registration is required by law, the assigned realty or chattel shall have been registered, while in case registration is not required, the delivery thereof shall have been accomplished.

In case, according to the preceding paragraph, an assignee obtains the ownership of a realty or chattel, the original owner may request the person unauthorized to dispose of the realty or chattel to compensate for his losses.

In case a related party obtains any other form of real right in good faith, the preceding two paragraphs shall apply by reference."

(d) The third party has obtained the trademark right at a reasonable price.
(e) The transfer act itself is valid and lawful. If the transfer is a result of duress or fraud, or that the parties involved are not capable to make a decision for itself, the assignee still has the obligation to return the underlying property given the good-faith principle is not met.
(f) The exclusive rights associated with the assigned trademark have been approved and published by the relevant trademark authorities.[102]

In addition to the above, the transfer of a registered trademark must also be approved by the trademark authorities. It is possible that the transfer can be invalidated by the court throughout the process due to certain acts carried out by the administrative authorities – in other words, the validity of the transfer can still be questioned (or in fact, invalidated) until the term to raise a challenge towards the approving administrative authorities has expired. Accordingly, the good-faith principle is still required during the term that the administrative procedure is subject to challenge and until the transfer of the underlying trademark can no longer be challenged.[103]

The good-faith principle is in place so as to ensure that the assignee has obtained the trademark in good faith under certain conditions; the satisfaction of this principle cannot however guarantee that the transfer will be completed especially when the rights associated with the trademark are not in existence in the first place. Article 39 of the 2013 Trademark Law states that "the valid term of a registered trademark is ten years (counting from the registration date of the underlying trademark)."[104] A trademark applicant can still transfer its pending trademark prior to the mark becoming registered (even though the mark is being opposed by a third party).[105] Accordingly, even though the transfer of the exclusive rights of a registered trademark must be carried out in good faith, the precondition is that the subject of the transfer – the exclusive rights of a registered trademark – must be in existence. If the transfer takes place prior to the mark becoming registered, and the trademark application does not mature to registration, the assignee is not entitled to the exclusive rights associated with the trademark even though the good-faith requirement has been met throughout the entire process. In the subject case, even though the Company did indeed obtain the Mark through legitimate channels, prior to the transfer becoming effective, the Mark was already denied registration by the Trademark Office; the relevant decision later became effective and was published. Under such circumstances, the Company's claim that it had obtained the 1359214 Trademark in good faith would not be supported by the courts.

102. Yuan Bo, *Legal Basis in Acquisition of Registered Trademark in Good Faith*, People's Judicature – Cases, Vol. 22, 2011 at 44–45.
103. As to the time limit for prosecution of the approval on the registered trademark assignment, please refer to the next chapter.
104. That is, Article 37 of the 2001 Trademark Law.
105. Article 17 Section 2 of the 2014 Implementing Regulation of the Trademark Law provides that "Trademark applicant that transfers its pending trademark application shall proceed with transfer formalities with the China Trademark Office."

9. Prosecution Time Limit to Challenge a Trademark Assignment

Administrative litigation filed by Li Guozong against the Trademark Office and a third party, Yang Cuixian, regarding the trademark assignment concerning the "Guo Zong in Chinese characters" trademark

- First Instance: Beijing No. 1 Intermediate People's Court (No. 374; 2014) - Decided on March 19, 2014
- Second Instance: Beijing High People's Court (No. 1515; 2014) - Decided on July 3, 2014

BACKGROUND

The approval on the assignment of "Guo Zong in Chinese characters" trademark (the "***Disputed Mark***") to Yang Cuixian was published in the Trademark Gazette No. 1260 on April 20, 2011. Dissatisfied with the decision made by the China Trademark Office (the "***Trademark Office***"), Li Guozong ("***Mr. Li***") - the original registrant of the Disputed Mark filed an administrative litigation with the court on November 11, 2013.

COURT DECISION

Pursuant to Article 41 Section 1 of the Interpretation of the Supreme People's Court on Several Issues Concerning the Implementation of the Administrative Procedure Law of the People's Republic of China (the "***Judicial Interpretation***"), Beijing No. 1 Intermediate People's Court (the "***Intermediate Court***") held that, when making specific administrative decisions and the administrative authority fails to inform the citizens, legal persons or other organizations of their appeal rights or the appeal time line, the appropriate starting date to calculate the appeal time frame should start from the date on which the citizens, legal persons or other organizations know or should have known about their rights. Despite the above, the appeal or prosecution time limit should not be more than two years. A publication in the Trademark Gazette is a legal way of making a public announcement concerning legal rights; it is deemed public and absolute. When a trademark assignment is published in the Trademark Gazette, the public - including the owner of the registration - is deemed notified of the approval. In this case, the approval of the trademark assignment was published in the Trademark Gazette No. 1260 on April 20, 2011; accordingly, Mr. Li had been imputed with the knowledge concerning the assignment of the Disputed Mark starting on April 20, 2011. Mr. Li's administrative lawsuit was filed on November 11, 2013; in other words, his litigation had exceeded the two-year time limit that was allowed to challenge the assignment of the Disputed Mark. In light of the above, the first instance court dismissed Mr. Li's lawsuit.

Mr. Li appealed the dismissal decision to the Beijing High People's Court (the "***High Court***"). In the appeal, Mr. Li pointed out that he was unaware of the assignment of the Disputed Mark until November 1, 2013 when the local Administration of

Industry and Commerce approached him and acquired about the Disputed Mark. Mr. Li pointed out that the starting date to calculate the appeal time line to challenge the assignment of the Disputed Mark should be November 1, 2013; his litigation was therefore timely.

The High Court reviewed the case and held that the Trademark Gazette is an appropriate legal medium in which the government can announce the approval of trademark assignment concerning a specific trademark registration to the society; accordingly, Mr. Li was deemed to be aware of the assignment of the Disputed Mark since April 20, 2011; his 2013 litigation was therefore not timely – it had exceeded the two-year time limit allowed in the Judicial Interpretation to pursue an appeal. The court of the second instance issued a final decision to dismiss the appeal and maintained the first instance's ruling.

ANALYSIS & INSIGHT

The key in this case involves the calculation and recognition of the start date and the appeal time frame in an administrative litigation concerning the approval of a trademark assignment. The time frame issue is closely related to the administrative body's approval of the underlying trademark assignment.

1. Definition of Specific Administrative Acts and Its Essential Elements.

It is stipulated in Article 5 of the Administrative Procedure Law that "*In handling administrative cases, the people's courts shall examine the legality of specific administrative acts.*" Based on the above, in an administrative litigation case, the scope of judicial examination is limited to the specific administrative act itself. The specific administrative act is relative to the abstract administrative act; it refers to the administrative act made by the administrative authorities concerning specific administrative audiences.[106]

A specific administrative act must include the following four key elements for it to become effective:

(1) the existence of administrative power;
(2) the practical exercise of administrative power;
(3) the existence of legal effects; and
(4) the existence of intention.[107]

The Trademark Office's approval of a trademark assignment is within its legal rights directly authorized by the Trademark Law. Accordingly, the Trademark Office's relative act concerning the applicant's trademark approval application should be

106. Jiang Ming'an, ed., ADMINISTRATIVE LAW & ADMINISTRATIVE PROCEDURE LAW, Beijing University Press, Higher Education Press, 178 (2005).
107. Jiang Ming'an, ed., *id.*, 223.

deemed a specific administrative act as long as it has corresponding legal effects. The so-called legal effect or legal meaning refers to certain rights or obligations that the subject applicant is seeking to determine, change or eliminate through its will and is seeking legal protection through its application. The "legal effect" discussed in this context must be the effect directing or targeting a specific relative person.[108] According to Article 31 Section 1 of the 2014 Implementation Regulations of Trademark Law,[109] the Trademark Office should issue relevant certificate or proof to the assignee once it approves the assignee's application to assign certain trademark registration. Based on the above, Trademark Office's act in approving the trademark assignment is a type of specific administrative act; it is therefore subject to the corresponding judicial examination.

2. Trademark Assignment Approval and the Publication Relating to a Trademark Assignment Approval.

Despite the fact that an approval of a trademark assignment is undoubtedly a specific administrative act, the content of such an administrative act and the completion of the administrative act - whether or not it is completed once the announcement is made - are often misunderstood by the public.

According to Article 42 Section 4 of the 2013 Trademark Law, "*once the assignment of a registered trademark has been approved, it shall be published. The assignee shall start enjoying the exclusive rights associated with the assigned trademark from the publication date.*"[110] The "publication" act comes after the application has been "approved." This explains why the public often misunderstands the publication act as separate and independent from the specific administrative act concerning the approval of trademark assignment. The misunderstanding should be clarified once we review this act in the context of the Trademark Law and the Implementation Regulations of the Trademark Law (the "***Implementation***").

First, Article 31 Section 1 of the 2014 Implementation stipulates that "*In order to seek an assignment of a trademark, both the assignor and the assignee shall submit a written application with the Trademark Office. The application procedures concerning an assignment of the registered trademark shall be processed jointly and involve both the assignor and the assignee. Once the assignment application has been approved by the Trademark Office, the Trademark Office shall issue an approval certificate and make a public announcement.*"[111] Based on the above, it is clear that in order to accomplish the

108. Jiang Ming'an, ed., *id.*, 226–227.
109. Article 25 Section 1 of the 2002 Implementation Regulations of the Trademark Law.
110. Article 39 Section 2 of the 2001 Trademark Law.
111. Article 25 Section 1 of the 2002 Implementation Regulations of the Trademark Law stipulates that "When applying for the assignment of a registered trademark, the assignor and assignee shall file with the Trademark Office an Application for Assignment of Registered Trademark. The formalities of applying for the assignment of the registered trademark shall be gone through by the assignor. The Trademark Office, upon examination and approval of the application, shall issue the relevant certificate to the assignee and make an announcement."

administrative act of approving a trademark assignment, the Trademark Office must complete two steps: (1) issue the corresponding approval certificate to the assignee, and (2) make a public announcement.

Second, although neither the 2001 nor the 2013 Trademark Law provided any clear guidance or stipulations concerning the specific act of publication (which therefore contributed to the public perception that the announcement act itself lacked proper legal foundation), the 2014 Implementation Regulations of the Trademark Law provided some clear guidance and rules in respect to the effects of the trademark publication based on Article 57 Section 2 of the 2002 Implementation Regulations of the Trademark Law.[112] Specifically, Article 96 of the 2014 Implementation states that "*The Trademark Office shall publish the Trademark Gazette to announce trademark applications that have matured to registration as well as other related trademark matters. The Trademark Gazette can be published either electronically or on paper. The public is deemed to know or should have known about the content included in the publication, except for service by publication, since the publication date.*" In other words, trademark announcement is a type of publication (except for service by publication); the public is deemed to know or should have known the content included in the publication. Furthermore, the Trademark Gazette's main audience is the public in general - the purpose of the publication is to ensure that the public in general are aware of trademark matters; in other words, the purpose of the Trademark Gazette is not to change any rights or obligation relationships between certain specific parties. In light of the above, the trademark publication is not itself an independent specific administrative act.

Third, trademark registration is to record relevant trademarks in the Trademark Register.[113] A trademark registration certificate along with other certifications are proof that a right holder enjoys exclusive rights relative to the mark registered.[114] The Trademark Law had specifically stated that an assignee shall enjoy exclusive rights associated with the assigned mark starting from the publication date of the approval of the trademark assignment. The assignee does not enjoy any trademark rights prior to the publication of the announcement. In other words, since the legal effect of a trademark assignment does not occur prior to the publication date, the corresponding specific administrative act is not considered to be completed prior to the publication date. This means prior to the approval publication, the claims relating to "relevant certificates or proofs" concerning the approval of the trademark assignment would not have any proper legal foundation.

112. Article 57 Section 2 of the 2002 Implementation Regulations of the Trademark Law stipulates that "The Trademark Office shall compile, print and distribute the Trademark Gazette to publish trademark registrations and other related matters."

113. Article 94 of the 2014 Implementation Regulations of the Trademark Law stipulates that "The Trademark Office shall prepare a Trademark Register to record registered trademarks and related registration matters."

114. Article 95 of the 2014 Implementation Regulations of the Trademark Law stipulates that "The Trademark Registration Certificate and other relevant certificates are proofs that a right holder enjoys the right to exclusive use of a registered trademark. The registration matters recorded on the Trademark Registration Certificate shall be consistent with those on the Trademark Register. In the event of any discrepancy thereof, the Trademark Register shall prevail unless there is evidence to prove that it is indeed erroneous."

Fourth, from the administrative law perspective, the approval act of a trademark assignment is a form of administrative confirmation. An administrative confirmation is a specific administrative act from the administrative authority to an administrative relative person concerning the latter's recognition, approval or denials of its legal status, legal relationships or relevant legal facts and the corresponding public announcement made by the administrative authority.[115] The approval of a trademark assignment, as discussed above, is a type of specific administrative act; it is a form of confirmation regarding the transfer of trademark rights between the assignor and assignee based on a trademark assignment agreement. The trademark announcement is simply the declaration part in this administrative act.[116]

In conclusion, the specific administrative act of approving a trademark assignment is composed of two parts: "approval" and "announcement." The "approval" is made by the trademark administrative authority confirming the substantive transfer of the trademark right from the assignor to the assignee; the "announcement" is the manifestation of the administrative approval.

3. Determine the Prosecution Time Period Relating to the Trademark Assignment Approval.

The determination of the prosecution time period in an administrative litigation regarding concerning the approval of a trademark assignment is a key issue; it directly impacts the parties because the outcome would determine whether or not the parties are entitled to any judicial reliefs. It is an important topic worth further discussion.

a. Relevant Regulations.

There are three primary judicial interpretations discussing the prosecution time period involving the specific administrative act concerning the approval of a trademark assignment:

Article 39 of the Administrative Procedure Law: "*If a citizen, legal person or any other organization brings a lawsuit directly before a people's court, except otherwise provided for by law, the lawsuit should have been instituted within three months from the day the plaintiff knows about the outcome of the specific administrative act.*"

Article 41 Section 1 of the Judicial Interpretation: "*When making specific administrative acts, and the administrative authority has failed to inform the citizens, legal persons or other organizations about their appeals rights or the prosecution time limit, the prosecution time limit shall be calculated from the date on which the citizens, legal persons or other organizations know or should have known about the right to appeal – the prosecution time limit, however, shall not exceed two years.*"

115. Jiang Ming'an, ed., ADMINISTRATIVE LAW & ADMINISTRATIVE PROCEDURE LAW, Beijing University Press, Higher Education Press, 282 (2005).
116. Luo Haocai, ed., ADMINISTRATIVE LAW, China University of Political Science and Law Press, 232 (1996).

Article 42 of the Judicial Interpretation: "*In situations where the citizens, legal persons or other organizations do not know about the content of the specific administrative decisions made by the administrative authority, the prosecution time limit shall be calculated from the date the citizens, legal persons or other organizations know or should have known about the content. Despite the above, the people's court shall not accept the case if the litigation is brought 20 years later involving real estate specific administrative acts, or 5 years later concerning other specific administrative acts.*"

b. Understanding and Applications of the above Regulations.

The three-month prosecution time limit stipulated in Article 39 of the Administrative Procedure Law is a general rule in administrative litigations where there are no specific laws governing the situations in the underlying litigations. In situations where the relevant laws including judicial interpretations have provided special rules governing the prosecution time limit, such "special" time limits should prevail.

Article 41 Section 1 of the Judicial Interpretation is a special rule that is provided in respect to Article 39 of the Administrative Procedure Law. Article 41 Section 1 is "special" for the following two reasons: (1) it stipulates the starting date for the prosecution time period in situations where the administrative authority has failed to notify the citizens, legal persons or other organizations of their appeal rights or the prosecution time limit. (2) The prosecution time period should be limited to two years, starting from the date the citizens, legal persons or other organizations know or should have known about their appeal rights or the prosecution time period. The longest prosecution time period is two years from the date on which the citizens, legal persons or other organizations know or should have known about the content of the specific administrative acts.

Article 42 of the Judicial Interpretation is a special rule made in response to Article 41 Section 1 of the Judicial Interpretation. Article 42 further stipulates the time limit for citizens, legal persons or other organizations to bring an administrative litigation. The two-year prosecution time period discussed in Article 41 Section 1 is calculated from the date the citizens, legal persons or other organizations know or should have known about the content of the specific administrative acts; the starting time period is not from the date the specific administrative acts were made. In other words, based solely on Article 41 Section 1 of the Judicial Interpretation, there exists a possibility that the citizens, legal persons or other organizations still could bring an administrative litigation a long time after the specific administrative acts were made because they did not have a chance to learn about the content until a later point; this possibility posts a risk to the stability of the judicial system. In order to maintain the stability in the judicial system, Article 42 of the Judicial Interpretation further limits the two-year prosecution time line by offering the following specifics:

(1) When the citizens, legal persons or other organizations do not know about the content of the specific administrative acts made by the administrative authority, the prosecution time limit shall be calculated from the date the citizens,

legal persons or other organizations know or should have known about the content of the specific administrative acts.

(2) The longest time limit for the citizens, legal persons or other organizations to bring an administrative litigation is twenty years if the specific administrative acts involve real estate, and five years for other specific administrative acts. The calculating point for both limitations is the date the specific acts are made by the relevant authorities.

Although Article 41 Section 1 of the Judicial Interpretation stipulates the longest prosecution period is two years from the date the citizens, legal persons or other organizations know or should have known about the content of the specific administrative acts, the longest prosecution period for other specific administrative acts (except for those involving real estate) is five years from the date the underlying administrative acts were made. Based on the above, if an administrative relative person knows or should have known about the specific administrative act on the third year after the act was made, the corresponding prosecution period to bring an administrative litigation would be less than two years. In other words, in the above situation, the prosecution time period would be less than the two-year time period allowed for citizens, legal persons or other organizations when the latter know or should have known about the content of the specific administrative acts.

As for the nature of the rules, the prosecution period discussed in Article 42 of the Judicial Interpretation is not independent from the two-year prosecution period discussed in Article 41 Section 1. Instead, Article 42 is supplementary to Article 41 Section 1 so that in situations where the citizens, legal persons or other organizations do not know about the content of the specific administrative acts but can bring an administrative litigation in the maximum time frame allowed under the law. This also brings finality to the relative administrative acts.

For example, suppose there was one specific administrative act and it was made on January 1, 2000; the administrative relative person did not learn about this act until January 1, 2001. Based on Article 41 Section 1 of the Judicial Interpretation, the prosecution period should be calculated from January 1, 2001, and the last day the administrative relative person can bring an administrative litigation is January 1, 2003. If the administrative relative person does not know about the specific administrative act until January 1, 2002, then the last date it can bring an administrative litigation is January 1, 2004. But if the two-year time limit from the date the administrative relative person knows about the specific administrative act has exceeded the five-year time limit from the date the specific administrative act was made, the two-year prosecution time limit no longer controls – instead, the prosecution time period should be calculated from the date the administrative relative person should have known about the specific administrative act until the 5th year anniversary from the date the specific administrative act was made. For example, the administrative relative person knows about the above-mentioned specific administrative act on August 12, 2003. In this situation, August 12, 2003, would be the starting date for the purpose to calculate the prosecution time period and the last date for the administrative relative person to bring the lawsuit is January 1, 2005 – i.e., the 5th anniversary when the administrative act was made. In this case, the actual prosecution period for the administrative relative person to bring a lawsuit is less than two years from the date it learns about the administrative act. On the other hand, if we calculate the prosecution time period based on the two-year limit, then the last day the administrative relative person can bring a lawsuit falls on August 12, 2005, which falls outside the five-year anniversary rule when the administrative act is first made. By the same token, even though a specific administrative relative person does not know about the administrative act until December 30, 2014, the last date it can bring a lawsuit still falls on January 1, 2005.

Based on the above, when determining the relevant prosecution time period of an administrative litigation regarding the specific administrative act of approving a trademark assignment, the two-year prosecution time limit discussed in Article 41 Section 1 of the Judicial Interpretation is still the general guiding principle. However, in situations where the citizens, legal persons or other organizations learn about the underlying specific administrative act and would therefore push the prosecution time period outside the 5th year anniversary window of the specific administrative act as discussed Article 42 of the Judicial Interpretation, the prosecution time period discussed in Article 42 controls.

4. The Legal Effect of the Trademark Gazette.

There was an article proposing the idea that the Trademark Gazette should be divided into two sections based on the published content: "public announcement" and "service announcement" – these two types of announcements would also have different legal effects. "Public announcement" refers to the type of announcement from the trademark office concerning the exclusive rights of a registered trademark – such as creation, extension, variation, or elimination of such exclusive rights. This type of announcement is made to the public in general without any specific groups in mind; its publication date is also deemed the date the public is imputed with the knowledge regarding the content of the announcement. "Service announcement" is a legal concept, a procedural requirement based on litigation law. It is simply one of the ways to "serve" a specific relative person or group of the underlying litigation. Such an announcement is one of the ways to "inform" the administrative relative person of the lawsuit (or result of a lawsuit). The announcement itself is not an independent administrative act; it is not a necessary part of the relevant administrative act either.[117]

Strictly speaking, serving legal documents to a specific relative person or group is not a statutory requirement of the Trademark Gazette. The purpose to include such information in the Trademark Gazette is only to facilitate the delivery of information – the information can also be published in carriers other than the Trademark Gazette. The goal to publish the Trademark Gazette is to announce trademark registration and related trademark matters and thereby, allow the public in general to be aware of trademark matters. The nature of the Trademark Gazette is public announcement; once

117. Jiang Shuwei, *The Differentiation and Analysis of the "Public Announcement" and "Service Announcement" in the Trademark Administrative Examination*, Chinese Patent and Trademark, Vol. 3, 2011 at 76.

the information is published, the general public is deemed to be aware of the published content and such an awareness is legally binding. In fact, different from the presumption in the procedure law, the relative person's or group's presumptive knowledge through the publication of the Trademark Gazette cannot be challenged or refuted by counter evidence. Although the Trademark Law and the 2002 Implementation Regulations of the Trademark Law did not provide clear guidance on the specific legal effect concerning the Trademark Gazette, Article 96 Section 3 of the 2014 Implementation Regulations of the Trademark Law has provided specific updates on the legal binding effects regarding matters published on the Trademark Gazette.

Therefore, the first instance court's view that the Trademark Gazette was merely a type of service was incorrect; this perspective was not confirmed nor supported by the second instance court. Despite this, it is a generally accepted view that the information once published in the Trademark Gazette does have legal binding effects. Except for a service announcement made in the Trademark Gazette (which is done for the purpose to facilitate the trademark procedures), any announcement made in the Trademark Gazette shall be deemed public knowledge – the public is deemed to know or should have known about the published content in the Trademark Gazette from the date of publication. Accordingly, in respect to the specific administrative act of the Trademark Office's approval of the underlying trademark assignment in this case, the assignor was deemed to know or should have known about the assignment approval from the date the Trademark Gazette carrying such information was published.

10. Transfer of a Trademark Based on Reasons other than an Assignment Agreement

Administrative litigation regarding the appeal of a trademark opposition concerning the "Bao Qing in Chinese characters and Design" mark; the litigation was brought by SU Qi'an against the Trademark Review and Adjudication Board and a third party Nanjing Baoqing Jewelry Co., Ltd.

- First Instance: Beijing No. 1 Intermediate People's Court (No. 578; 2013) - Decided on May 31, 2013
- Second Instance: Beijing High People's Court (No. 1579; 2013) - Decided on September 23, 2013

BACKGROUND

On September 26, 2005, a Chinese individual - Ms. Kong Lingli - filed a trademark application for "BAO QING in Chinese characters and Design" in connection with Class 35 services such as "outdoor advertising," "agency of commercial information," and "import-export services," etc. The mark was assigned an application number: 4916579 (the "***Opposed Mark***").

On December 19, 1985, Nanjing Metal Processing Factory applied for a trademark "BAO QING in Chinese characters and Design;" the mark was assigned an application number: 265875. The application was approved for registration on October 20, 1986, in connection with Class 14 goods such as "precious metal crafts," "jewelry," etc. (the "***Cited Mark***"). The Cited Mark was later assigned to Nanjing Baoqing Jewelry Co., Ltd. (the "***Company***"). The registration of the Cited Mark was subsequently renewed, and it is valid until October 19, 2016.

The Company filed an opposition against the Opposed Mark; the opposition action was timely filed with the China Trademark Office (the "***Trademark Office***"). The Trademark Office reviewed the case and denied the registration of the Opposed Mark. Ms. Kong filed an appeal to the TRAB under SAIC of PRC (the "***Appeal Board***"). On November 12, 2012, the Appeal Board issued a decision (the "***45554 Decision***") refusing Ms. Kong's appeal arguments. The Appeal Board agreed with the original Trademark Office decision and denied the registration of the Opposed Mark.

An individual named Su Qi'an ("***Mr. Su***") raised a timely administrative litigation challenging the 45554 Decision.

The case files revealed that Ms. Kong changed her first name to "Yiru" on October 25, 2011; Ms. Kong and Mr. Su were legally married. Mr. Su and Ms. Kong entered into a contract titled "Property Ownership Agreement relating to a Married Couple" (the "***Agreement***") on May 16, 2012. Section 2 of the Agreement states that "*all companies' shares – including shares that were held under Party A's (Mr. Su) name or shares from companies that Mr. Su controlled – and such companies' property (including but not limited to company shares and trademark rights) are Party A's personal property. Party*

B (Ms. Kong) agreed and expressly acknowledged that Party A enjoyed complete ownership over the above listed property." Ms. Kong passed away on May 20, 2012.

During the litigation process, Mr. Su provided a notarized document (the ***"599 Notarial Deed"***) issued by the Zhong Shan notary office in Nan Jing city, Jiang Su province (the "***Zhong Shan Notary Office***") on May 16, 2012. Based on the 599 Notarial Deed, Mr. Su and Ms. Kong signed the above-mentioned agreement after negotiation. Both parties had the capacity legally required by law to execute an agreement and to carry out the subsequent obligations. The agreement fully reflected the parties' intent and the content of the agreement was clear. The parties' signing acts complied with Article 55 of the Civil Law General Rules; the content of the agreement was legal and the signatures were genuine.

On March 25, 2013, the Zhong Shan Notary Office provided an acknowledgement to confirm a typo in the 599 Notarial Deed: "Explanation regarding a typo in the Property Ownership Agreement relating to a Married Couple" (the "***Revision***"). The Revision confirmed that the correct statement should be: "all companies' shares – including shares that were held under Ms. Kong's name or shares from companies that Ms. Kong controlled – and such companies' property (including but not limited to company shares and trademark rights) are Party A's personal property. Party B (Ms. Kong) agreed and expressly acknowledged that Party A enjoyed complete ownership over the above listed property."

COURT DECISION

Beijing No. 1 Intermediate People's Court (the "***Intermediate Court***") reviewed the case and held that Mr. Su had right to file an administrative litigation to challenge the 45554 Decision even after Ms. Kong's death because the agreement between the parties provided Mr. Su the standing to bring the lawsuit. The Opposed Mark and the Cited Mark did not constitute confusingly similar trademark in terms of the same or similar products and services. Accordingly, the Appeal Board's decision refusing the registration of the Opposed Mark violated Article 28 of the Trademark Law, and the decision was not supported by evidence. Meanwhile, given the designated goods and services covered by the Opposed Mark and the Cited Mark did not constitute the same or similar goods and services, Article 15 of the Trademark Law was not applicable to this case. In light of the above, the Intermediate Court decided to: (1) vacate the 45554 Decision; and (2) request the Appeal Board to issue a new decision.

Both the Appeal Board and the Company appealed the Intermediate Court's decision.

The Beijing High People's Court reviewed the case and decided not to consider the Revision issued by the Zhong Shan Notary Office for the following reasons:

- Zhong Shan Notary Office did not participate in the negotiation or drafting process when Mr. Su and Ms. Kong entered into the Agreement; the 599 Notarial Deed merely reflected the Agreement between the parties.

- The content in the Agreement was not fully incorporated in the 599 Notarial Deed.
- The Revision that was subsequently issued by the Zhong Shan Notary Office lacked proper factual and legal foundation.

Even assuming there is a typo or revision in the Agreement, Ms. Kong had expressly acknowledged the following: "All companies shares – including shares that were held under Ms. Kong's name or shares from companies that Ms. Kong controlled – as well as such companies' property are Party A's personal property; Ms. Kong expressly acknowledged and agreed that Mr. Su had complete control and ownership of her property." Despite the above, the rights associated with a registered trademark and a pending application should follow the standard practice as set out in the trademark register. Accordingly, even if Ms. Kong had transferred the Opposed Mark to Mr. Su or had expressly confirmed that any property rights associated with the Opposed Mark were now Mr. Su's personal property, such an acknowledgement did not comply with Article 17 Section (2) of the Implementation Regulations of the Trademark Law (the "***Implementation***"); accordingly, such a transfer was not lawful and did not have any legal effect. In light of the above and despite the evidence relating to the Agreement, the 599 Notarial Deed, and the Revision issued by the Zhong Shan Notary Office, Mr. Su was still not regarded, by law, as the applicant of the Opposed Mark; accordingly, Mr. Su did not have the standing to bring an administrative lawsuit to challenge the 45554 Decision. Despite the above, Article 24 Section 2 of the Administrative Procedural Law states that "any of the deceased's close relatives have the right to bring a lawsuit if the deceased party has the standing to bring the lawsuit in the first place." The 45554 Decision stated that the applicant of the appeal action was Kong Lingli; Kong Lingli later changed her first name to Kong Yiru. Kong Yiru later passed away. Accordingly, it was not a violation of the law if Mr. Su – as Ms. Kong's husband – stepped in and became the plaintiff to initiate the lawsuit after Ms. Kong's death.

The Appeal Board's review of the case was not improper because Ms. Kong's successor was not able to timely participate in the review process through a written declaration, and the Appeal Board would not have otherwise learned that the applicant of the appeal decision passed away. Yet it was a clear mistake when the Appeal Board still listed "Kong Lingli" as the applicant of the opposition review case in its 45554 Decision when the Appeal Board already knew that the original applicant was already deceased and had thereby lost her standing to bring a subsequent action.

The reason the Trademark Review Procedure is in place is to provide legal relief for the interested parties; the relief also includes the protection of the property rights associated with one's ability to apply for a trademark. Although the relevant law does not specify that the Appeal Board must take an active role to find out the successor of the deceased applicant and see if the successor is interested in participating in the subsequent appeals, Article 32, Section 1, Item 1 of the Rules for Trademark Review and Adjudication does expressly point out that the Appeal Board should terminate review of a pending case when the applicant is deceased or has been terminated and there is not a successor party, or the successor decides to abandon its rights to participate in the review process. In light of the above, although the Appeal Board does not have the obligation to confirm a deceased party's successor and to see if the successor is interested in participating in the subsequent review process, the Appeal Board should nevertheless have taken some affirmative actions in this case by, for example, seeking the opinion from the successor and confirming whether or not it should continue or suspend the appeal process based on the successor's interest in participating in the review process. This is because the Appeal Board was fully aware that the applicant in the appeal review was already deceased (through administration litigation or other objective factors), and the rights to participate in the appeal had transferred to its successor. Accordingly, in the subject case, since the Appeal Board was aware of the fact that Ms. Kong had passed away, it should have reached out to Ms. Kong's successor through the appropriate channel, inquired about her successor's intent in the proceeding and made a final decision as to continue reviewing the appeal case or terminating it. Similarly, Ms. Kong's successor should have made it clear to the Appeal Board in a timely manner, expressing its interest in participating in the review process concerning the Opposed Mark.

In light of the above, although the original decision did make some improper recognition of the facts, its conclusion was correct. Although the High Court did identify some of the errors made by the Intermediate Court, it did support the Intermediate Court's decision. The Intermediate Court refrained from commenting or making any decision in respect to the interested parties' legal rights given the Appeal Board had not yet made any response in accordance with Ms. Kong successor's opinion. Accordingly, the High Court rejected the appeal and maintained the Intermediate Court's decision.

ANALYSIS & INSIGHT

There are two ways to obtain exclusive rights associated with a registered trademark: through original application and through inheritance. The latter occurs when there has been some legal status changes in respect to the original owner of the trademark. The change can occur in one of the following two ways: (1) the change is a result of active transfer of the exclusive rights associated with a registered trademark; (2) the change is a result of transfer of the exclusive rights associated with a registered trademark for reasons other than a transfer.[118] In practice, a trademark can be transferred in the following ways:

(1) when the owner of the trademark is deceased;
(2) when the original trademark owner no longer exists due to separation, merger or change of corporate structure; the corporate successor after the separation, merger or change of corporate structure must then succeed and become the owner of the trademark;

118. Huang Hui, TRADEMARK LAW, Law Press, 191 (2004).

(3) when the original trademark owner declares bankruptcy, and the bankruptcy committee subsequently transfers the trademark of the bankrupt company to a third party;
(4) when a trademark is compelled to be transferred due to legal documents that have already become effective; and
(5) other situations.[119]

The transfer of exclusive rights associated with a trademark is a superordinate concept; assignment of a trademark is merely one of the situations where the rights associated with a trademark can be transferred.

A. Common Grounds.

A trademark can be transferred for various reasons such as through inheritance or a legal assignment agreement. Although the reasons that trigger the transfer may be different, they do share some common grounds:

(1) All transfers share the same legal consequence.
It is clear that although multiple reasons can trigger the transfer of a trademark, the legal consequence is the same: a trademark is transferred. In other words, after the triggering event, the subject owning the exclusive rights of a registered trademark has changed, and the original owner has lost its rights over the trademark. The assignee or the successor will then take the corresponding position and the original owner's rights in respect to the trademark.
(2) All transfers must be accompanied by a transfer application and be approved by the Trademark Office.
The 2014 Implementation Regulations of the Trademark Law states that: "To accomplish a trademark transfer, the assignor and assignee must submit a trademark transfer application to the Trademark Office . . . . Once the Trademark Office approves the application to transfer the registered trademark, it will issue appropriate proof to the assignee and publish the transfer of the subject trademark." For a trademark transfer that is triggered by inheritance or other reasons, "the successor should provide proof or legal documents and request the Trademark Office to review the associated transfer in connection with the exclusive rights of the trademark to be transferred . . . once the Trademark Office approves the application to transfer the registered trademark, it will publish the transfer." In other words, regardless of the triggering event, all trademark transfer must be accomplished by an application and be published by the Trademark Office once the application has been approved.

119. Zhang Cheng, *What Is the Matter for One Trademark Registration with Two Certificates?*, China Trademark Magazine, Vol. 8, 2008.

(3) All transfers become effective when the transfer notice is published by the Trademark Office.
In respect to the transfer of a trademark, the Trademark Law states that: "*the assignee will start enjoying the exclusive rights associated with a trademark as soon as the transfer is published.*" However, if the transfer is triggered by events other than an assignment agreement, neither the Trademark Law nor the 2002 Implementation Regulations of the Trademark Law provide any specific guidance in respect to the effective date when such a transfer will become effective. In light of the unclear status, some held the view that the assignee should enjoy the exclusive rights associated with a registered trademark as soon as the triggering event became legally effective.[120] The unclear status regarding the effective date of such a trademark transfer was finally put to rest by the 2014 Implementation Regulations of the Trademark Law. Article 32 Section 3 of the Implementation states that: "An application to transfer the trademark will be published once it has been approved by the Trademark Office. The party that is the recipient of the exclusive rights associated with the transferred trademark will start enjoying such exclusive rights since the publication date."

(4) All transfer is subject to the associated trademark rule.
Based on the Trademark Law and the Implementation Regulations of the Trademark Law, any other marks that are identical or similar to the mark to be transferred and cover the same or similar products or services must be transferred along with the subject trademark regardless of the underlying triggering event. For marks that fail to be transferred at the same time, the Trademark Office will issue a notification to ask the parties to transfer the marks within a certain time line. If the successor or assignee fails to transfer any of the associated marks within the specified timeline, the subsequent owner is deemed to abandon its trademark transfer application of the original transferred mark. The Trademark Office will also notify the subsequent owner in writing regarding the failed transfer application.

B. Characteristics Relating to a Trademark Transfer that Are Triggered by Reasons other than an Assignment Agreement.

Despite the common ground discussed above, there are still various differences between a trademark transfer that is triggered by inheritance and one triggered by an assignment agreement.

120. Xu Yi, *Legal Distinction Between Transfer and Assignment of a Registered Trademark*, People's Judicature – Cases, Vol. 10, 2011 at 99.

1. Legal Standing Difference.

When a trademark transfer is triggered by an assignment agreement, the assignor and the assignee are still validly in existence and in good standing. However, for a trademark transfer that is triggered by inheritance, bequeathal, bankruptcy, merger and acquisition, the original trademark owner has either deceased or disappeared - in other words, the original trademark owner no longer has the legal standing to serve as the owner of the trademark. In other situations where a trademark transfer is triggered by corporation separation or enforcement measures following a court decision, the original owner is still a legal entity.

2. Requirement of the Original Trademark Owner to Participate in the Transfer Process.

In a trademark transfer that takes place in accordance with an assignment agreement, the 2014 Implementation Regulations of the Trademark Law also requires the parties to submit a joint application to the Trademark Office in addition to their separate application. For trademark transfer that is triggered by other events, such as inheritance, the transfer can be accomplished without the participation of the original trademark owner. This is because the original trademark owner has either deceased or disappeared, in most trademark transfer situations. In light of the above, the Implementation only requires the assignee or the successor to handle the processing related to the transfer by itself.

C. Specific Facts Relating to the Trademark Transfer in the Subject Case.

Based on the Agreement between Mr. Su and Ms. Kong, the parties agreed that "all companies' shares - including shares that were held under Ms. Kong's name or shares from companies that Ms. Kong controlled - and such companies' property are Mr. Su's personal property; Ms. Kong agreed and expressly acknowledged that Mr. Su has complete control and ownership over such property." In light of the above, the statement in the Agreement can be regarded as the assignment agreement between Mr. Su and Ms. Kong. However, because the parties failed to submit associated trademark transfer application paperwork prior to Ms. Kong's death, Mr. Su did not become the assignee of the trademark and the applicant of the subject case concerning the Opposed Mark.

After Ms. Kong's death, Mr. Su - as Ms. Kong's successor - had rights to inherit the trademark application right that was originally enjoyed by Ms. Kong. However, given that Mr. Su and other successors failed to submit any transfer paperwork to the Trademark Office, the right to challenge the decision concerning the Opposed Mark did not transfer to Mr. Su. Accordingly, Mr. Su could only bring an administrative lawsuit as an interested party. The High Court considered the specific facts of this case, and asked the Appeal Board to inquire about all the successors' opinions, since the Board was already aware of Ms. Kong's death, and to make a corresponding decision.

Meanwhile, the High Court also asked Ms. Kong's successor to timely file a declaration to the Appeal Board in accordance with the Implementation Regulations of the Trademark Law and to express its interest in the review procedure in connection with the Opposed Mark. The High Court's approach was a good compromise because it fully considered the specific background of this case and also considered the relevant requirements under the Law.

CHAPTER 4
Cancellation of a Registered Trademark

11. Cancellation of a Registered Trademark due to the Death or Termination of the Trademark Registrant (Person or Company Registrant)

Administrative litigation filed by Tsui Fang Ming against the trademark office and a third party, Shunde Daliang Dongying Garment Factory, relating to the cancellation action of the trademark "XUE FEI LONG in Chinese characters and CHEVIGNON" due to the Death/Termination of the Trademark Registrant

- First Instance: Beijing No. 1 Intermediate People's Court (No. 392; 2012) – Decided on June 20, 2012
- Second Instance: Beijing High People's Court (No. 1888; 2012) – Decided on March 28, 2013

BACKGROUND

Shunde Daliang Dongying Garment Factory (the "***Company***") filed a trademark application for "XUE FEI LONG in Chinese characters and CHEVIGNON" under Application Number 1932719 (the "***Trademark***") on January 15, 2001. The TRAB under SAIC of PRC (the "***Appeal Board***") made a decision (No. 30882; 2009) on November 16, 2009, approving registration in respect to some goods covered by the Trademark. Beijing No. 1 Intermediate People's Court made an administrative decision on June 20, 2011, (No. 2588; 2010) maintaining the Appeal Board's decision. The Court's decision has since become effective.

On September 29, 2010, Tsui Fang Ming ("***Mr. Tsui***") applied to the China Trademark Office to cancel the Trademark due to death of the individual registrant or termination of the company registrant. Specifically, Mr. Tsui pointed out that corporate status of the registrant, a company, had been deregistered since December 25, 2003.

The Trademark Office did not consider the materials submitted by Mr. Tsui to be sufficient. On December 15, 2010, the Trademark Office requested that Mr. Tsui to provide more information relating to the Company's deregistration status in the administrative offices for industry and commerce in China as well as publication materials announcing the Company's deregistration status. On February 28, 2011, Mr. Tsui provided additional materials to the China Trademark Office, which included an original certified copy of the "private company's application to suspend/terminate its corporate status" (the "***Petition***"). The Petition is chopped with a seal from the "special stamp for profile query use of Fo Shan Shun De Marketing Safety Supervisor Bureau." The applicant's name shown on the Petition is the Company, and the Company is listed as a private company, established on June 20, 2001. Its business scope includes "clothing," and its address is listed as No. 68 Honggang Road, Daliang. The Petition also showed that the Company had been approved for deregistration on December 25, 2003. On May 18, 2011, the Trademark Office rejected Mr. Tsui's cancellation action (Cancellation No. 00243; 2010). Mr. Tsui filed a review with the Appeal Board. On November 4, 2011, the Appeal Board maintained the Trademark Office's decision (No. 206; 2011). Mr. Tsui appealed the decision to the court.

COURT DECISION

Beijing No. 1 Intermediate People's Court (the "***Intermediate Court***") was of the view that the applicant in a cancellation proceeding should provide sufficient and valid supporting materials evidencing the death or termination status of the trademark owner so as to meet its burden of proof under the law. Otherwise, the applicant shall bear the legal consequences of failure to meet its burden of proof. In the subject case, Mr. Tsui should have provided additional materials proving that the deregistered company listed in its supporting materials is the same party as the owner of the Trademark. Furthermore, Mr. Tsui should have provided the materials by the administrative management office when it approved the deregistration petition of the Company. Mr. Tsui did not provide the above materials and accordingly, the materials were not sufficient to show that the owner of the Trademark was no longer in existence. The Trademark Office made a correct decision to reject Mr. Tsui's cancellation action. In light of the above, there is insufficient factual and legal evidence to support Mr. Tsui's position; the Intermediate Court did not support the appeal and Mr. Tsui's request to vacate the Appeal Board's decision. The Intermediate Court therefore rejected Mr. Tsui's appeal based on Article 56(4) of the Interpretation of the Supreme People's Court on Several Issues Concerning the Implementation of the Administrative Litigation Law of the People's Republic of China.

Mr. Tsui appealed the Intermediate Court's decision to the Beijing High People's Court. The Beijing High People's Court reviewed the case and was of the view that the Intermediate Court's decision had fully considered the facts in the case, correctly applied the law and the decision-making process complied with the due process requirement under the law. The High Court therefore rejected the appeal and maintained the Intermediate Court's decision.

ANALYSIS & INSIGHT

Section 47 of the 2002 Regulation for the Implementation of the PRC Trademark Law ("***Implementation***") states that, "*anyone can petition to cancel a registered trademark due to the death of the trademark owner (an individual), or termination status of the trademark owner (a corporation), if the registered trademark has not been duly transferred to a third party within a year since the owner's death/termination. The applicant seeking to cancel a registered trademark on the above ground shall provide evidence relating to the death/termination of the trademark owner. The exclusive rights associated with a registered trademark shall be terminated on the date when the death or termination of the owner occurs.*" Under the law, although anyone can petition to cancel a registered trademark, it is important to keep the following points in mind when applying Section 47.

1. Burden of Proof and Evidence Requirements.

The administrative authorities bear the burden of proof in respect to legality of their specific administrative acts in the administrative lawsuits. Article 32 of the Administrative Litigation Law of PRC states that: "*the defendant bears the burden of proof regarding its administrative decisions; it shall provide the evidence and supporting administrative materials to support that decision.*" Although the authorities can cancel a registered trademark due to death or termination of the trademark owner, the trademark office is making the decision based on the applicant's petition. Cancellation of a registered trademark is a specific administrative act/decision. Accordingly, the Trademark Office must be careful in reviewing all relevant facts when making the decision so as to make sure that it has sufficient evidence to support its decision and its decision making process is in compliance with Section 47 of the Implementation. This explains why the Trademark Office has always taken a very careful approach in reviewing the evidence provided by the applicant so as to decide whether or not the evidence carries enough weight to support the cancellation of a registered trademark. Otherwise, the decision will be vacated by the courts in the later administrative lawsuits.

A decision in relation to the cancellation petition has two possible administrative outcomes: One is to approve the cancellation of a registered trademark and terminate all exclusive rights associated with the trademark; another is to reject the cancellation petition and the exclusive rights associated with the mark remain intact. Under the first scenario, the trademark owner has either deceased or become deregistered - it is no longer in existence and accordingly, there is little possibility of any further administrative lawsuits sought by the trademark owner to challenge the outcome of the case. For the applicant of the cancellation decision, given its petition had already been supported by the Trademark Office, it is not likely that it would pursue a further administrative lawsuit either. There is little possibility that any third parties would institute an administrative lawsuit due to the lack of standing (the decision has little impact on the third parties).[121] Under these circumstances, the only possibility of an administrative lawsuit comes from the trademark owner which is still alive or still maintains an active corporate status but is deemed otherwise by the Trademark Office. To avoid this (which requires an administrative lawsuit from a party taking a "passive" role in the prior actions), the Trademark Office should take a strict approach in requiring and reviewing the evidence. Furthermore, the standard of proof should not be the typical lower standard of proof in civil actions (i.e., "preponderance of the evidence"); the standard requirement should be similar to the higher evidence requirement, namely "beyond a reasonable doubt." Under the second scenario, there is no incentive for the trademark owner to institute an administrative appeal because its mark is still valid so are the exclusive rights associated with the registered trademark. Accordingly, only the applicant of the cancellation proceeding would have the incentive to start an administrative lawsuit seeking another review of the cancellation decision. A cancellation of a registered trademark means that the trademark owner would lose the exclusive rights it had obtained which would have a direct and significant impact on the trademark owner's civil rights. The court therefore will take a more strict approach, requiring a higher burden of proof when its decision may take away a trademark owner's civil rights. This explains why the lower standard of burden of proof, "preponderance of the evidence," would be replaced by the higher burden of proof requirement, "beyond a reasonable double."[122] If the petitioner of a cancellation action cannot prove beyond reasonable doubt that the trademark owner has indeed been deceased or become deregistered, its application is likely being rejected. If, on the other hand, the petitioner can provide such evidence and carry its burden of proof, it would naturally win the support of the trademark office before the administrative lawsuits.

Accordingly, in an administrative lawsuit concerning the cancellation action of a registered trademark due to death or deregistration of the trademark owner, the burden of proof is shifted from the Trademark Office (which is making administrative decision) to the applicant of the cancellation decision. In respect to the burden of proof requirement, in order to prove there is sufficient evidence to take away the exclusive rights associated with a registered trademark, the Trademark Office and the courts should impose the higher standard of proof - beyond a reasonable doubt - when reviewing the supporting materials in such actions.

Although the system designs the cancellation action so as to remove idle marks and allow the society to maximize the trademark resources, the system does not provide a channel for the trademark owner to become involved in the process (and the

121. Article 12 of the Interpretation of the Supreme People's Court on Several Issues concerning the implementation of the Administrative Litigation Law of the People's Republic of China states that where a citizen, a legal person, or any other organization with an interest in the specific administrative act could initiate an administrative litigation pursuant to the law.

122. "The adoption of standard of proof should take into account of the nature of the administrative cases and the degree of impact to the parties' rights and interests. And the standard of proof should correspond to the nature of the cases and the degree of impact. The more complicated the case is, the higher standard of proof is demanded." Jiang Ming'an, ed., ADMINISTRATIVE LAW & ADMINISTRATIVE PROCEDURE LAW, Beijing University Press, Higher Education Press, 535 (2005).

trademark owner is the party being impacted the most by the decision of the cancellation action). Given the trademark owner does not have an effective way to participate in the cancellation proceeding, there exists a possibility that a third party may take advantage of the system to cancel a registered trademark even though the trademark owner is still alive or in a good corporate standing.[123] On the other hand, the party instituting the cancellation proceeding is not always in the best position to access the evidence sufficient to verify the deceased or inactive status of the trademark owner. This explains why imposing a "beyond reasonable doubt" standard of proof requirement in the cancellation proceedings sometimes makes it impossible and impractical for anyone to cancel a registered trademark on this basis.

In reality, there are some practical issues when trying to enforce Article 47 of the Implementation:

(1) Companies in China with financial difficulties are most likely having their business licenses suspended. However, a suspension of the business license does not fall under the category in which the trademark owner should be deregistered or terminated. Accordingly, it is very rare that a cancellation action would be approved due to the trademark owner's business license being deregistered and this is not helpful to achieve the legislative objective to clear idle trademarks in China.
(2) There are also practical questions relating to the companies that are registered or incorporated outside China – i.e., the "foreign" entities. For example, the authorities often struggle to decide what situations would render a foreign entity "suspended" (i.e., being recognized as "deregistered/terminated" under the trademark law) and what type of laws are applicable to decide the deregistered/terminated status. Additionally, the authorities have not yet settled on the exact type of evidence required in order to prove an inactive corporate status relating to a foreign entity.
(3) For truly idle marks, the Trademark Law already provides a mechanism to remove such marks – i.e., the cancellation proceeding of a registered trademark due to three consecutive years of nonuse. This nonuse cancellation proceeding can entirely replace the cancellation proceeding where the trademark owner is deceased or no longer maintaining an active corporate status.
(4) The key to the cancellation proceeding where the trademark owner is either deceased or deregistered is that the owner fails to transfer the ownership of the mark to a third party within one year. In other words, the owner of the mark can avoid the cancellation proceeding so long as it completes the assignment process within the required time frame. However, this process

123. In practice, once there was such a case: the owner of a trademark was approved for deregistration according to the notification issued by the local administration for industry and commerce, and this deregistration status was published in the newspaper. While, later the local administration for industry and commerce issued another contrary notification to withdraw the previous deregistration notification, and expressed that the cancelled enterprise could exercise its rights relating to trademark opposition by holding the business license. Case Index: Beijing High People's Court, Gao Xing Zhong Zi [2012] No. 1209; Gao Xing Zhong Zi [2013] No. 1698.

may be delayed for some justifiable reasons but the owner is faced with the reality to lose all its rights associated with its trademark. The omission is therefore likely to trigger some disproportionate amount of "punishment" which understandably has been a concern among the legal community.[124]

In light of the above, Article 47 of the 2002 Regulation for the Implementation of the Trademark Law of PRC was deleted in its entirety in the 2014 amendments to the Regulation for the Implementation of the Trademark Law of PRC.

2. Article 47 Is Not Applicable in Situations the Trademark Owner's Business License Has Been Suspended.

Most of the cases these days involve the trademark owners having their business license suspended. Suspension of the business license is a form of administrative punishment;[125] it does not, however, result in deregistration or termination of the corporate status of the company, instead it will prevent the company from conducting further business activities. Accordingly, Article 47 of the 2002 Regulation for the Implementation of the Trademark Law of PRC does not apply in situations where the trademark owners merely have their business license suspended.

Suspension of the business license could impact a registered trademark in one of the two ways: First, the business license is suspended when the trademark is already registered in China. Second, the business license is suspended when the trademark has not yet been approved for registration.

In the first situation, given the trademark owner is still in existence and the exclusive rights associated with the trademark remain intact, the impact on the trademark is only in respect to the disposition of the trademark right. The mark, however, can still be cancelled if it has not been in use for three consecutive years.

In the second situation, even though the trademark owner is still in existence, the issues remain as to whether or not the mark can still be approved for registration and if the authorities would/should grant exclusive rights to the owner of the mark. In other words, in situations where the trademark owner's business license has been suspended and the mark is not yet approved for registration, there are concerns as to whether or

124. If the trademark owner has concluded a trademark assignment agreement with others before his/her death or its termination, however the assignee has not proceeded with the assignment formalities within one year from the death or termination of the trademark owner, the involved trademark may be cancelled according to Article 47 of the 2002 Regulation for the Implementation of the Trademark Law of PRC. This seems an overly strict approach against the assignee to directly cancel the registered trademark just because of its delay in not timely proceeding with the assignment formalities.

125. Article 8 of the Administrative Penalty Law of PRC states: administrative penalty shall include the following types: (1) disciplinary warning; (2) fine; (3) confiscation of illegal gains or confiscation of unlawful property or things of value; (4) ordering for suspension of production or business; (5) temporary suspension or rescission of permit or temporary suspension or rescission of license; (6) administrative detention; and (7) others as prescribed by laws and administrative rules and regulations.

not the Trademark Office and the judicial courts should conduct further searches and continue reviewing this issue prior to approving a trademark application for registration.

The court has gone through several different stages in its approach on the issues highlighted above. Initially, the courts were of the view that trademark registration should not be withheld simply because the owner of the mark had its business license suspended, and had not yet participated in the related trademark appeal and administrative litigation review process. For example, in the administrative litigation concerning the appeal of the trademark opposition involving the design trademark No. 1254967, the second level of court held that the Appeal Board can continue the review of the registration of the underlying mark even though the applicant had lost its business license and had not yet completed the deregistration process. The reason is because even though the company had lost its rights to operate the business, it had not yet lost its status as a company.[126]

However, there is a distinction between a corporate's ability to carry out its civil rights and its civil capacities. Suspension of one's business license does not mean the company has lost its capacity to exercise its civil rights. The suspension - however - does indicate that the company no longer has the rights and capabilities to operate businesses. Article 4 of the Trademark Law states that the application of a trademark registration is to carry out its business objectives, accordingly, the application no longer fulfills the requirement of this article when the trademark applicant has lost its business license. Accordingly, more and more courts are embracing the view that an opposed mark should not be granted for trademark registration when the applicant has lost its business license. In the appeal of a trademark opposition concerning "YA BO LE in Chinese characters and ABERLOUR" (Application Number 3551640), the court rejected the registration of this mark. The court pointed out that the basic function of a trademark is to operate as a source identifier for its goods and/or services. The goal of registering a trademark is to distinguish the goods and/or services provided by one party from those provided by other operators in the society. For the company where its business license has been suspended, this means that there are certain limitations for the company to continue operating business legally in China; it therefore no longer has the ability to provide goods and/or services to the market. In this case, the business license for the trademark application has been suspended for as long as four years. Furthermore, the company failed to carry out its legal obligation to deregister its corporate status and liquidate its assets; it also fails to transfer the mark to other companies with valid licenses to operate businesses in China. From the above, it can then be presumed that the company no longer has the subjective intent to use the mark. Furthermore, the opposed mark was still in the registration review period, it had not yet matured to a confirmed legal right in China. Considering the above and the overall objective to conserve social resources, the appealed mark was refused for registration.[127] With more and more precedents, the above view from the first level of court has

126. Case Index: Beijing High People's Court, Gao Xing Zhong Zi [2009] No. 484.
127. Case Index: Beijing No. 1 Intermediate People's Court, Yi Zhong Zhi Xing Chu Zi [2011] No. 1897.

gradually been accepted and supported by second level of courts. In the administrative litigation concerning the appeal of the trademark opposition for "REGITAR" (Application Number 3848227), the second level of court adopted the above first level court's view in the ABERLOUR case. The REGITAR mark was refused for registration because the applicant's business license had been suspended for four years, and it had not yet taken any steps to restore its ability as a business operator in China nor had the company been involved in any review and litigation processes.[128]

Beijing High Court has since offered some guidance in respect to the issues discussed above. Article 24 of the Guidelines of the Higher People's Court of Beijing Municipality for Hearing Administrative Cases on Trademark Authorization and Determination (No. 2014(37)) states that: "an opposed mark will be refused for registration based on Article 4 of the Trademark Law if the business license of the applicant company has been suspended, the applicant company has failed to carry out the necessary steps to deregister the company and there is an occurrence of the following:"

(1) The business license of the applicant of the opposed mark has been suspended for more than three years at the time the administrative decision is issued.
(2) There is no evidence to suggest that the opposed mark has been transferred or licensed for use by the applicant to any third parties.
(3) The applicant company has failed to participate in the review proceeding of its mark and the subsequent administrative litigations; the company has also failed to provide any explanation regarding its business status or the mark at issue.
(4) There are certain visual similarities between the opposed mark and the cited mark as well as the goods and/or services covered by both marks.

The above discussion from the Beijing High Court has provided clear guidance to ensure a consistent approach in respect to approval of the disputed mark where the business license of its owner had been suspended.

128. Case Index: Beijing High People's Court, Gao Xing Zhong Zi [2013] No. 111.

12. Cancellation of a Registered Trademark when It Has Become a Generic Term

Administrative civil action filed by Beijing Hua Qi Information Digital Technology Co., Ltd. to cancel the "YOU PAN in Chinese characters" trademark owned by Shenzhen Netac Technology Co., Ltd.

- Beijing No. 1 Intermediate People's Court (No. 1014; 2004) - Decided on February 20, 2006
- Beijing High People's Court (No. 358; 2007) - Decided on August 23, 2007
- Beijing No. 1 Intermediate People's Court (No. 2631; 2010) - Decided on July 31, 2011

BACKGROUND

Shenzhen Netac Technology Co., Ltd. (the "***Netac***") filed a trademark application for "YOU PAN in Chinese characters" under Application Number 1509704 (the "***Disputed Mark***") on August 23, 1999. The Mark covers Class 9 products such as "computer discs," "computer storage products," and "computers." The Disputed Mark was approved for registration on January 21, 2001.

Beijing Hua Qi Information Digital Technology Co., Ltd. (the "***Hua Qi***") filed a cancellation action against the Disputed Mark to the TRAB under SAIC of PRC (the "***Appeal Board***") on October 23, 2002. The cancellation ground was that the Disputed Mark was composed of two Chinese characters with the first character ("YOU") meaning "excellent" in Chinese and the second character ("PAN") referring to "discs" in the Chinese language. The second character is therefore a directly descriptive of the electronic storage device and is a standard term in the computer industry. Furthermore, the English term "USB" is an abbreviation for "Universal Serial Bus" and is a new standard description for the computer saving/storage device. Given the PAN character refers to a digital saving and storage device in the Chinese language, the name "U PAN" will naturally be accepted by the product promoters or the public and will almost always be incorporated in any product names involving mobile saving/storage devices with USB interface in the market. The English letter "U" is phonetically identical to the YOU Chinese character (i.e., the first character in the Disputed Mark; meaning "excellent" or "superior"). Accordingly, the Disputed Mark directly describes the underlying products and is indistinguishable from the general term "U PAN." The Disputed Mark has become a generic term for any flash memory devices, and it does not have any secondary meaning to allow consumers to distinguish its producers or retailers. In light of the above, Hua Qi sought to cancel the Disputed Mark.

Netac responded to the cancellation action by pointing out that the Disputed Mark was a special term for its patented technology; the Disputed Mark therefore bears no relationship to the generic term of flash memory devices. The Disputed Mark does not directly describe the functionality, purpose, and other characteristics of its underlying products and has therefore satisfied the distinctiveness requirement under the Trademark Law.

In response to the above defense, Hua Qi countered by pointing out that the Disputed Mark had violated Article 11 of the Trademark Law after it was registered; it is therefore irrelevant whether or not the Disputed Mark was composed of special terms at the time it was applied for registration. The Disputed Mark is descriptive of the quality, functionality, and purpose of the underlying product and is therefore a direct violation of Article 11(2) of the Trademark Law. Additionally, when using the mark, the trademark owner purposefully diluted the distinctiveness of the Disputed Mark; in fact, it had been actively using the Disputed Mark simply as a generic term. This had resulted in the public's perception and use of the characters in the Disputed Mark simply as a generic phrase. Indeed, over time, the Disputed Mark had become a generic term for the underlying products. The Disputed Mark had lost its distinctiveness; it had violated Article 11 of the Trademark Law after its registration and should be cancelled.

The Appeal Board made a decision on October 13, 2004 (No. 5569; 2004)(the "***First Appeal Decision***"). The Decision pointed out that the Disputed Mark had become a generic term for certain products in the market, and it should no longer maintain its registration as a trademark. Furthermore, the Decision noted that since the Disputed Mark had become a generic term for mobile saving/storage devices for computers, its registration in respect to computers and computer accessories was no longer distinctive. The Disputed Mark should therefore be cancelled in accordance with Article 11 Section 1(1) and 1(3), Article 41 Section (1), and Article 43 of the Trademark Law.

Netac filed an administrative action to challenge the First Appeal Decision.

COURT DECISION

Beijing No. 1 Intermediate People's Court (the "***Intermediate Court***") pointed out that the trademark dispute system was designed to protect legal rights of the trademark owner, and to prevent unfair competition in the trademark field. When reviewing the trademark dispute cases, examiners should abide by the fairness and just principle, follow the process and procedures as stated in the Trademark Law, the "Regulation for the Implementation of the Trademark Law of PRC" and the "PRC Trademark Review Rules;" the above rules and regulations are in existence to ensure and protect the legitimate rights of the parties involved. In the subject case, Hua Qi's initial position to have the Disputed Mark cancelled was different from that stated in its counter arguments. The former position was that the Disputed Mark lacked distinctiveness when it was seeking registration as a trademark; the latter, however, pointed out that the Disputed Mark should be cancelled due to the improper use by its owner, and the mark had therefore lost its distinctiveness after it was registered. The difference in both positions remains even though both arguments centered on the distinctiveness issue of a trademark. As a result of the different positions, the trademark owner would be required to take a different approach in defending its registration. The evidence the trademark owner submits may be helpful to defend the arguments advanced by the petitioner; however, the same evidence would not necessarily be helpful to defend or fully address the counter arguments later submitted by the petitioner. To allow an effective defense by the trademark owner, it should be given sufficient time to defend not only the arguments laid out in the initial cancellation decision, but also those submitted in the later arguments. The Appeal Board should have given the trademark owner more time to defend its registration in the event the petitioner in a cancellation action had changed its position and provided different arguments and evidence. The Trademark Law, the Regulation for the Implementation of the Trademark Law of PRC, and the Rules for the Review and Hearing of Trademarks did not provide a specific timeframe for the trademark owner to respond to the change in the petitioner's position in a cancellation action. In light of the lack of a specific time requirement under the law and based on the principle of fairness, the trademark owner should have been given sufficient time to provide further arguments in response to the counter arguments as, discussed under Article 32 of the Regulation for the Implementation of the Trademark Law of PRC - namely, "*any arguments and supplementary supporting materials should be referenced in the petition or the response brief, and should be provided in full within three months after the submission of the petition or response brief.*" In the subject case, the Appeal Board only gave Netac thirty days to provide its defense arguments and supporting materials; the short time frame therefore violated the fairness principle and the First Appeal Decision should therefore be vacated. In light of the above, the court did not discuss any substantive issues raised in the First Appeal Decision. Given the First Appeal Decision was an administrative decision rendered by the Appeal Board in response to the cancellation action filed by Hua Qi, the case would revert back to the review stage. The Appeal Board should make a decision with respect to Hua Qi's cancellation petition. The First Appeal Decision was cancelled based on Article 54 Section 2(3) of the Administrative Litigation Law.

Hua Qi filed an appeal to the Beijing High Court (the "***High Court***"). In the second court appeal process, Hua Qi petitioned to withdraw its appeal. On August 23, 2007, the High Court approved the withdrawal petition. Since then, Hua Qi has changed its name to Patriot Digital Technology Company ("***Patriot***").

On March 15, 2010, the Appeal Board made a decision (the "***Second Appeal Decision***") reaffirming its position in the First Appeal Decision to cancel the Disputed Mark. Netac decided to challenge the decision by filing an administrative lawsuit.

During the lawsuit, Patriot petitioned to withdraw its cancellation action against the Disputed Mark on July 11, 2011. The Appeal Board therefore reached a decision (the "***Third Appeal Decision***"); the Board notified the parties that it had decided to vacate the Second Appeal Decision given the withdrawal filed by Patriot; the Appeal Board also notified the parties that it had suspended the review of the cancellation action against the Disputed Mark. On July 13, 2011, Netac filed a formal withdrawal petition with the court. On July 31, 2011, the Intermediate Court approved Netac's withdrawal petition.

ANALYSIS & INSIGHT

According to Article 9 of the Trademark Law, a trademark application shall be distinctive in order to be approved as a trademark. However, once the mark is approved for registration, it can still lose its distinctiveness and become a generic term due to its owner's improper advertising, lack of management, ineffective protection of the trademark, or other factors (either involving competitors or the general public or both). A registered trademark will no longer function as a source identifier once it has become the generic term for the designated goods and or services; it therefore has lost its distinctiveness. Any third party (individual or organization) can file a cancellation action with the Trademark Office seeking to have the registrations cancelled.[129]

In the 2013 amendments to the Trademark Law, the amendments added one more situation in Article 49(2) where a registered trademark can be cancelled by any third party (individual or organization) if it has become a generic description for its designated products and/or services. The situation is generally referred to as the cancellation of a generic term degenerated from a registered trademark or "degeneration of a trademark."

Given there was no prior regulation in the Trademark Law, the Regulation for the Implementation of the Trademark Law of PRC and the related judicial interpretations, where a registered trademark could be cancelled due to its degeneration as a generic term, has no precedents. In the subject case, even though the petitioner in the cancellation action submitted arguments noting that the Disputed Mark lost its distinctiveness after registration, the court simply reviewed the procedural issues related to the case; the court did not take any clear position as to whether or not the Disputed Mark could and should be cancelled due to its degeneration status. Accordingly, we would need more judicial interpretations and guidance as to the exact requirements that would trigger a cancellation of a registered trademark due to its degeneration status as a generic term.

1. It Is a Value Proposition.

The Trademark Law respects the established order in the Marketplace by legally recognizing the distinctiveness associated with a trademark can be lost and thereby, allowing the mark to be cancelled.

Based on the related interpretations provided by the legislative Branch with respect to Article 49(2) of the Trademark Law,[130] the reason the new cancellation ground was incorporated was because the legislative Branch wanted to ensure a trademark would still be able to maintain its distinctiveness after registration. The principle function of a trademark is to function as a source identifier for the underlying goods and/or services; once a mark has degenerated to a common reference for some

129. The legislative affairs commission of the Standing Committee of the National People's Congress, ed., INTERPRETATION OF THE PEOPLE'S REPUBLIC OF CHINA TRADEMARK LAW, 97, Law Press (2013).

130. *Ibid.*

particulars products and/or services, it has become a common symbol referring to certain types of products and/or services recognized by the public and part of the public resources - accordingly, the mark can no longer function as a trademark to identify the specific goods and/or services. Generally speaking, a mark cannot serve both roles of being a trademark as well as a generic common description of the underlying products and/or services. In light of the above, when a mark has degenerated to become a common description of some of its designated products and/or services, one must strike a balance between the exclusive rights associated with the trademark (the rights that the trademark owner has already obtained and are legally effective) and the general public's interest to conveniently and efficiency use such a phrase to quickly reference the underlying products and/or services. Typically speaking, public interest comes before a private party's interest regarding the latter's rights for the trademark. The priority status given to the public interest is merely the outcome - the primary reason the public's interest is treated as the priority is because the objectives of the Trademark Law and the trademark system are meant to maintain and respect the market order that already has taken place and has already been established in the society. Based on the above premise, since it is already a market reality that the trademark had degenerated to become a generic phrase, the trademark law will respect such a market conclusion and the associated public interests.

In reality, the law's respect for the market order that had been objectively formed and established was a key factor in determining various conflicting values and interests in the trademark area - especially with respect to the distinctiveness associated with a trademark. For example, a mark that is inherently indistinctive can still become distinctive through use. In other words, the natural progression and evolution of the marketplace can be a primary contributing factor allowing a mark to "obtain" distinctiveness and thereby becoming a registered trademark.[131] Conversely, a mark can also lose its registered trademark status when its distinctiveness is "lost" in the marketplace - i.e., when the mark has become a generic phrase referring to its designated goods and/or services as part of the evolution of the marketplace. Given the marketplace has already made a choice, the Trademark Law respects such a natural objective evolution process and was amended to address this situation where a registered trademark can be cancelled when its distinctiveness has been "lost" and is part of the established market reality.

2. The Scope to Cancel the Degenerated Mark.

The scope should correspond to the level of degeneration.

One of the key issues in applying Article 49(2) of the Trademark Law is determining the proper scope to cancel the registered trademark. The scope of the mark to be cancelled as a registered trademark should be limited to the underlying products on which the mark is used as a generic term. If a mark is registered with respect to various kinds of products, and the mark has become a generic phrase only about one

131. Case Index: Beijing High People's Court, Gao Xing Zhong Zi [2012] No. 1750.

type of the products, the cancellation should be restricted to that certain type of product and not the rest. In other words, the cancellation should not apply to the remaining products where the mark still maintains its distinctiveness and therefore, should still be recognized as a registered trademark. Put simply, the extent of cancellation should correspond to the extent the mark has become a generic term; it is also important to take into account the extent to which the mark has lost its distinctiveness when making the determination. It would certainly be contrary to the legislative intent of the law if a mark had become a generic description simply to one of its designated products but is cancelled as a trademark in respect to all of its designated products. Take APPLE's Chinese mark as an example, the mark clearly does not have distinctiveness for fruit products; however, it is a distinctive trademark for portable communication devices. The mark therefore should not be cancelled or denied its distinctiveness in respect to the communication products simply because the mark is not a distinctive trademark in respect to fruit products. However, if the mark has lost its distinctiveness and has become a generic phrase for one type of product and such product is similar or related to the rest of the designated products, it is possible (and certainly logical) to cancel all of the registered products as long as the relatedness and similarities between the products have been duly considered.

3. Possible Reversion.

It is possible to avoid cancellation of a registered trademark as long as the mark has regained its distinctiveness.

As discussed above, although it is possible for a trademark to lose its registration status when it has become a generic term for certain types of products and/or services, the status is by no means set in stone. The possibility certainly exists to "reverse" this outcome. As discussed above, Article 49(2) of the Trademark Law has been included so as to respect the natural progression of the marketplace and to respect the already established market order – this is why the law has been amended to allow cancellation when a registered trademark has lost its distinctiveness in the marketplace. However, the end goal of the system is not meant to cancel a registered trademark. On the contrary, the system is in place to honor the established market order that is fluid and ever-changing. In other words, if the market order has undergone tremendous change prior to the mark at issue being cancelled – such as the owner launches a commercial campaign to revert the degeneration status of the mark, or a new generic term has been established to refer to the underlying products and/or services and that the relevant public is now using the new name instead to refer to such products and/or services – the mark should not be cancelled as a result of its supposedly degeneration status. This is because there have been some significant changes regarding the "loss" of distinctiveness associated with the trademark. The trademark owner has legally obtained the exclusive rights, with respect to the trademark, that are legitimate protectable property rights. In situations where there is no other right to which priority should be given, the owner's exclusive rights associated with the trademark should be respected, maintained and protected. It is not yet known whether or not the above situation is possible when the trademark owner can revert the degeneration status of its trademark prior to the cancellation action taking effect, it is nevertheless important to recognize this possibility which relates to the protection of the owner's rights to the trademark.

As pointed out by an American scholar: "A trademark should function as an adjective to the designated products and/or services; it should be used together with the noun referring to the designated products and/or services. If a product or service does indeed appear the first time, or that the current generic phrase describing the products and/or services is not memorable or cannot be easily pronounced such as the drug name "aspirin," the public will take the trademark and use it as a generic term which will then lead to the loss of distinctiveness and exclusive rights associated with the trademark. In order to prevent this from happening, it is advisable to create yet another generic term and to encourage the public to use this generic term rather than the trademark at issue to describe the underlying goods and/or services."[132]

132. Paul J. Lerner, Alexander I. Poltorak, Yu Dongzhi trans., ESSENTIALS OF INTELLECTUAL PROPERTY, China Renmin University Press (2004); quoted from Wu Xinhua, *Comparison of Trademark and Generic Name for Product – Note of Examining the Trademark Dispute over No. 1509704 "You Pan in Chinese characters,"* China Trademark, Vol. 10, 2007.

13. Cancellation of a Trademark Registration due to Three Years of Non-use

Administrative litigation filed by CONSOLIDATED ARTISTS B.V. seeking to cancel SONNETI INTERNATIONAL S.A.'s trademark registration for "MANGO"

- First Instance: Beijing No. 1 Intermediate People's Court (No. 10; 2011) - Decided on December 20, 2011
- Second Instance: Beijing High People's Court (No. 1820; 2012) - Decided on December 19, 2012

BACKGROUND

Da Yi International Co. Ltd. ("***Da Yi***") filed a trademark application for "MANGO" (the "***Disputed Trademark***") under Application Number 634764 on April 15, 1992. The application covers Class 25 clothing products, as well as underwear and hats. The Disputed Trademark was approved for registration by the Trademark Office on March 20, 1993; the exclusive rights of the Disputed Trademark expire on March 19, 2013.

On April 8, 2003, the Trademark Office accepted the application filed by CONSOLIDATED ARTISTS B.V. (the "***Art Company***") seeking to cancel the MANGO registration due to nonuse for three consecutive years.

On March 1, 2004, the Trademark Office decided to cancel the MANGO registration (Nonuse Cancellation Decision No. 2003002525) because Da Yi failed to timely submit any evidence to support the use situation of its trademark registration. Da Yi filed an appeal to the TRAB (the "***Appeal Board***") on March 19, 2004. In the appeal, Da Yi pointed out that its mark was in use during the challenged period (April 8, 2000–April 7, 2003) by its authorized licensee and sublicensee in Mainland China in respect to the challenged goods; products bearing the mark were even exported from China to Panama. Da Yi has submitted the below use evidence to the Appeal Board:

(1) A copy of the Trademark License and Use Permission Agreement between Da Yi and SONNETI INTERNATIONAL S.A. ("***Sonneti***") dated as of March 19, 1993. Da Yi has provided the agreement in its original English version and the corresponding Chinese version. The agreement states that Da Yi allows Sonneti nonexclusive rights to use the MANGO mark in respect to the clothing articles, underwear products, and footwear in Mainland China (excluding Taiwan, Hong Kong, and Macau). The agreement also allows Sonneti to grant further permissions to its sublicensees' retail providers. The term of the agreement is twenty years, from March 19, 1993 to March 19, 2013. On the top right corner of each page in the agreement, the following information is listed: "Telephone: 441-6796/6866/6286 Fax: (507)441-6340 E-MAIL: sonneti@sinfo.net" ("***Evidence One***").

(2) An original certified agreement between Sonneti (buyer) and Shaoxing Kai Li Ya International Trade Materials Co., Ltd. (seller). The agreement clearly

discusses the MANGO trademark registration and product model information bearing the mark, i.e., M-6602 and M-6603 showing the products being exported from Shanghai China to Panama ("***Evidence Two***").

(3) A certified invoice showing Sonneti purchasing products produced by Shaoxing Kai Li Ya International Trade Materials Co., Ltd. bearing the MANGO mark on November 26, 2001 ("***Evidence Three***").

(4) A certified invoice showing Sonneti purchasing products produced by Shaoxing Kai Li Ya International Trade Materials Co., Ltd. bearing the MANGO mark on March 3, 2003 (loading port: Shanghai/Ningbo; destination port: Panama); the product model includes the above-mentioned M-6603 along with pictures showing products bearing the MANGO mark ("***Evidence Four***").

On August 24, 2004, the Disputed Trademark was approved by the Trademark Office to be transferred to Sonneti. On December 29, 2009, Sonneti filed an application to the Appeal Board declaring its status as transferee (and owner) of the MANGO trademark and its involvement in the nonuse cancellation proceeding as well as its responsibility for the review consequences. The Appeal Board has approved the application and updated the record to reflect Sonneti as the applicant of the subject case.

Art Company filed response arguments to the Appeal Board questioning the authenticity of Evidence One; it further pointed out that the email address sonneti@sinfo.net listed in the 1993 agreement did not exist at that time since the website, sinfo.net, was not registered until 1995. To support this, Art Company has provided printout copies of the domain name record showing registration information relating to sinfo.net.

The Appeal Board made a decision concerning the MANGO registration on May 4, 2010 (No. 09112; 2010) (the "***Appeal Board's Decision***"). The Appeal Board's Decision maintained the registration of the MANGO registration in respect to clothing and underwear products because the evidence was sufficient to support use of the mark in respect to such products between April 8, 2000 and April 7, 2003. The Appeal Board, however, cancelled the trademark registration in respect to the hat products. The Appeal Board cited Articles 44(1)(4) and 49 of the Trademark Law and Article 41 of the Regulation on the Implementation of the Trademark Law to support its decision.

Art Company appealed the decision to the court along with the following evidence:

(1) Notarized evidence (No. 5966; 2010) showing the phone number in Panama has increased from six digits to seven digits in 1995.

(2) Notarized evidence (No. 1169; 2011) showing the phone number in Panama has increased from six digits to seven digits in 1995 and the domain information showing the sinfo.net domain was registered on August 24, 1995.

(3) The corporate record of Da Yi as reflected in Hong Kong; this evidence shows that the address information listed in the corporate record does not match the one provided in the supporting evidence that Da Yi submitted to the Appeal Board.

COURT DECISION

Beijing No. 1 Intermediate People's Court (the "***Intermediate Court***") was of the view that the Appeal Board could not justify its decision based simply on Evidence One. Furthermore, the Disputed Trademark was not transferred to Sonneti until August 24, 2004; this shows that the submitted evidence is insufficient to support that the mark was already put to use by Sonneti between April 8, 2000 and April 7, 2003. Even assuming Evidence Two, Three, and Four were sufficient to prove that Sonneti had indeed entrusted Shaoxing Kai Li Ya International Trade Materials Co., Ltd. to manufacture pants for men and other products bearing the MANGO mark during the relevant period, the evidence was not sufficient to show that Sonneti had legitimate and effective control regarding the use and granting use of the MANGO mark. Unauthorized use of a trademark means the mark has not been used in accordance with the trademark owner's control and permission, so the use shall not be deemed as a valid use of the mark at issue. Use in respect to other products (i.e., products that fall outside the scope of registration) is not a valid use of the registered trademark either; rather, it is use in respect to unregistered trademarks or use relating to other trademarks. Even assuming the products in use are similar to the registered products, such use is not sufficient to allow consumers to associate the registered products with the disputed trademark so as to allow the MANGO mark to function as a trademark; accordingly, it follows that the use in respect to unregistered products shall not be deemed as use of the disputed mark. In the Appeal Board's Decision, the board decided to recognize use on underwear as valid use sufficient to defend the nonuse cancellation action because the products in use (pants for men) were related to underwear – i.e., the registered products. The Appeal Board's Decision lacks proper factual and legal support. The Intermediate Court therefore decided to revoke the Appeal Board's Decision and request the Appeal Board to make a new decision.

The Appeal Board and Sonneti decided to challenge the Intermediate Court's decision and filed an appeal. Beijing High People's Court ("***High Court***") noted that the owner of the MANGO registration was Da Yi from April 8, 2000 to April 7, 2003. Although in the review proceeding, Da Yi provided the trademark license and use agreement between itself and Sonneti during the 2000–2003 period, the Art Company has provided sufficient evidence to challenge the authenticity of the 1993 agreement. The authenticity of the agreement therefore could not be verified, given Sonneti has not provided any response arguments to counter the Art Company's challenge. Even assuming the 1993 agreement between Da Yi and Sonneti could be authenticated, verified and confirmed, there is still insufficient evidence to show that there is valid trademark use agreement between Sonneti and Shaoxing Kai Li Ya International Trade Materials Co., Ltd. Even assuming Sonneti does obtain the right from Da Yi to grant further use of the MANGO mark to others and Shaoxing Kai Li Ya International Trade Materials Co., Ltd.'s use of the MANGO mark is sufficient to prove that it has obtained permission to use the mark from Sonneti, the use agreement and relationship between a trademark's authorized user and its sublicensee only, at best, proves the buyer-seller relationship; it does not constitute valid use of a trademark under the Trademark Law. The submitted evidence is insufficient to prove use of the MANGO mark by Shaoxing Kai Li Ya International Trade Materials Co., Ltd., nor is it sufficient to show that Shaoxing Kai Li Ya International Trade Materials Co., Ltd.'s use of the mark has obtained valid permission from the trademark owner and the use was carried out in accordance with the trademark owner's desire so as to constitute valid use of a trademark under the Trademark Law. In light of the above, the High Court maintained the original decision and rejected the appeal.

ANALYSIS & INSIGHT

Article 44(4) of the 2001 Trademark Law and Article 39(2) of the 2002 Regulation on the Implementation of the Trademark Law state that any third party can petition to the Trademark Office to cancel a trademark registration so long as the registered trademark has not been put to use for three consecutive years. The Trademark Office will then notify the trademark owner, and the owner would then have two months (from the receipt of notification from the Trademark Office) to provide use materials or explanations to justify the nonuse situation. The Trademark Office can cancel a registered trademark so long as the owner fails to provide any use material, or fails to provide any valid use materials or fails to provide a legitimate reason explaining the nonuse situation. Article 49(2) of the 2013 Trademark Law inherits the above-discussed nonuse cancellation action from the 2001 Trademark Law and provides two specific improvements:

(1) The 2013 Trademark Law has expanded the scope of coverage in the 2001 law by amending the following language: "[T]he Trademark Office shall order rectification of the situation within a specified period or shall revoke the registered trademark" to "the Trademark Office shall revoke the mark in accordance with a third party's application." This means that the Trademark Office would not actively survey the registrations and cancel any marks that have not yet put to use; the Trademark Office would only cancel marks based on nonuse in accordance with a third party's application.

(2) The 2013 Trademark Law has allowed an owner to maintain its registration so long as it can provide legitimate explanations. In other words, the Trademark Office will no longer cancel marks so long as the owner can provide legitimate explanations[133] justifying its three years' of nonuse. This situation typically

133. Author's footnote: 全国人民代表大会常务委员会法制工作委员会 [The legislative affairs commission of the Standing Committee of the National People's Congress, ed.], 中华人民共和国商标法释义[INTERPRETATION OF THE PEOPLE'S REPUBLIC OF CHINA TRADEMARK LAW] 98 (法律出版社[Law Press])(2013).

occurs when the use of the medicine is delayed due to the related governmental approval process.

In nonuse cancellation cases, the focus is on use so as to decide the exact types of use materials that can be accepted and recognized as valid use in defending a nonuse cancellation action. The consensus is that the use of the trademark must be "open, authentic, and legal" so as to allow the use to be recognized and accepted by the courts.[134] In practice, the following principles derived from the precedents should be very helpful in determining the validity of use materials when a trademark registrant is seeking to defend a nonuse cancellation action.

A. Use Must Be Sufficient to Allow the Disputed Mark to Function as a Source Identifier.

Use of a registered trademark includes the use of the mark by the registrant itself and through other authorized licensees. However, such use must allow the mark to commercially function as a source identifier, allowing consumers to distinguish the registered goods and/or services from those provided by other marks, in order to allow the use to be recognized as legally acceptable valid use of the mark. If the use is simply allowing others to use the mark or assigning the right to use the mark to others, and neither the transferor nor the transferee has put the mark to actual use, this should not be qualified as valid use of a registered trademark. The courts in fact have already provided a clear guidance in this respect: "*if the use simply governs the relationship between transferor and transferee, or between licensor and licensee, and does not allow the mark to function as a source identifier for consumers, such use shall not be regarded or accepted as valid use of a trademark.*"[135] In other words, the valid "legal" use of a registered trademark must be open, involving the general public, concerning the registered goods or services, and thereby, allowing the mark to function as a source identifier. Trademarks play the role of a social medium, bridging the gap between goods or services and consumers in today's market economy; trademarks therefore are not the target itself in a transaction. The use of a mark must allow it to function as a source identifier to carry out its legal purpose; otherwise, it is simply a type of "property" defined by the Property Law in today's world.[136]

Even though the agreement between licensors and licensees, or between the principle party and the party being entrusted to manufacture products bearing the mark, does allow commercial transactions involving products or services bearing the trademark at issue, such use is typically not recognized as valid use of a trademark.

134. Author's footnote: Case Index: the Supreme People's Court, Xing Jian Zi [2007] No. 184-1; 胡刚[Hu Gang],商标法意义上的使用：" 公开、真实、合法"——近期司法判例解读 [Trademark Use: "Open, Authentic and Legal" - Interpretation of Recent Judicial Precedents], 中国专利与商标[China Patent and Trademark] Vol. 3, 2012, at 80–87.
135. Author's footnote: Case Index: Beijing High People's Court, Xing Zhong Zi [2006] No. 78.
136. Author's footnote: 周波[Zhou Bo], 商标使用应发挥商品来源识别作用[Trademark Use Should Play the Role on the Identification of Products' Source], 中华商标[China Trademark] Vol. 1, 2013 at 72.

This is because this type of agreement involving use of the mark between certain parties in the market place and the relationship is not established with the goal to allow the disputed mark to function as a source identifier in the market place. It is therefore difficult to determine if the mark has indeed played the role as a source identifier and the use is therefore not likely to be accepted as a valid use of a registered trademark. The courts have expressed and supported the above view in the cancellation action concerning "T.U.F & Design" (Registration Number 1937137): "*[E]ven though the agreement between licensor and licensee involves products to be manufactured bearing the disputed mark and be used in the commercial transactions, this should not be deemed to allow the disputed mark to function as a source identifier. Accordingly, such a use shall not be regarded as valid use under the Trademark Law.*"[137] The subject case confirms the above view; it is undoubtedly yet another confirmation that the use of a trademark must be "open" in order to be accepted as valid use of a registered trademark.

B. Trademark Owner Should Have Real and Clear Intent to Use the Disputed Mark.

In most situations, valid use of a registered trademark should not be merely symbolic. In the appeal of cancellation action involving "BIG BRIDGE in Chinese characters, DAQIAO and Design" (Registration Number 1240054), the second level of court pointed out the following: "*[T]he use of a registered trademark should be authentic and offer some clear indication that the use of the mark is directed or under control by the trademark owner. Such use is sufficient to demonstrate the connection between the mark at issue and its registered goods or services so as to allow the public to establish association between the mark and its designated goods or services. Uses that are merely symbolic or are carried out primarily to maintain registration of a trademark shall not be deemed as a valid legal use of a trademark. To determine if the use of a trademark is merely symbolic, one should consider the subjective intent of the party carrying out the use of the mark, the way the mark is being used as well as other relevant factors.*"[138] In light of the above, the court decided to cancel the above BIG BRIDGE registration on the ground of nonuse. This is because the registrant only provided one-time advertisement on a newspaper concerning the use mark and the total sales revenue figure in the amount of RMB 1,800 (approximately USD 244); none of the above was deemed by the court to constitute valid use of the registered trademark. In the appeal of nonuse cancellation action concerning "TAMASHI" (Registration Number 1457817), the second level of court decided to cancel the registration. This is because the court did not consider mere one copy of the sales receipt was sufficient to constitute use of the trademark in the three-year period. Even assuming the sales receipt and its

137. Author's footnote: Case Index: Beijing High People's Court, Xing Zhong Zi [2011] No. 866.
138. Author's footnote: Case Index: Beijing High People's Court, Xing Zhong Zi [2010] No. 294.

corresponding sales figure can be verified, the use of the mark is merely symbolic and primarily carried out to maintain the trademark registration.[139]

Most of the courts today tend to regard a use merely symbolic if the use is carried out within a relatively short period of time prior to the filing of nonuse cancellation action. Even so, in order to decide whether or not the use of the trademark is "authentic," the focus should be on whether or not the trademark owner has a clear intent to use the disputed mark. The goal of a nonuse cancellation action is to remove trademark registrations that have not been put to use for a sustained period of time so as not to result in unnecessary waste and monopoly of the legal resources. Following the above principle, it is therefore important not to deprive a trademark owner's registration right by cancelling its registration even though there are not a large amount of evidence to support use, so long as the owner has demonstrated it has a clear intent to use the mark and the reason there is not a large amount of use evidence is due to some subjective and objective reasons. The 9th Circuit Court in the USA has offered some clear guidance in this respect: *so long as the use is authentic and can clearly demonstrate the owner's intent to use the mark, the information shall be deemed sufficient to defend a non-use cancellation action even though the mark has only been put to use in one occasion.*[140] Similarly, the Court of Justice of the European Communities also supports this view and notes that there should not be any minimum evidence requirement for a trademark owner to defend its registration; rather, the decision maker should consider all relevant factors and if there is a commercially legitimate reason to explain nonuse, some minimum use, or even an importer's use in certain countries would be sufficient to defend the cancellation action.[141] Accordingly, the key focus should be on whether or not the registrant has a clear intent to use the mark, and it plays an important role on distinguishing the minimum quantity of the trademark use and a merely symbolic use. Also, if the trademark owner has already put the mark to use before the filing of cancellation action and can provide valid evidence demonstrating the use of the mark has lasted a certain period of time, it should be sufficient to defend the cancellation action because such information has satisfied the legislative intent to supervise the use situation of a trademark. If so, the registration of the mark shall be maintained.

C. The Review Relating to Use of a Trademark Should Be Governed by Trademark Law Only.

The Law gives protection to the monopoly right of a trademark; the use of the trademark should therefore be lawful. However, what constitutes "lawful" use of a trademark is not straightforward - the view has since undergone some changes, as outlined below.

139. Author's footnote: Case Index: Beijing High People's Court, Xing Zhong Zi [2011] No. 264.
140. J. Thomas McCarthy: *McCarthy on Trademarks and Unfair Competition* (4th Edition). 2012: §17:14.
141. Author's footnote: 李顺德等[Li Shunde et al.], 欧盟知识产权法 [EU INTELLECTUAL PROPERTY LAW] (法律出版社 [Law Press] 484 (2010).

In the appeal of nonuse cancellation action for "KANG WANG in Chinese characters (康王)" (Registration Number 738354), the SPC held the following view: *"Based on Article 45 of the Trademark Law, the determination concerning whether or not the use of a trademark is lawful shall not be confined to Trademark Law alone and its related regulations. Recognizing use of a trademark in situations or activities that are not allowed under the mandatory and prohibited provisions of other types of law would be deemed as an encouragement or even condolence of such unlawful activities. This is clearly contrary to the intent of the Trademark Law."*[142] Following the above principle, the court did not recognize the use of the trademark as a valid lawful use because the use took place in activities that were in violation of the mandatory provisions in cosmetics manufacturing and sanitary license regulations.

Despite the above, the SPC modified its view in the appeal of nonuse cancellation action concerning "KA SI TE in Chinese characters (卡斯特)" (Registration Number 1372099). The Court held that the goal of Article 44(4) of the Trademark Law was to "liberate trademark resources, remove trademark registrations that have not been put to use." Accordingly, the cancellation action is merely a means to achieve the above goals rather than the objectives of the law. Following the above principle, so long as the trademark owner has openly put the trademark to authentic use in the commercial activities and the use of the trademark itself does not violate any trademark laws or regulation, the owner has fulfilled its obligation to use the mark. In respect to the issue concerning whether or not the underlying sales activities, the owner's business or the related import activities are lawful, it is outside the scope of Article 44(4) of the Trademark Law and should not be taken into consideration in determining the validity with respect to use of a trademark."[143]

Although different bodies of law should coordinate and work hand-in-hand with one another, each body of law has its own objectives. It is therefore inappropriate and impractical to require the subject of one body of law to also consider and fulfill its obligations under all types of law. Turning to the "lawful" use of a trademark, the decision maker should consider primarily the trademark laws and regulations. The SPC has decided to let go of some inappropriate and unnecessary considerations in the Ka SI TE appeal case and gave the Trademark Law its full control. We recognize and support the Supreme People Court's effort and decision in the Ka SI TE case.

D. The Use of the Mark Should Highlight the Prominent Elements of the Disputed Mark.

The use of a trademark in the everyday commercial life will necessarily involve some changes and variation from the registration form. The Trademark Law, however, has provided some clear guidance about this situation, i.e., the use of a mark should conform with its registration form. If the use is different from the registration form, the owner should also seek registration of the variations. In addition, the Trademark Law

142. Author's footnote: Case Index: the Supreme People's Court, Xing Jian Zi [2007] No. 184-1.
143. Author's footnote: Case Index: the Supreme People's Court, Zhi Xing Zi [2010] No. 55.

allows the trademark authorities to cancel registration of a trademark if the use is different from the form registered and the owner has failed to modify the use within the time limit. However, in respect to the nonuse cancellation action, the goal is to encourage use of a registered trademark so as to avoid unnecessary waste of the public resources. In such cases, so long as the use still incorporates the prominent elements of a registered trademark, the use would be deemed sufficient even though the mark in use has some slight differences from the form registered. On the contrary, if a use of the mark does not fully embody the prominent elements of a registered trademark, such use shall not be regarded as valid use to maintain the trademark registration. In the appeal of cancellation action involving "TIE LI SHI in Chinese characters (铁力士) and TINIT" (Registration Number 1092823), the court has decided not to recognize the use of the trademark. This is because, based on the evidence submitted by the trademark registrant, the mark in use in advertisement only includes a combined form of TIE LI SHI in Chinese characters（鐵力士） and the English "LISHIX." The second level of court held the view that although the use of the mark was sufficient to highlight the Chinese characters in the registration, there was sufficient difference between the English texts as shown in the trademark registration versus the text in use (*TINIT v. LISHIX*). The mark in use therefore was insufficient to embody the English text, which is also a prominent element in the original registration. Accordingly, the court did not support the evidence as valid use of the trademark and decided to cancel the registration despite that the registration number was marked in the advertisement.[144]

144. Author's footnote: Case Index: Beijing High People's Court, Xing Zhong Zi [2013] No. 303.

CHAPTER 5
Invalidation of a Registered Trademark

14. There Is no Time Limit for the Owner of a Well-Known Trademark to Bring an Invalidation Action Against a Bad-Faith Registration

Appeal of administrative litigation regarding the trademark invalidation action filed by Sichuan Mian-Zhu Jiannanchun Distillery Co., Ltd. against a trademark registration for "JINZHU in English and Chinese characters" – the registration belongs to Shenzhen Bao Song Li Industrial Co., Ltd.

- First Instance: Beijing No. 1 Intermediate People's Court (No. 3359; 2012) – Decided on December 18, 2012

BACKGROUND

Sichuan Bishan County Distillery applied for a trademark application for "JIN ZHU in English and Chinese characters and Design" (Registration Number 212759; *see* Image One below; the "***Disputed Mark***") on February 15, 1984; it was approved for registration on September 15, 1984, in connection with Class 33 alcohol and liquor products. The owner of the Disputed Mark later changed its name in March 1995 to Chongqing Bishan County distillery. The Disputed Mark was assigned to Sichuan Mian-zhu Mian Cellar Distillery in October 1999, to Chongqing Chuanshi Industrial Co., Ltd. in July 2000, and finally, to Shenzhen Bao Song Li Industrial Co., Ltd. (the "***Owner***") in September 2008.

Sichuan Mian-Zhu County distillery applied for "MIAN-ZHU in Chinese characters and Design" (Registration Number 112495; *see* Image Two below; the "***Cited Mark***") and the Cited Mark was approved for registration on October 31, 1979, in connection with Class 33 alcohol and liquor products. Through various assignment, renewals, and changes of ownership, Sichuan Mian-Zhu Jiannanchun Distillery Co., Ltd. became the owner of the Cited Mark (the "***Applicant***").

Image One	Image Two
Disputed Mark	Cited Mark

On June 7, 2010, the Applicant filed an invalidation action seeking to cancel the Disputed Mark. Its primary grounds to support the invalidation actions are summarized below:

The "Mian-Zhu" liquor has a long history in China, and the brand has been used exclusively by the Applicant since 1954 in China. The trademark application associated with the brand was approved for registration on October 31, 1979. In other words, the Mian-Zhu brand had already achieved the well-known status in China prior to the filing date of the Disputed Mark. The Owner adopted the Disputed Mark, which is closely similar to the Cited Mark; furthermore, the use of the Disputed Mark copies unique packaging design of the Applicant's Cited Mark which has already led to consumer confusion and caused a significant impact on the Applicant's legitimate rights. The above situation has fulfilled the situation described in Article 13, Section 2 of the 2001 Trademark Law. Accordingly, the Disputed Mark should be cancelled.

The Owner did not file any response to the invalidation action within the time period.

The TRAB under SAIC of PRC (the "***Appeal Board***") reviewed the invalidation action. The Appeal Board pointed out that the Disputed Mark was approved for registration on September 15, 1984; in other words, the Disputed Mark had been registered for more than five years by the time the Applicant raised the invalidation action on June 7, 2010. Despite this, based on Article 41 Section 2 of the 2001 Trademark Law, a trademark owner or any interested parties can raise an invalidation action to the Appeal Board to invalidate a registered trademark within the first five years of the disputed mark's registration on the ground that the registration of the mark has violated Articles 13, 15, and 31 of the Trademark Law. An owner of a well-known trademark, however, is not limited by the five-year time period and can raise an invalidation action at any time against a bad faith registration.

Based on the evidence provided by the Applicant, it is clear that Mian Zhu Da Qu has enjoyed a long history in connection with liquor and alcohol products in China. The Mian Zhu Da Qu branded liquor has been sold in the Sichuan province as early as 1992; the brand has received numerous awards, including industry excellence awards, and had been recognized by the government. The Mian Zhu Da Qu branded liquor continues to be manufactured and sold across China since PRC New China was established, and it continues to receive various awards. Since the Cited Mark was approved for registration in 1979, the Mian Zhu Da Qu branded products have been sold in many provinces in China and remain a popular choice for liquor products even today. In light of the consistent and extensive use of the brand, the Cited Mark has achieved a high level of fame among the relevant public. In fact, prior to the filing date of the Disputed Mark, the Applicant's Cited Mark – "MIAN-ZHU in Chinese characters and Design" – has fulfilled the well-known trademark requirements as defined by Article 14 of the Trademark Law.

The original and current owner of the Disputed Mark should have been aware of the Applicant, its Cited Mark, and the high level of fame associated with the Cited Mark in connection with Class 33 alcohol and liquor products in China. In fact, evidence had shown that the local administrative office had issued various punishment and notices to the past and current owner of the Disputed Mark in light of their copying of the packaging design concerning the Applicant's Mian Zhu Da Qu branded liquor. The above punishments were recognized by two courts in Mian-Zhu city and De-Yang city; the bad faith of the Owner of the Disputed Mark was therefore clear. The subject invalidation action therefore is not bound by the five-year time limit discussed in Article 41 Section 2 of the Trademark Law.

The characters in the Disputed Mark ("JIN ZHU") and the characters in the Cited Mark ("MIAN-ZHU") are very similar; these characters also have the same visual impact to consumers. Although the Disputed Mark is a senior registration, it has been assigned various times. Sichuan Mian-Zhu Mian Cellar Distillery and the Owner purposefully caused consumer confusion by taking advantage of the visual similarities between the two sets of characters and copying the overall design packaging of the Cited Mark. The Owner's unfair competition acts have caused confusion in the marketplace, had a negative impact on consumer interests, and detrimental effects on the Applicant's legitimate interests. In light of the above, the registration of the Disputed Mark should be cancelled in accordance with Article 13 Section 2 of the Trademark Law.

The Owner of the Disputed Mark disagreed with the Appeal Board's decision (No. 29989) and raised a trademark administrative litigation to the Beijing No. 1 Intermediate People's Court (the "***Intermediate Court***").

COURT DECISION

The Intermediate Court reviewed the case and pointed out the Disputed Mark was approved for registration on September 15, 1984; the Appeal Board reached a decision (No. 29989) on July 9, 2012; Article 13 and related sections of the 2001 Trademark Law were applicable to the subject case. Overall, 2001 Trademark Law was applicable to the subject case based on Article 5 of the Interpretation of the Supreme People's Court on the Relevant Issues concerning the Scope of Jurisdiction and on the Scope of Application of Laws for Hearing Trademark Cases and Article 59 Section 1 of the Rules for Trademark Review and Adjudication (2002 Revision).

Although the marks at issue cover the same type of products, the subject case did not exactly fall under the situation described in Article 13 Section 2 of the 2001

Trademark Law. The case should be granted a longer period of time to contest and invalidate any bad faith registrations for the legislative intent to give special protection to well-known trademarks. Thus, the 2001 Trademark Law should be applicable to this case.

Although the Trademark Law in China did not offer specific cross-class protection to well-known trademarks until after the 2001 revision, the determination of a well-known trademark was intensely fact-driven. The well-known status of a mark should consider the relevant public's awareness of the mark at a certain period of time. Accordingly, even though the Trademark Law did not specifically discuss the exact protection afforded to marks that had attained the well-known status, this did not take away from the fact that a trademark could still be considered well-known even in 1984.

Article 41 Section 2 of the 2001 Trademark Law states that an owner of a well-known trademark can raise an invalidation action against a bad-faith registration and there is no specific time limit in respect to the owner's right to challenge a bad-faith registration. The evidence in this case had shown that prior to the filing date of the Disputed Mark, the Cited Mark had attained the well-known status as discussed in Article 14 of the Trademark Law. In this case, the characters in the Disputed Mark "Jin Zhu" and the characters in the Cited Mark "Mian-Zhu" were very similar and had the similar visual impact on consumers. The original owner of the Disputed Mark and the owner of the Cited Mark were in fact located in the same province in China: Sichuan. Considering the proximity of the owners of the two marks, the owner of the Disputed Mark should have been well aware of the fame associated with the Applicant and the Cited Mark. The owner of the Disputed Mark can therefore be imputed with bad faith and its intention to trade on the goodwill and reputation of the Cited Mark because it still decided to register its mark despite its close similarities with a well-known trademark. Furthermore, although the Disputed Mark had been registered for a long time, it had been assigned and transferred multiple times as well. When the Disputed Mark was under the ownership of Sichuan Mian-Zhu Mian Cellar Distillery and Shenzhen Bao Song Li Industrial Co., Ltd., both companies were cited for violation for their intentional copying of the design packaging of the Cited Mark and their causing international consumer confusion given the overall design similarities and the similar nature between the characters in both parties' marks. Based on the assignment situation of the Disputed Mark and the intentional copying of its various owners, it is clear that the Disputed Mark was originally filed in bad faith; the Disputed Mark had become nothing but a convenient "tool" allowing its owners to obtain illegitimate profits by trading on the goodwill associated with the Cited Mark and profiting from consumer confusion. In fact, the Applicant's legitimate rights over the Cited Mark were further impacted due to the present and past owners' intentional copying of the Cited Mark, its overall packaging, and their deliberate causing of consumer confusion. In light of the above, the Disputed Mark should be invalidated in accordance with Article 13 Section 2 of the 2001 Trademark Law. Appeal Board's decision (No. 29989) is clear, the decision was rendered with due process and involves the correct application of the law. The Appeal Board's decision should therefore be maintained.

Neither party raised an appeal after their receipt of the Intermediate Court's decision. The decision is now effective.

ANALYSIS & INSIGHT

The current Trademark Law includes a number of articles offering special protection to well-known trademarks. For example, Article 13 Section 2 protects unregistered well-known trademarks over the same or similar products; Article 13 Section 3 protects registered well-known trademarks over products different or dissimilar from those registered; Article 45 Section 1 specifies the time limit for the owner of a well-known trademark to petition for protection. For this case, Article 13 Section 3 is applicable due to its discussion of the time period limitation for well-known trademarks.

Article 13 Section 3 of the Trademark Law states that "a junior mark should be refused for registration or be prevented from being used if it covers different or unrelated products so long as the junior mark is a copy, imitation or translation of third party's mark that is already a registered well-known trademark in China, and the use/registration of the junior mark would lead to consumer confusion, and could potentially damage the legitimate rights of the owner of the well-known mark." Three criteria must be fulfilled in order to apply the above article:

(1) The cited mark has already obtained the well-known status prior to the filing date of the disputed mark and is already registered in China.
(2) The disputed mark is a copy, imitation or translation of a third party's well-known trademark.
(3) The use or registration of the disputed mark is likely to lead to consumer confusion and potentially bring a negative impact on the well-known trademark owner's legitimate interests, despite the fact that the disputed mark covers different or dissimilar products from those registered by the well-known trademark.

In addition to the above, if the disputed mark has been registered for more than five years by the time the invalidation action is raised, it must be proven that the disputed mark was registered in bad faith. Accordingly, the focus of this case is twofold:

- The application of the above trademark law on the subject case in respect to the disputed mark's copying, imitation, or translation of the third party's well-known trademark registration in respect to the same or similar products.
- The determination of a bad faith registration.

A. Application of the Relevant Trademark Law to Protect a Well-Known Registered Trademark on the Same or Similar Products.

The legislative purpose of Article 13 of the Trademark Law is to afford a stronger protection to a well-known trademark (compared to a regular trademark) given that such marks are more likely to be copied so as to allow third parties to obtain improper profits and trade on the goodwill associated with the well-known trademarks. This level of protection is warranted so as to protect the well-known trademark owner's rights, maintain fair competition in the marketplace and to protect the legitimate rights of consumers. Given that Article 30 of the Trademark Law already covers the situation where the junior mark is similar to the senior mark visually and phonetically and in terms of the overall covered goods or services, Article 13 covers different situations. Specifically, Article 13 offers protection to unregistered well-known trademarks in terms of the same or similar goods/services; it also affords protection to registered well-known trademarks in terms of different or dissimilar goods/services. Accordingly, in order to maintain a balance between Article 30 and Article 13, the passive protection nature afforded for well-known trademarks (and the fact that such a protection is offered on as-needed basis), Article 13 is not applicable to all situations. Article 13 does not apply to situations where a junior mark is copying, imitating, or translating a registered well-known trademark if both marks cover the same or similar products. On the other hand, Article 30 is applicable to such a situation where a junior mark is similar to a senior well-known trademark.

Despite the above, in situations where the invalidation action is raised after the disputed mark has been registered for more than five years and the disputed mark is a bad-faith registration, one should not deprive the well-known trademark owner's rights by insisting Article 30 is the only applicable law (if so, the invalidation action would be refused, given that it was not timely raised). Considering the legislative intent of Article 13 of the Trademark Law, and the interpretation of the related law, a well-known trademark is more deserving of special protection in situations where the junior mark is copying, imitating, or translating a well-known mark and using it on the same or similar products, as opposed to situations involving different or dissimilar products/services. In light of the above, in situations where a junior mark is copying, imitating, or translating a registered trademark that is already well-known in China, and the two marks involve the same or similar products, Article 13 Section 3 of the Trademark Law (Article 13 Section 2 of the 2001 Trademark Law) is applicable when an invalidation is raised after the 5th registration anniversary of the junior mark and the junior mark is registered in bad faith.

B. Determination of a Well-Known Trademark.

Article 14 Section 1 of the Trademark Law states: the determination of a well-known trademark should consider the following:

(1) The level of awareness of the mark to the relevant public.
(2) The extensive nature and the period of time the mark have been used.
(3) The period of time and the extent the mark has been promoted and its geographical coverage of the mark that has been promoted.
(4) Any documentation to support that the mark has been recognized as well-known.
(5) Other factors relevant to consider whether or not the mark should be deemed well-known.

The determination of whether or not a mark should be considered as well-known should consider all the factors discussed above; it is, however, not a precondition that a mark must fulfill all criteria in order to be recognized as well-known. Key factors to consider include:

1. The Determination of "Relevant Public."

The concept of "relevant public" is important in order to decide whether or not a mark should be regarded as well-known. The relevant public concept has two key features: (1) territorial; and (2) relevance. "Territorial" refers to the public's perception of the mark at time of issue in China; it would not be reasonable to require that the mark should enjoy a similar well-known status in other countries or jurisdictions. Similarly, a mark should not be regarded as well-known in China simply because it has obtained such a status in other countries or jurisdictions. "Relevance" refers to the public's perception concerning the products or services at time of issue that are requested to be recognized as well-known. This includes, but is not limited to, the following situations: (1) the product manufacturers or service providers for the mark at issue; (2) the relevant consumers for the goods or services at issue; and (3) all the operators and related people that come in contact with the mark and its products (or services) during the channel of distribution process.

2. The Evidence Requirement.

In practice, the following evidence can be submitted to support the well-known status of a mark:

(a) Contracts, receipts, invoices, bills of lading (B/L), bank accounts or invoice information, import/export receipts concerning the goods/services bearing the mark at issue.
(b) Scope of distribution, sales networks and sales channels concerning the goods/services bearing the mark at issue.
(c) Advertising records on broadcasts, television, movies, newspaper, periodicals, Internet coverage, outdoor and multi-media advertising, media comments and other promotional activities and materials concerning the mark at issue.
(d) Materials showing the goods/services bearing the mark at issue being promoted or displayed at trade shows or other public exhibitions.
(e) The first use date regarding the mark at issue and information showing the continuous use of the mark.
(f) Proof of registration of the mark at issue in China, and countries or jurisdictions in other parts of the world.

(g) Official recognition by trademark authorities or administrative authorities regarding the well-known status of the mark (or why it deserves more protection) as well as information relating to the infringement situations of the mark.
(h) Sales revenue, profit and tax/asset information, output statistics, ranking information and advertising expenditures provided by authorities, industry associations, or trade groups.
(i) Awards the mark at issue has received over the years.
(j) Other relevant information that can prove the fame status of the mark at issue.

The above information should be published or become available prior to the filing date of the disputed mark. All the factors should be considered, and there is no need to fulfill all of the criteria discussed above before a mark can be formally recognized as well-known.

In the subject case, the Applicant had provided a large amount of evidence showing that the Cited Mark had obtained a high level of fame in connection with liquor products prior to the filing date of the Disputed Mark. The submitted evidence included:

(1) History relating to the trademark use (sufficient to prove a high level of fame in the related industry).
  - Mian-Zhu County Record states that in 1922, Mian Zhu Da Qu was the recipient of the first level of award at Industrial Association of Sichuan Province; in 1928, the brand was a recipient of a medal and a certificate showing that the brand was well received in the Sichuan Province domestic products exhibition.
  - Mian-Zhu AIC record states that the "MIAN-ZHU" in Chinese characters trademark used by Mian-Zhu distillery in 1954 is in fact the first trademark used by an enterprise in the county after the founding of Mainland China. The mark is still in use today.
  - Mian-Zhu AIC's summary table (1979) clearly shows Mian-Zhu distillery's use of the "MIAN- ZHU" trademark.
  - Mianyang Business Bureau of Sichuan Province document (No. 360; 1981) states that the "Mianzhu Daqu branded liquor was still in short supply; the demand continues to exceed the supplies."
  - Sichuan quality products compilation (1979–1985) included MIAN- ZHU liquor as one of its primary brands.
  - Chinese liquor magazine (published by Liaoning People's Publishing House) states that "the Mianzhu-branded liquor had long been a renowned and famous liquor brand before the Liberation; the manufacturing facilities were restored and resumed manufacturing of the famous liquor in 1951; the brand was named the premium product of the Sichuan province in 1963; since then, the brand has been the recipient of multiple awards."

(2) Tax record and payment history regarding the brand.
   - Mian-Zhu City State Administration of Taxation issued a written notification dated August 24, 2010; the notification stated that: "Tax No. 2920028 and No. 2920031 refer to special tax receipts under the Sichuan Province tax system" and both are related to tax payment and history for the MIAN ZHU DAD QU brand; "Erqu" means Mian-Zhu-Er-Qu. The notification further stated that "these two receipts were issued on January 6, 1984; and they covered the tax period of November 1983 and December 1983 respectively."

(3) Consumer awareness of the brand, protection of the brand and fame status associated with the brand.
   - Civil Judgment issued by the Hunan High People's Court (No. 11; 2010) stated that: the Mian Zhu Da Qu branded liquor started its production as early as the Qing Dynasty under the Emperor then named "Kangxi;" the MIAN ZHU DA QU liquor had already been selling and enjoying a high level of fame across China before the Liberation. The brand had been the recipient of multiple awards and was indeed a well-recognized brand in the marketplace.
   - The Cited Mark was the recipient of multiple awards such as, "The Premium White Wine of China" and recognized as a "Trustworthy" product due to the brand's high hygiene and production standards. The MIAN ZHU DA QU brand was also ranked third place in the second national brand reputation survey in the alcohol industry. The brand was one of the top ten best-selling national market leading brands in the Sichuan Province. In fact, the MIAN ZHU DA QU brand had been the recipient of various other awards that will not be listed in detail here.

Considering the evidence discussed above, the Appeal Board determined that the Cited Mark had fulfilled the criteria discussed under Article 14 of the Trademark Law and had become a well-known trademark prior to the filing date of the Disputed Mark.

C. Determination of Copying, Imitation or Translation of a Third Party's Well-Known Trademark.

Copying refers to the situation where the disputed mark is identical to the well-known trademark; imitation refers to the situation where the disputed mark adopts either all or parts of the distinctive elements of the senior well-known trademark; translation refers to the situation where the disputed mark uses a different language or characters to express the senior well-known trademark and the well-known trademark already enjoys an exclusive association between itself and such an "expression," and such an expression is known or used by the relevant public.

It is worth pointing out that although the words "copying, imitating or translating" are verbs with subjective meaning, it should not be inferred that such acts must be accompanied by subjective bad faith intent. The above words are in fact translation from Article 6 Section 2 of the Paris Convention. The special distinction regarding bad faith in Article 45 Section 1 of the Trademark Law also originated from Article 6 Section 2 of the Paris Convention. It can therefore be inferred from Article 45 Section 1 of the Trademark Law that there are two situations involving "copying, imitating or translating" other's well-known trademark: bad faith, or pure (innocent) coincidence. Otherwise, there would not be a need to enact two separate articles for an invalidation action where one must be brought within the first five years following the registration of the disputed mark (Article 13) and the other is not subject to any specific time limit (Article 41) when an owner of a well-known trademark is seeking to invalidate a bad faith registration.

In the subject case, the basic elements in the Disputed Mark are the same as those in the Cited Mark – all include Chinese characters, corresponding English phonetics, and the bamboo design. Also, the Chinese characters are the primary distinctive visual and phonetic elements in both marks and these characters are visually similar with roughly the same visual impact. Accordingly, it can be determined that the Disputed Mark is an imitation of the Cited Mark.

D. Determination of Consumer Confusion and the Possibility that the Owner's Interests in the Well-Known Trademark Would Be Negatively Impacted.

The current Trademark Law already has an article specifically designed to offer cross-class protection to a well-known trademark (Article 13 Section 3). However, it is important to note that simply because a mark is being recognized as well-known in one class, it is not automatically entitled to cross-class protection in the other 44 classes of goods and services. The premise in affording a well-known trademark cross-class protection is that the senior mark is registered to goods or services that are dissimilar or different from those covered by the disputed mark; accordingly, the use and registration of the disputed mark would lead to consumer confusion, and negatively impact the rights of the owner of the well-known trademark.

Article 9 of the Interpretation of the Supreme People's Court on Several Issues Concerning the Application of Law to the Trial of Cases of Civil Disputes over the Protection of Well-Known Trademarks explains that Article 13 Section 2 of the Trademark Law is applicable to the following situation where the use or registration of a disputed mark is likely to mislead the public and negatively impact the interests of the well-known trademark owner: [the use or registration of the disputed mark] is enough to cause the relevant public to believe the disputed mark is connected to some extent with the well-known mark, and it would "diminish the distinctiveness of the well-known trademark, negatively impact the market reputation of the well-known trademark, or improperly trade off the goodwill or reputation of the well-known trademark."

In practice, the more well-known and distinctive the mark is, and the more the mark is being used in connection with daily consumer products or services (and its relevant public is in fact the general public), the scope of protection for such a mark will be broadened, especially in the situation where the disputed mark is closely similar to the well-known trademark. For example, in several trademark administrative litigation cases, the court recognized the YILI mark as a well-known trademark for milk and dairy products, and the mark was later afforded cross-class protection to unrelated products, such as shampoo and computers. The court recognized the mark "BAIDU" as a well-known trademark in connection with Internet search engine services; the mark was later afforded cross-class protection over unrelated products, such as condoms. The court recognized the mark "GIORDANO" as a well-known trademark for clothing products; it was later afforded cross-class protection over products such as sanitary napkins, Hada, and shrouds. The court recognized the mark "SEVEN WOLVES in Chinese characters and Design" as a well-known trademark in connection with clothing products; the mark was later afforded cross-class protection over products such as faucets and radiator sections. The court recognized the mark "Mobil" as a well-known trademark in connection with petrochemical products; the mark was later afforded cross-class protection over products such as fertilizer. The mark "CASIO" was recognized as a well-known trademark in connection with electronic calculators, electronic watches, and electronic music instrument products; the mark was later afforded cross-class protection for unrelated products such as floor drains. The marks "OU BO LAI in Chinese characters" and "AUPRES" are recognized as well-known trademarks for cosmetic products; they were afforded cross-class protection over unrelated products, such as sausage casings and condom products. The mark "Zhong Xin in Chinese characters" was recognized as a well-known trademark in connection with financial services; it was later afforded cross-class protection for toilet products. The mark "Chanel" was recognized as a well-known trademark in connection with cosmetics and clothing products; it was later afforded cross-class protection over unrelated products such as sanitary napkins.

In the subject case, although the Cited Mark and the Disputed Mark were both approved for registration in respect to the same products, in light of the specific requirements under Article 13 Section 2 of the 2001 Trademark Law, further analysis was still needed to see if the registration of the Disputed Mark would mislead the public and cause a negative impact on the Cited Mark owner's rights. The evidence submitted to the Court was sufficient to show that the prior and current owner of the Disputed Mark purposefully caused consumer confusion by taking advantage of the visual similarities between the characters in the Cited Mark and those in the Disputed Mark, and their deliberate adopting of a packaging design similar to that of the Cited Mark was also a gesture aimed to create market confusion. As such, the use of the Disputed Mark had already triggered negative impact on the marketplace; it had therefore damaged the Cited Mark Owner's legitimate rights.

E. Determination of a Bad-Faith Registration.

According to Article 45 Section 1 of the Trademark Law, the owner of the well-known trademark or any interested party can file an invalidation action to the Appeal Board in the first five years of the disputed mark's registration date seeking to invalidate its registration if the mark was filed based on copying, imitation, or translation of a third party's well-known trademark. However, if the disputed mark is in fact a bad faith application, the owner of the well-known trademark and any interested parties seeking to invalidate the bad faith disputed mark are not bound by the five-year time limit. Accordingly, for any invalidation action that is raised after the 5th registration anniversary of the disputed mark, it is important to first establish the disputed mark is a bad faith application before the invalidation action can be reviewed for its merits.

Below are the relevant factors to consider when determining whether or not the owner of the disputed mark filed the mark in bad faith:

(1) whether or not the owner of the disputed mark has any contact or business connection with the owner of the cited mark;
(2) whether or not the owner of the disputed mark is located in the close proximity with the owner of the cited mark, or if the products/services of both marks have the same channel of trade and are sold within the same geographic area;
(3) whether or not the owner of the disputed mark has ever encountered any disputes with the owner of the cited mark so that the former should be imputed with knowledge of the cited mark;
(4) whether or not there is any connection between the people working for the cited mark and those working for the disputed mark;
(5) whether or not the owner of the disputed mark has used its mark for improper business purposes such as purposefully causing consumer confusion by trading off the goodwill and reputation of the cited mark, compelling the owner of the cited mark to cooperate with it or to extort an unreasonably high assignment fee, licensing fee, or compensation fee from the owner of the cited mark or any third parties;
(6) the cited mark is an inherently strong distinctive trademark;
(7) other factors that are helpful to determine the disputed mark was filed based on bad faith.

In the subject case, the Applicant had submitted a large amount of evidence establishing trademark infringement committed by the prior and current owner of the Disputed Mark. Selective supporting evidence included:

(1) In the decision rendered by the People's Court in Mian-Zhu City, Sichuan Province (No. 9; 2000), the decision recognized the Applicant's Mian-Zhu Brand product, Mian Zhu Da Qu, as a famous product. The packaging of Jin Zhu branded Jin Zhu Da Qu products was closely similar to that of the Applicant's famous brand, and the Owner's acts have constituted unfair competition.
(2) In the decision of administrative penalty rendered by the AIC in Mian-Zhu City, Sichuan Province (No. 20; 2009), it was identified that Sichuan Mian-Zhu Mian Cellar Distillery entrusted another party to manufacture and process the Jin Zhu Da Qu liquor products and delivered them to Shenzhen Bao Song Li Industrial Co., Ltd. for distribution; the Jin Zhu Da Qu liquor

products adopted the packaging design similar to that of the Applicant's Mian Zhu Da Qu liquor products. This decision was upheld in the two instances.

(3) In the decision rendered by the People's High Court in Hunan Province (No. 11; 2010), the "Jin Zhu Da Qu" characters were closely similar to those characters – i.e., "Mian Zhu Da Qu" – that were adopted and used by the Applicant; the Owner's deliberate use of these characters had therefore constituted an infringement against the Applicant's trademark and name rights;

(4) The Hong Kong High Court's decision to remove the following characters – JIANNANCHUN in English and Chinese characters – from the corporate file of the company, Sichuan Province Jian Nan Chun Distillery (Hong Kong) Limited Company. The company was established by the legal representative of the Owner: XIE Yuechang.

The present case was not subject to the five-year limitation because the Disputed Mark was a bad faith registration which was supported by the following facts: (1) the Cited Mark had been put to use for a long time and had enjoyed a high level of fame prior to the filing date of the Disputed Mark; (2) the owner of the Disputed Mark and the owner of the Cited Mark were located in the same area, Sichuan Province; and (3) a series of infringements committed by the prior and current owner of the Disputed Mark.

15. Recognition and Analysis Involving the Agent's or the Representative's Bad-Faith Application/Registration of Its Principal's Trademark

Administrative litigation regarding the trademark invalidation action filed by Chongqing Zheng Tong Health Products Co., Ltd. against a trademark registration for "TOU BAO XI LING in Chinese characters and English phonetics (TOUBAOXI-LIN)" – the registration belongs to Sichuan Huashu Animal Health Products Co., Ltd.

- First Instance: Beijing No. 1 Intermediate People's Court (No. 437; 2005) - Decided on December 8, 2005
- Second Instance: Beijing High People's Court (No. 93; 2006) - Decided on April 3, 2006
- Third Instance: SPC (No. 2; 2007) - Decided on August 31, 2007

BACKGROUND

Chongqing Zheng Tong Health Products Co., Ltd. ("***Zheng Tong***") obtained the name "*TOU BAO XI LIN in Chinese characters*" for its veterinary medicine after the use was approved by the Agriculture Bureau in Chong Qing City. Zheng Tong subsequently entered into an agreement with Sichuan Hua Shu Animal Health Products Co., Ltd. ("***Hua Shu***"), which was titled, "Exclusive Sales Agreement relating to the TOU BAO XI LIN branded products" (the "***Exclusive Sales Agreement***"). In the Exclusive Sales Agreement, Zheng Tong licensed to Hua Shu the right to exclusively sell the powder injection products named "TOU BAO XI LIN" in the PRC. Zheng Tong was not allowed to sell the products, and Hua Shu was not allowed to manufacture the products; otherwise, it would be considered a breach of the Exclusive Sales Agreement. Hua Shu was also responsible for the packaging design, sales, promotional strategies, and pricing of the products. During the term of the Exclusive Sales Agreement, Hua Shu applied for and successfully registered the trademark "TOU BAO XI LIN in Chinese characters and English phonetics (TOUBAOXILIN)" (the "***Disputed Mark***"), Registration Number 3304260, without authorization from Zheng Tong. The Disputed Mark was confusingly similar to the product name Hua Shu and was licensed to sell under its Exclusive Sales Agreement with Zheng Tong. The Disputed Mark was approved for registration in connection with Class 5 products such as "veterinary preparations, veterinary drugs." After the Exclusive Sales Agreement was terminated, the parties agreed that Zheng Tong was not allowed to manufacture any products bearing Hua Shu's trademark, i.e., the "TOU BAO XI LIN" products. The parties also agreed that Hua Shu was restricted from manufacturing the "TOU BAO XI LIN" products or from including any labeling information that the products were manufactured by or bore the approval stamp of Zheng Tong.

Zheng Tong later filed an invalidation action with the TRAB under the SAIC of PRC (the "***Appeal Board***"), seeking to invalidate the Disputed Mark. After review, the

Appeal Board was of the view that the "agent" discussed in Article 15 of the Trademark Law included dealers and distributors that would become familiar with the principal's trademark through commercial business transactions. The Exclusive Sales Agreement between the parties confirmed that Zheng Tong and Hua Shu were involved in an agency relationship. Hua Shu's application and registration of the Disputed Mark were therefore in violation of Article 15 because it was carried out without Zheng Tong's authorization. The Appeal Board decided to invalidate the registration of the Disputed Mark. Hua Shu challenged the Appeal Board's decision and raised a timely administrative litigation with the court.

COURT DECISION

The Beijing No. 1 Intermediate People's Court (the "***Intermediate Court***") reviewed the case and supported the Appeal Board's interpretation and application of Article 15 of the Trademark Law. The Intermediate Court therefore affirmed the Appeal Board's decision. Hua Shu raised yet another appeal to the Beijing High People's Court (the "***High Court***"). The High Court reviewed the case and pointed out that the agency relationship discussed in Article 15 of the Trademark Law was limited to "trademark agent[s]" and "trademark representative[s]." The relationship between Hua Shu and Zheng Tong was not an agency relationship. Hua Shu was responsible for the packaging design, sales, and promotion of the products, and for commercializing the TOU BAO XI LIN branded products. The "TOU BAO XI LIN" marks were therefore regarded as Hua Shu's unregistered trademarks. The High Court vacated the Intermediate Court's and the Appeal Board's decisions.

The Appeal Board and Zheng Tong challenged the High Court's decision and sought an appeal from the SPC (the "***Supreme Court***"). This case was in fact the first retrial case after China's Trademark System adopted the judicial review process on trademark authorization and determination. The Supreme Court reviewed the case and held that the "agent" and "representative" terms discussed under Article 15 of the Trademark Law also included special agency relationships such as distributor (exclusive distributor) relationships and licensing (exclusive licensing) relationships. The Exclusive Sales Agreement between the parties had transformed the relationship into an exclusive sales and distribution relationship. Hua Shu was awarded the rights to exclusively sell the TOU BAO XI LIN products in China based on the Exclusive Sales Agreement. The parties' relationship was therefore considered and fell under the definition of "sales agency" discussed under Article 15 of the Trademark Law. "TOU BAO XI LIN" was the specific name awarded to Zheng Tong with respect to the powder injection products after its application was approved by the administrative review authorities in China. The ownership of the name should not, and did not, change simply because the parties were involved in the Exclusive Sales Agreement, or the agent was authorized to use the name during the term of the Exclusive Sales Agreement. Accordingly, the ownership over the TOU BAO XI LIN name still belonged to Zheng Tong after the Exclusive Sales Agreement expired. In light of the above, the Supreme Court vacated the High Court's decision and affirmed the Intermediate Court's decision.

ANALYSIS & INSIGHT

There are three key issues in this case: (1) the interpretation of the "agent" and "representative" relationship under the Trademark Law; (2) the relationship between a product reference and a trademark; and (3) the recognition of ownership between a product name and the corresponding trademark.

A. "Agent" and "Representative" as Defined under Article 15 of the Trademark Law.

Article 15 of the Trademark Law states that *"an agent or a representative seeks registration of a trademark under its own name and the mark belongs to the entity that the agent or representative represents; the registration and use of the mark shall be refused if the principal opposes the application."*

There are three different interpretations with respect to the definition of "agent" and "representative" in Article 15 of the Trademark Law:

(1) The term "agent" is limited to a trademark agent, i.e., an agent who is specifically authorized by the trademark applicant or the trademark registrant to handle related matters in connection with the trademark at issue (the scope of representation may include the handling of a trademark application, trademark enforcement, or any other matters related to the trademark at issue). The term "representative" is limited to a trademark representative, i.e., an individual who represents a company to handle the trademark registration and other matters associated with the mark.

(2) The agent and representative are limited to the roles as defined under civil law. The definition does not include dealers and distributors.

(3) The term "agent" includes not only an "agent" as defined under the General Rules of Civil Law and Contract Law, but also dealers and distributors who become familiar with the principal's trademarks through the normal course of business transactions. The term "representative" refers to an individual who becomes familiar with the principal's trademark during the course of carrying out his or her responsibilities on behalf of the principal. The term "representative" therefore includes legal representatives, directors, supervisors, managers, and executive partners, etc. In the subject case, the key issue was that the second level of the court and the Appeal Board had a different understanding than the first level of the court with respect to the scope of the term "agent" as defined under Article 15 of the Trademark Law. It is therefore important to analyze this different point of view from the vantage of legislative intent and purpose. It is also important to consider relevant international

rules and customs so as to properly define the scope of the terms "agent" and "representative" under Article 15 of the Trademark Law.

1. The Interpretation of "Agent" and "Representative" Should Be Consistent with International Rules and Customs.

Article 25, Section 1(3) of the 1993 Implementing Rules of the Trademark Law states that "an agent who seeks to register the principal's trademark without authorization" falls under the category where a trademark registration is obtained through improper means. Such action should not be tolerated. The 2001 amendments formally incorporated the above and became Article 15 of the Trademark Law. The 2001 amendments also considered Articles 6–7 of the Paris Convention and incorporated the provision that, in addition to the "agent," the "representative" is also forbidden to register its principal's trademark without proper authorization. The 2013 amendments kept the original wording as written in the 2001 amendments. However, bad-faith trademark applications have expanded where the applicant can become familiar with the principal's mark not only through the agent's or representative's contract, but also through other channels such as general commercial contracts and business relationships. In light of the above, the amendments incorporated some updates in light of changes in Chinese society. Those updates are reflected in Article 15, Section 2. Article 15, Section 2 states that "a trademark application should be refused if an applicant is seeking to register a mark that is similar or identical to that of a third party and covers the same or similar products, and the applicant had prior dealings with the third party through contracts, business relationships or any other relationship which allows the applicant to become aware of the third party's trademark and the third party has opposed the trademark application."

As pointed out in the Supreme Court's decision, "Article 15 of the Trademark Law is not only to carry out the obligations as discussed under Articles 6–7 of the Paris Convention, but also to prevent the agent or representative from obtaining the principal's trademark in bad faith." The legislative history of Article 15 of the Trademark Law was considered, as well as Article 9 of the Provisions of the Supreme People's Court on Several Issues Concerning the Hearing of International Trade Administrative Cases, which stipulates that "the people's court should choose the interpretation that is consistent with the relevant international rules and customs if the court is asked to decide on international trade administrative cases and there exist more than two reasonable logical interpretations of the laws or administrative rules. The above principle is not applicable to rules and regulations where the PRC has expressly reserved the rights to give its own interpretation." In light of the above, the interpretation of "agent" and "representative" in Article 15 of the Trademark Law should be consistent with relevant international rules and customs.

Articles 6–7 of the Paris Convention states that "if the trademark agent or representative seeks to register its principal's trademark without proper authorization in one or multiple member countries, the principal has the right to challenge the application or seek to invalidate the registration; or, if there is applicable law in the destination country, the principal can request to have the trademark registration assigned to itself unless the representative or agent can provide evidence proving that its trademark application is proper." In fact, the Guidelines of the Paris Convention for the Protection of Industrial Property points out that the "agent" and "representative" in Articles 6–7 should not be narrowly construed. The articles are also applicable to situations where the distributor uses its own name to apply for a trademark without first obtaining the principal's authorization.[145]

The purpose of Articles 6–7 of the Paris Convention is to address the situation where the agent or representative in one member country seeks to register or use the principal's mark in another member country. Articles 6–7 prevent an agent or representative from obtaining its principal's trademark unless proper authorization is first obtained. The terms "agent" and "representative" discussed in Articles 6–7 refer to distributor agents and distributor representatives in the international trade context. The way the distributor seeks to register its principal's trademark without authorization is a classic example where the "agent/representative seeks to register the principal's mark in bad faith." The interpretation of the above international rules and customs also lists "distributor" as one of the examples that falls under the category of "agents" and "representatives." In other words, international rules and customs do not narrowly construe the definition of agents and representatives. Accordingly, the first and second interpretations of Article 15 of the Trademark Law are not consistent with international rules and customs. The third interpretation is consistent with the understanding and interpretation under international customs of "agent" and "representative."

2. The Interpretation of "Agent" and "Representative" Should Conform with the Legislative Intent and Legislative Purpose.

Article 15 of the 2001 Trademark Law protects the principal's trademark in an agent-principal and representative-principal relationship. Article 15 of the 2001 Trademark Law - together with Article 13, Section 1, which seeks to protect unregistered, well-known senior marks, and Article 31, which seeks to protect senior marks that have been put to use and have obtained a certain level of influence among the relevant public - is therefore one of the basic frameworks in China's trademark system to protect unregistered trademarks. The above articles are in place to prevent bad-faith trademark applications and registrations. The precondition of Article 13, Section 1 is that the unregistered trademark must be "well-known." The precondition of Article 31 is that the senior mark must have "obtained a certain level of influence." Similarly, the

145. Bodenhausen G.H.C., Tang Zongshun, Duan Ruilin trans., GUIDELINES OF PARIS CONVENTION FOR THE PROTECTION OF INDUSTRIAL PROPERTY, 306, China Renmin University Press (2003).

precondition to apply Article 15 is that the parties must have been involved in an agency or representative relationship. The above articles ensure that the applicant or registrant is aware of the third party's mark. The legislative principles that are reflected in these articles are good faith, honesty, and integrity, and the legislative purpose is to prevent unfair competition from trademark squatting. The agent or representative in the distributor/dealer relationship is fully aware of the principal's trademark. Accordingly, the distributor's application or registration of the principal's mark is also a violation of the good-faith honesty principle and a form of unfair competition. Accordingly, the legislative intent of the "agent" and "representative" terms discussed in Article 15 of the Trademark Law was to include the principal's distributor and dealer.

The first interpretation, where "agent" is narrowly construed to mean "trademark agent," not only changes the legal term and concept, but it also contradicts the legislative intent and purpose of Article 15 of the Trademark Law. This is because the only term included in Article 15 is "agent." The first interpretation confines the definition of "agent" to a "trademark agent" and seeks to provide an interpretation on that basis. The definition of "agent" clearly exceeds the definition of "trademark agent." The first interpretation therefore is not in conformity with the legislative intent and improperly narrows the applicable scope of Article 15.

The second interpretation defines "agent" as a "civil law agent," which would be correct, as trademarks should follow civil law interpretations. However, a distributor is excluded from such a "civil law agent" definition. Under this interpretation, the law is not capable of preventing situations where a distributor seeks to apply or register a principal's trademark. The second interpretation is therefore not helpful in promoting honesty, integrity, and fair competition in the marketplace, and fails to fulfill the legislative intent.

On balance, the "agent" and "representative" terms in Article 15 of the Trademark Law should be broadly construed. They should not only include civil law agents and representatives (including trademark agents and representatives), but also agents and representatives in a commercial distributor and dealer relationship.[146] In the subject case, the Exclusive Sales Agreement between Zheng Tong and Hua Shu qualified the parties to be in an exclusive agency relationship. In this relationship, Zheng Tong was the manufacturer and Hua Shu was the exclusive sales agent of Zheng Tong's TOU BAO XI LIN products. This relationship fell under the sales distribution agent relationship as defined in Article 15 of the Trademark Law.

146. In the retrial decision, the Supreme Court held that in order to stop the trademark squatting acts of sales agents or representatives who know or use other's trademarks due to special agency relationships, the "agent" and "representative" terms in Article 15 of the Trademark Law should be broadly construed. They should not only include civil law agents and representatives (i.e., trademark agents and representatives), but also agents and representatives in a commercial distributor and dealer relationship. In the subject case, since Hua Shu was the exclusive sales agent, there were no dissents on the Supreme Court's interpretation of the "agent" and "representative" terms. However, for trademark squatting cases involving (subordinate) sales agents, there may be discrepancies on the understanding of the "agent" and "representative" terms.

B. Relationship Between a Product Reference (Product Name) and a Trademark.

The name of the product is essential in explaining or indicating the quality, functionality, purpose, ingredient(s), or raw material(s) of the product. The purpose of a trademark is to directly state and identify the source of the products. According to Article 11, Section 1(1) of the Trademark Law, a generic reference of the underlying product cannot be registered as a trademark. However, there is a corresponding effect between the reference of the product and its trademark. In other words, through improper use, a trademark can be lost when it can no longer serve as a source identifier and becomes a generic product reference. Conversely, a noncommon product name can eventually function as a trademark either through long-term use or when the reference is itself capable of functioning as a source identifier. An example of a product reference functioning as a trademark through long-term use is the specific reference to some famous products based on Article 5, Section 2 of the Anti-unfair Competition Law.[147] An example of a product reference that is capable of functioning as a trademark when it is itself a source identifier is the specific product name for the pesticide[148] or the veterinary medicine product when the name has been approved by the relevant authorities and the owner enjoys exclusive rights over such a name. The product names under both examples are entitled to the protection of the law.

In the High Court's decision, it pointed out the following: "Zheng Tong's rights over the TOU BAO XI LIN product name was [sic] limited to its approval license in connection with the manufacturing of the veterinary medicine; Zheng Tong's rights over the name did not include its trademark rights. . . . [T]he fact that the product name TOU BAO XI LIN also functioned as a trademark enabling the consumers to identify the underlying Zheng-Tong-manufactured products from those produced by others was due to Hua Shu's prominent use of such a phrase during its promotional and sales effort." In other words, "the fact that the TOU BAO XI LIN term was able to transition from a product reference to a trademark was solely due to the effort of Hua Shu." The High Court's erroneous conclusions were because it believed that the reference of the veterinary medicine product could not become a trademark unless (and until) the reference had become famous; in other words, it was confused between the relationship of the following three names: the product reference, the specific name of a famous product, and the trademark.

Based on Articles 2 and 3 of the Notification to Strengthen the Management of Veterinary Medicine Names (issued on March 10, 1998), "the references or names

147. According to Article 2 of the Interpretation of the Supreme People's Court on Some Issues Concerning the Application of Law in the Trial of Civil Cases Involving Unfair Competition, the name of a product that has notable characteristics to distinguish the source of product shall be regarded as the "specific name."

148. According to Article 6 of the Pesticide Management Regulation, China applies the pesticide registration system. Article 12 of the Implementing Measures of the Pesticide Management Regulation states that "[w]hen proceeding with pesticide registration, pesticide manufacturers can apply for product names of pesticide which should be in accordance with naming conventions and should not be obviously descriptive as well as misleading. The applicant (pesticide manufacturer) is entitled to exclusive use of the pesticide product name after it is officially approved by the Ministry of Agriculture."

listed for any specific veterinary medicine as stated in the National Veterinary Medicine, Professional Standard of the Agricultural Department, Local Standards of the Veterinary Medicine is the legal name of such underlying veterinary medicine (i.e., the common reference). . . . [T]he common reference of a veterinary medicine cannot be registered as a trademark . . . . [E]ach manufacturer of the veterinary medicine can create its own name for the products, and it should include such a name in the application paperwork to the Management Department of Veterinary Medicine when the manufacturer is seeking approval of the underlying products or the serial number of their products. Once the name is approved by the authorities, the company can then apply to register the name as a trademark to the Trademark Office. The name of the veterinary medicine should not be used as a general reference for the product." In light of the above, the exclusive name of the veterinary medicine is itself capable of functioning as a source identifier; it is therefore an unregistered trademark. In other words, the name does need to become famous before it can be registered or used as a trademark.

C. The Recognition of Ownership Between a Product Name and the Corresponding Trademark.

1. The Original Obtaining of the Product Name.

Zheng Tong's veterinary medicine application was approved by the Agriculture Bureau in Chong Qing City on May 28, 2002, with the following approval certificate number: Chong Qing Veterinary Medicine No. 533 (2002). The certificate states that "the common reference requested by the applicant and approved by the Chong Qing City Agriculture Bureau is 'penicillin potassium compound for injection purpose (Type 1),'" and the name of the product is "TOU BAO XI LIN powder injection." Based on the above, it is clear that the core element in Zheng Tong's product name is "TOU BAO XI LIN" since "powder injection" simply describes the type of medicine. The exclusive rights associated with the phrase "TOU BAO XI LIN" as a product name were therefore first obtained by Zheng Tong. The interest associated with the TOU BAO XI LIN name as an unregistered trademark also started out with Zheng Tong. No change in ownership over the TOU BAO XI LIN product name would occur unless it was first jointly consented by Zheng Tong and Hua Shu or some other specific legal event took place.

2. The Difference Between a Manufacturer Trademark and a Distribution Trademark.

Producer's trademarks, also called "manufacturer trademarks," refer to the type of marks used for underlying products that are produced by the producer itself. Retailer's trademarks, also called "distribution marks," refer to the type of marks used by retailers to identify products sold by the retailer itself. Distribution marks are not as common as manufacturer trademarks. Distribution marks are only relevant (and used) when the responsible manufacturers are relatively weak and the retailers are in a better financial and commercial position.

Based on the Exclusive Sales Agreement, Zheng Tong and Hua Shu were in an exclusive sales agency relationship. In this relationship, Zheng Tong was the manufacturer and Hua Shu was the retailer. TOU BAO XI LIN was the unregistered trademark first obtained by Zheng Tong. Zheng Tong therefore had exclusive rights over the name. Hua Shu's use of the TOU BAO XI LIN mark on the packaging was licensed under the specific consent of Zheng Tong. It did not constitute use of its own trademark unless and until Hua Shu was using the "HUA SHU" prefix mark. Through the HUA SHU prefix trademarks, consumers learned that the TOU BAO XI LIN branded products were sold by Hua Shu. Through the TOU BAO XI LIN trademark, consumers were notified that such products were manufactured by Zheng Tong. If Zheng Tong licensed the use of the TOU BAO XI LIN mark to various retailers and each retailer was capable of selling and distributing the TOU BAO XI LIN branded products, consumers would not be able to identify the retailers of the TOU BAO XI LIN branded products if all retailers included their own trademarks and the veterinary medicine reference "TOU BAO XI LIN" on the packaging. The consumers could only immediately identify Zheng Tong as the manufacturer of the TOU BAO XI LIN branded products. In light of the above, the HUA SHU mark on the packaging was the distribution mark. TOU BAO XI LIN was the manufacturer (unregistered) trademark. The TOU BAO XI LIN mark was used to identify the source of the products, i.e., Zheng Tong, as opposed to its retailer (Hua Shu).

3. The Nature and Legal Consequences to Carry Out the "Use" Obligations as Required under an Agreement.

One of the reasons the High Court believed Hua Shu was the rightful owner of the Disputed Mark was that *"there was no evidence to support that Zheng Tong sold any veterinary medicine under the product name of 'TOU BAO XI LIN' from the time it obtained the approval certificate from the Agriculture Bureau to the date the two parties signed the Exclusive Sales Agreement."* The High Court also pointed out that *"from the time Zheng Tong obtained the product name to the time Hua Shu sought trademark registration over the Disputed Mark, Zheng Tong did not include any use of the product name of 'TOU BAO XI LIN' in its external sales effort."* It was implied that if Zheng Tong had been interested in obtaining (and maintaining) the rights associated with the TOU BAO XI LIN mark as an unregistered trademark, it had to either have sold some of the TOU BAO XI LIN branded products before any business partnership or it had to have been involved in the retail effort for the TOU BAO XI LIN branded products after the signing of the Exclusive Sales Agreement, but before Hua Shu sought to register the Disputed Mark. Based on business customs, the manufacturer does not have the obligation to be immediately involved in the production or retailing of the products that it invented; the product produced by the manufacturer can be sold by itself or through a third party. The first clause in the Exclusive Sales Agreement expressly stated that

Zheng Tong licensed to Hua Shu the exclusive rights to sell the TOU BAO XI LIN branded products in the PRC. Hua Shu's sales and use rights involving the Disputed Mark originated from Zheng Tong. The parties were therefore in a sales agency relationship. In other words, Zheng Tong was engaged in a sales effort of its products through Hua Shu. Any sales made by Hua Shu were deemed a sale made on behalf of Zheng Tong. The fact that the High Court requested Zheng Tong to start selling the TOU BAO XI LIN branded products before the partnership (with sales being conducted by Zheng Tong itself) was an obvious contradiction of business customs. This in fact forced the manufacturer to become disengaged from its role as a product producer to become a retailer - in fact, an exclusive and sole retailer - of its own products. Furthermore, the High Court's decision requesting Zheng Tong to be engaged in external sales involving the Disputed Mark was an obvious violation of Article 1 of the Exclusive Sales Agreement between Zheng Tong and Hua Shu.

The second reason the High Court believed Hua Shu was the rightful owner of the Disputed Mark was that "*Hua Shu had used the TOU BAO XI LIN mark in a prominent way in its packaging design,*" and "*Hua Shu admitted that it had been engaged in sales and promotional efforts concerning the TOU BAO XI LIN branded products.*" The above line of reasoning was not tenable to support the High Court's conclusion.

First, Hua Shu was not involved in the manufacturing of veterinary medicine products. It merely designed the packaging of such products based on the agreement between the parties. Furthermore, the prominent use of the Disputed Mark involved the use of an exclusive product name that was created by Zheng Tong. Third, Hua Shu admitted that its sales and promotional efforts (and the associated costs) concerning the Disputed Mark were in fact its obligation under the Exclusive Sales Agreement - the goal was to maximize the profits. By Hua Shu carrying out its obligation under the Exclusive Sales Agreement, it did promote the fame associated with the Disputed Mark; however, its actions should not be construed as a justification to change the ownership recognition with respect to the product name and the unregistered trademark rights associated with the Disputed Mark. Assume that Zheng Tong licensed multiple retailers to sell its TOU BAO XI LIN branded products, and each retailer were then required to package and promote the products. Following the High Court's line of reasoning, the unregistered mark "TOU BAO XI LIN" would then be jointly owned by each and every licensed retailer, while the manufacturer does not retain or own any rights at all. This line of reasoning would therefore lead to an unfair outcome. The High Court's conclusion that the rights associated with the unregistered trademark "TOU BAO XI LIN" belonged to Hua Shu simply because it was first used by Hua Shu lacked a factual and legal foundation. Hua Shu's use and promotion of the product name "TOU BAO XI LIN" were merely results of its fulfilling its obligation under the Exclusive Sales Agreement between the parties. Although Hua Shu's use did in fact add significant value to the fame status associated with the product name "TOU BAO XI LIN," Hua Shu also financially benefited from it based on the Exclusive Sales Agreement between the parties.[149] In conclusion, Zheng Tong specifically and expressly consented to Hua

149. Contract consideration included the qualification of exclusive sales agency and profits gained from distributing Zheng Tong's "TOU BAO XI LIN" products.

Shu's use of the product name. Its use, however, was not sufficient to change the ownership with respect to the TOU BAO XI LIN product reference name.

4. Ownership Should be Consistent with Respect to the Product Reference and the Corresponding Trademark.

Based on Articles 1 and 10 in the Exclusive Sales Agreement, Hua Shu was not allowed to manufacture the TOU BAO XI LIN branded products. Upon the expiration of the agreement or if the parties decided to terminate the agreement before term, Zheng Tong still had the right to continue manufacturing the TOU BAO XI LIN branded products. The only restriction was that Zheng Tong was not allowed to use Hua Shu's HUA SHU trademark (the parties in fact confirmed this restriction when terminating the Exclusive Sales Agreement).

Despite the above, following the High Court's decision, it was concluded that Hua Shu could still - Zheng Tong could not at all - manufacture the TOU BAO XI LIN branded products after the termination of the Exclusive Sales Agreement simply because Hua Shu had obtained the specific product name and the unregistered trademark rights associated with TOU BAO XI LIN by using the phrase in a prominent way. This clearly violated the Exclusive Sales Agreement between the parties. Again, following the High Court's decision, Hua Shu obtained the unregistered trademark rights associated with TOU BAO XI LIN while Zheng Tong was still the rightful owner over the TOU BAO XI LIN phrase as a product reference. This conclusion not only failed to correctly address the trademark dispute between the parties, but it also created new conflicts involving the ownership recognition regarding the trademark and product name.

D. The Difference Between Article 15 of the Trademark Law and the Relevant Regulations in the Paris Convention.

There are several differences between Article 15 of the Trademark Law in China and Articles 6–7 of the Paris Convention.

First, the two bodies of law involve different usage terms. The term in the Paris Convention involves the concept of a "trademark owner." Under the Trademark System in China, the corresponding concept is "the person or entity being represented." This term difference has resulted in a discrepancy in interpretation, which can be entirely avoided when one of the interpretations of the agency/representation relationship is defined to include a "trademark agency and trademark representation relationship only." Second, the two bodies of law involve a different scope of protection. Under the law in China, the disputed mark shall be denied for use and registration "if the party being represented does raise an opposition." The Paris Convention, on the other hand, not only grants the principal (or those being represented) the rights to oppose an application or challenge a trademark registration, but also the right to request the disputed mark to be transferred to any member country as long as the law in the respective country so allows. Third, no exception is provided under the system in China. Under Paris Convention, the agent or the representative is allowed to defend its trademark registration so long as there is a reason to justify the registration. In other words, there are possible ways to defend such an action under Paris Convention. In China, however, no exception is allowed.

16. Trademark Squatting Involving a Senior Trademark Which Has Been First Put to Use (But Not Yet Registered) and Has Obtained a Certain Level of Influence in China

Appeal of administrative litigation regarding the trademark invalidation action filed by ZHANG Xueli against a trademark registration for "TIAN PI TANG ZHANG in English and Chinese characters and Design" – the registration belongs to WANG Yuxia.

- First Instance: Beijing No. 1 Intermediate People's Court (No. 3340; 2010) – Decided on November 20, 2010
- Second Instance: Beijing High People's Court (No. 30; 2011) – Decided on February 28, 2011

BACKGROUND

An individual, WANG Yuxia (the "***Owner***") filed a trademark application for "TIAN PI TANG ZHANG in English and Chinese characters and Design" (Registration Number 3522359; *see* Image One below; the "***Disputed Mark***") on April 11, 2003; the mark was approved for registration on October 7, 2004, on Class 30 products including candy, fondants [confectionery], chewy candy, candy of popped rice, sugar coated nuts (confectionery), and candy crisp.

Image One

An individual, ZHANG Xueli (the "***Applicant***"), raised an invalidation action to the TRAB under SAIC of PRC (the "***Appeal Board***") seeking to cancel the registration of the Disputed Mark. The Applicant's primary grounds include:

- "Pi Tang ZHANG" candy shop (the "***Candy Shop***") is an iconic brand with more than 100 years of operation history in Tianjin City, China; the Applicant is the third generation and successor to the Candy Shop. Through generations' of development, the PI TANG ZHANG brand enjoys a high level of fame in connection with candy products such as chewy candy and candy crisp in China. The products are famous not only in China but have been exported for sale outside China for multiple years.

- The Applicant used his daughter's name (ZHANG Qi) to establish a candy shop company called "Tianjin City Hongqiao District Pi Tang ZHANG Candy Shop" (the "***Company***") on December 21, 1995. The Owner is in fact the former daughter-in-law of the Applicant, and she was employed to work at the Company.
- The Applicant took an absence from his management duty for health reasons in 1998; the Applicant therefore handed over the management of the Company to his son and daughter, ZHANG Kuan and ZHANG Qi.
- The Owner's application of the Disputed Mark was clearly motivated by bad faith because she was trying to become the owner of a brand which has more than a 100 years' of history and has been passed down for generations in the Applicant's family. The Disputed Mark should therefore be invalidated because it has "improperly obtained a third party's mark which has been put to use and has obtained a certain level of fame and influence [among the relevant public]."

In order to support its claim, the Applicant provided the following supporting evidence:

(1) A news media report by *China Food Newspaper* in June 2003 regarding the Applicant's PI TANG ZHANG brand.
(2) A copy of the business operation license for the Company - Tianjin City Hongqiao District Pi Tang ZHANG Candy Shop - showing the Company was established on December 21, 1995.
(3) Certificate copies regarding the quality, health standards and food safety standards of the Applicant's products in 2001 and 2002.
(4) A certificate copy approving the Company's products and certifying its products level dated on June 8, 1996.
(5) Shipping orders and sales invoices concerning the Candy Shop's products.
(6) Award certificates in 2000 regarding the PI TANG ZHANG-branded candy products;
(7) Evidence materials supporting Zhiyong Huang's - the Applicant's son-in-law - obtaining of design patents for the related products.
(8) Third parties' declaration and notarized copies affirming the Applicant is the true successor of the PI TANG ZHANG brand.
(9) Evidence copies showing that the Owner worked at the Company and received wages from the Company.
(10) Evidence materials evidencing that the PI TANG ZHANG brand was formally recognized as one of the oldest brands in Tianjin city.

The Owner responded by pointing out that: the Owner and the Applicant's Son - ZHANG Kuan - used to be a married couple. The Applicant and his daughter had once agreed that the Owner and her former husband could use the PI TANG ZHANG brand. In 1998, when the Owner established the factory named "Tianjin City the ZHANG's Family Pi Tang Factory" (the "***Factory***"), it was operated by the then-married couple:

the Owner and the son of the Applicant. Accordingly, it did make sense that the Owner applied for the Disputed Mark – the Applicant was also aware of the application of the Disputed Mark at that time. When the couple divorced in 2006, ZHANG Kuan expressly stated that the Factory, its sales center, and the Disputed Mark belonged to the Owner. The Owner had started using the Disputed Mark as early as the establishment date of the Factory, and her use of the Disputed Mark was the subject of numerous awards. In light of the above, the Owner's use and registration of the Disputed Mark was legal, logical and reasonable; furthermore, the use of the Disputed Mark by the Owner did not result in any level of consumer confusion or deception and has not had any negative impact on the Applicant and his daughter's use of the PI TANG ZHANG brand. Since the Owner's use and registration of the Disputed Mark had not and would not have any negative effect on the Applicant and his rights; the authorities should therefore maintain the registration of the Disputed Mark.

The Owner has provided the following supporting evidence:

(1) The approval acknowledgement provided by the Company – namely, Tianjin City Hongqiao District Pi Tang ZHANG Candy Shop – by ZHANG Qi and the Applicant ZHANG, Xueli.
(2) The notarized copy of the civil mediation decision issued by the Tianjin Hongqiao District People's Court.
(3) Pictures bearing the Disputed Mark showing how the Mark was used by the Owner in everyday life.
(4) The government registration materials for the Factory and product sales center.
(5) Award copies to the Owner, her company and products.

The Appeal Board reviewed the case and found that the submitted materials were sufficient to prove that the PI TANG ZHANG brand was one of the oldest and most iconic brands in Tianjin city. The brand was created by the Applicant's ancestors and the Applicant was the third generation using the brand. For many years prior to the registration of the Disputed Mark, the Applicant and his daughter had been using the Disputed Mark to run their family business to produce and sell the iconic candy products. The Owner should have been aware of this background and the Applicant's family's operation of the Disputed Mark given she used to belong to the family and used to work at the Company. In addition, given the Owner had obtained approval from ZHANG Qi prior to using the PI TANG ZHANG brand in the manufacturing and sales of candy products, it showed that the owner was aware of the influence of the PI TANG ZHANG brand and that the family had not yet sought trademark registration of the brand. The Disputed Mark was applied for under the Owner's personal name; furthermore, the characters in the Disputed Mark – "TIAN PI TANG ZHANG" – and the PI TANG ZHANG brand are confusingly similar; the use and registration of the Disputed Mark on candy products would easily lead to consumer confusion. The Owner's arguments pointed out that its use and registration of the Disputed Mark was approved by the Applicant and that the divorce agreement showed that the Disputed Mark belonged to the Owner and could not serve as a valid defense to her ownership of the

Disputed Mark. The Disputed Mark was in fact "a third party's senior influential (but unregistered) mark that was obtained by the Owner through improper means." The registration of the Disputed Mark was therefore a violation of Article 31 of the 2001 Trademark Law and should be invalidated.

The Owner filed an administrative litigation to the Beijing No. 1 Intermediate People's Court (the "***Intermediate Court***") to appeal the Appeal Board's decision.

COURT DECISION

The Intermediate Court reviewed the case and pointed out the PI TANG ZHANG brand was created by the Applicant's family and was one of the oldest brands in Tianjin city; the Applicant was the third generation and successor of the brand. The PI TANG ZHANG characters have been used prominently on the chewy candy product packaging – the use of the PI TANG ZHANG characters is trade name use, as well as trademark use; these characters are capable of functioning as source identifiers because they do allow consumers to distinguish between the products offered by the ZHANG's family from those offered by others. The Disputed Mark fully includes the characters PI TANG ZHANG and covers the identical products as the ZHANG's brand – accordingly, the two trademarks are not only visually closely similar, but also identical or highly similar in terms of the product functionality, purpose and the targeted groups of consumers. Given the Owner used to be married to the son of the Applicant, she should therefore be very aware of the ZHANGs' and the Applicant children's use of the PI TANG ZHANG mark. Accordingly, the Owner applied for the Disputed Mark in bad faith in light of her prior knowledge and awareness of the ZHANGs' use of the brand. The certificate provided by the Owner – of the brand being the "2001 Popular Brand of the Tianjin city" (awarded by the Tianjin City Commercial Industry Committee) – in fact proved the high level of fame and popularity as well as the objective positive market perception of the brand. The registration of the Disputed Mark had therefore violated Article 31 of the 2001 Trademark Law and the Appeal Board's decision should be maintained.

The Owner appealed the decision to the Beijing High People's Court (the "***High Court***"). The High Court reviewed the case, rejected the appeal and maintained the Intermediate Court's decision.

ANALYSIS & INSIGHT

The subject case is a classic illustration of Article 31 of the 2001 Trademark Law (Article 32 of the 2013 Trademark Law) where a registration should be invalidated if it has "improperly obtained a third party's mark which has been put to use and has obtained a certain level of fame and influence [among the relevant public]." The legislative objective of Article 31 is to make sure that all trademark registrations should be based on honesty and integrity. The Article also seeks to protect marks that have been put to use and have obtained a certain level of fame but whose owners have not yet sought to register the mark as a trademark. The Article is therefore seeking to prevent any bad faith trademark registrations that may be allowed due to the inadequacies of the trademark system. Four conditions must be met in order to apply Article 31 to invalidate an existing registration:

(A) The senior mark must have obtained a certain level of influence prior to the filing date of the disputed mark.
(B) The senior mark and the disputed mark must be identical or closely similar.
(C) The products or services covered by the disputed mark must be identical or closely similar to those covered by the senior mark.
(D) The applicant of the disputed mark must have bad faith.

A. Determination Relating to the Senior Mark "Being Put to Use and Has Obtained a Certain Level of Influence."

1. Determination of Use.

The "has been put to use" language should be taken literally – that is, the senior mark has been put to use prior to the filing date of the disputed mark. The determination of "use" involves the following four areas.

a. The Interested Party that Has the Standing to Bring the Action.

The party that can seek to invalidate the disputed mark based on Article 45, Section 1 of the 2013 Trademark Law (Article 41, Section 2 of the 2001 Trademark Law) must be interested parties – namely, either the owner of the senior mark or parties that would have been directly impacted by the outcome of the decision. Accordingly, the evidence submitted must be sufficient to establish that the claimant is an interested party in order for Article 45, Section 1 of the 2013 Trademark Law to apply.

In the subject case, the Applicant – Mr. ZHANG Xueli – is the third-generation successor of the famous brand "PI TANG ZHANG;" Mr. ZHANG has been manufacturing and selling PI TANG ZHANG branded candy products through his family business. The Applicant is therefore qualified as the interested party to the PI TANG ZHANG trademark and has the standing to file the invalidation action.

b. The Geographic Areas Relating to Use.

Trademark protection is territorial. Generally speaking, the "has been put to use" clause refers to the use within the PRC's territory – such as the subject case where the use of the PI TANG ZHANG mark involves Tianjin city. However, if the use of the mark is outside China, but the relevant public in China is nevertheless familiar with the use, the use can still satisfy the "has already been put to use" requirement for the senior unregistered trademark.

For example, in the appeal of a trademark opposition case[150] involving the "NUXE" mark under Application Number 3747592, LABORATOIRE NUXE ("***Nuxe Company***") provided a large amount of use evidence relating to its mark "NUXE PARIS and TREE DESIGN" - however, these use evidence and promotional materials concentrated on the use in the US, European countries, Hong Kong and Taiwan. Nuxe Company also provided archived information showing Chinese consumers visiting its website, www.nuxe.com, as well as Chinese cosmetics media discussions relating to the NUXE brand and products prior to the filing date of the opposed mark. The Appeal Board rejected Nuxe Company's opposition on the ground that the submitted evidence was not sufficient to prove that its trademark had obtained a certain level of fame and influence prior to the filing date of the opposed mark; accordingly, the opposed mark should be allowed for registration. The first instance Court was of the view that the submitted evidence was in fact sufficient to prove that Nuxe Company's trademark - NUXE PARIS and Tree Design - had obtained a high level of fame in the US, European countries, Hong Kong and Taiwan prior to the filing date of the opposed mark. Furthermore, through Nuxe Company's use and promotion, the brand had in fact acquired a high level of commercial value and had become an influential brand. Given cosmetics products are consumer products and they enjoy a high level of attention and the relevant public's awareness of the NUXE brand was higher than those of other brands, and the fact that a large number of consumers from China continued to purchase NUXE-branded cosmetics products from foreign countries and bring them back to use in China, the Court held that the above evidence was sufficient to support the relevant public's awareness of the brand and its fame and also the TREE design prior to the filing date of the opposed mark. Given the applicant of the opposed mark was involved in the same cosmetics business, and used to hold a director position in its companies in Hong Kong, and its actual use of the disputed mark involved a variation of the mark (i.e., NUXE was changed to nu-xe [in lower cases]) and in combination of the tree design), the opposed mark was determined to be in violation of Article 31 of the 2001 Trademark Law where a junior mark should be invalidated because it has "improperly obtained a third party's mark which has been put to use and has obtained a certain level of fame and influence [among the relevant public]." The Court overruled the Appeal Board's decision; the second instance Court maintained the original Court decision.

c. The Way the Senior Unregistered Mark Was Put to Use.

According to Article 48 of the 2013 Trademark Law, the use of the senior unregistered mark must involve "using the mark on products, product packaging, or containers and documentation involving the transaction of the underlying products;" the use can also

150. Case Index: Trademark Review & Adjudication Board [2011] No. 21498; Beijing No. 1 Intermediate People's Court, Yi Zhong Zhi Xing Chu Zi [2012] No. 1053; Beijing High People's Court, Xing Zhong Zi [2013] No. 86.

be in the form of "advertising promotion, exhibition and other commercial activities" - the above use should be deemed qualified use as long as it allows consumers to distinguish products or services provided by the owner as opposed to those provided by others. The evidence submitted for review must prove that the unregistered mark seeking protection has been put to open and public use that satisfies use as a trademark prior to the filing date of the disputed mark.

One of the key issues involving use is in respect to the "OEM" (Original Equipment Manufacturer) use and whether or not such "use" satisfies the use requirement under the trademark law. In the administrative lawsuit involving "GATEHOUSE" under Registration Number 4458183,[151] two levels of Courts reached a different conclusion regarding OEM use.

The first level of Court recognized and approved the OEM use. The Court's view was that although the use involved manufacturing of products which were exported and sold outside China, it did not negate the fact that the mark at issue still enjoyed a certain level of fame at the geographic areas where the manufacturing facilities were located, and among the people that are involved in the OEM business. The second level of Court, however, reached a different conclusion. It stated that the use of a trademark can only occur when the products or services bearing the mark go through the marketplace - the mark would not otherwise function as a source identifier until the underlying products or services reached this stage. Accordingly, the "use" discussed under Article 31 of the Trademark Law must be open use, in connection with the mark at issue, and go through the marketplace so as to allow the relevant public to associate the underlying products or services bearing the mark with the manufacturers or service providers. In the GATEHOUSE case, the submitted evidence was insufficient to prove that the mark at issue had entered into the market place in PRC China; accordingly, the evidence was not sufficient to demonstrate the fame associated with LF Company's GATEHOUSE mark or that the mark had been put to "use" prior to the filing date of the disputed mark.

It has been a controversial topic as to whether or not an OEM use constitutes use of a trademark. The inconsistent view is especially pronounced and has a greater impact particularly in cases involving trademark infringements. There is not yet a consistent, uniform and clear view on this topic. Despite the inconsistency, the determination regarding OEM use should be consistent when the use takes place in a trademark licensing context, as well as in a trademark infringement case. In other words, if the OEM use is not considered to be trademark use in China, then the OEM use involving a mark at issue should not be regarded as trademark infringement - the same action in the trademark licensing context should not be regarded as use either. In other words, the OEM use does not satisfy the "use" requirement under Article 31 of the 2001 Trademark Law (Article 32 of the 2013 Trademark Law); otherwise, the inconsistency would lead to double standards and lack legal basis.

---

151. Case Index: Beijing No. 1 Intermediate People's Court, Yi Zhong Zhi Xing Chu Zi [2012] No. 2195; Beijing High People's Court, Xing Zhong Zi [2013] No. 94.

d. The Protection Scope of the Products/Services.

The Article does not offer a clear requirement on the products that have been put to use in connection with the mark at issue. However, from the legislative intent, purpose and in an effort to balance the different articles in the Trademark Law, the protection scope for an unregistered famous mark should be the same as a regular trademark that has been registered in China. In other words, the protection for both types of marks should be limited to the same or similar products/services. Accordingly, the protection of unregistered marks that have enjoyed a certain level of fame is limited to the products or services that are either the same or similar to those of the disputed mark.

In the subject case, the prior unregistered yet famous mark - PI TANG ZHANG - has been put to use for chewy candy products; such products are the same or similar to those covered by the Disputed Mark: candy, soft sweets, candied cake of popped rice, chewy candy, candy crisp, etc.

2. Determination Relating to the "Certain Influence" or "Certain Level of Fame" of the Prior Unregistered Mark.

China's Trademark Law is based on the first-to-file system; in other words, the protection of a trademark is based primarily on its registration right. In light of the above, in order to make sure all marks are registered with honesty and integrity and in an effort to supplement the existing Trademark Law, the Article is put in place in order to afford protection to unregistered trademarks. It is however still important to obtain registration as early as possible, so as to maintain the stability of the trademark registration system. To balance the scope of protection afforded to different types of trademarks, the prior unregistered trademark can only be protected when the mark has obtained "a certain level of influence" prior to the filing date of the disputed mark.

The following situations should be considered, as a whole, in order to determine whether or not the prior unregistered trademark has obtained a certain level of influence. Despite the listing of the criteria, it is not a "must" to require a senior mark at issue to fulfill all of the following before it can be deemed obtaining a certain level of fame to enjoy protection.

(1) The relevant public's awareness of the mark.
(2) The length of time the mark has been put to use and the relevant geographic area.
(3) Promotional effort concerning the mark such as duration of time, promotional channel, extent of promotion, and geographic area.
(4) Any other factors that would impact the influence of the mark.

The above requirements can be supported by the following evidence:

(1) The agreements, invoices, receipts, purchase orders, bank notes, import/export information relating to the products/services bearing the mark.

(2) The geographic reach, sales channel, promotion method concerning the products/services bearing the mark.
(3) Any promotional commercial materials such as media coverage, movie trailers, television commercials, newspaper/media coverage, magazine articles, online promotional materials, outdoor media promotional or media reviews concerning the mark at issue.
(4) Exhibit or trade show materials relating to the products or services bearing the mark at issue.
(5) Supporting materials evidencing the earliest use date of the mark and consecutive use of the mark through different periods of time.
(6) Award information relating to the mark.
(7) Any other supporting materials that can provide evidence of the fame/ influence of the mark.

Any supporting materials to use as evidence of the use of the mark should be able to demonstrate the mark in use, the associated products or services, use dates and the parties that are using the mark.

In the subject case, the evidence submitted by the Applicant was sufficient to show that PI TANG ZHANG was one of the oldest and most iconic brands in the Tianjin area; the brand was created by the Applicant's ancestors with the Applicant being the third generation owner of the brand. The Applicant's daughter established the Company in 1995 and since then, the Company has been producing and selling PI TANG ZHANG branded products. The above was sufficient to show that the PI TANG ZHANG mark had obtained a certain level of fame prior to the filing date of the Disputed Mark.

B. Bad-Faith Determination.

One of the necessary conditions to apply Article 31 of the 2001 Trademark Law is that the owner of the disputed mark must have exhibited bad faith - *the owner of the disputed mark used "improper means.... to register" the senior unregistered mark*. The so-called bad faith refers to the fact that the owner of the disputed mark knew or should have known the influence associated with the senior mark first used by others. Despite its knowledge, the owner of the disputed mark still sought to register an identical or highly similar mark and intended to use the mark on products or services that were identical or similar to those covered by the senior mark. Its primary goal in registering and using the disputed mark was to trade on the goodwill or commercial reputation associated with the senior mark, or for improper purposes - such as preventing the senior mark owner from obtaining registration unless it first receives an unreasonable assignment fee, licensing fee or infringement compensation fee.

The determination of bad faith is subjective - it therefore needs objective evidence to support the finding. The following factors should be taken into account so as to determine whether or not the owner of the disputed mark seeks to register the mark in bad faith:

(1) whether or not the owner of the disputed mark has commercial ties or a business relationship with the owner of the senior mark;
(2) whether or not the owner of the disputed mark is located in the same geographic area as the owner of the senior mark or that the two parties' products or services enjoy the same geographic reach and channel of trade;
(3) whether or not the owner of the disputed mark was involved in any disputes with the owner of the senior mark so that the former was aware of the latter's mark;
(4) whether or not there is an overlap in terms of personnel between the owners of the respective marks;
(5) whether or not the owner of the disputed mark seeks to use the mark for improper business purposes after registration – such as seeking to create market confusion by trading on the goodwill or market reputation of the senior mark, compelling the senior right holder to enter into a business partnership, or seeking to obtain an unreasonably high assignment fee, licensing fee or infringement compensation fee from the senior right holder;
(6) the senior mark is highly unique and is closely similar to the disputed mark;
(7) other factors that can be directly contributed to the bad faith of the disputed mark owner.

In the subject case, the Owner once belonged to the Applicant's family and used to work in the Company. In addition, the Owner had used the PI TANG ZHANG trademark on her products by seeking the permission of the Applicant's daughter. Accordingly, the Owner was aware of the iconic brand status of PI TANG ZHANG, that the Applicant was the third-generation successor of the mark, and that the Applicant's ZHANG family had been manufacturing and selling the PI-TANG-ZHANG-branded candy products for years. The Owner then registered the Disputed Mark that was highly similar to the PI TANG ZHANG mark in connection with candy products. The Owner's bad faith can therefore be imputed based on the facts stated above.

C. The Balance Between "Certain Level of Influence" and "Bad Faith."

Based on the way Article 31 is written, two conditions must be satisfied in order for the Article to apply: the senior mark must have obtained "a certain level of influence" and the disputed mark owner must have exhibited "bad faith" in registering the mark. Yet in practice, there are endless creative ways where the bad faith squatters try to register senior influential marks through "improper means." In light of this market reality, it is therefore important to strike a balance between the above two requirements – this is also a difficult point in trying to invalidate bad faith registrations in China through this Article in the everyday practice. Striking a balance between these necessary requirements is also the key to fulfilling the legislative purpose and effectively preventing the ever-growing bad faith registrations in today's society in China. Article 31 of the 2001 Trademark Law is in fact one of the most common and important articles in the

Trademark System and has been used consistently to remove bad faith registrations in China. Through years of communication with different administrative and judicial trademark authorities in China, a consensus has been reached – that is, when the bad faith of the disputed mark owner is clear, the required burden of proof can be reduced accordingly on the part of the senior right holder.

In the appeal review concerning the opposition action against "SOUGOU in English and Chinese characters" (Application Number 4205184),[152] the Sohu Company formally introduced to the market one of the first Chinese search engine websites named "Sou Gou" (www.sogou.com) on August 3, 2004; the company was then the first third-generation Chinese interactive search engine service provider globally and the news was a headline grabber at that time. An individual applied for a trademark registration for the above opposed mark on August 4, 2004, designating the following Class 42 services: computer programming, computer software design, website creation and maintenance of others, and website hosting, etc. Although the filing date of the opposed mark was only one day later than the announcement of the So-Gou website, the Appeal Board concluded that the applicant of the opposed mark was or should have been aware of the website launch given the launch event was widely and extensively covered by the Chinese media – including prominent media such as Xinhua News, Wuji News, CCIDNET, eNet, Daily Messenger, Guangzhou Daily, Beijing Youth Daily, West China City Daily, Beijing Morning Post, and Xinhua Times; given the speed the news travelled nowadays (especially stories that were widely and extensively reported by media), the relevant public was already aware of the launch of the website and its popular yet unregistered mark: SOU GOU. The services covered by the opposed mark (i.e., computer programming services) belong to the same internet service area as that provided by the Sohu Company (i.e., network client services); both marks therefore cater to the same group of consumers and have the same or highly similar service content. The applicant of the opposed mark can therefore be imputed to have applied for the mark in bad faith because its application was identical or highly similar to a senior unregistered mark that had been put to use and had obtained a certain level of influence. The situation violated Article 31 of the 2001 Trademark Law where a third party had obtained registration of a senior influential mark; the opposed mark was therefore refused for registration. The decision became final when the applicant of the opposed mark failed to raise a timely appeal to the Court.

In order to further deter any bad faith registrations and to maintain the honesty and integrity of the China Trademark System, the 2013 Trademark Law incorporated Article 7, Section 1 in the General Guideline. Article 7, Section 1 states, "any trademark use or application should follow the honesty, integrity and good-faith principle." The 2013 Trademark Law further includes Article 15, Section 2 which expressly states, "a trademark application which is identical or closely similar to a third party's existing but not yet registered trademark, where both marks cover the same or similar products or services, and the applicant has had a contractual relationship, business relationship or any other relationship that allowed the applicant to know or be in a position to have

152. Case Index: Trademark Review & Adjudication Board [2013] No. 10365.

known the existence of the third party's unregistered trademark, shall not be allowed for registration when the senior right holder raises an opposition against it." In other words, if the applicant of a bad faith trademark application knew or should have known about a third party's senior mark (which has been put to use but not yet become a registered trademark) due to the special relationship between the parties, the "influence" prong is no longer a necessary requirement of the senior unregistered trademark. Based on the honesty/good faith principle stated in the General Guidelines, Article 33 will be used in conjunction with Article 15, Section 2 so as to effectively deter any bad faith squatting and will maintain a fair and just trademark registration system.

17. Refusal of Trademark Application due to Its Negative Impact on Prior-Existing Copyright

Appeal of trademark opposition filed by NBA PROPERTIES, INC. against a bull design trademark application applied for by Huang Weidong[153]

- First Instance: Beijing No. 1 Intermediate People's Court (No. 3818; 2012) - Decided on December 4, 2012
- Second Instance: Beijing High People's Court (No. 343; 2013) - Decided on September 5, 2013

BACKGROUND

Huang Weidong ("***Mr. Huang***") filed a trademark application for a bull design (*see* Image One) under Application Number 4539238 on March 15, 2005 (the "***Opposed Mark***"). The Trademark Office preliminarily approved the Opposed Mark in respect to its designated products, such as tea products.

NBA PROPERTIES, INC. ("***NBA***") filed an opposition against Mr. Huang's bull design mark on the ground that it violated NBA's prior copyright. The Trademark Office reviewed the opposition and rejected the Opposed Mark. Mr. Huang appealed the decision to the TRAB under SAIC of PRC (the "***Appeal Board***"). Mr. Huang pointed out that NBA did not provide sufficient evidence to show that NBA enjoyed copyright over the bull design and that the Opposed Mark was unique and inherently distinctive and accordingly, it should be approved for registration.

NBA responded to the appeal by pointing out that NBA enjoyed trademark rights for the team logo for the Chicago Bulls and had obtained trademark registrations for the design in a number of countries and jurisdictions across the globe prior to the filing date of the Opposed Mark. The fact that NBA already enjoyed the copyright for the team logo for the Chicago Bulls had been recognized by the Trademark Office and the Appeal Board on numerous occasions and such decisions had long become effective. According to relevant provisions of China's Trademark Review and Adjudication Rules and allocation of burden of proof, Mr. Huang should have borne the burden of proof to show that NBA did not enjoy copyright for the bull design. The Opposed Mark should not be allowed for registration because it would otherwise damage NBA's senior copyright over the design. NBA had submitted copies of decisions rendered by the Trademark Office and the Appeal Board that recognized NBA's copyright for the bull design.

The Appeal Board recognized that it did issue a decision on March 23, 2009 (Decision No. 06207; 2009; "***Decision 06207***") recognizing NBA's copyright for the bull

153. Prior right holder or interested party is entitled to raise opposition or invalidation on the ground that its prior copyright will be negatively impacted by the junior mark. This case is an appeal of trademark opposition instead of an invalidation action; nevertheless, it is a great illustration of the law at point. This is why the case was selected as an example to illustrate situations when prior copyright is negatively impacted.

design as shown in Image Two below. The decision has since become effective. The Trademark Office has also made similar decisions recognizing NBA's copyright for the bull design in a number of opposition decisions. In the absence of contrary evidence, the Appeal Board recognized and concluded it as a fact that NBA did enjoy the copyright for the bull design that had been recognized by numerous decisions. The Bull Design applied for by Mr. Huang is essentially the same design as that over which NBA enjoys copyright; the two designs are therefore substantively similar. Mr. Huang applied for the Opposed Mark without NBA's prior approval; the Opposed Mark therefore violates Article 31 of the 2001 Trademark Law: *"an application shall not damage a third party's prior existing rights."* In light of the above, the Appeal Board rejected the application of the Opposed Mark.

Image One	Image Two
	CHICAGO BULLS

Mr. Huang appealed the decision by raising an administrative litigation to the Beijing No. 1 Intermediate People's Court (the "***Court***"). The Court maintained the Appeal Board's decision to refuse the Opposed Mark. Mr. Huang appealed the decision to Beijing High People's Court (the "***High Court***").

COURT DECISION

Article 11 of the Copyright Law states, *"in the absence of contrary evidence, the individual, legal entity or other organization upon which the work bears its signature/ seal shall be deemed as author of the work."* The "signature/seal" wording in this article refers to a message from the author to the public conveying itself as the creator of the work. The applicant and registrant information reflected in the trademark gazette and trademark registration certificates merely confer the exclusive ownership of the trademark. Such information should not be equated as having the same importance as the "signature" or "seal" to indicate the author information as discussed in the above Copyright Law.. Accordingly, one cannot conclude NBA does enjoy copyright for the bull design or the team logo of Chicago Bulls by simply relying on its pending and registered trademarks for the same design.

Although Article 68(1)(4) of the "Provision of the Supreme People's Court on Several Issues concerning the evidence of Administrative Litigation of PRC" allows the court to directly recognize certain backgrounds as "facts," as long as such facts have already been "legally proven." There is not yet any clear guidance in the relevant laws or judicial interpretations discussing whether or not findings identified by administrative authorities would constitute "legally proven" facts and can therefore be directly recognized by the courts. Accordingly, one should not rely solely on the administrative decisions and need to consider other evidence prior to recognizing certain backgrounds conclusively as "legally proven" facts. In the subject case, there was insufficient evidence and, accordingly, it would have been premature to recognize NBA's copyright ownership for the bull design or the team logo for the Chicago Bull simply based on the 06207 Decision and effective decisions issued by the Trademark Office.

In accordance with Article 30 of the 2001 Trademark Law, anyone can raise an opposition to a published trademark within the prescribed period. Accordingly, any third parties - which include not only the copyright owner, but also any parties that can be directly or indirectly impacted by the prior work or, in fact, any third parties which may or may not be impacted at all - can raise an opposition against a published trademark in China. It is a commonly known fact that the bull design is the team logo for the Chicago Bulls in the American National Basketball League. This bull design falls under the definition of "work" under the Copyright Law, and is therefore protectable under the Copyright Law. The copyright of the bull design would not have belonged to Mr. Huang. Furthermore, the design in the Opposed Mark was closely similar with that in the team logo for the Chicago Bulls in terms of design, visual representation, and overall impression impact. The only difference was that the team logo for the Chicago Bulls included additional English text, "CHICAGO BULLS." In light of the above, the bull design in the Opposed Mark was substantively similar to the design owned by NBA. Mr. Huang sought to register a publicly known bull design which was closely similar to the design in the team logo for the Chicago Bulls and would undoubtedly damage the creator's copyright. The trademark application of the Opposed Mark therefore violates Article 31 of the 2001 Trademark Law, as it would "damage a third party's senior rights" and should not be approved for registration. Although the Appeal Board and the first instance court decisions did not reach the conclusion through the same accurate analysis, their decisions are nevertheless sound. In addition to correcting the mistakes, the High Court does support the earlier decisions and would therefore maintain both decisions to reject the Opposed Mark filed by Mr. Huang.

ANALYSIS & INSIGHT

The subject case is an excellent illustration of Article 31 of the 2001 Trademark Law (which is Article 32 of the 2013 Trademark Law) where a trademark application is refused so as to protect a third party's senior copyright as noted in the above law: "*an application shall not damage a third party's prior existing rights.*" Without proper authorization, a trademark inclusive of a third party's copyright shall be deemed a violation to the third party's senior copyright, and the trademark application shall be refused or invalidated. Under the current Trademark Law, three conditions must first be met prior to rendering the work at issue is entitled to copyright protection:

(1) The disputed mark is the same or substantively similar to the work over which a third party enjoys copyright.
(2) The applicant of the disputed mark has access or has the possibility to access the work over which a third party enjoys copyright.
(3) The applicant has never obtained permission from the copyright owner to apply for the disputed mark as a trademark.

A. Legislative Intent.

The general explanation of the legislative intent to the provision "*an application shall not damage a third party's prior existing rights*" is to seek the resolution of the "conflict" between junior and senior rights. However, it is important to clarify what constitutes a "conflict" between different rights so as to gain a clear understanding of the legislative intent.

A precondition of a "conflict" is that one party owns various legal rights; these legal rights also belong to various different parties. A conflict exists when the legal boundaries surrounding such rights are uncertain, vague, or one party is abusing its rights, and such an abuse would cause for limiting or damaging a third party's rights when seeking to enforce its rights. General approaches to resolve a conflict include legislation (so as to clarify the boundaries between respective rights) or to limit different rights so as to strike a balance between different parties' interests. For example, the fact that the owner of a senior trademark is allowed to provide counter arguments with respect to use of its trademark as discussed in Article 59 of the 2013 Trademark Law fully embodies the legislative spirit to resolve conflicts and to prevent abuse of trademark rights. The conflict exists between legitimate rights. The way to resolve conflicts mainly involves clarifying the legal boundaries between the competing rights, or limiting the competing rights so as to balance the interests between the parties. In fact, the idea to "resolve conflict" is itself a false statement for the trademark article at issue. Take the senior copyright issue as an example. The trademark application itself is a violation of the good faith and honesty principle if the applicant has had access or is likely to get in contact with the copyright work at issue but still chooses to seek trademark registration of the same or highly similar design of the copyright without the owner's prior authorization. Such a "trademark right" is therefore not obtained through legitimate means. If so, there is no "conflict" between legitimate competing rights among the senior copyright and trademark, but instead a conflict between a bad faith attempt to register a trademark and a legitimate senior copyright. The way to resolve the "conflict" is not to limit rights through the legislative channel, but to refuse or invalidate the bad faith trademark registration. Similarly, if a junior trademark registration does not negatively impact a third party's senior copyright and the fact that the two competing rights are not visually identical or substantively similar or that the owner of the junior right does not have any legitimate means to get in touch with the prior design, then there is no "conflict" between the junior trademark and the senior copyright.

The legislative intent of this trademark section is not to resolve conflicts between competing rights; instead, its goal is to protect the senior rights of a third party and to prohibit any trademark registrations that are in violation of the good faith principle. It is therefore important to understand the legislative goal of the subject trademark section with regard to the protection of the senior copyright under the Trademark Law.

According to the Berne Convention, a copyright exists the moment a work is "fixed" by citizens of any of its member countries or anyone that first publishes its work in its member countries. The work is then automatically protected in all signatory countries of the Berne Convention. Accordingly, different from the protection of trademark rights, the protection of copyright is not territorial among the members of the Berne Convention. Furthermore, different from the protection of regular trademark rights where it is limited to the same or similar products and services, the protection of copyright covers goods and services irrespective of their related nature, so long as the applicant of the trademark does not obtain prior authorization of the copyright owner; and if so, the trademark application should be refused or invalidated. In light of the above, some believe that it is necessary to take a strict approach to require the uniqueness of the senior copyright and burden of proof to show evidence of the ownership of the senior copyright; otherwise, the protection of the senior right would exceed that of a well-known trademark in that the protection is granted irrespective of the underlying products and/or services. This would then lead to a monopoly, overprotection of some work, and disruption of the overall trademark system.

The above is in fact an incorrect view of the legislative intent of the Trademark Law, where a trademark application shall not *"damage a third party's prior existing rights."* The legislative objective of this section is to protect the legitimate senior rights of a third party by limiting any applications that are not filed in good faith. Accordingly, if one's senior copyright would be damaged as a result of a third party's bad faith trademark application, the copyright owner can request to have the junior trademark application refused or trademark registration invalidated. This is certainly not the situation where the design at issue has been registered as a trademark and therefore has deprived or limited the owner of the senior copyright to seek protection of its rights. Besides, the protection of copyright and trademark involves two distinct legal systems where the former seeks to protect intellectual work while the latter is to prevent confusion. The copyright protection is preconditioned on the fact that the designs at issue must be "substantively" similar, while the protection for the trademark would be granted so long as the designs at issue are simply "similar." A well-known trademark is entitled to a cross-class protection so long as the junior mark closely resembles the well-known trademark. Furthermore, the more well-known the senior mark is, the more demanding it is that the junior mark must resemble the senior mark so as to allow the latter to enjoy the cross-class protection. However, in terms of a protection of a senior copyright work, the examination standard is "substantial similarity." In light of the above, one cannot conclude that a design trademark is entitled to more protection than a well-known trademark simply because the former is also protected under the copyright law.

On balance, when applying the subject section to protect the senior copyright, the standard should be based on the copyright standard itself, rather than the characteristics of a trademark and, it should demand a higher standard of proof for the purpose of maintaining the integrity of the trademark system. Also, when applying the law, it is important to keep in mind the good faith principle so as to prevent bad faith applications and to prevent any trademark applications and/or registrations that would negatively impact a third party's senior copyright.

B. Definition of "Work" under the Copyright Law and the "Substantively Similarity" Examination Standard.

In order to qualify for copyright protection, the design must satisfy the "work" definition under the copyright law. Article 2 of the Regulation on the Implementation of the Copyright Law of the People's Republic of China defines "work" under the copyright law to mean "*creative intellectual works in the literary, artistic and scientific fields that are unique and capable of being reproduced in certain forms.*" Based on the law, the "work" must be unique and capable of being reproduced in the form of words, music, art, movies, architecture, and photography, etc. The "uniqueness" of the work is the key to determine whether or not a certain design is capable of being defined as "work" under the copyright law. In practice, there are two schools of thought to help shape the definition. (1) The first school of thought emphasizes the originality of the work. Under this school of thought, a "work" should be completed by the author's own choice, preference, arrangement, design, and it is therefore a unique reflection of the author.[154] The unique value of the work is independent from its value in literature, art, or science.[155] Accordingly, this school of thought has refused to set any standards regarding the requirement for the work to be unique. A work should be regarded as unique so long as it has its own character and originality; it does not matter how small a part the creator's choice, preference, arrangement, and design plays in completing the work, so long as the creator plays a part, the work should be regarded as unique.[156]

(2) Another school of thought holds the view that the work should be independently created and completed by its creator, and the work must have attained a certain level of intellectual creativity in order to be regarded as a type of "IP" work. For example, in Decision No. 38 (2012), the SPC supported this school of thought. The decision states that the works protected by the Copyright Law are those that "have been independently created and have attained the minimum requirement of originality." A work must fulfill the above two criteria in order to be regarded as "work" and become protectable under the Copyright Law. In other words, the type of work protected under the Copyright Law must not only be independently created, but also have obtained a certain level of intellect. Such IP must fully embody the creator's unique intellectual

154. Liu Chuntian, INTELLECTUAL PROPERTY LAW (3rd Edition), Beijing University Press, Higher Education Press, 46–48 (2007).
155. Chen Jinchuan, *Judicial Judgment of Originality of Work*, People's Judicature, Vol. 9, 2008 at 89–92.
156. *Ibid.*

judgment and decisions, and represent the creator's character to a certain extent. Both requirements must be satisfied in order to be qualified for copyright protection. For example, the disputed mark as shown in Image Three below has been determined to not be entitled to copyright protection. This is because the stylization of the characters in Image Three is not unique – in other words, the stylization of these characters is not substantively different from the regular fonts to represent these two characters and has not reached a certain level of creativity. This shows that the work has not yet attained the inherent intellectual requirement. Due to different, and to some extent, subjective, interpretations of the originality requirement for the work protected under the Copyright Law, there have been some rather inconsistent administrative and judicial decisions. For example, some designs composed strictly of simple lines, such as Images Four, Five, and Six below, have been determined to satisfy the definition of "work" under the Copyright Law. On the other hand, there have been some contrary administrative and judicial decisions which disregard Images Seven, Eight, and Nine below as "work" under the definition of the Copyright Law, because these designs are too simple and accordingly, they do not constitute "work" intended under the Copyright Law.

Image Three	Image Four	Image Five	Image Six

Image Seven	Image Eight	Image Nine

The legislative goal of the Copyright Law is essentially to protect copyright, encourage the public to create and to promote knowledge sharing and creativity so as to bring on more and more positive societal and cultural developments. Following the legislative intent, in order to encourage the public to create, the condition to grant protection should not be rooted in the literature, artistic or scientific value of the work. The work should be entitled to the copyright protection so long as the work has been independently created and completed, possesses a certain aesthetic value, is the author's creative expression, and is the result of the author's intellectual effort. This is especially important in respect to the trademark design. The simple eye-catching designs typically are more distinctive than those that are complicated. Accordingly, one should not disregard a design as "work" under the Copyright Law simply based on the views that the design components as shown are too simple or the intellectual value of the design must be low. For example, the NIKE, ADIDAS, and LI-NING logos - depicted below as Images Ten, Eleven, and Twelve, and also the aforesaid Image Seven - are composed of relatively "simple" designs. However, these "simple" designs are nevertheless a clear representation of each author's creativity and their underlying intellectual hard work. If a design can be deprived of copyright protection simply because it is composed of straightforward design or that it does not have "sufficient" intellectual value, then such an interpretation of the law is clearly contrary to the legislative intent where the law was created, which was to encourage creation and to protect any intellectual work. However, similar to the practice that the scope of protection varies accordingly due to the differences on the fame of the trademarks, it is important to recognize that there is a difference in terms of the protection scope for works that involve "higher" intellectual value. It is therefore important to utilize the "substantial similarity" standard so as to properly define the scope of protection for the senior work. For work that is composed of more "simple" designs, the "substantial similarity" standard should be more stringently applied as opposed to work that is composed of more "complicated" designs. In other words, the senior work that is composed of more simple designs is only entitled to copyright protection when the junior work clearly copies the senior work in terms of the basic design, color choice or image representation, and that the two works are substantially similar or almost identical.

Image Ten	Image Eleven	Image Twelve

In the subject case, the Bull Design, which is the team logo for the Chicago Bulls in the American National Basketball League, is unique and of aesthetic value; it has therefore met the definition of "artwork" under the Copyright Law. Comparing the Opposed Mark with the Bull Design, the two marks are almost identical in terms of the overall design composition, expression, and visual effect; the only difference is that the senior NBA design includes the additional English words: CHICAGO BULLS. Accordingly, the Opposed Mark is therefore "substantially similar" with the senior Bull Design.

Let us look at the appeal of the trademark opposition case[157] involving the DKK Design No. 4445480 (*see* Image Thirteen below). The senior DKK Design registration (*see* Image Fourteen below) is a relatively simple design and it only involves some slight stylization of the DKK letters. Despite this, the stylization nevertheless represents the author's effort in trying to increase the aesthetic value of the mark, because the design embodies the author's choice preference, specific arrangement, and design effort; the work therefore has constituted a unique expression and IP of the author and therefore should be regarded as "work" under the Copyright Law. However, the senior mark is in fact a relatively simple design; this means the threshold to satisfy the "substantial similarity" standard is high in that the junior design should be closely similar or nearly identical to the senior design. The opposed mark in this case is a common English letter combination mark and it has some overall design and visual differences when compared with the senior design. The two designs therefore do not constitute "substantial similarity" under Copyright Law. This is why the opposed mark in this case is not deemed a violation to a third party's senior copyright. It is not because the senior design fails to reach certain intellectual height due to its simple design and thus fails to be protected as work under the Copyright Law.

Image Thirteen	Image Fourteen

By the same token, in the appeal of the trademark opposition case involving the design in Image Fifteen under Application Number 3950331 (*see* image below),[158] the senior design (*see* Image Sixteen) involves a relatively simple design. It is nevertheless a design that should be regarded as "work" under the Copyright Law, because the lines in Image Sixteen are stylized and have aesthetic value. In other words, the senior design should not be deprived of any copyright protection simply because it involves straightforward lines and that the design has therefore failed to attain a certain intellectual height. The reason that the junior design is not deemed a violation of the senior work should be that there are substantial differences between the two designs. Such differences include the design composition and the shape of the lines.

157. Case Index: Trademark Review & Adjudication Board [2012] No. 29064; Beijing No. 1 Intermediate People's Court, Yi Zhong Zhi Xing Chu Zi [2012] No. 3157; Beijing High People's Court, Gao Xing Zhong Zi [2013] No. 728.
158. Case Index: Trademark Review & Adjudication Board [2011] No. 30053; Beijing No. 1 Intermediate People's Court, Yi Zhong Zhi Xing Chu Zi [2012] No. 732; Beijing High People's Court, Gao Xing Zhong Zi [2012] No. 1471.

Image Fifteen	Image Sixteen

It is important to interpret the requirement for uniqueness under the Regulation on the Implementation of the Copyright Law of the People's Republic of China from the standpoint of originality. One should not demand a high level of uniqueness so long as a design is created and completed by its author and the work fully embodies the author's unique design and intellectual effort. It should therefore be deemed as "work" under the definition of the Copyright Law. Take the above-mentioned two cases as an example. The junior marks in both cases should be regarded as similar to the senior designs under the trademark similarity examination standard. However, under the examination standard of the Copyright Law, to decide whether or not the junior mark is "substantially similar" to the senior "work," the threshold is high for senior marks that are composed of simple designs and the junior mark must be closely similar or nearly identical to the senior mark for the copyright law to apply. In situations where the two designs are different, the "substantial similarity" threshold is clearly not met.

As the above shows, one should not require the uniqueness of the work to attain a certain intellectual height before the underlying design is protectable under the Copyright Law. Instead, in lieu of this "intellectual height" requirement, the application of the law is in line with the original legislative intent (i.e., encourage creation), and the application of the Copyright Law is not disruptive of the trademark system where a work may be entitled to a broader protection than a well-known trademark.

In addition to the above, a trademark application which copies a senior design without any changes, when the applicant has been (or is likely to be) exposed to the senior design but still chooses to seek a trademark registration without any prior authorization, should be regarded as a prima facie bad faith application. Such an application either covets the aesthetic value of the senior design, seeks to trade off the goodwill associated with the senior design or is itself an opportunistic bad faith application. This type of application is therefore inappropriate, lacks goods faith, and should be refused. Article 32 of the Trademark Law provides the refusal basis where a trademark application should be based on integrity and good faith: *"a trademark application shall not damage a third party's existing prior rights."*

C. Determination of "Prior Copyright."

The focus, and sometimes the difficulties, involving copyright cases is the secrecy associated with creation of a work. Because of the inherent secrecy in connection with creation of a work, it is typically difficult to ascertain the creation time, to preserve any evidence and accordingly, to determine the ownership of the underlying work. According to Article 7 of the Interpretation of the Supreme People's Court Concerning the Application of Laws in the Trial of Civil Disputes over Copyright, *"any drafts, documentation, publications, copyright registration certificates, documents provided by any certification organizations, and contract agreements provided by the relevant parties in connection with the copyright ownership dispute can serve as evidence."*

In reality, many designs are originals and unique, and thus qualified as "work" under the Copyright Law. The owner's intent to create the design at issue is to use it as a trademark. Accordingly, once the creation stage is completed, the creator typically will not have any signed publication in addition to seeking trademark registration of the design at issue and use it as a trademark. The creator typically will not preserve any drafts or paperwork in connection with creation of the design. Under such circumstances, when the "owner" is unable to provide any creation documents, agreements in connection with creation of the design or any publication evidence associated with the design, the owner will provide either the copyright registration certificate or a prior trademark registration certificate inclusive of the design at issue so as to show evidence that it enjoys "senior copyright" over the disputed design. However, there are still some uncertainties regarding the probative effects of ownership of the copyright, if any, in connection with the copyright registration certificate and the trademark registration inclusive of the design at issue.

1. Evidentiary Value of a Copyright Registration Certificate.

A copyright registration certificate is the preliminary affirmation afforded by the copyright offices in countries around the world. It can therefore serve as a public notification and carries a certain level of credibility afforded by the respective governments. The registration certificate carries a significant impact on the burden of proof so as to show evidence of the creation date of the copyright work. Based on the relevant regulations outlined in the aforementioned Interpretation of the Supreme People's Court Concerning the Application of Laws in the Trial of Civil Disputes over Copyright, the certificate serves as the preliminary evidence showing the claimant's rights over the work at issue. In practice, owners of a copyright work typically provide two types of copyright registration certificates so as to evidence their ownership. The first type is the registration certificate showing that the copyright work has already obtained copyright registration in China or other member countries of the Berne Convention, and the copyright registration date is earlier than the application date of the disputed trademark (the "**Prior Copyright Registration Certificate**"). The second kind of copyright registration is also registered as a copyright in China or other member countries of the Berne Convention, but the creation date, as reflected on the copyright registration certificate, is later than the filing date of the disputed trademark (the "**Subsequent Copyright Registration Certificate**").

In respect to the evidentiary value of the Prior Copyright Registration Certificate, given its registration date is earlier than the application date of the disputed mark, it serves as prima facie evidence and completes the owner's preliminary burden of proof responsibilities in respect to its "senior" copyright. This is a valid piece of evidence and is sufficient to shift the burden of proof from the copyright owner to the other party, even though this might be the only evidence provided by the copyright owner. And the creation date, as reflected on the copyright registration certificate, is provided by the owner itself to the copyright office. If the other party cannot provide valid contrary evidence to disprove the senior creation date of the copyright work, it can then be established that the copyright owner does enjoy senior copyright in respect to the work at issue.

In respect to the evidentiary value of the Subsequent Copyright Registration Certificate, it is not as certain as that of the Prior Copyright Registration Certificate. This is because our country, like with many countries in the world, adopts the "voluntary" approach system so that copyright owners are not required to register their work when it is created. The creation date, as reflected in the copyright registration certificate, is provided by the owner itself, and the copyright office does not carry out any substantive review of the copyright application either prior or subsequent to the registration of the copyright. Accordingly, if the party simply provides a copyright registration certificate that is registered after the filing date of the disputed mark (although the creation date listed on the certificate is earlier than the filing date of the disputed mark) but is unable to provide further documentation to show evidence that the work has indeed been created prior to the filing date of the disputed application, the copyright certificate is insufficient to show that the owner does enjoy "senior" copyright. Under such circumstances, the owner of the copyright has not fulfilled its preliminary responsibilities so as to shift the burden of proof from itself to the other party. As such, the other party does not have any legal responsibilities to provide contrary evidence to refute the copyright certificate.

2. Evidentiary Value of an Earlier-Registered Trademark Registration.

Article 11(4) of China's Copyright Law states that *"a citizen, legal entity or other organization which signs a certain work shall be deemed as the author unless proven otherwise."* In other words, the person or entity that signs a copyright work should be regarded as the creator of such work, unless there is valid evidence to prove otherwise. In light of the public nature and the constructive notice value of a trademark registration, some trademark examiners have held the view that unless there is valid evidence to prove otherwise, a trademark owner should also be deemed as the copyright owner in respect to some unique designs included in its trademark registration. The above view has been supported by some courts such as in the administrative litigation involving the disputed mark "Shang Dao in Chinese characters and Design" under Application Number 1207183.[159]

159. Case Index: Trademark Review & Adjudication Board [2004] No. 3135; Beijing No. 1 Intermediate People's Court, Yi Zhong Xing Chu Zi [2004] No. 686; Beijing High People's Court, Gao Xing Zhong Zi [2005] No. 111.

Despite the above, the courts have started to adopt the view since 2010 that a senior trademark registration is not conclusive evidence in respect to the copyright ownership of the work at issue. For example, in the subject case, the Beijing High Court has supported the above view and noted that the "signatory" statement in the Article 11(4) of China's Copyright Law refers to a direct and clear signature that should be concluded as a public message, conveying the ownership of the design to the public. The applicant information reflected in the trademark gazette when a trademark application is published, or the registrant information in a trademark registration certificate when a mark is registered, deals with the exclusive rights of a trademark. This exclusive ownership information is not the same as the ownership/creator information discussed under the Copyright Law (where an author signs its work). Accordingly, one cannot reach the conclusion that NBA owns the copyright of the Bull Design simply because it owns pending or registered trademarks for the design in China.

Based on the evidence requirement in respect to the ownership of a senior copyright, there is insufficient evidence to establish that a design is still within the copyright protection period or that the registrant of a trademark is also the copyright owner of the work at issue simply based on a senior trademark registration. A senior trademark registration is insufficient to show that the registrant enjoys senior copyright over the design at issue. The message to the public concerning the registrant information as reflected on a trademark registration certificate is strictly about the exclusive ownership about the mark itself; it is not a message to the public similar to an author putting its signature on the work as intended in the Copyright Law. In practice, it is not uncommon that people are seeking trademark applications inclusive of designs that are already publicly available. A trademark registration certificate is not a "proof issued by certification organizations;" accordingly, an owner of a trademark cannot be equated as an owner of a copyright simply based on a trademark registration certificate. Furthermore, a trademark owner should not be automatically considered as owner of the work inclusive in the trademark, even though the mark had been in fact "published" prior to it becoming a registered trademark. This is because a trademark owner would be deemed to fulfill its initial burden of proof, unless proven otherwise, if and when it continues to use the mark after registration. Given the very use of the mark shows that the mark has not been (successfully) opposed and invalidated (i.e., being challenged by contrary evidence). However, there is a time limitation concerning a work protected by the Copyright Law. Accordingly, in addition to proving the ownership of work, it is also necessary to prove that the work at issue is still within the protective period afforded under the Copyright Law. There is insufficient evidence to prove that a work is still within the protective period under the Copyright Law simply based on a trademark registration inclusive of the design.

In practice, many designs included in trademark registrations are intended to be used as trademark only. The owner in most circumstances is unable to provide any documentation supporting the fact that its work has been made public or any original drafts supporting the creation date of the design at issue. In light of this reality, imposing an overly harsh burden of proof requirement would make it practically impossible to protect the senior copyright that falls under the definition of "senior existing rights" under the Trademark Law. A harsh requirement is also contradictory to the legislative intent where a trademark application should be filed in good faith, following the honesty and integrity principle, and a bad faith trademark application should be refused. In the subject case, the second level of the court ruled that NBA did not have a senior copyright over the Bull Design simply based on its trademark registrations and other relevant and prior administrative decisions concerning the Bull Design. On the other hand, it would obviously be contradictory to the legislative intent of the Trademark Law where "senior existing rights" should be protected if a Chinese individual is allowed to register a trademark inclusive of the Bull Design which is a publicly known team logo belonging to the Chicago Bulls in the American National Basketball League. In light of the above and the fact that there was no standing requirement for an opposition action under the 2001 Trademark Law, the second level of the court recognized the following: (1) it is a publicly known fact that the Bull Design is the team logo and it belongs to the Chicago Bulls in the American National Basketball League; (2) the Bull Design therefore falls under the definition of "work" under the Copyright Law; (3) the copyright of the Bull Design does not belong to Mr. Huang. In light of the above, the registration of the Opposed Mark would negatively impact the owner's copyright over the Bull Design, because Mr. Huang did not obtain valid permission from the owner of the copyright and sought to register a publicly known Bull Design (or a design that has been deemed substantially similar to the senior Bull Design) as a trademark. The decision therefore avoided addressing the issue of whether or not the Bull Design was still within the protective period under the Copyright Law. The decision essentially follows the legislative intent and uses the "senior existing right" protection clause in the Trademark Law and reduces the burden of proof requirement for the senior copyright. Despite this, under the 2013 Trademark Law where an opposition or invalidation action should be raised by the owner or affected parties, the court would no longer be able to follow the way the subject case was handled and avoid the issue of whether or not the owner of the senior trademark is also the copyright owner of the design.

It is therefore important to divide the burden of proof responsibilities between the parties in a reasonable way so as to fulfill the legislative intent to protect "existing senior rights" under the Trademark Law and to satisfy the evidence requirement for the senior copyright under the Copyright Law. On one hand, if the claimant can only provide a senior trademark registration certificate or a copyright registration certificate that is junior to the disputed mark, it has not fulfilled its burden of proof so as to shift the evidence requirement to the applicant of the disputed mark. On the other hand, in situations where the disputed mark is identical or substantively similar to the earlier design, the court should take into account the legislative intent of the law, the practical difficulties for the claimant to provide documentation supporting the creation of the design, and the nature of the dispute (civil rather than criminal). As such, the court should consider shifting the burden of proof where appropriate, rather than imposing a high and overly harsh evidence requirement on the claimant. If the claimant can provide not only the senior trademark registration certificate, but also the later-registered copyright registration certificate, as well as creator's declaration, creation materials, agreements that give rise to the design at issue or assignments in connection with the design, this should be sufficient to cause the shifting of the burden of proof. In other words, taking into account all the evidence presented, the court should consider shifting the burden of proof to the applicant of the disputed mark so long as the overall evidence presented has satisfied the "reasonable believable" standard. If the applicant of the disputed mark is not able to provide sufficient evidence showing that the registrant of the senior trademark is not the owner of the copyright or that the applicant of the disputed mark has independently created the design at issue, the court should feel comfortable ruling that the senior trademark owner does also enjoy a copyright of the design at issue.

D. Determination of "Possible Access."

Work that is entitled to Copyright Law protection must be "unique" and capable of being "reproduced." The requirement relating to a work being unique means that the work should be independently created, rather than a result of copying. It is possible that two works have been independently created by different authors but are nevertheless similar. If so, both works should be entitled to equal protection under the Copyright Law so long as it is provable that both have been independently created. As such, the bad faith requirement under Copyright Law is different from that in the Trademark Law, where it can be inferred that a trademark has been filed in bad faith so long as the two marks involve unique designs or wordings, and the two marks are closely similar. In order to for Copyright Law to apply, the following two requirements must both be fulfilled: (1) the junior work is "substantively similar" to the earlier work; and (2) "possible contact." The two requirements must be proven on their own; in other words, simply because the junior work is substantively similar to the senior work does not mean the applicant of the junior work does enjoy access to the senior work.

In the subject case, the second level of the court noted that the fact the Bull Design is the team logo for the Chicago Bulls in the American National Basketball League is a "publicly known" fact; based on the above, the court inferred that there exists the possibility that Mr. Huang had "possible access" to the Bull Design. Given the public nature of a trademark registration, most practitioners hold the view so long as the work at issue has been included and published in a trademark, it is then possible that the applicant of the disputed mark would have had the access to the work. Publication of the senior trademark is not limited to China only, but also includes publication in foreign countries or as an international registration. For example, in the administrative litigation of the appeal of trademark opposition concerning "SHI CHENG DA YAO FANG in Chinese and English phonetics and Design" (Application Number 1962902),[160] both levels of the courts held the view that it is reasonable to infer

160. Case Index: Beijing No. 1 Intermediate People's Court, Yi Zhong Zhi Xing Chu Zi [2010] No. 3223; Beijing High People's Court, Gao Xing Zhong Zi [2012] No. 595.

that the applicant of the disputed mark could have had access to the senior mark where it had been published as a trademark in other countries or jurisdictions prior to the application date of the disputed mark and there was no contrary evidence to prove otherwise.

18. Invalidation of a Trademark Registration on the Ground of Another Individual's Existing Personal Name Rights

Appeal of an administrative litigation regarding a trademark invalidation action filed by Storm Model Management Limited against a trademark registration for "KATE MOSS in English and Chinese characters" that belongs to an individual named Jing Shengqiang

- First Instance: Beijing No. 1 Intermediate People's Court (No. 534; 2010)
- Second Instance: Beijing High People's Court (No. 723; 2011)

BACKGROUND

Jing Shengqiang (the "***Owner***") applied for a trademark application for "KATE MOSS in English and Chinese characters" (Application Number 3271558; *see* Image One below) (the "***Disputed Mark***") on August 12, 2002. The Disputed Mark was approved for registration on February 28, 2004, covering clothing, shoes, and sock products.

Image One

Storm Model Management Limited (the "***Company***") filed an invalidation action on September 20, 2006, to the TRAB under the SAIC of PRC (the "***Appeal Board***") seeking to cancel the Disputed Mark. Its primary grounds included:

- KATE MOSS is the name of a famous model based in the UK. She is so famous that she has been referred to as "the Reincarnation of Marilyn Monroe."
- The Disputed Mark fully includes the personal name of KATE MOSS. The combination of these two English words is by no means a coincidence but a direct violation of the personal name rights of Kate Moss, the famous model.
- The Disputed Mark violates Article 31 of the 2001 Trademark Law, which states that "a trademark registration shall not damage or negatively impact others' prior existing rights."

To support the grounds listed above, the Company submitted an authorized document signed by Kate Moss with certified originals provided by the Chinese Embassy in the UK. The Company also provided images, photographs, and promotional pages in color from the website "Supermodel of the World," as well as trademark applications and registration materials relating to KATE MOSS in the US, the EU, etc.

The Owner responded by pointing out that although "KATE MOSS" is the name of a famous model, she should not be considered a "public figure" and her name is rather unfamiliar to the general public in China. Furthermore, it is a common first and last name combination that is shared by many people in the English-speaking world. "KATE" in fact is a common first name for non-Chinese consumers, which directly corresponds to the two Chinese characters in the Disputed Mark based on the transliteration of the English name Kate. The word MOSS has multiple meanings, such as the "green moss on a plant" (which corresponds to the same Chinese characters in the Disputed Mark) or a male first name (which does not correspond to the same Chinese characters in the Disputed Mark). The Chinese characters in the Disputed Mark are the primary distinguishing element of the entire mark. These characters can be easily understood and serve as a distinguishable trademark for consumers in China. The Disputed Mark is therefore unique. It was not filed in bad faith and is not a violation per se or copy of the personal name of the famous model. In light of the above, the registration of the Disputed Mark does not negatively impact any third party's personal name rights and should be maintained.

The Appeal Board was of the view that the evidence provided by the Company (e.g., a media report on the Alibaba website stating that Kate Moss was to be the spokesperson for Ports in June 2002, plus coverage by fashion magazines) was sufficient to prove that KATE MOSS was a name with sufficient fame recognition in the fashion industry. The Disputed Mark includes the exact English name "Kate Moss" and the Chinese transliteration for Kate Moss. Any use of the Disputed Mark in the designated products was likely to negatively impact a third party's personal name rights, which is a violation of Article 31 of the 2001 Trademark Law (stating that a registration shall not be allowed when it impacts a third party's prior-existing rights).

In light of the above, the Appeal Board decided to cancel the registration of the Disputed Mark. The Owner disagreed with the decision and raised a trademark administrative litigation to the Beijing No. 1 Intermediate People's Court (the "***Intermediate Court***").

COURT DECISION

The Intermediate Court reviewed the case and disagreed with the Appeal Board's decision. The primary argument raised by the Company to support its invalidation action was that the registration of the Disputed Mark would negatively impact Kate Moss's personal name rights. In order to show that the Company had standing to file the invalidation action, it had submitted relevant authorization documents, including a power of attorney signed by Kate Moss. The power of attorney specifically stated that "*the Company (Storm Model Management Limited) is Kate Moss' agent and representative authorized to handle her modeling business and other commercial activities. . . . [T]his includes the handling of the invalidation action concerning Reg. No. 3271558 in Class 25 in China . . . and to act on behalf of Kate Moss regarding . . . sign[ing] and submit[ting] all necessary documents in connection with the action.*"

Based on the above-mentioned power of attorney, Kate Moss only entrusted the Company with handling the subject invalidation action. She did not entrust the Company with any substantive rights in connection with the name KATE MOSS. Based on the power of attorney alone, the Company could not prove that it was an interested party in the case. The Company therefore lacked standing to raise an invalidation action based on Kate Moss's prior-existing name rights. As a result, the Intermediate Court concluded that the Appeal Board had made a mistake with respect to the standing in this case.

The Company had submitted an Alibaba website printout titled "Famous Model Kate Moss is the New Spokeswoman for Ports" in order to prove that Kate Moss was famous in the fashion industry. The article described Kate Moss as a mega model in the 1990s and that she had once again become the new favorite model for all the major brands in the fashion industry. Kate Moss was the spokesperson for the 2002 spring and summer collection for Ports. Although this article was published prior to the application date of the Disputed Mark, it alone was insufficient to prove the fame of the KATE MOSS name in China.

Despite the above, in light of the fact that the KATE MOSS combination is not an usual/common combination and the Owner had yet to provide a satisfactory answer as to how he came up with that combination, his filing of the Disputed Mark did suggest bad faith. Given that the Owner was an operator in the clothing industry, he should have had a higher level of awareness than the average consumer concerning the famous models in his industry (this is especially so when Kate Moss was selected and promoted as the spokesperson for the 2002 spring and summer collection for Ports). In light of the above, it was concluded that the Owner had improperly registered the Disputed Mark for commercial purposes in connection with Class 25 clothing products, and the use and registration of the Disputed Mark would have a negative impact on the model Kate Moss's name rights.

The Intermediate Court therefore overruled the Appeal Board's decision. The Owner, the Company, and the Appeal Board all appealed the decision to the Beijing High People's Court (the "***High Court***").

The High Court held that Kate Moss (the model) had fully entrusted the Company to raise the invalidation action on the ground of her personal name rights based on the power of attorney submitted by the Company and the declaration provided by Kate Moss. More importantly, the Company was and would be directly and commercially impacted by the name KATE MOSS, which fell under one of the definitions of an "interested party" under Article 41(2) of the 2001 Trademark Law. The Company could therefore raise an invalidation action based on Article 41(2). The Intermediate Court, therefore, came to an incorrect conclusion regarding the Company's standing in the subject invalidation case, where the primary arguments were based on Kate Moss's prior-existing name rights. This needed to be corrected. The High Court, however, agreed with the Intermediate Court's conclusion, which inferred that the Owner had registered the Disputed Mark for improper commercial purposes and violated Kate

Moss's prior-existing name rights under Article 31 of the 2001 Trademark Law (which states that a registration shall not negatively impact a third party's prior-existing rights). The High Court overruled the decision in the first instance and affirmed the Appeal Board's decision.

ANALYSIS & INSIGHT

Article 31 of the 2001 Trademark Law forbids a registration where it would negatively impact a third party's prior-existing rights (now Article 32 of the 2013 Trademark Law). The subject case is a classic illustration of Article 31 where the "prior-existing rights" are aimed to protect existing personal name rights. A disputed mark cannot be registered or its registration shall be invalidated if the application of a trademark is based on a third party's name without prior authorization and the registration of the mark has caused or is likely to cause damage to such rights.

1. Definition of "Prior-Existing Name Rights."

"Personal name rights" refer to the rights an individual enjoys to decide, change, and use his or her personal name. Based on Article 99(1) of China's General Rules on the Civil Law, "all citizens enjoy personal name rights and rights to decide, use and change their own names and to prevent others from intervening or using their names without permission."

In cases involving trademark oppositions and invalidation actions, violations to personal name rights primarily occur when an applicant seeks to register a third party's name as a trademark without the owner's consent or license. A prior-existing name can take several forms, such as an individual's name, nickname, stage name, acting name, or alias, etc. Because an individual's name rights are personal, such rights can only be asserted when the individual is alive. In cases where a trademark application includes a deceased person's name without proper authorization and such use is likely to lead to consumer confusion, the "other negative effects" discussed under Article 10, Section 1(8) are more applicable.

For example, in a trademark invalidation action involving Registration Number 3858717 for "LIXINGFA in Chinese characters and in English phonetics,"[161] Guizhou Meijiuhe Distillery Co., Ltd. sought to register the name "LI XING FA." This three-character combination is in fact the name of the deceased former vice director of the Mou-Tai Distillery. The registration covered alcoholic beverages (excluding beer). Li Changshou, the son of Li Xingfa, raised an invalidation action seeking to cancel the registration on the grounds that the mark would negatively impact his father's name rights and the registration of the mark would result in "other negative impacts" as

161. *See* Trademark Review & Adjudication Board (No. 3390; 2010); Beijing No. 1 Intermediate People's Court (No. 2154; 2010); Beijing High People's Court (No. 1503; 2010); Supreme People's Court (No. 11; 2012).

discussed under Article 10, Section 1(8) of the Trademark Law. The Appeal Board dismissed the personal name ground because Li Xingfa was no longer alive when the invalidation action was raised. Despite this, the evidence did show that Li Xingfa was the former vice director of the Mou-Tai Distillery and he was successful in leading the company's scientific effort in developing three classic types of famous Chinese Mou-Tai wine/spirits in 1964. Mr. Li was therefore influential in getting recognition for the skills needed to make traditional Mou-Tai spirits, including recognition from the local provisional government and the wine/spirits industry. The results of his efforts were widely publicized, and he was also the recipient of various awards between 1984 and 1992. Mr. Li was therefore an influential figure in the history of making Mou-Tai wine/spirits, and his name carries a certain level of fame and impact overall in the Chinese wine/spirits industry. The disputed registration consisted of Mr. Li's name, LI XING FA, and covered wine/spirits products. This registration was therefore likely to mislead consumers into believing that the products bearing the mark share some connection either with Mr. Li himself or the Mou-Tai factory or both. In other words, the registration of the mark was likely to mislead consumers and have a negative impact on the Chinese wine/spirits industry. The Appeal Board's decision to invalidate the registration was supported by the Intermediate Court and the High Court. Guizhou Meijiuhe Distillery Co., Ltd. sought to appeal the decision to the SPC (the "***Supreme Court***"). The Supreme Court agreed with the Appeal Board and the two other courts' decisions, and refused the appeal request.

2. Standing Requirement to Assert Personal Name Rights.

Name rights are "personal" in nature - in other words, actions involving personal name rights are typically brought by the actual individual. Despite this, a third party is allowed to assert an individual's name rights so long as it can prove that it will be directly impacted by the outcome of the case. Besides any direct impact, a third party is also allowed to assert an individual's name rights as long as it can provide sufficient documentation showing that it has been specifically authorized by the individual. If this is the case, the third party is allowed to raise a trademark opposition or invalidation action on the basis of an individual's name rights. Any other third party would not be allowed to have standing to assert an individual's name rights in a trademark invalidation action except for the situations discussed above.

In the subject case, the power of attorney signed by Kate Moss specifically authorized the Company to be her "agent and representative in charge of her modeling affairs and other commercial activities." The power of attorney also authorized the Company to have full authority to handle the trademark invalidation action concerning the trademark "KATE MOSS in English and Chinese characters" under Registration Number 3271558 in Class 25 in China, as well as the power to "provide any documents and carry out any actions as may be required to fulfill its duty to handle and litigate the invalidation action of the said registration." When the first level of court rejected the standing of the Company, the Company further submitted a notarized declaration provided by Kate Moss. The Company specifically pointed out that, in the declaration,

Kate Moss fully authorized the Company to handle "her personal name rights, image rights, biography, nickname and any use of her trademarks." Based on the power of attorney and declaration, the High Court reached the conclusion that the Company was directly impacted by the outcome of the case with respect to the personal name rights of Kate Moss. This relationship therefore qualified the Company to be an "interested party" as defined by Article 41, Section 2 of the 2001 Trademark Law. Accordingly, it was allowed to raise the invalidation action asserting Kate Moss's personal name rights.

In a trademark invalidation action concerning Registration Number 3546462 for "Zeta-Jones in English and Chinese characters,"[162] the party bringing the action was Cariad Properties Ltd (the "***Applicant***"). In order to prove that the company would be directly impacted by the outcome concerning Zeta-Jones's personal name rights, the company provided copies of its applications for the trademark "CATHERINE ZETA-JONES" in connection with products and services in Classes 3, 9, and 41 in China. These applications were filed on April 15, 2005 with the China Trademark Office. Both the Appeal Board and two levels of courts in Beijing refused to recognize the company as an interested party concerning the name rights for "Zeta-Jones." These application materials at best could only show that the company had filed trademark applications for Zeta-Jones's name in China. Accordingly, in this case, the company had no rights to bring a trademark invalidation action on the basis of personal name rights concerning Catherine Zeta-Jones.

3. Similarity Analysis Concerning the Disputed Mark and the Prior Personal Name of a Third Party.

To obtain protection in a trademark opposition or invalidation action on the basis of personal name rights, the disputed mark is or should be identical to the prior third party's name. In situations where the two parties' marks are phonetically identical but involve different characters, Article 10, Section 1(8) of the Trademark Law is applicable to invalidate the disputed mark where the prior third party's name enjoys a high level of fame and, accordingly, the use and registration of the disputed mark may mislead the public and result in a negative impact on the public's interests. If the disputed mark consists of common surnames or first names - and typically cases like this involve foreign names - and the disputed mark is not identical to the third party's existing name, the protection of personal name rights would often be denied. In the subject case, the disputed mark included English and Chinese characters for KATE MOSS. The English portion of the dispute mark was identical to the model's existing name; the Chinese portion was a transliteration based on the English name Kate Moss. In light of the above, the disputed mark was regarded as an unauthorized use of a third party's personal name and was invalidated.

162. *See* Trademark Review & Adjudication Board (No. 37158; 2010); Beijing No. 1 Intermediate People's Court (No. 2027; 2011); Beijing High People's Court (No. 1237; 2012).

4. Damage Assessment (Including Possible Damage) to a Third Party's Existing Personal Name Rights.

Most "personal name rights" cases involve unauthorized trademark applications or registrations of names of famous people in today's society. Accordingly, the fame status of the third party (or rather, the fame status of the third party's name) is a key factor in determining whether or not the unauthorized trademark application/registration would have a (possible) negative impact on his or her name. However, is it a necessary condition that the name must be famous or recognizable among the relevant public in China prior to it being protected as a personal name? The relevant clause of the Trademark Law states that "an application of a trademark shall not negatively impact a third party's prior existing rights." The purpose of this clause is to resolve conflicts among competing rights, maintain the rights of the senior party, and prevent trademark registration of any unauthorized use of a prior-existing name. Article 99, Section 1 of China's General Rules on the Civil Law specifically states that "all citizens enjoy personal name rights; all citizens have rights to prevent others from intervening or using their names without permission." In light of the above, any trademark application should be deemed a violation of a third party's personal name as long as such an application involves an unauthorized use of the public figure's personal name or a name of a third party that the applicant should have known but nevertheless decided to seek trademark registration of that name.

In the subject case, the evidence of fame provided by the Company was a printout of an article titled "Famous Model Kate Moss will be the new spokesperson for Ports" from the Alibaba website. This evidence alone was insufficient to prove that Kate Moss enjoyed a high level of fame in China. However, the combination of KATE MOSS is not a common combination in English, and the Owner of the Disputed Mark had not provided any satisfactory answer as to how he created or adopted this English combination. Furthermore, considering the fact that the Owner was involved in the fashion industry, he was or should have been imputed to have a higher level of knowledge and awareness about the fashion industry than the average consumer in China. Considering the above and the fact that Kate Moss was the spokesperson for the 2002 Ports spring and summer collection, it can be concluded that the Owner of the Disputed Mark knew or should have known that the combination KATE MOSS was a third party's personal name, but nevertheless still decided to seek a trademark registration of that name for his own unjust commercial benefits. The use and registration of the Disputed Mark in connection with Class 25 clothing products would have a detrimental impact on the model Kate Moss's personal name rights.

In an administrative litigation involving the appeal of a trademark opposition concerning "ZANG TOI & DESIGN" (Registration Number 3973136),[163] the Intermediate Court specifically pointed out that a person's name rights would be protected regardless of whether or not the relevant public in China was aware of such a name. The Intermediate Court stated that, "based on the law of PRC China, the relevant factor

163. *See* Beijing No. 1 Intermediate People's Court (No. 1954; 2012).

to determine the protection scope of an individual's personal name right is whether or not a third party has the intent to improperly use the name at issue. If the applicant does have such an intent, its act can and will be regarded as a violation of the prior individual's name rights. Although the fame status of the prior personal name among the relevant public is a relevant factor, it is however not a necessary condition before the granting of personal name right protection."

5. Scope of Protection of Personal Name Rights where Different Individuals Share the Same Name.

In practice, some of the personal name cases involve a situation where the applicant of the disputed mark shares the identical name as the prior individual. Although the right to an individual's personal name is "personal" in nature, such a right is equally shared by all individuals. Based on Article 99, Section 1 of China's General Rules on the Civil Law, all individuals enjoy rights to decide, use, and change their names, as well as rights to prevent others from intervening, using, or copying their names without authorization. In other words, the rights between individuals sharing the same name are equal regardless of the fact that one individual might enjoy a higher level of fame than the other in society. Accordingly, the violation of a person's name rights will not be supported if the applicant of a disputed mark in fact shares the same name of the individual who claims that his or her personal name rights are being violated. On the other hand, an individual should not abuse his or her rights. The boundary of an individual exercising his or her rights is limited, and such exercising of rights should not negatively impact a third party's legitimate rights and the public's interest as a whole. The above principle also applies to the scope of protection for personal name rights. If the individual asserting the personal name rights enjoys a higher level of fame among the relevant public in society, and the use of the disputed mark in connection with the registered goods can be seen as a free ride of the other party's fame and influence so as to mislead the relevant public into believing there is a certain level of connection between the disputed mark and the other individual, such a use would be prohibited based on the "other negative impact" clause under Article 10, Section 1(8) of the 2001 Trademark Law.

In the invalidation action concerning the "LIU DE HUA in Chinese characters" trademark (Registration Number 4143917),[164] an individual named Liu Dehua applied for the mark on June 29, 2004. The application was approved for registration on July 28, 2007, in connection with Class 3 facial cleansers, leather protection products (polishing), cosmetics, shampoos, soaps, mousse, and toothpaste products, etc. The disputed mark was subsequently assigned a number of times. The mark was then finally transferred to a Chinese company named Guangzhou Gold Boli Health Products Co., Ltd. The Hong Kong actor, Liu Dehua, authorized Hengtai Universal Ltd. (the "***Applicant***") to raise an invalidation action to the Appeal Board in China. The

164. *See* Trademark Review & Adjudication Board (No. 09341; 2011); Beijing No. 1 Intermediate People's Court (No. 2272; 2011).

Applicant sought to have the registration invalidated on the grounds that it violated the Hong Kong actor's personal name rights and it was likely to have a negative impact on society. To support its claim, the Applicant provided proper authorization from the Hong Kong actor (which included the actor's authorization to have the Applicant handle all his trademark matters in China) as well as relevant evidence of the Hong Kong actor's fame. The Appeal Board rejected the invalidation action on the ground that, although the disputed mark was the name of the famous actor in Hong Kong, it was also the name of the original individual who first applied for and registered the mark. Both individuals therefore enjoyed equal rights to the name LIU DE HUA. Accordingly, the use and registration of the disputed mark did not constitute a violation of the actor's name rights.

Despite the above, the submitted evidence had shown that the name LIU DE HUA was the stage name of the Hong Kong actor. The actor had long been a famous singer and movie/TV star in China, and had been actively involved in charity events in China. The actor's involvement in movies and television series, as well as his songs, made him long popular prior to the application date of the disputed mark. The actor himself had also obtained a high level of fame and reputation among the Chinese public. Although the original individual applicant did enjoy personal name rights over the disputed mark, the mark was identical to the Hong Kong actor's stage name. Furthermore, the actor's name had obtained a high level of fame in China prior to the filing date of the disputed mark. The registered products of the disputed mark were in fact closely related to the actor's movie and acting career. Accordingly, the owner of the disputed mark would have enjoyed a great windfall by getting a free ride on the actor's reputation. In light of the actor's high fame and popularity among Chinese consumers, the use of the disputed mark in connection with the above-referenced products would mislead consumers into believing that the mark was connected with the Hong Kong actor. The use and registration of the disputed mark would therefore cause a disruption to the market order and have a negative impact on the actor's reputation. In light of the above, the registration of the disputed mark had exceeded the legal boundary of the original owner's personal name rights. The mark, therefore, would impact the legitimate rights of the Hong Kong actor as well as the general public. The disputed mark was therefore invalidated based on Article 10, Section 1(8) of the 2001 Trademark Law. The case was later appealed to the Intermediate Court, which affirmed the original Appeal Board's decision. The decision is now final.

In the third amendment to the Trademark Law, the phrase "*exaggeration and deceptive promotion*" in Article 10, Section 1(7) was changed to "*deceptive, easily mislead the public regarding the quality, quantity characteristic of a product or its origin.*" The new phrase was in fact one of the specific situations outlined in the "other negative impact" clause under Article 10, Section 1(8) of the 2001 Trademark Law. The phrase is now being incorporated in Section 1(7) to offer better guidance. It is not yet certain if Section 1(7) of the 2013 Trademark Law is applicable to the personal name rights situation discussed above where the same name was shared by different individuals. However, it would be more appropriate to use the subject clause to regulate this type of situation.

19. Invalidate a Trademark Registration on the Ground that It Negatively Impacts Others' Senior Trade Name Rights

Trademark invalidation administrative litigation concerning the trademark "Xi Bei You Mian Village;" the action was brought by Beijing Xi Bei You Mian Village Restaurant Company against the individual Xi Jia-Jun

- First Instance: Beijing No. 1 Intermediate People's Court (No. 222; 2012) – Decided on May 10, 2012
- Second Instance: Beijing High People's Court (No. 1358; 2012) – Decided on October 16, 2012

BACKGROUND

An individual, *Xi Jia-Jun* ("***Mr. Xi***"), filed a trademark for "XI BEI YOU MIAN VILLAGE" in Chinese characters (*see* Image One below; the ***Disputed Mark***) on August 29, 2003 with the Chinese Trademark Office. The Disputed Mark was approved for registration on June 7, 2005, covering Class 30 products such as biscuits, bannock, starch products for food, seasonings and beverage preparation.

Image One
西贝莜面村

Beijing Xi Bei You Mian Village Restaurant Company (the "***Applicant***" or the "***Company***") filed an invalidation action on November 26, 2009 with the TRAB under SAIC of PRC (the "***Appeal Board***") seeking to cancel the Disputed Mark. Its primary ground was that the Company was a registered company with the Beijing Administrative Authority for Industry and Commerce; it was a registered restaurant company since December 3, 2001. Through the Company's management and continuous promotion, the company name – Xi Bei You Mian Village – had enjoyed a high level of fame. The Disputed Mark was identical to the Company's trade name. In fact, Mr. Xi had been in contact with the Applicant on multiple occasions seeking to sell to the Company the Disputed Mark; the Company had declined. Mr. Xi's Disputed Mark had infringed upon the Company's senior trade name right and violated relevant laws in China such as Article 31 of the 2001 Trademark Law where a trademark application or trademark registration "shall not negatively impact a third party's senior rights." The Company sought to invalidate Mr. Xi's Disputed Mark on the above-discussed grounds.

To support its claim, the Applicant provided the following supplementary documents: its copy of the business license, certificate, photocopies of advertisement agreements and commercial receipts, copies of articles in the *Beijing Daily News, China Trade News*, photocopy of certificate of being one of China's Tier One Hotels, photocopies of certificates issued by the Beijing City showing the Company met the restaurant regulation standards and being a credit-worthy corporation, certificate copies showing the donation efforts made by the Company and certificates showing that the Company was one of the handful of restaurants offering China ethnic-flavor cuisine.

Mr. Xi did not file any defense within the time limit.

The Appeal Board reviewed the case and recognized that trade name rights fell under the scope as discussed under Article 31 of the Trademark Law as "a third party's other senior and legitimate rights" other than the trademark rights. The Appeal Board pointed out that based on the supplementary documents provided by the Company, they were sufficient to prove that the Xi Bei You Mian Village phrase was already a validly registered trade name and had already been put to use prior to the filing date of the Disputed Mark. Besides, through media reports and advertisement efforts in various channels, the Company's trade name had attained a certain level of fame among the relevant public as well as in the restaurant service industry. Consumers were therefore familiar with the Company's trade name. Furthermore, the Chinese characters of the Company's trade name – Xi Bei You Mian Village – was not a common phrase in modern Chinese language; the trade name therefore involved certain unique characters and was therefore a coined phrase, indicative of the services provided by the Company. Third, it was hardly a coincidence that Mr. Xi happened to register a trademark that was comprised of the same characters as those of the Company's trade name and the trade name was already put to use and obtained a certain level of fame prior to the filing date of the Disputed Mark. In addition, the Disputed Mark covered products such as bannock which were closely similar to and connected with the restaurant services provided by the Company. The Appeal Board therefore concluded that the use and registration of the Disputed Mark were likely to cause consumer confusion among the relevant public; it would easily mislead consumers into believing that the products in connection with the Disputed Mark were originated from the Company or from a company that was affiliated with the Company. In light of the above, the use and registration of the Disputed Mark would have a negative effect on the Company's "senior and legitimate" interests as discussed under Article 31 of the 2001 Trademark Law.

The Appeal Board accepted the Company's arguments and decided to cancel the Disputed Mark. Mr. Xi disagreed with the decision and raised a trademark administrative litigation to the Beijing No. 1 Intermediate People's Court (the "***Intermediate Court***").

COURT DECISION

The Intermediate Court reviewed the case and pointed out that the Disputed Mark was comprised of five Chinese characters: Xi Bei You Mian Village. The Disputed Mark was therefore identical to the Company's trade name. Based on the evidence provided by the Company during the trademark invalidation proceeding, the evidence was sufficient to prove that the Company's trade name was already a popular name among the relevant public prior to the filing date of the Disputed Mark; in fact, the name had already obtained a certain level of fame among the restaurant industry through the Company's continuous promotional efforts. The Disputed Mark covered Class 30 products, such as bannock and beverage preparation, which were closely related to the restaurant field in which the Company was involved. Accordingly, the two parties' products share a great connection in terms of target (service) consumers, and sales channel; in other words, the two parties were involved in providing similar products and services. The use and registration of the Disputed Mark were likely to result in consumer confusion, mislead the consumers into believing that the products covered by the Disputed Mark were originated from the Company or a party affiliated with the Company and accordingly, resulted in damages to the Company's legitimate interests. In light of the above, the Intermediate Court maintained the Appeal Board's decision where the Appeal Board recognized the Disputed Mark would negatively impact the Company's senior trade name rights.

Mr. Xi appealed the Intermediate Court's decision and filed an appeal with the Beijing High People's Court (the "***High Court***"). The High Court reviewed the case, rejected the appeal and maintained the Intermediate Court's decision.

ANALYSIS & INSIGHT

The subject case is a classic illustration to protect a third party's trade name rights on the ground of Article 31 of the 2001 Trademark Law, where it invalidates a trademark registration if it would negatively impact a third party's prior-existing rights. Under the framework of China's Trademark Law, three criteria must be met in order for a trade name to be protected under this law: (1) the use and registration of a trade name should be prior to the filing date of the disputed mark; (2) the trade name seeking protection must have obtained a certain level of fame among the relevant public in China; (3) the use and registration of the disputed mark are likely to result in consumer confusion among the relevant public and thereby, damage the trade name holder's interests.

1. Definition of Prior Trade Name Rights.

The "senior rights" discussed under the phrase "a trademark registration shall not negatively impact a third party's existing senior rights" in Article 31 of the 2001 Trademark Law (i.e., Article 32 of the 2013 Trademark Law) refer to rights *in addition to* trademark rights. Based on the legislative purpose of Article 31 which is to resolve disputes between trademark rights and other legitimate rights, the "senior right" clause should be read to include not only legal rights, but also legal interests that warrant protection because the right holder has followed the relevant procedures as required by the law.

A trade name, also known as a company name, refers to the name that a company refers to itself when it conducts business or manufactures products; the name is reflected in the company's registration form. A company's trade name falls under the "industrial property" right as defined under the Paris Convention for the Protection of Industrial Property; accordingly, a company's trade name warrants protection once the company follows the legal requirements and registers its trade name with the respective offices in China. Despite the above, China's law does not yet have clear guidance with respect to a company's trade name rights. The "trade name" concept is different from a person's name right and portraiture right; they do not belong to the same legal rights. Despite this, a trade name warrants protection in accordance with China's Anti-unfair Competition Law and relevant judicial interpretations.

Article 5 Section 3 of the Anti-unfair Competition Law states that: "*an operator shall not engage in unfair competition in using a third party's company name without authorization and thereby, misleading the public to believe the products produced by itself are somehow connected with the other party so as to negatively impact its market competitors.*" Article 6 Section 1 of the Interpretation of the Supreme People's Court on Some Issues Concerning the Application of Law in the Trial of Civil Cases Involving Unfair Competition states that: "*a trade name that has been validly registered with the authorities in China, as well as any foreign trade name that has been put to use for the purpose of commercial transactions that occur within domestic China, shall be deemed as the "trade name" as discussed under Article 5 Section 3 of the Anti-Unfair Competition Law. As for trade names that have obtained a certain level of fame in the market place and are widely recognized by the relevant public, it is qualified as a "trade name" as discussed under Article 5 Section 3 of the Anti-Unfair Competition Law.*"

If one is seeking to invalidate a registered trademark on the basis of a trade name, the said trade name should be registered and put to use prior to the filing date of the disputed mark. The fact that the trade name has been put to use prior to the disputed mark can be proven by its company registration record, products (services) transaction documents, and advertisement promotional materials. In the subject case, the Company had provided sufficient documentation showing that its company was validly registered with the authorities in China as early as December 3, 2001; its business registered scope included: restaurant services for Chinese foods, retail for tobacco, wine, and beverage. The above information showed that the trade name was already in use prior to the filing date of the Disputed Mark: August 29, 2003. In other words, the above evidence was sufficient to prove that the Company's trade name was senior to the Disputed Mark.

2. Definition of the Fame Associated with the Prior Trade Name.

A trade name must have obtained a certain level of fame among the relevant public in China for it to warrant protection. In order to determine whether or not the senior trade name has met the fame requirement, the following factors should be considered: the date the trade name is registered, and the duration, geographic reach, operation revenue, advertising/promotional efforts in respect to the business using the underlying trade name.

In the subject case, based on the supplementary evidence provided by the Applicant during the examination proceeding at the Appeal Board, the Applicant and its related companies had already engaged in a broad advertisement effort concerning its trade name and the restaurant services prior to the filing date of the Disputed Mark: Beijing Traffic Radio Station, Beijing People's Radio Station, 108 Lift-Hall, China Hou-Che-Ting Advertisement Network, Taxi, Beijing TV stations (BTV-1, BTV-2, BTV-3, BTV-4, BTV-7). There was also an article with the title of the Company's trade name that was written based on the interview with the Company; the article was published in the Beijing Daily on December 26, 2002. On September 11, 2003, China's Hotel Examination Committee issued a national first level hotel certificate to the Company. The above evidence was sufficient to show that the Company's trade name – Xi Bei You Mian Village – was already popular and widely known among the relevant public, and had obtained a certain level of fame in the restaurant industry prior to the filing date of the Disputed Mark.

3. Definition that the Disputed Mark Is Likely to Cause Consumer Confusion Among the Relevant Public and Lead to Negative Impact on the Senior Trade Name Holder's Legitimate Interests.

Article 31 of the 2001 Trademark Law states the following: "*...is likely to cause consumer confusion among the relevant public, and have a negative impact on the senior trade name holder's legitimate interests.*" The focus in Article 31 refers to the use and registration of the disputed marks that are likely to cause consumer confusion among the relevant public and lead the public into believing that the products or services bearing the disputed marks come from the trade name owner, or a party that is affiliated with the trade name holder. This confusion would therefore have a negative impact on the trade name holder's senior interests. In order to determine whether or not confusion is likely among the relevant public and the effect is likely to have a detrimental effect on senior trade name holder's interests, one should take a balanced approach in considering the unique nature and fame status associated with the senior trade name, the similarities between the trade name and the disputed mark, the similarities in respect to the goods and services offered by the trade name holder and those offered by the owner of the disputed mark. Generally speaking, the products or services provided by the owner of the trade name should either be the same or highly similar to those designed by the disputed mark. However, over time and considering the diversified operation approach by many businesses these days and the market reality, consumers are very used to the modern business operational and management approach, where it typically crosses multiple industries. If the senior trade name enjoys a high fame status, the disputed mark is closely similar to the senior trade name and the disputed mark owner's subject bad faith is clear, the scope of protection for the senior trade name should not be rigidly limited to the business' original and exact products or services – the scope of protection should be broadened accordingly and correspond to the industries where there is a close correlation with the senior trade name in the owner's original industry and the industry in which the disputed mark owner is engaging in business activities and the relationship is such that consumer confusion is likely.

In the subject case, "Xi Bei You Mian Village" in Chinese characters is not a common phrase in modern Chinese language and is therefore a unique and "original" phrase. After the Company's extensive advertisement and promotional efforts, its company name – "Xi Bei You Mian Village" – had obtained a certain high level of fame in the restaurant industry prior to the filing date of the Disputed Mark. It is hardly a coincidence for Mr. Xi to apply for a trademark registration that was entirely identical to the Company's established trade name. Although China's Products and Services Guidebook – The Classification Table of Goods and Services – clearly states that the products covered by the Disputed Mark (e.g., bannock, seasoning and beverage preparation) are and should be considered "formally different" from the products and services that the Company provides, such products are nevertheless closely related in real life and both integral part to today's restaurant industry. In light of the above, it is clear that the use and registration of the Disputed Mark are likely to cause confusion among the relevant public and result in damages to the Company's legitimate interests. The Court had made a careful and thorough consideration of the following factors in the case: (1) the unique nature and distinctiveness related to the Company's trade name: "Xi Bei You Mian Village;" (2) the Company's trade name had already obtained a high level of fame prior to the filing date of the Disputed Mark; (3) the identical nature between the Disputed Mark and the Company's trade name; and (4) Mr. Xi's clear bad faith in pursuing registration of the Disputed Mark.

4. Other Relevant Issues to Consider in Order to Protect the Senior Trade Name Rights.

A. Protection for the Abbreviation of the Company's Trade Name.

If a company name includes a distinctive trade name, the general approach is to treat the distinctive senior trade name as a priority for the purpose of protection. However, for company names that do not include distinctive trade name elements, the general public would typically refer to or identify the business by the abbreviation of its company name. If the submitted evidence is sufficient to show that the abbreviation of a company name has been recognized and widely popular among the relevant public through the company's continuous and extensive use and promotional efforts and that its abbreviation has enjoyed a high level of fame in the relevant industries (in fact the fame status is sufficient to allow consumers to identify and distinguish the company from other similarly situated service/product providers; in other words, the abbreviated name essentially functions as a trademark), the abbreviated name is entitled to protection just as much as other senior trade name.

The above is reflected in the trademark invalidation case involving the mark: "JIN GUI LUN" in Chinese characters (Registration Number 6635873).[165] The applicant of the trademark invalidation action was Gui-Zhou Province Tire Company; it pointed out that GUI-LUN in Chinese characters was its trade name and the name was senior to the trademark owner's registered mark and had enjoyed a high level of fame in the tire industry. The owner of the JIN GUI LUN trademark was an individual named "Zhao Jian-Bing." In the earlier 2009 litigation brought by the applicant against Guizhou Jia-Tong United Rubber Company (its legal representative is the same individual in the trademark invalidation case: Mr. Zhao Jian-Bing), both the intermediate court and the high court in Gui-Zhou province recognized and affirmed the defendant's unauthorized use of the applicant's trade name. Turning back to the trademark invalidation case involving Registration Number 6635873, the Appeal Board held that the submitted evidence was sufficient to show that the GUI-LUN trade name had enjoyed a high level of fame in the tire manufacturing industry through the applicant's continuous promotion efforts; the fame evidence also showed that the relevant public in fact already recognized the exclusive connection between the GUI-LUN trade name and the applicant. The applicant was involved in the tire manufacturing industry; its products were therefore identical or highly similar to those designated by Mr. Zhao's disputed trademark. In light of the above, the registration of Mr. Zhao's disputed trademark would negatively impact the applicant's senior trade name rights. Mr. Zhao's disputed mark should therefore be invalidated. Mr. Zhao appealed the Appeal Board's decision to the Beijing No. 1 Intermediate Court. The court maintained the Appeal Board's decision.

B. Protection for Iconic Company Names.

For cases involving the protection of senior trade name rights, they usually get more complicated if the senior trade name that the owner is seeking protection concerns an iconic brand that has been passed down generations after generations, as opposed to a regular trade name that is newly or recently established. Such cases are usually more complicated because the designated successor of the iconic brand is typically not the owner of the brand. It is therefore important to strike a balance between the successors' rights and those of the brand's current legal owner; it is important to consider multiple factors, including the history, and succession stories involving the iconic name, the operation history and its current business situation.

In the trademark invalidation action concerning the registration "DA-NING-TANG 1644 in Chinese characters and Design" (Registration Number 4570166),[166] a Chinese company named "Tai-Yuan DA-NING-TANG Pharmaceuticals Limited

165. Case Index: Trademark Review & Adjudication Board, [2012] No. 08260; Beijing No. 1 Intermediate People's Court, Yi Zhong Zhi Xing Chu Zi [2012] No. 1695.
166. Case Index: Trademark Review & Adjudication Board, [2012] No. 08260; Beijing No. 1 Intermediate People's Court, Yi Zhong Zhi Xing Chu Zi [2010] No. 3539; Beijing High People's Court, Gao Xing Zhong Zi [2011] No. 339; the Supreme People's Court, Zhi Xing Zi [2013] No. 62.

Company" ("***Tai-Yuan***") sought to register the mark in connection with Class 5 medicine products. Another Chinese company named "Shan-Xi Pharmaceuticals Company" ("***Shan-Xi***") filed a trademark invalidation action with the Appeal Board seeking to invalidate Tai-Yuan's trademark registration. Shan-Xi's invalidation action was filed on the ground that Tai-Yuan's trademark registration negatively impacted its senior trade name rights. The Appeal Board reviewed the case and pointed out that based on the evidence submitted by Shan-Xi, it was sufficient to prove that the DA-NING-TANG in Chinese mark (i.e., "DA-NING-TANG" in Chinese characters) was in fact one of China's oldest and most iconic brands; the brand had enjoyed with a long operation history in connection with the pharmaceutical industry. In fact, the SPC of China had issued a retrial decision concerning the infringement lawsuit in relation to the DA-NING-TANG in Chinese registration. The Supreme Court pointed out that Shan-Xi should be regarded as the owner of the brand (specifically, the owner of the DA-NING-TANG brand after the brand had been jointly operated by public and private entities in 1956); accordingly, Shan-Xi was regarded as the successor of the trade name and commercial reputation associated with the DA-NING-TANG iconic brand. Shan-Xi and Tai-Yuan are located in the same province in China and are both involved in the pharmaceutical industry; they are both deeply involved in the manufacturing and retailing of medicine products in China and should have been aware of or very similar with one of the most well-known pharmaceutical brands in China. The use and registration of Tai-Yuan's DA-NING-TANG in Chinese character mark would have had a negative impact on Shan-Xi's senior trade name rights; Tai-Yuan's registration should be invalidated. The case subsequently went through two levels of court reviews and both courts (in Beijing No. 1 Intermediate People's Court and Beijing High People's Court) supported the Appeal Board's decision to invalidate the DA-NING-TANG in Chinese character registration. Tai-Yuan sought an appeal with the SPC; the SPC rejected the appeal request on the ground that the earlier decisions had a clear understanding of the facts, and had applied the correct laws to the facts.

In the appeal of trademark opposition decision concerning the "San-Duo-Xuan" registration (which roughly translates to "Three Plus Hall" in English) (Registration Number 3320195),[167] the Appeal Board rejected the brand's successor's claim and awarded the mark to a different party. The San-Duo-Xuan mark was registered by an individual named Huang Jin-Qi (the "***Owner***"). However, the SAN-DUO-XUAN brand was the brand name for the applicant because the applicant had been operating various stores using the San-Duo-Xuan name. The applicant brought an opposition action to the Appeal Board in China seeking to refuse the Owner's registration. The Appeal Board pointed out that although there was sufficient evidence to prove that the brand was indeed created by the Owner's grandfather, the Huang family lost control over the brand as well as all assets associated with the brand when the brand was nationalized, and the brand had been jointly operated by private and public entities since 1957. In other words, despite the brand being created by the Huang family, the family no longer

167. Case Index: Trademark Review & Adjudication Board, [2010] No. 15449; Beijing No. 1 Intermediate People's Court, Yi Zhong Zhi Xing Chu Zi [2010] No. 2933; Beijing High People's Court, Gao Xing Zhong Zi [2011] No. 685.

had any ownership nor commercial control over the brand.. Fast forward to October 18, 1985, business operation was resumed under the brand, and there were multiple stores opened during this period bearing the SAN-DUO-XUAN characters. The revival of the brand and the commercial activities associated with the brand were largely due to the government collective efforts – specifically, the Guangzhou City, East Mountain district – was the reason behind the reopening of multiple SAN-DUO-XUAN stores and the revival of the brand. The San-Duo-Xuan characters (meaning: "Three Plus Hall" in English) were the primary distinctive element of the applicant's trade name of its San-Duo-Xuan stores, and its stores have been using these characters until now – in fact, because of the applicant's continuous use of these characters for its stores, the San-Duo-Xuan brand was recognized by the Guangzhou People's Government as one of Guangzhou's oldest and most iconic brands. The Owner's registration of the SAN-DUO-XUAN characters, therefore, had a negative impact on the applicant's senior trade name rights; additionally, the Owner's registration would have had a negative impact on the applicant's senior trademark which had already been put to use and obtained a certain level of influence among the relevant public. Based on the above, the Appeal Board decided to refuse the Owner's registration. The Owner challenged the Appeal Board's decision and filed an administrative appeal to the Beijing No. 1 Intermediate People's Court. The first level of court vacated the Appeal Board's decision. Specifically, the court pointed out that the submitted evidence was sufficient to prove that the SAN-DUO-XUAN name was created around the Qing dynasty by the Owner's great grandfather Mr. Huang Qi-Pei. The brand was primarily used in connection with stationery products such as pen, ink, paper and ink-stone. Although the applicant of this case – San-Duo-Xuan stores – had enjoyed trade name rights associated with the brand since 1957, the stores had not always used the SAN DUO XUN name over the years. In fact, the stores only used the name between 1985 and 2000. Furthermore, there was insufficient evidence to prove that the use of the SAN-DUO-XUAN characters by the store (the applicant of the opposition action to the Appeal Board) had resulted in any level of increased brand influence among the relevant public in China. The evidence further showed that the stores were not open for business after the year 2000. This means that the stores had stopped using the SAN-DUO-XUAN characters in the year 2000. In addition to the above, the evidence submitted by the Owner showed that the fame and popularity associated with the SAN-DUO-XUAN brand were primarily due to the Owner's family; it was the Huang family's collective efforts over generations that had contributed to and increased the level of fame in connection with the brand over the years. Although the applicant's management of its SAN-DUO-XUAN stores was awarded with a certificate by the Guangzhou government, recognizing the brand was one of the most iconic brands in the area, the certificate itself was not sufficient to prove that it was because of the stores ownership and management of the brand that led to the fame status and popularity associated with the SAN-DUO-XUAN brand. It was, however, very clear that the Huang family had always been a major force behind the success of the brand, especially during the time that the stores were closed for operation. In other words, the evidence was insufficient to show that the applicant's inclusion of the SAN-DUO-XUAN characters was directly and exclusively associated with the popular SAN-DUO-XUAN brand.

The Owner is the great-grandson of the creator of the brand and sought to register the brand in connection with Class 16 stationery products; the Owner's registration was supported by valid reasons, and his registration should be approved for registration and maintained accordingly. The court decided to vacate the Appeal Board's decision. The Beijing High People's court rejected an appeal request and maintained the Intermediate Court's decision to approve and maintain the Owner's registration.

In the appeal of trademark opposition case concerning the "HENG DE LI in Chinese characters" (Registration Number 1780508) (the "***Heng De Li Mark***"),[168] China Commerce Enterprise Management Association Hengdeli Clocks and Watches Branch (the "***Branch***") sought to register the Heng De Li Mark in connection with watches and clock products. During the opposition period, Beijing City Watch and Clock Eyeglasses Company opposed the Branch's registration over the Heng De Li Mark. The China Trademark Office supported the opposition and refused the registration of the mark. The Branch raised an appeal to the Appeal Board. The Appeal Board reviewed the case and pointed out that, based on the evidence and other relevant decisions made by the board, it was clear that the HENG DE LI brand was one of the most iconic brands in China; the fame, commercial reputation and market value of the brand were in fact jointly created by multiple Heng De Li stores across China; accordingly, the brand should not belong to, be owned or become monopolized by, one single organization. The evidence submitted by the Branch was insufficient to show that the Branch was representative of all Heng-De-Li companies across China to obtain trademark rights for the mark. The registration of the mark, therefore, negatively impacted all the other Heng-De-Li companies' legitimate and senior rights over the mark; the Heng De Li Mark was therefore refused for registration. The case was reviewed by two levels of the courts; both Beijing No. 1 Intermediate People's Court and Beijing High People's Court agreed with the Appeal Board's decision to refuse the mark's registration.

168. Case Index: Trademark Review & Adjudication Board, [2010] No. 09608; Beijing No. 1 Intermediate People's Court, Yi Zhong Zhi Xing Chu Zi [2010] No. 3180; Beijing High People's Court, Gao Xing Zhong Zi [2011] No. 132.

20. Determine the Validity of a Trademark Registration that Is "Obtained Through Other Improper Means"

Administrative litigation brought by Futabasha Publishers Ltd. against Jiang Su La Bi Xiao Xin Clothing Co., Ltd. relating to the invalidation action against the registered trademark "La Bi Xiao Xin" in Chinese characters

- First Instance: Beijing No. 1 Intermediate People's Court (No. 1230; 2011) – Decided on: June 26, 2011
- Second Instance: Beijing High People's Court (No. 1428; 2011) – Decided on: December 9, 2011

BACKGROUND

Guangzhou City Cheng-Yi Eye Glasses Company (the "***Eyeglasses Company***") applied to register the trademark "LA BI XIAO XIN" in Chinese characters on January 9, 1996; the application was assigned a filing number – 1026606. These four characters are the Chinese name for the famous cartoon character, Crayon Shin-Chan; it is a Japanese manga series that follows the adventures of the five-year old. Crayon Shin-Chan is the name of the five-year old; the four characters are the five-year old's Chinese name. A cartoon adaptation of the series began airing on TV Asahi in 1992 and is still ongoing. Crayon Shi-Chan has been one of the most popular cartoon characters in Asia. The application was approved for registration on June 14, 1997, in connection with Class 18 travel bag products (the "***Disputed Mark***"; *see* Image One). The Disputed Mark was later assigned to Shanghai Si-Jia Trading Development Company and was approved by the China Trademark Office. The Disputed Mark was subsequently assigned to *Jiang Su La Bi Xiao Xin Clothing Co., Ltd.* (the "***Clothing Company***").

Image One
蠟筆小新

On January 26, 2005, *Futabasha Publishers Ltd.* (the "***Japanese Company***") filed an invalidation action with the TRAB under SAIC of PRC (the "***Appeal Board***") to cancel the Disputed Mark based on the following grounds: (1) the registration of the Disputed Mark was motivated by clear bad faith; (2) the Disputed Mark infringed the Japanese Company's senior copyright; (3) the registration of the Disputed Mark was therefore a bad faith squatting and it violated the Japanese Company's rights in its unregistered well-known trademark. Based on when the Japanese Company brought the action, the invalidation action was subject to the 1993 Trademark Law. Even assuming the case was subject to the 2001 Trademark Law, the Japanese Company pointed out that the relevant term to calculate the invalidation action should start from the effective date of the 2001 Trademark Law itself.

The Appeal Board reviewed the case and its decision was discussed under No. 4646 (2005). The Appeal Board pointed out the following. First, the invalidation action was raised after the implementation of the 2001 Trademark Law so the case was subject to Article 41 Section 2 of the 2001 Trademark Law. The Japanese Company's invalidation request was raised pursuant to Article 31 of the Trademark Law and accordingly, it had exceeded the five-year time limit so its request was dismissed. Furthermore, there was insufficient evidence to support the Japanese Company's requests to cancel the Disputed Mark based on Article 13 Section 1 and Article 41 Section 1 of the Trademark Law; accordingly, the invalidation request was dismissed.

The Japanese Company challenged the Appeal Board's decision by raising an administrative appeal; the first level of the court maintained the Appeal Board's decision. The Japanese Company raised another appeal. The second level of the court made an administrative decision (No. 392; 2006) (the "***No. 392 High Court Decision***"). The second level of the court pointed out that although the five-year term discussed under the new Trademark Law was applicable to the subject case, the five-year term did not start until December 1, 2001, – any other starting point would not be fair to the "senior right holders;" it would also violate the nonretroactivity principle discussed under China's Legislation Law. In light of the above, the second level of the court pointed out that the Appeal Board and the first level of the court both made a mistake in calculating the starting point of the five-year term and this should be corrected. Based on the evidence provided by the Japanese Company, which included the Eyeglasses Company's past and present trademark records, the Eyeglasses Company had exhibited a systematic pattern to apply for and register a large number of infringing trademarks so as to sell such marks later for profits; the evidence was sufficient to prove that the Eyeglasses Company was an egregious and repeat offender. The Disputed Mark and its corresponding design were unique; and the Disputed Mark had already obtained a high level of fame in Japan, Taiwan, and Hong Kong, prior to the filing date of the Disputed Mark. The Eyeglasses Company copied the Japanese Company's famous cartoon character and sought to register it as a trademark in Mainland China. In light of the Disputed Mark and the Eyeglasses Company's systematic squatting and infringing registration of other famous brands in the world, it can be established that the Eyeglasses Company intended to register famous marks in bad faith. This was a clear violation of the integrity principle and violated Article 41 of the 2001 Trademark Law. The court, however, did not make a ruling on this part because the Japanese Company did not present the above-mentioned evidence during the Appeal Board review period. Although the Appeal Board and the first level of court made some incorrect determination on the facts of the case, they did make a correct application of the law. Accordingly, the court dismissed the Japanese Company's appeal grounds and maintained the original decision.

The Japanese Company sought a further appeal to the SPC (the "***Supreme Court***"). The Supreme Court ruled that the 2001 Trademark Law was applicable to the subject case in accordance with Article 5 of the Interpretation of the Supreme People's Court on the Relevant Issues concerning the Scope of Jurisdiction and of the Scope of Application of Laws for Hearing Trademark Cases. The Japanese Company did not raise the invalidation action until January 26, 2005, which was more than seven years after the registration of the Disputed Mark. In other words, the invalidation was not timely because it had exceeded the five-year time limit discussed under Article 41 Section 2 of the Trademark Law. The Appeal Board and the first level of the court's decisions to dismiss the Japanese Company's action on this ground were therefore lawful. The second level of the court's belief that the five-year term should not start until December 1, 2001 lacked legal ground; however, the court still reached the same conclusion. Accordingly, there was no need to restart the supervisory procedure to correct the decision made by the second level of the court.

On March 8, 2007, the Japanese Company raised another invalidation action to the Appeal Board to cancel the Disputed Mark on the ground that the Disputed Mark was the registration "obtained through other improper means" discussed under Article 41 Section 1 of the 2001 Trademark Law.

The Japanese Company submitted a large amount of evidence to the Appeal Board. The evidence could be summarized into four groups:

(1) Evidence proving that the Japanese Company was the legal copyright owner of Crayon Shin-Chan, the popular cartoon character in the Japanese manga series.
(2) Evidence showing that the Crayon Shin-Chan manga series was published and enjoyed a wide circulation in Taiwan, Hong Kong, Mainland China, as well as, many other countries in the world.
(3) Evidence showing that the Japanese Company was successful in obtaining trademark registrations for Crayon Shin-Chan (in both texts and design) in countries around the world including China. There was also a large amount of evidence showing that such trademarks had obtained a high level of fame.
(4) Evidence showing that the original owner of the Disputed Mark – the Eyeglasses Company – had subjective bad faith in seeking to register many famous brands in China.

The Clothing Company responded to the invalidation action by pointing out the following:

(1) The second invalidation action violated the double jeopardy principle; accordingly, it should be dismissed.
(2) There was no evidence to support that the registration of the Disputed Mark was motivated by bad faith and would lead to unfair competition between the parties.

In light of the above, the Disputed Mark failed to meet the criteria discussed under Article 41 Section 1 of the 2001 Trademark Law and its registration should be maintained.

In Decision No. 39811 (2010), the Appeal Board decided to invalidate the registration of the Disputed Mark on the following grounds:

- The characters in the Disputed Mark - i.e., the Chinese name for Crayon Shin-Chan (the famous cartoon character based on the popular Japanese manga series) - and the corresponding design enjoyed strong originality and distinctiveness.
- The cartoon and the name of its main character, Crayon Shin-Chan, already enjoyed a high level of fame in Japan, Hong Kong, and Taiwan prior to the filing date of the Disputed Mark;
- The original owner of the Disputed Mark - i.e., the Eyeglasses Company - was located in Guangzhou which is very close to Hong Kong. In other words, the Eyeglasses Company should have been intimately familiar with the fame and popularity associated with the cartoon and its main character.
- The Eyeglasses Company registered nine trademarks inclusive of the same characters in the Disputed Mark in Classes 9, 16, 18, 25, and 28; in fact, the Eyeglasses Company had registered close to fifty famous brands in Class 9 including well-known international brands such as COLGATE in Chinese, SNOOPY in Chinese, and 7 Up. In fact, the Trademark Office and the Appeal Board had recognized the Eyeglasses Company's bad faith in opposition, opposition appeal, and invalidation proceedings on multiple occasions.

The Appeal Board believed that the Eyeglasses Company's trademark squatting had violated the integrity and honesty principle, disturbed the trademark registration system and public order, and severely damaged the public interests. Accordingly, the Disputed Mark satisfied the criteria discussed under Article 41 Section 1 of the 2001 Trademark Law where a registration was "obtained through other improper means" and should be invalidated.

The Clothing Company was dissatisfied with Appeal Board's No. 39811 Decision and raised an administrative litigation to the Beijing No. 1 Intermediate People's Court (the "***Intermediate Court***").

COURT DECISION

The Intermediate Court reviewed the case and decided to maintain the decision to invalidate the Disputed Mark. Specifically, the Intermediate Court pointed out that the manga series and the subsequent cartoon series on television featuring Crayon Shin-Chan (whose name was the Disputed Mark in the subject case) were already published, widely distributed, and enjoyed a huge popularity among consumers in Japan, Hong Kong, and Taiwan. The fame and popularity of the cartoon series occurred prior to the filing date of the Disputed Mark. The registrant - the Eyeglasses Company - was located in Guangzhou which was close to Hong Kong. Given the proximity and the speed of information exchange between the two cities, the Eyeglasses Company should have been aware of the fame and popularity associated with Crayon Shin-Chan's Chinese name. Rather than respecting the Japanese Company's rights in Crayon Shin-Chan, the Eyeglasses Company sought to register its Chinese name and its cartoon image as a trademark in China – the above was sufficient to infer the Eyeglasses Company's bad faith.

In addition, based on the evidence provided by the Japanese Company during the second invalidation action, it showed that the Trademark Office and the Appeal Board had recognized the Eyeglasses Company's bad faith on multiple occasions in the opposition, opposition appeal and invalidation decisions. Combining the above with the Eyeglasses Company's trademark portfolio, which included a large number of world-famous trademarks, it supported the court's finding in No. 392 High Court Decision where the court believed the Eyeglass Company had been engaged in large and systematic trademark squatting behaviors with the sole purpose to assign such marks later for profits. The Eyeglasses Company had violated the integrity and honesty principle, damaged the Japanese Company's interests, and disturbed the trademark management system and public order and resulted in an extreme waste of the administrative review and judicial resources as well as public interests. The Intermediate Court maintained the Appeal Board's decision.

The Clothing Company appealed to the Beijing High People's Court. The High Court reviewed the case, dismissed the appeal and maintained the original decision.

ANALYSIS & INSIGHT

The subject case is a classic example of Article 41 Section 1 of the 2001 Trademark Law where a registration is "obtained through other improper means." The law is in existence so as to prohibit situations where a third party has registered a large number of famous or unique trademarks (or seek to register such marks on multiple occasions), and such registrations are sought not for commercial use purpose but for improper profits.

A. Legislative Source for "Registration that Is Obtained Through Other Improper Means."

Article 41 Section 1 of the 2001 Trademark Law states that: "*The Trademark Office can cancel a registration if the registration violates Article 10, Article 11, Article 12 of the Trademark Law, or that it is obtained through deceptive means or other improper means; any organizations or individuals can request the Trademark Review & Adjudication Board under State Administration for Industry & Commerce of PRC to cancel such trademark registration.*" Article 41 Section 1 of the 2001 Trademark Law was originated from Article 27 Section 1 of the 1993 Trademark Law and Article 25 of the Detailed Implementation Guideline of the Trademark Law ("***Detailed Guideline***"). Article 27 Section 1 of the 1993 Trademark Law states that "*The Trademark Office can cancel a registration if the registration violates Article 8 of this Trademark Law, or has been* *obtained through deceptive means or other improper means. Any organizations or individuals can request the Trademark Review & Adjudication Board under State Administration for Industry & Commerce of PRC to cancel such trademark registration."* Article 25 of the Detailed Guideline states that: "*any trademark that is registered through any of the following ways fulfills the deceptive or other improper means as discussed under Article 27 Section 1 of the Trademark Law:*

(1) A trademark that is registered through fabricated or fraudulent trademark application documents or other related materials; or that the application documents have omitted relevant facts.
(2) A trademark that is a violation of the integrity and honesty principle because it copies, imitates, or translates a third party's popular mark.
(3) A trademark that is registered by the trademark agent under the name of itself without prior authorization of the trademark owner.
(4) A trademark registration that violates a third party's prior-existing legal rights.
(5) A trademark registration that is obtained through other improper means.

The 2001 Trademark Law incorporated Article 25 of the 1993 Detailed Guideline by taking the following steps:

- Article 25 Section 2 of the 1993 Detailed Guideline was incorporated in the 2001 Trademark Law; it was further divided and became Article 13 which aimed to protect well-known trademarks and Article 31 which aimed to protect senior unregistered trademarks that have been put to use and have obtained a certain level of fame.
- Article 25 Section 3 of the 1993 Detailed Guideline was incorporated in the 2001 Trademark Law; it became Article 15 of the 2001 Trademark Law where a trademark registration should be invalidated if the registration was obtained under the name of the trademark agent or representative without the trademark owner's consent.
- Article 25 Section 4 of the 1993 Detailed Guideline was incorporated in the 2001 Trademark Law; it became Article 31 of the 2001 Trademark Law where a trademark shall not be registered if it violates a third party's prior-existing legal rights. With respect to a trademark that is "obtained through deceptive or other improper means," the specific section that forbids this is maintained in Article 41 Section 1 of the Trademark Law.

The 2013 Trademark Law distinguishes between a trademark invalidation action and a trademark cancellation action. The title of the fifth chapter of the 2001 Trademark Law is: "Determination in respect to Disputes of a Registered Trademark." The title was changed to "Invalidation Action of a Registered Trademark." All the disputed actions thus became invalidation actions under the new law. Article 44 Section 1 of the 2013 Trademark Law is essentially the same as Article 41 Section 1 of the 2001 Trademark Law – both formally include violation of Article 10, Article 11, Article 12 and any registration that is obtained through deceptive or other improper means as ground to support invalidation of a registered trademark.

B. Understanding and Application of a Registration that Is "Obtained Through Other Improper Means."

One of the issues that the Appeal Board and judicial authorities has long struggled with is the idea of whether or not the section - a registration that was "obtained through other improper means" - could be utilized to protect private parties' rights; the authorities have also struggled to define the proper criteria to apply this section of the law. Based on the legislative origin of the section, Article 27 of the 1993 Trademark Law was aimed to forbid any registration that essentially was a lie to the trademark registration authorities, any registration that was a violation of a third party's legal rights, and to stop any improper trademark registration that would otherwise negatively impact the public interests and trademark registration order; the law was also in existence to protect certain parties' civil rights. Despite the above, Article 41 of the 2001 Trademark Law included the language - a registration that was "obtained through other improper means" - with other absolute grounds such as a registration that was obtained through deceptive means or that the registration was obtained with violations of Article 10, 11, and 12 of the Trademark Law. Further, Sections 2 and 3 of Article 41 of the 2001 Trademark Law included relative grounds where a certain right holder's legal interests were impacted. In light of the above, the literal language in respect to the "other improper means" section included in Article 41 of the 2001 Trademark Law should logically be aimed to protect public interests and registration order only - it was not applicable to protect the relevant third parties' legal interests.

The 2001 Trademark Law did not include the general honesty/integrity section or save clauses - accordingly, there lacked specific legal foundation to govern trademark registrations that were motivated by clear bad faith but were not otherwise applicable under Article 13, Article 15 and Article 31 of the Trademark Law. The Appeal Board considered the legislative background of Article 41 Section 1, the practical needs during the examination process and considered various expert opinions after its in-depth discussions with trademark experts during 2004–2005, and promulgated an examination standard specifically focusing on Article 41 Section 1. This examination standard governed situations where the trademark at issue did not fall under Article 13, Article 15, and Article 31 of the 2001 Trademark Law. Despite the inapplicable nature of the above clauses, the applicant - on the other hand - did collect and was able to submit sufficient evidence that showed the owner of the disputed trademark knew or should have known the third party's prior trademark which had been put to use. Despite the above, the owner still sought or did register the disputed mark which was a clear violation of the honesty and integrity principle and the action negatively impacted the other parties' legal interest as well as the market order.

The 2005 Trademark Examination and Review Standard outlines four criteria prior to invalidating a trademark registration that was obtained "through other improper means:"

(1) the cited mark was already put to use and in fact was used prior to the filing date of the subject disputed mark in China;
(2) the products covered by the cited mark and those covered by the disputed mark are the same or similar type of products;
(3) the disputed mark and the cited mark are either identical or similar;
(4) the owner of the disputed mark knows or should have known about the cited mark.

In cases involving the GAP or the MUJI in Chinese trademark, the Appeal Board relied on Article 41 Section 1 to stop unfair competition where the trademarks were registered or applied for with clear bad faith. The Appeal Board's application of Article 41 Section 1 in the above cases was well received and widely applauded by the society; the Appeal Board's decisions in the above cases were also supported by the courts in the subsequent judicial proceedings.

Despite the society's welcoming and acceptance of the Appeal Board's reliance on Article 41 Section 1 in the above cases, China's Supreme Court issued Notification on Dismissing the Retrial Application (No. 118-1, 2006) (the "***Notification***") in September 2008. In the Notification, the Supreme Court pointed out that "*Article 41 Section 1 of the Trademark Law is mainly focused on the absolute grounds to invalidate a trademark registration; such grounds are aimed to protect the social order and public interests, or to prevent actions that would otherwise upset the proper order of the trademark registration system and the trademark management system. In respect to trademark invalidation cases that involve senior third parties' rights, the proper grounds should be Section 2 or Section 3 of Article 41 of the Trademark Law.*" The above position was further explained in the Opinions on Several Issues Concerning the Trial of Administrative Cases Involving the Authorization and Determination of Trademark Rights (the "***Opinions***") that were issued by the Supreme Court in April 2010. Article 19 of the Opinions states that "when the people's courts are reviewing and examining cases to cancel a trademark registration on the ground that it was registered through improper means, the courts must consider factors in addition to fraud and if the registration was obtained through means that would disturb the trademark registration order, negatively impact the public interest, improperly occupy the public resources or had been sought primarily for unjust interests. However, in trademark cancelation actions where the trademark merely impacted certain parties' civil rights, such cases should be examined under Section 2 and Section 3 of Article 41 of the Trademark Law as well as other relevant laws under the Trademark Law."

After the issuance of the Opinions, the issue as to whether or not the protection against registration that was "obtained through other improper means" was applicable to protect private interests was finally settled. Through the progress of the Trademark Law and the market reality, the Appeal Board and the courts have reached a consensus that in cases where a disputed trademark is registered not for commercial use purpose, and the trademark registrant has applied for a large number of famous or unique trademarks (or has applied for such marks on multiple occasions) so as to seek improper interests, such a situation should be deemed an act to disturb the order of the trademark registration system; it is therefore a situation that satisfies the clause where a registration is obtained "through improper means" and the registration can be invalidated accordingly.

In the subject case, the Eyeglasses Company knew or should have known about the Crayon Shin-Chan character, and the Japanese Company's copyright for the character. Despite its knowledge and the fame status associated with Crayon Shin-Chan, the Eyeglasses Company still sought to register Crayon Shin-Chan's Chinese name - "LA BI XIAO XIN" in Chinese characters - in Classes 9, 16, 18, 25, and 28. There were nine trademark registrations in total (the Disputed Mark was included) and these registrations included not only the word marks for Crayon Shin-Chan's Chinese name, but also image marks for Crayon Shin-Chan itself. Furthermore, the Eyeglasses Company had sought to register the following marks in Classes 9, 18, 25 and 44: "SNOOPY," "SNOOPY in Chinese characters," "Meng Di Jiao in Chinese characters," "Meng Te Jiao in Chinese characters," "LONGINES in Chinese characters," "Burberrys," "CHANEL," "WALT DISNEY," "POLO CLUB," "Gillette," "VOLVO," "COLGATE in Chinese characters," "GUESS," "Calvin Klein," "BETU," "BETU in Chinese characters," and "FENDI." The above registrations had already been challenged by relevant trademark owners in opposition, opposition appeal, and invalidation proceedings by claiming those marks were applied for registration through improper means. The Trademark Office and the Appeal Board had also recognized the Eyeglasses Company's bad faith in seeking to imitate/copy the world's famous trademarks and supported the legitimate owners' various actions. With the above in mind, it is clear that the original owner of the Disputed Mark sought multiple trademark registrations not for commercial use purpose, but for the goal to profit from its large number of infringing registrations. This had satisfied the "registration obtained through other improper means" clause discussed under Article 41 Section 1 of the 2001 Trademark Law because such an action had a negative impact and destructive effect on the overall trademark registration system.

Similarly, in the administrative litigation involving a trademark invalidation case against the registration, "Haitang Bay in Chinese characters,"[169] the court invalidated the registration on the same ground discussed above. Specifically, the Supreme Court reviewed the case and considered the legislative spirit discussed in Article 4 of the Trademark Law. The Supreme Court concluded that the trademark registrant - Li Long Feng - sought to register the mark and determined its purpose was not for commercial use. The Supreme Court was able to reach this conclusion after reviewing Mr. Li's interview where he discussed his plan in seeking to register the disputed mark, and he included his thirty other trademark registrations that were famous tourist spots on the Han-Nan island. Mr. Li's registration was therefore an improper use of the public resources and a disturbance to the trademark registration system. The situation satisfied Article 41 Section 1 and Mr. Li's registration was cancelled because it was obtained "through improper means." In the end, the Supreme Court supported the second level court and the Appeal Board's decision.

169. Case Index: Supreme People's Court, Zhi Xing Zi [2013] No. 42.

In a separate case, the Appeal Board also utilized Article 41 Section 1 to cancel a trademark registration. In the trademark invalidation action concerning the ERE trademark (Registration Number 4809737),[170] the Appeal Board considered:

- the fame associated with the ERE brand;
- the fact that the mark was already put to use by the petitioner;
- the owner of the disputed mark did not have any ability to manufacture aluminum ingots;
- the owner had demanded a high compensation payment for the so-called trademark infringement; and
- finally, the pattern that was demonstrated by the owner of the disputed mark and its brother in law in seeking to register famous marks in bad faith.

The Appeal Board concluded that:

- the owner of the disputed mark did not register the mark so as to continue carrying out its commercial operation;
- its action violated Article 4 of the Trademark Law where a trademark registration should be sought for commercial operation purpose;
- the owner of the disputed mark had in fact caused disturbance to the trademark management system and market economy and it had therefore satisfied the "other improper means" criteria discussed under Article 41 Section 1 of the 2001 Trademark Law.

The Registration of "ERE" was therefore cancelled for all of its designated goods.

The 2013 Trademark Law in fact had specifically included Article 7 Section 1 in the General Rule section so that it is clear that "all trademark applications, registrations and use of the trademarks should follow the good faith principle." This clause is an important guidance to the executive and judicial authorities when seeking to interpret the law and to stop any improper trademark applications/registrations. Following the good faith principle, and in an effort to continue maintaining this principle in all trademarks in China, Article 44 Section 1 of the 2013 Trademark Law also includes the following clause – "a trademark that is registered through other improper means." This clause will for sure have a greater and more effective impact on stopping bad faith registrations in China.

C. Time Limit to Seek an Invalidation Action on the Ground that a Registration Was "Obtained Through Other Improper Means."

A registration that is obtained through "other improper means" is listed together with Article 10, Article 11, and Article 12, and deception as the absolute grounds to invalidate a trademark registration in Article 44 Section 1 of the 2013 Trademark Law

170. Case Index: Trademark Review & Adjudication Board, [2009] No. 35663. This case does not get into judicial proceeding and the adjudication has become effective.

(Article 41 Section 1 of the 2001 Trademark Law). The time limit to invalidate a trademark registration on absolute grounds is different than it is to invalidate a trademark registration on relative grounds which has a five-year time limit counting from the date the trademark at issue becomes registered. Specifically, an invalidation action seeking to remove a trademark registration on the absolute grounds is not subject to any time limit. Accordingly, although the date the Japanese Company sought to invalidate the registration the second time it presented to the Appeal Board did not occur until March 8, 2007 (more than ten years after the registration date of the Disputed Mark, June 14, 1997), the Appeal Board did not refuse to examine the invalidation petition. This is because the action was brought on the ground to cancel a registration that was obtained "through other improper means" and based on Article 41 Section 1 of the 2001 Trademark Law, there is no time limit to invalidate a trademark registration on such grounds.

D. The Type of Cases that Are Applicable Based on the "Improper Means to Obtain Registration" Ground.

There are still lingering disputes regarding whether or not the ground that the disputed registration is "obtained through other improper means" is available to cases going through the opposition appeal process. Some hold the view that because the clause is located in Chapter 5 "dispute determination regarding registered trademarks" in the 2001 Trademark Law, the clause is only applicable to invalidation actions seeking to cancel a trademark registration and is not applicable to the appeal of opposition cases. Others hold the view that the legislative spirit of the law is to maintain a good market order based on the good faith principle, and to prevent and discourage bad faith trademarks of any kind (pending application or registered trademark). This principle should therefore be used throughout all stages concerning a trademark regardless of the fact as to whether or not the mark is at the examination stage, approval stage, opposition and invalidation stage. If the examiner in the Trademark Office or the Appeal Board discovers a trademark applicant/owner is seeking to obtain a registration through fraud, deception or other improper means, the mark can be immediately invalidated on the basis of the above-discussed clause. In other words, in order to maintain the good faith and honesty principle throughout the trademark system, the examiner can simply reject such a trademark application - i.e., one does not need to wait until the mark is first registered then start the action to invalidate it.

According to Section 4 of the Trademark Law, a civil party should have legitimate reasons to register a trademark - such as the need to identify or to promote its business operations. The 2013 Trademark Law further specifies this point in the general section where it states, "any effort to register and use a trademark should follow the good faith principle." Despite the above, the reality is that there are many trademark dealers and squatters in the market in China these days and they have sought to register a large number of trademarks. These trademarks are registered not for the purpose of promoting legitimate business needs; instead, they are registered for the purpose of monopolizing legal resources, or obtaining illegitimate profits (or both). In other words, the owners register such trademarks not to use them, but to seek illegitimate profits. These types of trademark registrations not only fail to benefit the overall economic development, but also disrupt the fair competition and market order while contributing to a tremendous amount of waste of the administrative resources. Overall, such trademark registrations are likely to result in a detrimental effect on the society. Accordingly, these types of trademarks should be immediately refused (or invalidated) regardless of the stage they are in: application, opposition, or registration stage. In other words, one should not avoid the application of the clause and refuse to invalidate or reject a trademark application/registration on the ground that the mark is registered "through other improper means" simply because the law is incorporated in Chapter 5 under the section titled, "invalidation of a registered trademark" in the 2013 Trademark Law, and the fact that it is not specifically incorporated as one of the grounds to support opposition of a trademark in Article 35. The above rigid interpretation and application of the law will not only disrupt the trademark order in China, but will also result in "unusual" and "illogical" results where a mark at issue can be approved for registration during the opposition process but will be immediately invalidated once it is registered - an obvious violation of Article 4 Section 1 and Article 7 Section 1 of the 2013 Trademark Law.

E. Protection Against Double Jeopardy.

Article 35 of the 2002 Regulation for the Implementation of the Trademark Law of PRC states that: *"an applicant who has withdrawn the application for trademark appeal examination shall not seek to apply again on the basis of the same ground; anyone should not request a second appeal examination on the basis of the same grounds along with the same supporting documents if the Trademark Appeal Board has already made a decision regarding such a case."* The above reflects the protection against double jeopardy in the trademark administrative process in China.

In the subject case, although the Japanese Company filed two trademark invalidation proceedings with the Appeal Board concerning the same Disputed Mark; these two invalidation actions were based on different grounds and legal arguments. The first invalidation proceeding sought to invalidate the Disputed Mark on the ground that the registration of the Disputed Mark negatively affected its copyright and was a copy, reproduction, and translation of its unregistered trademark. Such a claim was not supported by the actions of the Appeal Board and two levels of the court. The second invalidation proceeding was filed on the ground that the Disputed Mark was registered "through other improper means" as discussed under Article 41 Section 1 of the 2001 Trademark Law. This is a new basis to invalidate the Disputed Mark and accordingly, the Appeal Board's acceptance and review of the case did not violate the double jeopardy concern as discussed in the above Article 35 of the 2002 Regulation for the Implementation of the Trademark Law. The Appeal Board's action in Decision No. 39811 (2010) recognized the Clothing Company's response, and it argued that the second invalidation proceeding violated the double jeopardy principle was not supported by the law.

In order to allow flexibility in the opposition proceeding and to ensure the opposition applicant's procedural rights, Article 62 of the 2014 Regulation for the Implementation of the Trademark Law preserved the protection against double jeopardy as articulated under Article 35 of the 2002 Regulation for the Implementation of the Trademark Law. Specifically, Article 62 of the 2014 Regulation for the Implementation of the Trademark Law states that the double jeopardy protection principle is not applicable to "any trademark application that is approved for registration by the Trademark Appeal Board through the opposition appeal process but is subject to yet another invalidation action that is filed with the Trademark Appeal Board."

F. Protection of Good-Faith Assignee's Interests.

In the subject case, there was insufficient evidence to prove that the current registrant of the Disputed Mark - i.e., the Clothing Company - had obtained the Disputed Mark in bad faith. Despite this, given the purpose of the trademark invalidation system under the 2001 Trademark Law (which was equivalent to the invalidation of the registered trademark under the 2013 Trademark Law) was to prevent and to discourage bad faith actions during the application process, the determination involving whether or not the disputed mark should be invalidated in accordance with Article 41 Section 1 of the 2001 Trademark Law should be based on the subjective state *during the application proceeding involving the disputed mark*. If so, in this case, there *was* sufficient evidence to prove that the original applicant of the Disputed Mark - i.e., the Eyeglasses Company - had applied for the mark in bad faith. In light of the sufficiency of the bad faith evidence, the Disputed Mark should be invalidated and the fact that the mark was later assigned to a third party and the third party had accepted the assignment in good faith would not serve as valid defense arguments.

Article 36 of the 2002 Regulation for the Implementation of the Trademark Law states, "any trademark registration that has been cancelled in accordance with Article 41 of the Trademark Law, the exclusive rights associated with the said trademark would be deemed as nonexistent from the very beginning. The cancellation decision, however, would not be traced back and retroactively affect any past judgments, adjudications or decisions which have been executed already - such as those rendered by the civil people's courts and local authorities for industrial and commercial administration where decisions have been issued and executed either by the courts or local authorities for industrial and commercial administration - as well as any trademark assignment or licensing agreement concerning the said mark that has been performed already. Despite the above, the registrant should still be held responsible for any loss that is caused by its bad faith registration." The effects of Article 36 are threefold:

(1) it specifically states that any exclusive rights associated with a trademark would be deemed as nonexistent from the very beginning pursuant to Article 41;

(2) the decision to invalidate the trademark will not be retroactively applied to past decisions and judgments;
(3) nevertheless, Article 36 also holds the trademark registrant is accountable: "the trademark registrant shall be responsible for any damage or losses caused by its bad faith registration."

This compensation language in Article 36 has generally been understood and interpreted as the legal basis for the senior right holder to seek compensation from a bad faith registrant. In practice, however, this means it would be difficult to protect the interests of a good faith assignee. In order to strengthen the protection of a good faith third party, to increase the costs associated with a bad faith trademark registration and to maintain the fairness principle, Article 36 of the 2002 Regulation for the Implementation of the Trademark Law was amended during the third amendment to the Chinese Trademark Law. The amendment added a third section to Article 47 where it reads, *"any bad faith registrant that has refused to pay the compensation caused by its infringing acts, the trademark assignment fees, or the trademark license fees shall be required to return either the entire or partial amount if the refusal is a clear violation of the fairness principle."* This new section of the law - Article 47 Section 3 - is therefore the legal basis upon which the good faith assignee can rely when requesting the entire or partial payment of the trademark assignment fees from the original trademark registrant after the assigned mark has been cancelled.

CHAPTER 6

Protection of Trademark Right

21. Infringement Recognition Involving Pay-Per-Click Advertising and Confusion Determination Involving Pre-sale Efforts

Civil trademark infringement action brought by Beijing Volitation Information Technology Co., Ltd. against 800APPs (Babaike) Beijing Software Technologies Co., Ltd.

- First Instance: Beijing Haidian District People's Court (No. 26988; 2009) - Decided on: January 16, 2009
- Second Instance: Beijing No. 1 Intermediate People's Court (No. 2779; 2010) - Decided on: May 6, 2010

BACKGROUND

Beijing Volitation Information Technology Co., Ltd. ("***Company***") owns a registered trademark "XTOOLS & Device" (the "***Disputed Mark***") covering Class 42 services such as computer software upgrading services, and maintenance services of computer software. 800APPs (Babaike) Beijing Software Technologies Co., Ltd. ("***800APPs***") participated in the pay-per-click competition hosted on the platform, www.baidu.com ("***Baidu Website***"); Baidu Website was provided and operated by a third party named Beijing Baidu Netcom Science Technology Co., Ltd. ("***Baidu Company***"). 800APPs purchased a keyword encompassing the Disputed Mark and used the keyword to participate in the competition. As a result of 800APPs' ownership of the keyword involving the Disputed Mark, when the internet users searched the word "XTOOLS" on the Baidu Website, the 800APPs' website would appear and in fact, it was listed as the top search results on the Baidu Website. In the link information associated with the 800APPs' website, it included the following subject line: "the most professional XTOOLS in China" as well as the following advertisement message listed below the

800APPs' website: "800APPs (Babaike) is the best CRM service provider in China; the provision of a standard service package is complimentary; over 5,000 successful cases and the service package includes additional features such as one-to-one video which is offered on a complimentary basis as well." Despite the above advertisement phrases, when the user entered the 800APPs' website, the website itself did not include any use of the Company's Disputed Mark.

The Company was of the view that 800APPs' above act infringed its exclusive rights of the Disputed Mark and filed a trademark infringement civil action to the court in China. The Company's primary grounds to support its trademark infringement claim included:

- 800APPs is a competitor in the same industry as the Company in China and should have been aware of the Company's exclusive ownership of the "XTOOLS" mark, and the fact that the Disputed Mark had obtained a higher fame status in the relevant markets in China. However, instead of respecting the Company's exclusive rights regarding the Disputed Mark, 800APPs selected a keyword encompassing the "XTOOLS" term on purpose to participate in the pay-per-click program hosted by the Baidu Website. 800APPs furthered the infringement by incorporating misleading information such as "800APPs (Babaike) is the best CRM service provider in China; the provision of a standard service package is complimentary; over 5,000 successful cases and the service package includes additional features such as one-to-one video which is offered on a complimentary basis as well."
- By purchasing a keyword involving the Disputed Mark, 800APPs intended to mislead the consumers and thereby, divert the internet traffic from the legitimate XTOOLS website to its own website; this was sufficient to cause consumer confusion and deception between the services provided by the Company and those provided by 800APPs.

The Company concluded that the 800APPs' above act had infringed its trademark rights over the Disputed Mark. The Company requested 800APPs to immediately stop its infringement and to compensate the Company its economic loss in the amount of RMB 200,000 (around USD 30,000).

800APPs defended its position by noting that its use of the "XTOOLS" term in the pay-per-click advertising was not a trademark use – in other words, the use of the XTOOLS term was not connected with 800APPs' products or services; its use of the term was different from using it as a trademark in the commercial advertisements. Accordingly, 800APPs' use of the "XTOOLS" term did not constitute trademark infringement against the Company's exclusive rights over the Disputed Mark, and the action should be dismissed by the Court.

COURT DECISION

Beijing Haidian District People's Court (the "***Trial Court***") reviewed the case and concluded that 800APPs deliberately chose the term "XTOOLS" as its keyword on the

Baidu Website and the key word was closely similar to the Company's registered Disputed Mark: "XTOOLS & Device." 800APPs also included a misleading subject line - "800APPs (Babaike) is the most professional XTOOLS providers in China" - as well as other similarly misleading descriptions on its webpage. 800APPs' above actions had resulted in its website being listed as the top search results on the Baidu Website when using "XTOOLS" as a key search term. The search result also revealed misleading information such as the subject line discussed above, which then directly pointed to 800APPs' own website. This had led to consumer confusion and deception among the relevant public regarding the CRM software services provided by the Company as well as those provided by 800APPs. 800APPs' action had also mislead the confused users to its own website when such users searched under XTOOLS to look for the Company's website or look for CRM software services. 800APPs actions had also greatly increased the exposure of its own website and its CRM software services which in turn attracted more internet users and greater attention to the services provided by 800APPs, and thereby, more business opportunities and the potential for greater revenue. In other words, 800APPs action had negatively impacted the Company's exclusive rights over the Disputed Mark and should be held accountable for the corresponding civil liabilities. Despite the above, in light of the fact that 800APPs had already stopped its infringing acts (this was also acknowledged by the Company), the Court would not issue an order to request 800APPs to immediately stop its infringing acts. The Trial Court had considered all factors involving the fame and distinctiveness associated with the Disputed Mark in the CRM software service industry, the business scale of 800APPs, the nature, duration, scope, and consequences of its infringement and decided *not* to support all of the reliefs requested by the Company.

Therefore, in accordance with Article 52 Section 5 and Article 56 Section 2 of the Trademark Law, the Trial Court ordered 800APPs to compensate the Company its economic loss in the amount of RMB 50,000 (approximately USD 7,500); the Trial Court, however, dismissed other reliefs requested by the Company.

800APPs filed an appeal with the Beijing No. 1 Intermediate People's Court (the "***Intermediate Court***"), seeking to vacate the Trial Court decision and all the reliefs requested by the Company. 800APPs' primary appeal arguments were that its actions did not constitute an infringement to the Company's Disputed Mark.

The Intermediate Court reviewed the case and held that 800APPs' use of the term "XTOOLS" had in fact constituted trademark use; the use involved a term that was the same or similar to the Company's registered trademark in respect of the same or similar services; the use had also caused consumer confusion among the relevant public. 800APPs' acts had therefore constituted a trademark infringement and the Trial Court's decision was not improper. In accordance with Article 153 Section 1(1) of the Civil Procedural Law of China, the Intermediate Court thereby ruled to uphold the Trial Court's decision and dismissed 800APPs' appeal.

ANALYSIS & INSIGHT

This case involves the determination with respect to trademark infringement in the context of the online pay-per-click advertising. Although there is no substantive criteria difference in terms of infringement recognition for this type of action, the underlying actions are uniquely associated with the internet world and accordingly, different from the traditional behaviors. This type of internet action is different specifically in terms of the nature of the action and the exact time frame, which ultimately leads to consumer confusion. Accordingly, it is worth exploring the application of the general trademark infringement rules in this context and the legality concerning the actions at issue.

A. The Essential Criteria to Recognize a Trademark Infringement.

In terms of recognizing trademark infringement, one would still need to follow and apply the general rules before concluding whether or not the actions at issue do constitute a trademark infringement. Accordingly, it is worth exploring the essential criteria that would constitute a trademark infringement. Generally speaking, the following criteria should be evaluated before making a trademark infringement determination.

1. Whether or Not the Underlying Actions Constitute Trademark Use.

Trademark use refers to use of a mark on the alleged infringing products or services that is sufficient to allow the relevant public to identify and distinguish the underlying goods/services, or to allow the relevant public to perceive the mark as a trademark.

If the defendant's use of a mark is not sufficient to allow the relevant public to identify and distinguish the goods and services associated with the mark, the use should not be deemed as a trademark use. Under such circumstances, even assuming the disputed mark is identical or highly similar to the plaintiff's registered trademark, and that the two parties' marks involve the same or similar goods/services, it will not constitute trademark infringement because the use did not involve the protected area of a registered trademark.

The use requirement is not rooted in any specific legal stipulation; instead, it is based on the basic principle of the Trademark Law. Although the existing Trademark Law and judicial interpretations do not explicitly require "trademark use" as one of the criteria prior to recognition of trademark infringement, it does not mean the use should then not be considered and evaluated. In practice, daily goods and services usually bear multiple marks; however, not all of the marks in use should be deemed as a trademark. Similarly, the protection scope of a trademark does not involve (nor should it extend to) all marks. The type of marks that warrant protection should only extend to the type of actions that satisfy use of a trademark and if so, the underlying mark should be protected as a trademark. As everyone knows, the essence of a trademark is to allow the relevant public to identify and distinguish the underlying goods and services (i.e., the relevant public can distinguish the products or services provided by different providers by relying on the trademark). In light of the above, for a mark to warrant protection, it must be capable of functioning as a source identifier. If the mark used by the defendant is not able to function as a source identifier, its use would not be deemed as trademark use and such an action does not fall under the scope protectable by the law. Accordingly, using a mark as a trademark is one of the essential criteria prior to reaching the trademark infringement conclusion.

In practice, many courts have already regarded a trademark use as one of the key criteria prior to finding trademark infringement. For example, in the trademark infringement case involving "REN AI in Chinese characters," the plaintiff enjoyed ownership over the trademark "REN AI in Chinese characters;" the mark was registered in connection with education services and publication of textbooks. The plaintiff published its English textbooks under its trademark "REN AI in Chinese characters." The defendant in the case was Bilingual Newspaper - the defendant published a teaching reference newspaper called "*Student Times.*" In such newspaper, the defendant used "Student Times in Chinese characters and Device" as the trademark; however, the newspaper included the following phrases in its upper right corner: "2004-2005 Academic Year; Issue No. 37; Version for 7th Grade of REN AI." The plaintiff was of the view that the defendant's use of the REN AI characters on its newspaper was an infringement to its registered trademark and pursued a court action. In reviewing the case, the court pointed out that trademark infringement is possible only when the mark at issue is being used as a trademark, without authorization, by an individual, legal entity or other organizations; and if so, trademark infringement was possible if the use involved a registered trademark and the use was not permitted by the trademark registrant. In the newspaper published by the defendant, the REN AI characters were being used descriptively. In other words, the REN AI characters, as they appeared in the defendant's newspaper, were not sufficient to operate as a source identifier for the defendant's newspaper. These characters were there simply to emphasize that the content of the newspaper was related to the English teaching materials provided by the REN AI teaching institute; in other words, the characters were included only to assist the readers understanding of the content of the materials. The use did not satisfy the legal requirement of a trademark use and accordingly, the defendant's use of these characters did not constitute trademark infringement of the plaintiff's exclusive rights over these characters.[171] In addition to the above, the courts in the following cases have also identified that the underlying use must first satisfy the trademark use criteria before one can move on to the analysis of trademark infringement: a trademark infringement case of "WAN HUI DA Intellectual Property in Chinese characters,"[172] and the trademark noninfringement confirmation case involving the trademark of "PETER RABBIT" in Chinese characters.[173]

171. Case Index: Beijing No. 1 Intermediate People's Court, Yi Zhong Min Zhong Zi [2006] No. 15091.
172. Case Index: Beijing No. 1 Intermediate People's Court, Yi Zhong Min Chu Zi [2008] No. 4574.
173. Case Index: Beijing No. 1 Intermediate People's Court, Yi Zhong Min Chu Zi [2003] No. 6356.

2. Likelihood of Confusion.

Likelihood of confusion is the core element in deciding a trademark infringement; this requirement has already been confirmed by our country's legislations, legislations of other countries, as well as the international treaties. Despite the consistency, there have been some changes leading to the establishment of this principle in China's Trademark Law. Article 52 of the 2001 Trademark Law did not explicitly include the likelihood of the confusion factor as an element to decide trademark infringement cases; Article 52 of the 2001 Trademark Law only outlined two elements in determining trademark infringement cases - similarity with respect to the disputed mark and the cited marks, as well as the similarities of the underlying goods or services.[174] In order to address the deficiency in the law, Section 9 and Section 11 of the "*Interpretation of China's Supreme People's Court Concerning the Application of Laws in the Trial of Cases of Civil Disputes Arising from Trademarks*" formally introduced the concept of "confusion and misidentification" to the law. However, despite this formal introduction of the confusion concept, this element was only regarded as one of the factors when the courts and examiners considered the similarities with respect to the disputed mark and the cited mark, and the similarities concerning the underlying goods (or services). In other words, confusion was not yet regarded as the sole element utilized by the courts or the examiners to determine trademark infringement cases.[175] This was finally "corrected" in the 2013 Trademark Law. Specifically, Article 59 of the 2013 Trademark Law explicitly states that "confusion and misidentification" was the key element in determining trademark infringement cases, Article 59 of the 2013 Trademark Law made it clear that the similarities of the marks at issue or goods (services) at issue were

174. Article 52 Section 1 of the 2001 Trademark Law stipulates that: *"any of the following acts shall be an infringement of the exclusive right to use a registered trademark: ... ... to use a trademark that is identical with or similar to a registered trademark in respect of the same or similar goods without authorization of the proprietor of the registered trademark."*

175. Section 9 of the Interpretation of the Supreme People's Court Concerning the Application of Laws in the Trial of Cases of Civil Disputes Arising from Trademarks provides that: "identical marks as provided in Article 52 Section 1 of the Trademark Law refers to that the alleged infringing mark and the plaintiff's registered trademark are without distinction in principle from visual perspective. Similar marks as provided in Article 52 Section 1 of the Trademark Law refers to that the alleged infringing mark is similar to the plaintiff's registered trademark in respect of the font, pronunciation, meaning of the word, or the pattern and color of the device, or the composites of all elements, or its 3-dimensional shape, combination of color, which is like to cause confusion to relevant public about the source of goods or think there being certain relation between the source of its goods and that of the plaintiff."

Section 11 of the Interpretation of the Supreme People's Court Concerning the Application of Laws in the Trial of Cases of Civil Disputes Arising from Trademarks provides that: "similar goods as provided in Article 52 Section 1 of the Trademark Law refers to goods that share the same aspects in respect of function, usage, manufacturing department, sales channels, consumers, etc. or goods that relevant public may generally think there being certain relations and are likely to cause confusion. Similar services refers to services that share the same aspects in respect of the purposes, contents, ways and objects of services, etc. or services that relevant public may generally think there being certain relations and are likely to cause confusion. Similar goods and services refer to goods and services have certain relations and are likely to cause confusion among relevant public.

merely factors to consider and they were by no means the only and deciding factors. In fact, they were both factors that would contribute to the "likelihood of confusion" analysis.[176]

Although under the framework of the 2001 Trademark Law, likelihood of confusion was not the sole element in determining infringement, it was widely regarded as the only element in recognizing infringement by the courts in many cases. For example, in the trademark infringement case involving the mark "QIAN JUN" in Chinese characters, the court found infringement. Specifically, the court held that the confusion element was met because the defendant's cartoon image was identical to the prominent element of the plaintiff's trademark, the defendant's use was carried out without any prior authorization and the use was in connection with the same goods covered in the plaintiff's registration. The above factors were sufficient to show that the relevant consumers were likely to be confused by the defendant's use of the trademark and accordingly, the use infringed upon the plaintiff's exclusive rights over its trademark.[177] In the trademark infringement case involving the trademark "NEC," the court ruled that the defendants, Leetac Company and Ri Dian Company, used their marks, which were identical or highly similar to four of the plaintiff's "NEC" registered trademarks; the defendants' trademark was also used in connection with the same products covered in the plaintiff's trademark registrations and the use was carried out without any prior permission of the plaintiff. The court then concluded that the above factors were sufficient to mislead the relevant public to believe there was a certain connection between the products offered by the defendants and those offered by the plaintiff; in other words, confusion was likely as a result of the defendants' unauthorized use of the trademark. In light of the above, the court ruled in favor of the plaintiff and found trademark infringement.[178] From these cases, it is clear that the court regarded the "likelihood of confusion" prong as the final key element in evaluating a trademark infringement case.

The factor "likelihood of confusion" in fact has multiple meanings; the concept can be understood and categorized into multiple different "types" of confusion by applying different standards. There are five common categories for "likelihood of confusion:" direct confusion, indirect confusion, presale confusion, confusion during the course of transaction, and post-sale confusion.

Direct confusion and indirect confusion are divided based on the different content that ultimately leads to confusion. For direct confusion cases, the relevant public is misled into believing that the products or services provided by the defendant are in fact provided by the plaintiff. For indirect confusion cases, consumers generally are not misled into believing that the products or services provided by the defendant

176. Article 57 of the 2013 Trademark Law stipulates that: "*any of the following acts shall be an infringement of the exclusive right to use a registered trademark: ... ... to use a trademark similar to a registered trademark in respect of the same goods or to use a trademark identical with or similar to a registered trademark in respect of similar goods, without authorization of the proprietor of the registered trademark, where such use is likely to cause confusion.*"
177. Case Index: Beijing No. 1 Intermediate People's Court, Yi Zhong Min Chu Zi [2002] No. 1212.
178. Case Index: Shanghai Pudong New District People's Court, Pu Min San Zhi Chu Zi [2009] No. 269.

are in fact provided by the plaintiff; however, the relevant public is nevertheless misled into believing that there is a certain level of connection between the plaintiff or the defendant such as investment, sponsorship, business cooperation or that the two parties are in fact affiliated.

In addition to using the underlying products or services as a way to differentiate the type of confusion, one can also use the timing that causes the confusion as a differentiating factor. There are three types of confusion based on the difference in timing in which the confusion arises: presale confusion, confusion in buying, and post-sale confusion. "Confusion in buying" (presale confusion) refers to the type of confusion that occurs during the course of a sales transaction or when the products or services are circulating in the marketplace – this is the classic type of confusion and the most traditional sense of confusion understood by the public. Traditionally, the protection of trademark rights is limited to the process of providing products or services (i.e., in the transaction process). The fact that the confusion concept has been extended to protect beyond the transaction itself and is now also protecting the presale and post-sale period (i.e., presale confusion and post-sale confusion) is due to the expansion of the traditional trademark concept.

Presale confusion refers to the confusion that occurs prior to the offering of products or services to the relevant public. One unique feature about this type of confusion is that although confusion does occur *prior to* the actual offering of the underlying products or services, confusion does not occur during the transaction process itself. In other words, consumers have a clear understanding that the underlying products or services are not actually provided by the trademark owners; or that these products or services are not provided by a party related to the trademark owners. In other words, despite the initial confusion, there is no confusion during the transaction process.[179]

In practice, there is still controversy with respect to whether or not "presale confusion" should be formally recognized as trademark confusion in China. This is because China's Trademark Law and other laws or regulations have not yet formally adopted the literal language "presale confusion." This explains why there is not yet a consensus with respect to whether or not a presale confusion should be recognized as a form of trademark infringement, either in practice or in academia. Despite the above, there are already cases that recognize "presale confusion" as a type of trademark infringement. This recognition was illustrated, for example, in the case involving the "ZHONG FA WANG" trademark in Chinese characters (a case similar to the facts in the subject case). The characters ZHONG FA WANG can be roughly translated to mean "China Legal Network." In this case, the plaintiff was the owner of the registered trademark: "ZHONG FA WANG" in Chinese characters. However, when the public searched the internet using Zhong Fa Wang in Chinese characters as a search term, the defendant's website, which was related to legal education, appeared at the top of the

179. If others cause confusion among consumers not only before providing products or services, but also during the process of providing products or services, it should be categorized into confusion in buying, not initial interest confusion since it can be deemed as having been absorbed into confusion caused during the process of providing products or services.

search results. Furthermore, the defendant's website appeared with the following subject line: "Zhong Fa Wang is a website dedicated for people interested in studying the law - Our website is China's largest legal education website providing remote learning tools and resources for people interested in studying the law remotely." The court found in favor of the plaintiff and confirmed trademark infringement in this case. In the court's view, the defendant's use of "ZHONG FA WANG" in Chinese characters as a key word made it difficult for consumers to identify the source of service provider; the defendant's use of the key word evidently cased confusion among the relevant public. The court therefore confirmed infringement over the defendant's key word use involving the China Legal Network characters.[180]

The incorporation of (or rather, the expansion to incorporate) "presale confusion" to the trademark protection scope is justified whether the justification is based on the literal language of the law, or on the trademark's principle goal to protect the consumers.

First and foremost, one can deduct the protection of "presale confusion" is warranted from reading the Implementing Regulation of the Trademark Law provisions. A trademark infringement act generally refers to use of a registered trademark without prior authorization from the trademark owner. The key issue is therefore on what type of uses would be deemed "trademark use." Article 3 of the 2001 and 2004 Implementing Regulation of the Trademark Law directly addresses this issue by providing examples of uses that would be deemed as "trademark use" under the law. The examples include presale use of a trademark prior to the actual transaction of the underlying goods or services - such presale use includes advertising and promotional efforts. The examples also include trademark use during the process of transaction - such as using the trademark on the product packaging or product containers. Although the communication efforts to introduce and promote a trademark occur prior to the actual product or service transaction, such use involving a trademark can still lead to consumer confusion. Accordingly, if such use takes place without the trademark owner's permission, infringement can still be recognized despite the fact that it is a "presale confusion;" the recognition of infringement can be based on the above-referenced legal provisions. In light of the above, it is clear that China's Trademark Law does not take an opposing view if "presale confusion" is incorporated under the trademark protection scope. In other words, the Chinese Law is in agreement to protect such a use even though the use occurs prior to the actual transaction.

In addition to the legal basis discussed above, "presale confusion" can also cause damages and result in harmful effects to the trademark holders despite the fact that the confusion occurs prior to the actual transaction stage.

One school of thought that refuses to consider "presale confusion" as a type of trademark infringement, points out that in the "presale confusion" scenario, there is no confusion in the actual transaction process. Accordingly, although the third party may have benefited from the original trademark holder's commercial reputation or its goodwill associated with the brand, there is no ultimate damage to the trademark

180. Case Index: Beijing No. 1 Intermediate People's Court, Yi Zhong Min Zhong Zi [2006] No. 3739.

owner because consumers are aware of the fact that the product or service provider is not the trademark owner itself during the transaction stage.

Despite the above point of view, "presale confusion" can equally cause damage and negative impact on the exclusive rights associated with a trademark, and this is precisely why use that occurs in the presale stage warrants protection. The damage is mainly exemplified in two ways. First, presale use of a trademark results in business opportunity loss that would have otherwise belonged to the trademark owner. Take the above Zhong Fa Wang case (the China Legal Network mark) as an example. Although the internet users may eventually realize the defendant's website is not associated or affiliated with the plaintiff (the trademark owner for the ZHONG FA WANG characters), they were nevertheless interested in the plaintiff's website and the services provided by the plaintiff in the first place and this was why they were searching specifically for the plaintiff's trademark. However, due to the defendant's key word use which involved the plaintiff's registered trademark, these interested prospective customers were diverted to the defendant's website instead. Although these prospective customers may eventually realize the defendant's website was not what they intended to visit, this does not mean that the consumers would immediately click away and research the plaintiff's website again. In other words, in the presale scenarios where the consumer loyalty is not particularly high (or has not yet been established), it is very likely that the initially misled consumers may/would continue browsing the defendant's website. This means loss of business opportunities to the plaintiff because such consumers would have been visiting the plaintiff's website with the intention of purchasing the products or services provided by the plaintiff. In addition to the loss of potential sales opportunities, presale unauthorized use of one's trademark would also lead to dilution, and accordingly, directly damaging the exclusive association between the trademark and the trademark owner. This exclusive association between the trademark and the trademark owner is in fact the key source from which the financial interests to the trademark owners. Take the same Zhong Fa Wang case as an example. If the defendant's website did not engage in unauthorized use of the plaintiff's Zhong Fa Wang trademark, the internet users using ZHONG FA WANG as a key word to conduct the search, or when such users are confronted with the search results, they will always be directed to the exclusive source: the plaintiff's website. However, if multiple parties are engaging in the same unauthorized presale use of the plaintiff's trademark as the defendant (i.e., using the plaintiff's trademark as a key word search term and displaying the plaintiff's trademark in the search results), the exclusive relationship between the mark and the plaintiff's website will be destroyed. This is because the internet consumers will eventually understand the website is not necessarily the plaintiff's website despite the key word search result confirmed it should be. Over time, the internet users will simply believe that when clicking a key word search result connected with the plaintiff's trademark, it would actually lead to unrelated third parties' websites. Once this understanding takes hold, the exclusive connection between the trademark and the plaintiff is diluted and will eventually disappears.

B. Whether or Not the Alleged Infringing Act Constitutes a Trademark Use as Required by the Trademark Law.

Turning back to the subject case, one still needs to analyze the two elements discussed above prior to determining whether or not the pay-per-click advertising use in the subject case has constituted trademark infringement. The Intermediate Court provided a detailed analysis in this respect.

In the final judgment, the Intermediate Court first discussed whether or not the defendant's unauthorized use of the "XTOOLS" trademark in the pay-per-click advertisement was a form of trademark use. Generally speaking, trademark use refers to use of a trademark in connection with the underlying products or services, or such use is incorporated in the advertising or promotional efforts for the underlying trademark. In the subject case, however, the use was mainly incorporated in the key word search results (in the subject title and information summary). The use of the trademark clearly was not associated with the underlying products or services. Even assuming the defendant's use of the XTOOLS trademark would be deemed as an advertisement effort, such promotional effort was quite different from the usual advertisement effort, as commonly understood by the public. The court therefore pointed out that given the unique circumstances of the case, one cannot and should not quickly jump to conclusion in deciding that the defendant's use of the mark was not trademark use because it did not meet the traditional criteria.

The Intermediate Court then pointed out that whether or not the defendant's use of the trademark would constitute trademark use should be examined from the relevant public's perspective. Generally speaking, the relevant public's perspective is the key in determining whether or not a particular use falls under the scope of trademark use.

However, in this case, the alleged infringing act is quite different from the traditional understanding because the infringing act in the case is a result generated by the internet users when they used XTOOLS as the search word. Accordingly, the relevant public in this case was not the general internet users nor *all* of the relevant public that would otherwise be directly impacted by a third party's unauthorized use of the Disputed Mark. In other words, the relevant public concept in the subject case should be limited to a portion of the internet users who have specifically used XTOOLS as an internet search word. In other words, the relevant public in the case should not involve the entire public that would otherwise be associated with the Disputed Mark; instead, they are limited to a particular section of the internet users who have specifically used XTOOLS as the search term.

Once the "relevant public" in the subject case was determined, the court then pointed out that it should be this particular group's perception as to whether or not they conducted the key word search with the understanding that the term "XTOOLS" was a trademark. If this particular group perceived "XTOOLS" as a trademark when conducting the keyword search, they would naturally perceive the defendant's use of the "XTOOLS" word as a trademark use when they reviewed the search results. If so, the alleged infringing webpage's use of the XTOOLS term should be regarded as trademark use as defined by the law; it should not otherwise be concluded as trademark use if the internet users conducted the keyword search without this understanding.

In order to determine the internet user's perception of the XTOOLS term when they conducted the keyword search, it is necessary to consider whether or not XTOOLS has any other fixed meanings. Although "XTOOLS" is the textual element of the Disputed Mark, it remains possible that the term has other meanings. However, it should be the defendant's burden to prove and to show that the "XTOOLS" term has other fixed meanings. In this case, the defendant failed to provide any evidence showing that the "XTOOLS" term has other meanings except as a textual element in the Disputed Mark. Furthermore, it is clear that the XTOOLS term was not a fixed word with any specific meaning in the English language. Based on the above, the second instance court reached the reasonable conclusion when the internet users used XTOOLS as a search term, they perceived the "XTOOLS" term as a trademark in the sense that the term was the textual elements incorporated in the Disputed Mark.[181]

With the above understanding, although 800APPs' use of the "XTOOLS" term on its website did not point to any specific products or services, it is clear that the products or services intended by 800APPs' website involved the same computer software services as those included in the Disputed Mark. Specifically, despite the fact that 800APPs' use of the XTOOLS term was limited to the subject line in the search results: "800APPs (Babaike) – the Most Professional XTOOLS in China" and the promotional information listed directly below the subject line: "www.800app.com" and the following promotional information: "800APPs (Babaike) is the best CRM service provider in China; the provision of standard service package is complimentary; over 5,000 successful cases and the service package includes additional features such as one-to-one video which is offered on a complimentary basis as well," it was clear that the scope of services from the website and the above promotional phrases involved computer software which was the same type of services that the internet users had in mind when they were searching the "XTOOLS" term. Accordingly, for the relevant public in the subject case, they would inevitably conclude that the XTOOLS term used on 800APPs' website was in fact the Disputed Mark in connection with the computer software services. The second instance court therefore concluded that 800APPs' use of the "XTOOLS" term had constituted trademark use because the use was indicative of the origin of the underlying product/service provider.

C. Likelihood of Confusion Determination: Presale Confusion.

In the subject 800APPs case, the Disputed Mark was merely used in the Internet search results – specifically, on the subject line of the search results and the information summary. When the internet users actually clicked on 800APPs website, they would not be confronted with a website involving any use of the Disputed Mark. In other words, 800APPs did not engage in any actual use of the Disputed Mark in connection with computer software services. If confusion was possible in the subject case, it would only occur and stay limited to the presale stage (as opposed to confusion during the

181. While reviewing this case, the author conducted search on the internet by using "XTOOLS" as the keyword, and the first few pages of the search results are mostly related to the plaintiff and its registered trademark, which proves the meaning of this term to some extent.

actual transaction stage). As discussed above, "presale confusion" also falls under the scope of trademark protection; accordingly, the court in the subject case would still need to determine whether or not confusion was likely in the presale stage. Many factors are likely to influence the confusion analysis, regardless of whether the underlying scenario involves presale confusion or confusion during the process of a transaction. Among these multiple factors, the similarities of the underlying trademarks, and the goods and services provided by both parties would have a direct substantive impact on the confusion determination.

The textual element in the Disputed Mark, XTOOLS, was used by 800APPs on the Internet subject line and information summary. Accordingly, 800APPs was involved in using a highly similar mark as the Company's registered trademark despite the fact that the Disputed Mark includes not only the word XTOOLS but also a design element. In addition to the similarities of the trademarks, it is clear that from the search results (the title and the summary information) that the services provided by 800APPs were identical or highly similar to those included in the Disputed Mark: upgrading services of computer software, and computer software maintenance services. The above similarities between the trademarks and the services involved are likely to convince the relevant public that the "actor" in this case (800APPs) was in fact the owner of the Disputed Mark. Put simply, 800APPs' use of the XTOOLS term was likely to result in consumer confusion among the relevant public with respect to the origin of the underlying products/services.

Although the infringing website in the subject case did include the defendant's trade name, "800APPs (Babaike)," this inclusion would not necessarily guarantee that the internet users would automatically understand or perceive that 800APPs was the company name associated with the website. Even assuming the relevant public could immediately understand that 800APPs was in fact the defendant's company name, it still does not negate the infringement recognition. This is because likelihood of confusion determination does not require the relevant public to precisely identify the exact party providing the underlying products or services. Confusion will be recognized as long as the relevant public would be misled into believing that the defendant is the same party as the trademark owner or that the two parties are associated to some extent. In other words, even assuming the relevant public would know and perceive the term "800APPs" (Babaike) as the name of the defendant, this understanding still does not impact the confusion recognition in the subject case.

22. Infringement Recognition Involving Use of the Same or Similar Marks in Connection with the Same or Similar Products

Civil action involving trademark infringement and unauthorized use of a third party's company name brought by Dale Carnegie & Associates, Inc. against Beijing Haidian District Carnegie Training School for Success

- First Instance: Beijing No. 1 Intermediate People's Court (No. 16511; 2011) - Decided on: December 19, 2011
- Second Instance: Beijing High People's Court (No. 4545; 2012) - Decided on: June 18, 2014

BACKGROUND

Dale Carnegie & Associates, Inc. (the "***Dale C. Company***" or the "***Company***") registered "DA-ER-KA-NEI-JI" (one of the transliterations for "DALE CARNEGIE" in Chinese characters) under Registration Number 772658, and the English mark "DALE CARNEGIE" under Registration Number 772672 in connection with Class 41 educational services (the "***Carnegie English and Chinese Trademarks***"). The Dale C. Company registered additional trademarks - namely, "KA NAI JI TRAINING" (CARNEGIE TRAINING in Chinese characters; note that this version involves a different middle character for Carnegie: *Nei v. Nai*) - under Registration Number 3497814 on September 7, 2004, and "KA-NEI-JI TRAINING" in Chinese characters under Registration Number 3531415 on November 14, 2004, in connection with education, teaching, and adult education services. The above registrations have been renewed and were valid registrations in China.

From 2001 to 2005, the Dale C. Company had signed various license agreements and authorized different companies across China in provinces and cities such as Beijing, Tianjin, Hebei, Jiangsu, Shanghai, Shandong, and Zhejiang to provide Carnegie training courses; the Dale C. Company had also licensed the use of various trademarks, such as "DALE CARNEGIE" in English and Chinese characters, to its licensees across China. From 2003 to 2004, Dale C. Company's licensees in China signed training agreements with more than forty companies across China. These forty plus companies included sizable and state-owned entities such as China National Offshore Oil Corporation, Ideal (Beijing) Co., Ltd., China Development Bank. In addition to the above, Dale C. Company provided multiple witness declarations showing that Dale C. Company had been involved in licensing contracts with companies in China, authorizing such companies to offer DALE CARNEGIE branded training classes and use its name: "DALE CARNEGIE" in China since as early as 1994.

Beijing Haidian District Carnegie Training School for Success (the "***School***") was approved of its corporate status in December 1999. In its operation, the School used "Beijing KA NAI JI School" and "KA NAI JI School" phrases on signage on the first floor of its building, its front desk, posters on the wall, and top left corner of its promotional brochures. The School's articles on its website (such as those introducing the School's teachers, principal and the School itself), its print media and newspaper articles all identified itself as "Beijing KA NAI JI School," "KA NAI JI School," and/or "Beijing KA NAI JI national branch school" and the above as the source of publication. In fact, the top left corner of the website for "Beijing Carnegie Training School for Success (Guangzhou) School" used the stand-alone "Carnegie" word and logo.

Dale C. Company believed the School had infringed its trademark rights and its infringing acts had constituted unfair competition; Dale C. Company brought a lawsuit to the court in China.

COURT DECISION

Beijing No. 1 Intermediate People's Court (the "***Intermediate Court***") reviewed the case and rejected Dale C. Company's trademark infringement and unfair competition claims. The Intermediate Court was of the view that the School followed the industry's customs and abbreviated its company name to simply "Beijing KA NAI JI School" and "KA NAI JI School" (the "***Abbreviated Names***"). The School's use of its Abbreviated Names did not involve any prominent use of Dale C. Company's registered trademarks in China; the use of the KA NAI JI characters in the Abbreviated Names, i.e., one of the transliterations of Carnegie in Chinese characters, did not involve any special font or stylization. Accordingly, the School's use of the Abbreviated Names did not constitute any prominent use of its company name. The School's use of its company name was earlier than the registration date of Dale C. Company's trademarks - specifically, Registration Number 3497814 and Registration Number 3531415. Since the School's company name was registered prior to Dale C. Company's registered trademarks, it enjoyed legitimate rights over the name. Accordingly, the School's use of its Abbreviated Names for its facilities, promotional brochures, and websites fell under the legitimate and reasonable use of its company name. The use did not fall under the category where it involved the prominent use of characters that were identical or highly similar to those of Dale C. Company's registered trademarks, and the School therefore did not infringe Dale C. Company's trademarks. The Intermediate Court did not support Dale C. Company's trademark infringement claim and rejected Dale C. Company's request for relief.

Dale C. Company pursued an appeal to the Beijing High People's Court (the "***High Court***"). During the appeal, Dale C. Company submitted the following (final) decisions issued by the China Trademark Office (the "***Trademark Office***"):

- No. 52272 titled "Opposition Decision against the "KA NAI JI School" Trademark (2011).
- No. 60043 titled "Opposition Decision against "KA NAI JI• KA-ISM TRAINING in Chinese characters" (2012) (collectively, the "***Opposition Decisions***").
- The Opposition Decisions were submitted so as to prove that the School's trademark applications for "KA NAI JI School" (in Chinese characters; Application Number 4745544) and "KA NAI JI• KA-ISM TRAINING" (in Chinese

characters; Application Number 7892110) were denied for registration in connection with Class 41 educational services.

Beijing High People's Court ("***High Court***") reviewed the case and pointed out that Dale C. Company's exclusive rights over its trademark registrations covering educational services in Class 41 in China were entitled to protection under the Chinese Law. The prominent element of its trademarks focused on the word "KA-NEI-JI" or "KA NAI JI" in Chinese characters. Both versions were variant transliterations of the last name of Dale Harbison Carnegie, who was from the USA and was the founder and developer of famous courses in self-improvement and interpersonal skills. He was a world renowned master in interpersonal relationships and was instrumental in developing modern relationship education. The Company's Carnegie trademarks, "DALE CARNEGIE" under Registration Number 772672 and "DALE CARNEGIE" in Chinese characters under Registration Number 772658, were filed prior to the establishment of the School. The fact that the School and Dale C. Company were involved in the same or similar type of educational training industry meant that the School was or should have been aware of the reputation in connection with the training services offered by the Company. The School used "Beijing KA NAI JI School" and "KA NAI JI School" phrases on signage on the first floor of its building, its front desk, posters on the wall, and promotional brochures, as well as the School's articles on its website (such as those introducing the School's teachers, principal and the School itself), its print media and newspaper articles. It turned out that the School's use of its Abbreviated Names indicated its prominent use of the KA NAI JI characters. These characters were therefore the prominent distinctive source identifiers in the School's training services, because the word "SCHOOL" is less distinctive and, in fact, generic in this context. The School's use of its Abbreviated Names would therefore easily mislead the relevant public into believing that it was associated with the Company. Also, it was clear that the School had subjective intent to purposely use the KA NAI JI characters because its website used the "Carnegie" logo and it had sought to register "KA NAI JI SCHOOL" in Chinese characters in connection with Class 41 educational services. The School should have used its complete company name. "KA NAI JI" and "KA-NEI-JI" were both coined phrases based on foreign language. Given that the Company already owned exclusive trademark rights over such characters, the School should have been more careful in using characters that were identical or highly similar to the Company's registered trademarks. It should have at least avoided using the same or similar characters by themselves or in a prominent manner. Furthermore, based on the evidence provided by the Company, its registered trademarks had obtained a certain level of fame through consistent use in China. Such use involved its long-term involvement in China to provide training services, and it had provided training to employees of many established companies, etc. The School should therefore bear the corresponding civil responsibilities because its use of the Abbreviated Names for its business operation, promotional materials, business cards, and websites had infringed the Company's trademark rights. The Company, however, did not provide any supporting evidence showing its actual loss or the School's profits on the basis of the School's infringing acts. The High Court therefore calculated the damage amount based on the fame associated with the Company's trademarks, the duration of the School's infringing acts, the nature of the infringement, and the subjective intent of the parties involved in operating the School. The High Court also considered reasonable legal expenses paid by the Company in order to protect its rights under the Chinese system.

Dale C. Company was a US-based company and its commercial use of its company name in China was therefore entitled to protection under the Law in China. However, the primary subject in the licensing agreements between the Company and its counterparts in China was its trademarks, as opposed to the Company's name – in other words, the licensees did not offer training classes under the name of Dale C. Company. Furthermore, the Company's English and Chinese names were not validly recorded company names with the relevant authorities in China. Therefore, it was insufficient to prove Dale C. Company's commercial use of its company name in China. In light of the above, the High Court did not support the Company's claim that the School was engaged in unauthorized use of its company name and it was therefore unfair competition.

The High Court's decisions were:

(1) vacate the Intermediate Court's decision;
(2) the School should properly use its entire/complete company name; it was ordered to stop using the Abbreviated Names or any other closely similar marks of "Beijing Carnegie School" and "Carnegie School" in connection with education, training, and adult education services. The School must stop its infringing acts against the Company's following registered trademarks: Registration Numbers 772658, 772672, 3497814, and 3531415;
(3) the School was ordered to pay RMB 400,000 (approximately USD 60,000) to the Company to reimburse its economic loss and reasonable expenses;
(4) rejected the Company's other requests for relief.

ANALYSIS & INSIGHT

There are a wide variety of ways one's trademark rights would be infringed upon; however, the Trademark Law mainly concentrates on the protection of the exclusive rights associated with a registered trademark. The protection of an unregistered trademark, however, is limited to certain types of cases only.[182] Accordingly, trademark infringement cases typically involve actions that infringe upon one's exclusive rights associated with its registered trademarks.

Article 57 of the 2013 amended Trademark Law states that: "Any of the following actions shall be deemed an infringement to the exclusive rights of one's registered trademark:

182. For example, the infringing acts against unregistered well-known trademarks can be prohibited under relevant provisions of the China Trademark Law.

(a) A third party's use of a mark that is identical to one's registered trademark and the use involves the same products or services covered by the registered trademark and the use is without the trademark owner's authorization.
(b) A third party's use of a mark that is highly similar to one's registered trademark and the use involves the same or similar products or services as those covered by the registered trademark; and the use is without the trademark owner's authorization and is likely to lead to consumer confusion.
(c) A third party's sale of products that constitutes a violation of the trademark owner's exclusive rights over its trademarks.
(d) A third party's copying and manufacturing of the trademark owner's trademark or its sale of the counterfeited trademark or manufactured trademark without the owner's authorization.
(e) A third party's altering of the trademark owner's registered trademark without authorization and use of the altered trademark in the marketplace.
(f) A third party's provision of services that are aimed to or facilitate others to infringe upon the exclusive rights associated with the registered trademarks.
(g) A third party's acts that have caused other damages to others' registered trademark rights."

Depending on whether or not the acts would have a direct impact on the practical functionality of a trademark, the infringing acts can be further divided to two primary categories: (1) acts that directly and negatively impact the exclusive rights associated with a registered trademark; and (2) acts that infringe one's exclusive rights associated with a registered trademark. The first category of acts are the classic infringement acts - i.e., one's use of a mark that is identical or highly similar to a third party's registered trademark, and the former has put the use of the mark on the same or closely similar products or services as those registered by the third party's trademark. The above use is without the trademark owner's authorization and the use is likely to lead to consumer confusion as to the origin of the products or services among the relevant public. Article 57 Sections 1 and 2 points out that any actions that will negatively impact one's trademark rights should be deemed the direct acts that would impact the exclusive rights of one's registered trademark. The second category of acts refers to the types of actions that are derivative, an extension or an expansion, from the original acts that are directly harmful to one's exclusive rights of its trademark. Article 57 of the Trademark Law states that "other acts that are harmful to one's trademark rights" belong to this category.[183] The second category of infringing acts is attached to the actions that are directly harmful to one's exclusive trademark rights and accordingly, it can take various forms. Due to the wide variety of the specific acts that may lead to a trademark infringement, it is advisable to evaluate each act in question by determining if such an act has a direct negative impact on one's trademark rights.

183. Kong Xiangjun, TRADEMARK AND UNFAIR-COMPETITION LAW — THEORY AND CASES, Law Press, 170–172 (2009). Chen Zhaohua, THEORY AND PRACTICE OF TRADEMARK LAW, Angle Publishing Co., Ltd., 183–184 (2013).

1. Necessary Conditions to Qualify an Act as an Infringing Act to One's Registered Trademark Rights.

In addition to fulfilling the usual conditions such as bad faith, the ability to establish causation relationship between the infringing act and impact on one's registered trademark rights, and the negative consequences,[184] the infringing acts in question must also satisfy the following conditions.

a. The Infringing Act Must Involve Using the Mark in Question as a Trademark.

The basic functionality of a trademark is to enable consumers to distinguish the source of the underlying products or services. In other words, through a trademark, a business operator is able to distinguish its products or services from those provided by others in the market. Accordingly, the use of the underlying mark as a trademark is a necessary condition to ensure that the mark at issue is equipped with sufficient distinctiveness and capable of functioning, in substance, as a trademark.[185] In practice, through the process of obtaining the exclusive rights associated with a trademark, the public's perception of the mark at issue - i.e., whether or not the mark will be recognized and perceived as a trademark - has a direct impact on the distinctiveness associated with the mark and whether or not the mark will be approved for registration. Similarly, in determining whether or not a particular act has constituted an infringing act, one must consider if the mark has been put to use before making the determination whether or not the act itself is an infringement to a third party's trademark.[186]

The reason that use is a precondition prior to determining whether or not an act is an infringing act to one's trademark is because the trademark protection is aimed to protect the "association" between a trademark and the underlying products or services. The ability to allow the relevant public to "associate" the mark with the underlying products or services is therefore the primary characteristics of a trademark.[187] If the actions in question do not intrude upon the interests protected by the law and do not lead to any negative impact between the trademark itself and its association with the

184. Wang Jiafu, ed., CHINA CIVIL LAW — CREDITOR'S RIGHTS, Law Press, 407–491 (1991). Jiang Ping, ed., CIVIL LAW, China University of Political Science and Law Press, 481–496 (2011).

185. Wen Xue, STUDY ON TRADEMARK USE AND TRADEMARK PROTECTION, Law Press, 21 (2008).

186. Case Index: Beijing No. 1 Intermediate People's Court, Yi Zhong Min Zhong Zi [2006] No. 3739; Beijing High People's Court, Gao Min Zhong Zi [2006] No. 1429; Beijing No. 1 Intermediate People's Court, Yi Zhong Min Chu Zi [2007] No. 470; Beijing No. 2 Intermediate People's Court, Er Zhong Min Chu Zi [2007] No. 10758; Guangdong Province Guangzhou Intermediate People's Court, Sui Zhong Fa Min San Zhong Zi [2009] No. 42; Chongqing High People's Court, Yu Gao Fa Min Zhong Zi [2009] No. 43; Zhejiang High People's Court, Zhe Zhi Zhong Zi [2009] No. 140. Of course, there are also views that whether the trademark is being used or not does not constitute a necessary precondition in determining trademark infringement, *see* Xu Jie, ed., CASE ANALYSIS OF INTELLECTUAL PROPERTY RIGHTS, People's Court Press, 125 (2010).

187. Zheng Qibin, ON THE ESSENCE OF TRADEMARK RIGHT, People's Court Press, 89 (2009). Xu Jie, ed., CASE ANALYSIS OF INTELLECTUAL PROPERTY RIGHTS, People's Court Press, 125 (2010).

underlying products or services, the acts should not be deemed as infringing acts. To use a mark as a trademark means the mark at issue is capable of functioning as a source identifier. It is therefore an embodiment of its "association" function. Other than using a mark in a trademark sense, the mark is not entitled to any protection and is therefore available for use by anyone unless it is otherwise qualified for other legal protection, such as copyright or patent.[188] In light of the above, it is therefore reasonable and logical to require the defendant to first use the mark as a trademark (i.e., use it as a source identifier) before one can move onto the next step of examination as to whether or not the defendant's act has constituted an infringement towards the plaintiff's exclusive rights over the trademark.

A trademark is an unique and particular symbol to one's business operation, and the objective of a trademark is to enable a business owner to distinguish its products or services from those offered by others in the marketplace.[189] Accordingly, a use of a trademark must involve commercial use. "Commercial use" refers to the use of a registered trademark in the channel of commerce; the purpose in using the mark must be for profit and the activities are aimed to facilitate the business reputation associated with the mark at issue so as to allow the mark to function as a source identifier.[190] The Paris Convention also supported the above view and offered a similar explanation by stating, "use of a trademark refers to the commercial sales activities of offering goods or services bearing the mark at issue in the marketplace."[191] In situations where a mark is mentioned in newspaper reports, authority decisions or official/government documents, these do constitute "use" but the use should not be regarded as "commercial use." The above uses are simply objective and factual descriptions of the mark at issue. In fact, these uses are "fair use," and such uses should not be regarded as an infringing use to one's exclusive rights over its registered trademark. On the other hand, if a third party changes, removes, alters, or covers a third party's trademark while the trademark is going through the channel of commerce, the action will be regarded as a form of trademark infringement and should be prohibited. This is why trademark reverse passing-off acts should be prohibited as well.[192]

188. Kong Xiangjun, TRADEMARK AND UNFAIR-COMPETITION LAW — THEORY AND CASES, Law Press, 189 (2009).
189. Li Mingde, ed., LAW OF INTELLECTUAL PROPERTY RIGHTS, Social Science Document Press, 311 (2007).
190. IP Tribunal of Beijing No. 1 Intermediate People's Court, STUDY OF DIFFICULT QUESTIONS IN ADMINISTRATIVE TRIAL IN RESPECT OF TRADEMARK RIGHT CONFIRMATION, Intellectual Property Press, 176 (2008).
191. Bodenhausen G.H.C., Tang Zongshun & Duan Ruilin trans., GUIDELINES OF THE PARIS CONVENTION FOR THE PROTECTION OF INDUSTRIAL PROPERTY, Renmin University of China Press, 50 (2003).
192. Xu Jie, ed., CASE ANALYSIS OF INTELLECTUAL PROPERTY RIGHTS, People's Court Press, 119 (2010). Besides, in legal practice, the first case that was included and protected by the concept of reverse confusion is the business reputation and unfair competition infringement lawsuit brought by Beijing Jing Gong Clothing Industry Group No. 1 Factory against Beijing Bai Sheng Light Industry Limited Company, Hong Kong Crocodile International PTE and China Development Council. Case Index: Beijing No. 1 Intermediate People's Court, Zhong Jing Zhi Chu Zi [1994] No. 566. In this case, the basic principle was established, and it was included in the Trademark Law and has become the basis for Article 52 Section 4 of the 2001 Trademark Law. Afterwards, other courts ruled the reverse confusion acts based on this provision in the

As to the proper factors to determine whether or not a particular use should be deemed a commercial use of the trademark at issue, the court offers a clear explanation in the civil trademark infringement action brought by Shannxi Mao Zhi Entertainment Company against DreamWorks Animation SKG, Inc., Paramount Pictures, China Film Group Corporation, and Beijing Hua Ying Tian Ying Cinema Management Corporation. Specifically, the plaintiff pointed out that the defendants infringed upon its trademark registration for "Kung Fu Panda in Chinese characters & Device" under Registration Number 6353409 because the defendants used its registered trademark during the manufacturing, distribution, and showing of the movie Kung Fu Panda 2. In the second level of the court decision, the Beijing High People's Court pointed out that in order to determine whether or not the defendants' above acts had infringed upon the plaintiff's exclusive rights over its trademark, it is necessary to first determine whether or not the defendants' actions involving the mark were in fact "trademark use" as contemplated and discussed under the Trademark Law and the Regulation on the Implementation of the Trademark Law.[193] The court pointed out that in order to properly examine whether or not the defendants' act had constituted trademark use, the following factors should be considered:

(a) whether or not the acts in question were motivated by good faith;
(b) whether or not the acts in question were carried out with the goal to identify the actor's products or services;
(c) whether or not the acts in question were merely carried out with the goal to describe or explain the features and characteristics associated with the underlying products or services.

In the KUNG FU PANDA case, the defendants' use of the mark in the movie KUNG FU PANDA 2 was to explain and describe the specific features and content of the movie and that the movie was manufactured, distributed, or shown by itself. In other words, the defendants' use of the KUNG FU PANDA characters was not to identify the movie production services and to distinguish such services provided by itself and those by others. The defendants' use of the KUNG FU PANDA characters therefore did not constitute commercial use of the plaintiff's trademark. Furthermore, the use of the characters is likely to be perceived by consumers and the relevant public as merely the title of the movie (as opposed to a trademark). In fact, the relevant public was not likely to be confused by the defendants' use of the characters because, based on information disseminated by the defendants' group and the popularity of the movies in China, the relevant already public knew that the movie was manufactured and distributed by US companies, such as Paramount Pictures, DreamWorks, and DreamWorks Animation. The above-mentioned public's knowledge is tied to the legal concept of copyright in

---

Trademark Law, such as the trademark infringement civil lawsuit brought by Hang Zhou Jiang Nan Bu Yi Clothing Co., Ltd. against Hang Zhou Shan Shui Ren Jia Clothing Co., Ltd. Case Index: Hangzhou People's Court, Hang Min San Cu Zi [2006] No. 301; Zhejing High People's Court, Zhe Min San Zhong Zi [2007] No. 43.

193. Article 52 Section 1 of the 2001 Trademark Law and Article 19 of the Regulation on the Implementation of the Trademark Law.

connection with the perception and confirmation of the movie work products; the public's knowledge is not at all related to the trademark perception where a name is used to identify the source of the products or services. Overall, the plaintiff's infringement claim was denied because the defendants' use of the KUNG FU PANDA characters was not commercial use of the plaintiff's trademark; accordingly, the defendants' use of these characters did not constitute trademark infringement under the law in China.[194]

b. The Infringing Act Must Involve Using the Same or Similar Trademarks in Connection with the Same or Similar Registered Products or Services.

Article 56 of the 2013 Trademark Law states, "the exclusive rights associated with a registered trademark are limited to the goods or services registered to the mark."[195] In light of the above, the acts that involve an infringement of a registered trademark must involve use of the products or services that are either identical or similar to those registered to the mark at issue. The Trademark Law, however, does not offer any clear guidance as to the specific factors that would qualify two products, services, or marks to be regarded as similar. Accordingly, the Supreme Court offered judicial interpretation regarding the factors that allow the authorities to conclude that the two marks or two products/services can be deemed similar. This judicial interpretation offered by the Supreme Court has therefore become a key guidance in practice when the examiners or judges are asked to determine whether or not two marks, products, or services are similar.

The Supreme Court's judicial interpretation points out that "two products should be deemed similar if they share the same functionality, purpose, manufacturing process, distribution channel, target groups of consumers; and if the relevant public will believe the two are related or confusion is likely due to their similar nature." Based on the Supreme Court's judicial interpretation, "two services should be deemed similar if they share the same purpose, content, method, and target audience; and if the relevant public will believe the two are related or confusion is likely due to their similar nature . . . ;" "specific products should be deemed similar to some specific services if there are certain connections between such products and services and such a connection is likely to result in consumer confusion among the relevant public."[196] According to the Supreme Court, two marks are identical (or should be deemed as such) if "there are few visual differences when putting the plaintiff's registered mark and the mark used by the defendant side by side;"[197] two marks are similar (or should be deemed as such) if "the text font, pronunciation, concept, components of a design, color combination, three-dimensional shape, overall visual impact under the combination of each

194. Case Index: Beijing High People's Court, Gao Min Zhong Zi [2013] No. 3027.
195. Article 51 of the 2001 Trademark Law.
196. Section 11 of the Interpretation of the Supreme People's Court Concerning the Application of Laws in the Trial of Cases of Civil Disputes Arising from Trademarks ([2012] No. 32).
197. Section 9(1) of the Interpretation of the Supreme People's Court Concerning the Application of Laws in the Trial of Cases of Civil Disputes Arising from Trademarks ([2012] No. 32).

key element of the plaintiff's registered trademark is similar to the mark used by the defendant, and the similarities between the two marks are likely to either confuse the relevant public or mislead the relevant public into believing that there is a certain connection between the two marks."[198]

Although the similarity requirement in terms of the marks and products at issue should both be present in a trademark infringement case (given both are necessary conditions), there is in fact a priority difference order in practice. In other words, the judges and examiners must first determine whether or not the products (or services) involved are similar, and if they are, move onto the next level of examination to determine if the marks at issue are similar. If the products (or services) provided by the defendant are not similar to those provided by the plaintiff or covered in the plaintiff's registered trademark, there is no need to determine whether or not the marks at issue are similar.

Based on the International Classification of Goods and Services for the Purposes of the Registration of Marks (the Nice Classification) provided by the WIPO, the Trademark Office has released the Table for the Purpose of Differentiating Similar Goods and Services ("***Subclass Guidance***") so as to become a reference to judge the similarity of the involved productions or services. Although the Subclass Guidance is one of the important references in determining whether or not specific products or services are similar, the Subclass Guidance is not itself the only or exclusive guidance to determine the similarities between the products and services in the world. The process should take into account the specific backgrounds and facts in each case; it is a fluid process. Most importantly, the similarity determination should also involve the market condition of the products at issue, as well as the relevant public's perception.[199]

The above point is amply illustrated in the civil lawsuit related to trademark infringement involving the "Gui Fei Vinegar" ("Gui Fei" characters can be roughly translated to mean "royal senior concubine") between Beijing Fang Tai Xin Yi Hua Food Distribution Co., Ltd. and Changsha Yang Shi Drinks Company. The vinegar product is not specifically covered in the Subclass Guidance book. The defendant believed the product was a Class 32 nonalcohol beverage (given its vinegar content). Its use of the above three characters was therefore a mere reference to the product name as opposed to a trademark use. The plaintiff believed that the underlying products were a vinegar type of product which fell under the Class 30 category. The product was therefore similar to its registered products, as discussed under Subclass Guidance. The Trademark Office had issued a letter to Hu Nan Province Administrative Authority For Industry And Commerce discussing this specific issue on June 3, 2003. In the letter, the Trademark Office pointed out that "the vinegar drinks are nonalcoholic drinks and should be categorized under International Class 32, the second subclass. This subclass classification of such beverage therefore dictates that the product is not similar to the vinegar products covered in International Class 30, the 15th subclass." Despite the above, the 1st and 2nd level of the courts did not accept the above views advanced by

198. *Ibid.*
199. Kong Xiangjun, TRADEMARK AND UNFAIR-COMPETITION LAW — THEORY AND CASES, Law Press, 211 (2009).

the defendant or discussed in the 2003 letter. The court pointed out that the products used by the defendant and those registered by the plaintiff should be deemed similar because they shared some important common grounds in respect to the raw materials, drinking method, functionality, purpose, and channel of trade. In addition to the above, the plaintiff's trademark enjoys a high level of fame and is rather distinctive among the relevant public. Its fame and popularity would dictate the distributors and the relevant public associate any vinegar type of drinks with the plaintiff's trademark. There is not yet a uniform approach to the vinegar products discussed above because it is a new type of drink in today's marketplace. Despite this, and regardless of the product names to refer to such a product (and whether or not it is a Class 30 or Class 32 product), the fact is that the products offered by the plaintiff and those offered by the defendant do share some common key features. Accordingly, despite the legal classification of such products, the general public would still regard them as the same or similar type of products. The court therefore supported the plaintiff's infringement claim because the defendant engaged in a prominent use of the GUI FEI characters that the plaintiff had made famous. The defendant's use was sufficient to cause consumer confusion among the relevant public, and was ordered to bear its civil responsibilities due to its infringement.[200]

The judicial interpretation confirmed the following in respect to the identical nature or similarities between two marks:[201]

(a) The determination basis should be the general perception of the relevant public.
(b) The comparison process should compare the two marks as a whole, as well as key elements in both marks (the comparison should be carried out in a vacuum without the influence of any relevant public's perception).
(c) The similarity examination should also take into account the fame and distinctiveness associated with the mark for which the plaintiff is seeking protection.

The "relevant public" refers to the consumers or distributors that would come in contact with the products or services bearing the mark at issue.[202] As for the comparison for the marks, the key is to compare the distinctive and prominent elements of each mark and use these distinctive elements as a guide to compare both marks as a whole. In the trademark infringement and unfair competition case brought by Jing Hua Bao Dao (Beijing) Eye Glasses Co., Ltd. against Fuzhou Bao Dao Eye Glasses Co., Ltd. and WANG Zaiwu, the plaintiff enjoyed trademark rights over "BAO DAO" in simplified Chinese characters (Registration Number 1394775), "BAO DAO in traditional Chinese characters and Design" (Registration Number 772859), and "BAO

200. Case Index: Hunan Changsha Intermediate People's Court, Chang Zhong Min San Chu Zi [2002] No. 272; Hunan High People's Court, Xiang Fa Gao San Zhong Zi [2003] No. 34.
201. Section 10 of the Interpretation of the Supreme People's Court Concerning the Application of Laws in the Trial of Cases of Civil Disputes Arising from Trademarks ([2012] No. 32).
202. Section 8 of the Interpretation of the Supreme People's Court Concerning the Application of Laws in the Trial of Cases of Civil Disputes Arising from Trademarks ([2012] No. 32).

DAO in traditional Chinese characters and Design" (Registration Number 3110047). The marks or names used by the defendants were "Bao Dao Eye Glasses (Chain Store)" and "Bao Dao Eye Glasses Chain Store." The court pointed out that the use of "eye glasses" characters lacked distinctiveness when the subject products and services were related to ophthalmic products, because such a term was incapable to function as a source identifier. The characters for "Chain" or "Chain Store" were not distinctive either because they merely pointed out the way the business operated. Accordingly, the distinctive characters - and the prominent element - in the defendant's name were the Bao Dao characters that were identical or similar to the primary elements in the plaintiff's registered trademarks. Given the defendant's prominent use of the BAO DAO characters, the use was likely to lead to consumer confusion and its infringement was therefore acknowledged by the court.[203]

(3) The Acts Are Likely to Lead to Consumer Confusion Among the Relevant Public.

Article 57 Section 1 of the Trademark Law states that if "a third party is using a mark that is identical to the prior registration and is using the mark on the same registered products or services and the use is without the trademark owner's permission," it would constitute a trademark infringement.[204] Despite the situation described in Article 57 Section 1 of the Trademark Law, not all unauthorized use of a trademark - including use of a mark similar to the prior registration on the same products or use of the same or similar mark as a prior registration on the similar products - would constitute a trademark infringement. The above uses would not necessarily constitute a legal infringement unless the use is also accompanied by confusion among the relative public.[205]

Although the confusion concept was not formally introduced and included in the Trademark Law until 2013, it has always been a necessary requirement prior to the court recognizing a particular act as trademark infringement. The above observation was reflected in the court's approach in the civil trademark infringement lawsuit brought by Jiang Ya Mei against Chen Yun Kui, Si Chuan Zhang Fei Beef Company Limited, and Cheng Du Zhang Fei Beef Sales Company Limited. In the lawsuit, the plaintiff was the owner of the trademark registration for "ZHANG FEI" in Chinese characters (*see* Image One) under Registration Number 3261397 in connection with Class 43 restaurant and hotel services. The plaintiff was also the restaurant owner and operator for Ha Er Bin City Zhang Fei Barbeque Restaurant. The defendants were the authorized licensees of the following four trademark registrations as shown in Images

203. Case Index: Beijing No. 2 Intermediate People's Court, Er Zhong Min Chu Zi [2012] No. 8648; Beijing High People's Court, Gao Min Zhong Zi [2013] No. 773.

204. Article 16 Section 1 of the Agreement of the World Trade Organization on Trade-Related Aspects of Intellectual Property Rights (TRIPs) stipulates that "in case of the use of an identical sign for identical goods or services, a likelihood of confusion shall be presumed."

205. The legislative affairs commission of the Standing Committee of the National People's Congress, ed., INTERPRETATION OF THE PEOPLE'S REPUBLIC OF CHINA TRADEMARK LAW, 108 Law Press (2013).

Two, Three, Four and Five (Registration Numbers 653173, 3471308, 6780511 and 3567843).

Image One (Registration Number 3261397)
张飞

Image Two (Registration Number 653173)	Image Three (Registration Number 3471308)
	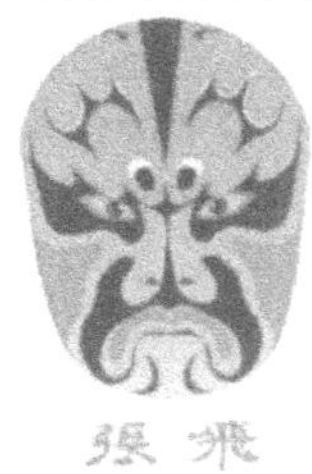
Image Four (Registration Number 6780511)	**Image Five (Registration Number 3567843)**

After reviewing the case, the court held that although the defendants' use of the ZHANG FEI mark was identical or closely similar to the plaintiff's registration both visually and phonetically, and the two marks were in fact "legally similar" trademarks under the Chinese Law, the defendants' use of the ZHANG FEI trademarks were nevertheless not infringing the plaintiff's trademark rights. The primary reason was because of the differences between the two parties' actual uses of the marks. The court held that the uses of the two marks were unlikely to lead to confusion among the relevant public. Specifically, the court pointed out the following differences to support its noninfringement finding:

(a) Actual use of the two parties' marks.
The defendants had included their trademarks in multiple promotional materials such as print copies, tableware in the defendants' restaurant, restaurant signage, and restaurant decorations. Most of the uses, however, did not involve the use of the stand-alone ZHANG FEI characters. Instead, most of the defendants' uses of the marks include ZHANG FEI characters, along with the Chinese characters for "BEEF," the classic silhouette of Zhang Fei facial makeup in Peking Opera, or the portrait of Zheng Fei. The use therefore involved the prominent elements in each of the defendants' registrations such as the Peking Opera design in Registration Number 3471308, and Zhang Fei portrait in Registration Number 653173. Furthermore, the character combination of "ZHANG FEI" and "BEEF" or "ZHANG FEI" and designs were more prominent and distinctive than the stand-alone ZHANG FEI characters, as shown in the plaintiff's trademark registration.

Fame Associated with the Two Parties' Trademarks.

Although "ZHANG FEI BARBEQUE" was a unique dining choice in the Northeastern region of China (particularly in the Ha Er Bing city Hei Long Jiang Province where the plaintiff's restaurant was located), the reputation of the brand was limited to Hei Long Jiang Province in the Northeastern region of China. On the other hand, the defendants' trademark "ZHANG FEI BEEF" was in fact a well-known brand. It enjoyed a long history in the Si Chuan province and had been the recipient of multiple provincial or national level awards. Due to the defendants' use of the mark and its consistent marketing and long-standing promotional efforts, the brand had in fact enjoyed a higher level of fame than that of the plaintiff's brand in Mainland China. In fact, the defendants' mark had been officially recognized as a well-known trademark in China. In light of the above, it was clear that there was a big difference in connection with the fame status associated with the two parties' brands.

(b) Restaurant operation features difference.
The plaintiff's restaurant featured grilled meat and traditional Northeastern Chinese cuisine. The defendants' restaurant, on the other hand, features a fast-food style of Chinese food and focuses on rice noodles and other types of beef noodles. The two parties' restaurants are therefore clearly distinctive from each other.

(c) Restaurant decoration difference.
The two parties' restaurants were decorated differently. The plaintiff's restaurant was set up more like a traditional Chinese dining restaurant, while the defendants' restaurants were set up in a fast-food style.
(d) Location difference.
Some of the defendants' restaurants were located in Beijing, an area where the plaintiff's restaurant did not have any commercial involvement. Accordingly, there was no overlapping of the two parties' business operations in China.
(e) The defendants' Beijing Fei General Restaurant was operated as a boutique store where it offered regular meals, as well as various types of beef products such as prepackaged Zhang Fei branded beef products. Furthermore, this restaurant offered cuisine which included pulled beef, original flavor beef, and other fresh cut beef meat. The defendant had legitimate rights to use its registered trademarks in its store; its use of the ZHANG FEI characters was therefore logical and appropriate.[206]

Along with the introduction and formal inclusion of the consumer confusion concept in the 2013 Trademark Law, the requirement is receiving more attention during the process to determine trademark infringement. Despite the attention to this requirement, it is important to bear in mind that, in some instances, the possibility of finding consumer confusion was sufficient to satisfy this requirement, as opposed to the submission of actual consumer confusion evidence. The above observation was reflected in the civil trademark infringement case brought by Dai Hong against Zhe Jiang Sen Chuang Clothing Company and Bai Sheng Business Development Company. The plaintiff's trademarks were "SEC" under Registrations Numbers 4754048 and 4753865. Both marks were approved for registration in 2009; however, the plaintiff had not used the marks. The defendants were two clothing companies. One of the defendants Zhe Jiang Sen Chuang Clothing Company was established on January 30, 2007. The defendant sought to register the mark "SEC Sculpture Element Collection" covering Classes 18 and 25 products on March 2, 2007. The defendant's applications were refused on the basis that they were deemed similar to the plaintiff's prior registrations. Despite the Trademark Office's refusal decision in 2009, the defendant had already started using their mark in connection with the sales of their clothing products. The plaintiff filed a trademark infringement lawsuit with the court. The court agreed with the plaintiff's trademark infringement claim even though the plaintiff had not yet started using its trademark in commerce. Specifically, considering the similarities of the two parties' marks and the overlapping goods, consumer confusion could be expected even though the plaintiff had not started using its trademarks.[207] The finding

206. Case Index: Beijing Changping District People's Court, Chang Min Chu Zi [2012] No. 3064. Both parties did not appeal and this judgment has become effective.
207. Case Index: Beijing Xicheng District People's Court, Xi Min Chu Zi [2010] No. 4468. Zhe Jiang Sen Chuang Clothing Company appealed to Beijing No. 1 Intermediate People's Court. In the appeal proceeding, Zhe Jiang Sen Chuang Clothing Company withdrew the appeal, and it was

of consumer confusion in the above case was not supported by any actual confusion evidence. In other words, actual consumer confusion evidence was not a necessary condition to satisfying the consumer confusion requirement.

2. Certain Specific Situations Not Outlined in the Law but Would Nevertheless Constitute Trademark Infringement in Practice.

Although there are only a few situations listed under the Trademark Law that could be deemed as a violation to one's trademark rights, Article 57 Section 7 of the Trademark Law provides a catch-all provision where certain "unanticipated" situations can also be deemed as a trademark infringement despite the fact that they are not specifically listed in the Law. Additionally, in practice, there are a wide variety of acts that would be deemed as a violation to one's trademark rights. Below are listed a few situations where trademark infringement can be found despite the fact that these situations are not included in the Trademark Law.

a. Prominent Use of a Trade Name that Has or Is Likely to Lead to Consumer Confusion.

Although a company name is protected under the Anti-unfair Competition Law and is a type of civil right different from those protected by the Trademark Law, the use of a company name should be legal and comply with the basic rules and commercial customs. If one's use of its trade name involves prominent use of certain elements, and such use is likely or has led to confusion among the relevant public, the use can be deemed an infringement to one's trademark rights. The above observation has in fact been formally recognized in practice. For example, some legal interpretations have provided the following: *if one is using its trade name in a way that involves prominent use of certain elements that are identical or closely similar to a third party's registered trademark, and the use involves the same or similar products as those covered by the prior trademark, and such a use is likely to lead to consumer confusion among the relevant public, the use can be deemed a violation of the third party's trademark rights.*[208]

In the subject case, for example, although the School enjoyed trade name rights over its name "Beijing Hai Dian Ka Nai Ji Success Element Training School," it was still found to infringe the Company's trademark rights. This is because the School's actual use of its name was either "Beijing Ka Nai Ji School" or "Ka Nai Ji School." The word "school" clearly lacked distinctiveness when it was used in connection with training services and, accordingly, the characters "KA NAI JI" were the prominent distinctive element of the School's name as well as the services provided by the School. Through the Company's long and consistent use, its trademarks, such as "DALE CARNEGIE"

approved by the second instance court with the ruling ([2010] No. 12741). Under such circumstances, the first instance judgment has become effective.

208. Section 1(1) of the Interpretation of the Supreme People's Court Concerning the Application of Laws in the Trial of Cases of Civil Disputes Arising from Trademarks ([2012] No. 32).

under Registration Number 772672 and "DALE CARNEGIE" in Chinese characters under Registration Number 772658," had acquired a certain level of fame. Under such circumstances, the School's use of the KA NAI JI characters in its name was likely to mislead the relevant public as to the original source regarding the underlying training services. Accordingly, despite the School's ownership of its trade name, its use nevertheless was still found to infringe upon the Company's trademark rights.

b. Use that Has Violated the Owner's Rights in Connection with Its Well-known Trademark.

The discussion relating to a well-known trademark is already included in the "general section" of the Trademark Law, either in the original version of the Trademark Law or the amended version. There is not yet a clear consistent application of the Law in respect to a well-known trademark. This is because Article 57 of the Trademark Law limits the protection to a registered trademark when a third party is using the same or similar products or services, and also the Law does not include any specific section discussing the protection in respect to a well-known trademark. In light of the above, there is not yet a consistent application of the law in situations where a third party's use of its mark involves products or services that are different from those covered by the well-known trademark. The SPC of China provided a judicial interpretation to address this. Specifically, the Supreme Court pointed out that "one's imitation, copying, or translation of a third party's registered well-known mark or the prominent element of such a well-known mark can be found a violation of the third party's exclusive trademark rights even though the imitation, copying or translation involves dissimilar or different goods and services from those covered by the senior registered well-known mark so long as the action is likely to mislead the public, and negatively impact the third party's rights."[209] Despite the above, the infringement recognition should be preconditioned on the basis that the senior mark was registered and recognized as a well-known trademark in China. On that basis, if the defendant's action satisfies other elements that are required to protect a well-known trademark, then such an action can be deemed a violation of its trademark rights.

In the civil action brought by Swarovsky Aktiengesellschaft against Beijing SWANROV Wedding Company regarding the latter's alleged trademark infringement and its unauthorized use of a third party's company name, the court supported the plaintiff's claims. Specifically, both the first instance and the second instance courts recognized the defendant's stand-alone and/or prominent use of "SWAROV in Chinese characters" either in the simplified or traditional version, and its use of the English mark such as "SWAROV" and "SWAROVSKI" in its stores, signage, display windows, price information, invoices, display picture album, advertising promotional materials, and websites, were imitations of the plaintiff's well-known trademarks, namely "SWAROVSKI" (Registration Number 384001) and "SWAROVSKI in Chinese

209. Section 1(2) of the Interpretation of the Supreme People's Court Concerning the Application of Laws in the Trial of Cases of Civil Disputes Arising from Trademarks ([2012] No. 32).

characters" (Registration Number 385013). The defendant's actions were sufficient to mislead the relevant consumers into believing that the services provided by the defendant were somehow connected to those provided by the plaintiff, and thereby impacted the plaintiff's legitimate interests.[210]

c. Infringe a Third Party's Exclusive Trademark Rights Through Domain Name Registration.

With the advancement of Internet technologies, there are an increasing number of trademark infringement cases involving a third party's use and registration of its domain names. It took some time for the society to form a consensus regarding this type of infringement given the characteristics associated with the ownership and use of a domain name are different from those of a trademark. At the very beginning, a domain name would not be deemed as a trademark infringement unless the senior mark at issue was a well-known registered trademark. In the civil lawsuit brought by Du Pont against Beijing Guo Wang Information Technology Limited regarding domain name issues, the Beijing High People's Court articulated the following point of view: "*a domain name is a specific user's name and address in the internet world; it is therefore a mark that identifies one from others – accordingly, a domain name is capable of functioning as a source identifier. When a user registers and/or uses a third party's well-known trademark as a domain name, the user is therefore capable of transfering the commercial benefit, function and goodwill associated with the well-known trademark outside the internet world to the internet. Any unauthorized use or registration of a domain name inclusive of a well-known trademark therefore has converted the legitimated benefits associated with a well-known trademark from its legitimate owner to itself. If such an action does not have prior authorization from the owner of the well-known trademark, it should be deemed an infringement to the well-known trademark.*"[211] Although the mark the judges had in mind in the above decision was the well-known DU PONT trademark, the analysis was applicable to other types of trademarks. Accordingly, in the subsequent judicial interpretations, the protection was extended from well-known trademarks to regular trademarks. Furthermore, the subsequent judicial interpretations also provided a clear guidance for the situations where a domain name registration would be deemed trademark infringement: "*a domain name registration involving the same or similar elements of one's registered trademark, and the domain name is carrying out electronic commerce involving the same or related products or services similar to those of the registered trademark, and the use of the domain name is likely to lead to consumer confusion among the relevant public.*"[212]

Despite the above, it is important to note that a domain name registration is protected under the law so long as the party has obtained the registration through the

210. Case Index: Beijing No. 2 Intermediate People's Court, Er Zhong Min Chu Zi [2008] No. 10067; Beijing High People's Court, Gao Min Zhong Zi [2008] No. 1376.
211. Case Index: Beijing High People's Court, Gao Zhi Zhong Zi [2001] No. 47.
212. Section 1(3) of the Interpretation of the Supreme People's Court Concerning the Application of Laws in the Trial of Cases of Civil Disputes Arising from Trademarks ([2012] No. 32).

legitimate legal channel. Accordingly, there exists a conflict in situations involving a prior registered domain name and a subsequently registered trademark. This issue was explored and discussed in the domain name case brought by Travel Group Company against Li Yong. In this case, the disputed domain, www.travelzoo.com.cn, was registered on November 29, 2004; the defendant's domain name registration was therefore earlier than the plaintiff's trademark registration because the plaintiff's International Registration numbered 863101 for "TRAVELZOO" in connection with Class 39 travel services was not extended to and registered in China until August 25, 2005. Despite the later registration date of the trademark, the Beijing High People's Court pointed out that one of the functions of a trademark was to operate as a source identifier, and all registered trademarks had gone through the public notification process with the relevant trademark authorities in China. This publication process informed the public of the owner's exclusive rights associated with their respective registered trademarks in China. In light of the above, the Court noted that when the use of the domain name was sufficient to establish a connection between the domain itself and the services that the domain provided – that is, when the domain name is capable of functioning as a source identifier for the products and services the domain provides – the owner of the domain should avoid continuing to use the same domain if a third party had already obtained exclusive trademark rights over the domain in China. Following this analysis, the Court did not support the defendant's defense that it obtained and was using the domain in a legitimate way. Specifically, the Court pointed out that, based on the submitted evidence, the defendant did not start using the disputed domain until July 16, 2007. In other words, the defendant did not use the disputed domain prior to the plaintiff obtaining its trademark registration in 2005. Put simply, the defendant did not use the disputed domain early enough to obtain any legitimate rights protectable under China's Anti-unfair Competition Law so as to afford the defendant some rights to compete with the plaintiff's trademark rights. In light of the above, the High Court held that the defendant's use of the disputed mark was an infringement of the plaintiff's trademark rights.[213]

d. Infringe a Third Party's Unregistered Well-Known Trademark Rights.

The protection of an unregistered well-known trademark is a special case under the Trademark Law in China. Accordingly, the protection afforded to such a trademark should carefully follow the parameters discussed in the judicial interpretations: "*one should be held civilly responsibly for the associated legal consequences if one copies, imitates, or translates a third party's unregistered well-known trademark or the primary elements of such a trademark, and has used the mark for the same or closely similar products or services, and the use is likely to lead to consumer confusion.*"[214] With the above judicial interpretations in mind, in addition to requiring the senior mark to be

213. Case Index: Beijing High People's Court, Gao Min Zhong Zi [2011] No. 1713.
214. Section 2 of the Interpretation of the Supreme People's Court Concerning the Application of Laws in the Trial of Cases of Civil Disputes Arising from Trademarks ([2012] No. 32).

well-known in China, the protection should also be limited in the situation where the party is using the well-known mark in the same or similar products or services.

In the trademark infringement lawsuit brought by Sotheby's Auction against Si Chuan Su Fu Bi Auction Company Limited, the court supported the plaintiff's infringement claim because the evidence was sufficient to prove that the SOTHEBY mark in Chinese characters was an unregistered well-known mark in connection with auction services. Under such circumstances, the defendant should have been aware of the mark. Its prominent use of the SOTHEBY characters was sufficient to mislead the relevant public regarding the source of the auction services or to believe that the parties were somehow connected. The defendant's use of the SOTHEBY characters was deemed an infringement, despite the unregistered status of such a mark in China.[215]

215. Case Index: Beijing No. 2 Intermediate People's Court, Er Zhong Min Chu Zi [2007] No. 11593; Beijing High People's Court, Gao Min Zhong Zi [2008] No. 322; the Supreme People's Court, Min Shen Zi [2010] No. 1182.

23. Infringement Recognition Involving a Design Patent Application that Includes the Same or Similar Primary Element as a Third Party's Registered Trademark

Civil action involving trademark infringement brought by Louis Vuitton Malletier S.A. against GUO Biying

- First Instance: Beijing No. 1 Intermediate People's Court (No. 8048; 2008) - Decided on: December 16, 2008
- Second Instance: Beijing High People's Court (No. 2575; 2009) - Decided on: July 16, 2009

BACKGROUND

Louis Vuitton Malletier S.A. (the "***LV Company***" or the "***Company***") registered an LV trademark under Registration Number 241025 on January 15, 1986, (the "***LV Trademark***") - *see* Image One. The mark was registered in connection with Class 28 products such as toys, checker games, backgammon games, golf gloves. The exclusive right associated with the mark had been renewed by LV Company until January 14, 2016.

GUO Biying sought to register a design patent with the State Intellectual Property Office of the PRC on November 13, 2003. The name listed on the design patent is "MAHJONG in Chinese character and Number 23;" the application number is 200330116816.3 (the "***Design Patent***"). The Design Patent was published on July 14, 2004 with publication number CN3379670. The 200330116816.3 Patent includes five views, i.e. the front view; the left-side view; the rear view; the top view and the perspective view as shown on Image Two. LV Company believed Guo's design patent had infringed upon its trademark rights and brought a civil litigation to the court on June 16, 2008.

Image One	Image Two

COURT DECISION

Beijing No. 1 Intermediate People's Court (the "***Intermediate Court***") reviewed the case and supported LV Company's infringement lawsuit. Specifically, the Intermediate Court believed that the civil courts can make a determination in situations where a registered but not yet put to use design patent has a conflict with a third party's prior rights. The Company's LV Trademark enjoyed rights that were senior to Guo's Design Patent. The products covered by Guo's Design Patent - mahjong - were similar to the products such as checker games covered by the LV Trademark. Both parties' registrations included the same LV letters and design, and accordingly, the relevant public would be easily misled into believing that the products bearing Guo's Design Patent were in fact the LV Company's products. Clearly, Guo's Design Patent would therefore impact the Company's exclusive rights over its LV Trademark. Although there was no evidence to support that Guo had put its Design Patent into use, the underlying objective to register a design patent is to use it. Therefore, the impact to the Company's exclusive trademark rights were inevitable and predictable once the Design Patent was put to use with Guo's Design Patent being deemed an infringement to the Company's trademark rights. Specifically, Guo's Design Patent fell under the "other trademark infringement situations" discussed under Article 52 Section 5 of the 2001 Trademark Law. In light of the above, the Intermediate Court ruled that Guo should not use its registered Design Patent.

Guo appealed the decision to the Beijing High People's Court ("***High Court***").

The High Court reviewed the appeal and decided to maintain the Intermediate Court's decision for the following reasons: The High Court pointed out that an infringing act to a third party's exclusive trademark rights typically refers to an unauthorized action involving use of the third party's trademark. The use of the trademark refers to the combined action in using the mark and its registered products or services in connection with sales or promotional activities with the consumers. A design patent application involving a third party's trademark (or similar elements in a third party's trademark) is not per se a trademark infringement act because the application action itself does not involve consumer-facing aspects. Accordingly, Guo's appeal arguments pointing out that her action to apply for the Design Patent did not infringe upon the Company's exclusive trademark rights in the LV Trademark were supported by the High Court. The Intermediate Court's decision that recognized the action to apply for the Design Patent itself an act of trademark infringement was improper and lacked legal foundation. Despite this, the LV Trademark was senior to Guo's Design Patent. Furthermore, the products registered under Guo's Design Patent fell under the same international class, Class 28, under International Classification of Goods and Services (the Nice Classification; Tenth Edition). In other words, there were no substantive differences in terms of the functionality, purpose, manufacturing process, channel of trade and target consumers in respect to the two products covered by the LV Trademark and Guo's Design Patent. The mahjong products covered under Guo's Design Patents are regular square cuboids; there was no difference between Guo's mahjong and regular mahjong products except for the LV design. The LV stack design in Guo's Design Patent was identical to that in the Company's trademark registration. Although there was no evidence to support that Guo already put the Design Patent to use, as the Intermediate Court pointed out, the underlying purpose to seek a design patent was to put it to use in commerce. Once Guo's Design Patent was put to use, the relevant public would be easily confused and misled into believing Guo's products were in fact from, or associated with, the LV Company. Accordingly, Guo's Design Patent conflicted with the Company's LV Trademark. On balance, although part of Guo's appeal arguments were supported by the High Court, her primary claim lacked factual and legal foundation so the Court decided to reject the appeal and maintain the Intermediate Court's decision.

ANALYSIS & INSIGHT

There are still some inconsistent views regarding whether or not a design patent would constitute an infringement to a third party's trademark if the former includes the primary element of a third party's trademark. If the products or services registered under the disputed design patent are dissimilar from those registered for the senior trademark, and the senior trademark is not itself a well-known trademark, the application to register the design patent should not be deemed a violation given there were no conflicting rights in this situation. In other words, under the above circumstances, the act to apply for the design patent and to use the disputed design patent does not constitute a trademark infringement. The key issue is therefore whether or not a design patent would constitute trademark infringement if the two rights involve the same or similar products.

1. Approach One – Infringement Recognized Regardless of Whether or Not the Party Has Put the Disputed Design Patent to Use.

The first school of thought believes that the action itself of applying for a design patent registration is a type of trademark infringement whether or not the design patent has been put to use. This view supports the recognition of infringement so long as the design patent includes the same or similar element of a third party's trademark and covers the same or similar products.

In the trademark infringement action brought by the LV Company against an individual, WANG Jun, the court supported the Company's infringement claim. LV Company enjoyed four trademark registrations in connection with "travelling bags, small handbags for women, shopping bags" – namely, Registration Numbers 241000, 241081, 1106237, 1106302 as shown in Images Three, Four, Five, and Six. Without LV's permission, Wang incorporated the identical textual and design elements in its design patent application as shown in Image Seven; Wang's design patent was called "handbag." The LV Company pointed out that Wang's design patent covered the same products as those covered by its trademark registrations. Accordingly, once Wang put its design patent to actual use in commerce, it would cause irreparable harm to LV Company's trademark rights; the LV Company therefore asked the court to enjoin Wang's design patent.

Image Three	Image Four	Image Five
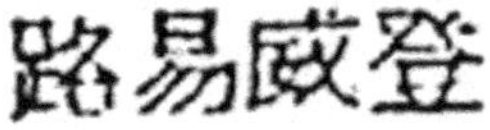	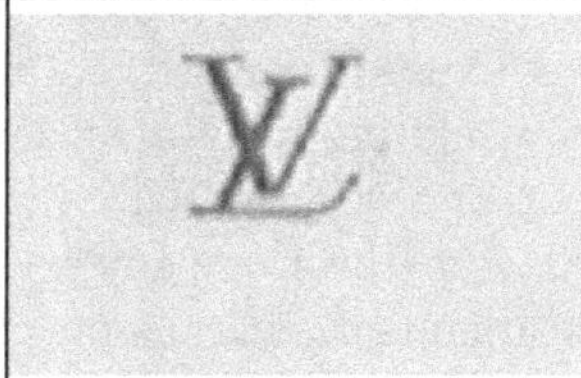	
Image Six	Image Seven	
	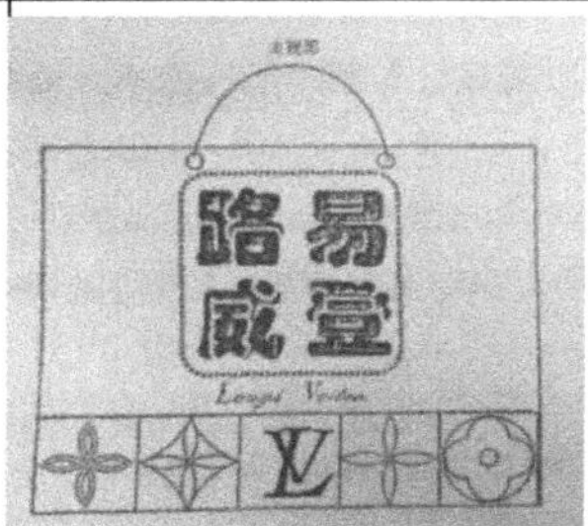	

Both the first and second levels of the courts in the case supported the LV Company's infringement claim. Specifically, the courts pointed out that Wang's design patent covered handbag products that fell under the same international class as those covered by the Company's prior trademark registrations. Wang's design patent not only included the same or similar elements as those included in the LV Company's trademark registrations, but those elements were in fact the primary design elements in Wang's design patent. Consumer confusion could be easily anticipated once Wang started to use its design patent in the marketplace. Accordingly, Wang's design patent had conflicted with the LV Company's trademark rights. Although Wang had not yet put its design patent to use, the court agreed the objective to apply for a design patent was to use it in the marketplace. In order to avoid harm to the LV Company's trademark rights caused by Wang's design patent, the courts ruled that Wang's action to seek a design patent application had constituted "the other actions that would infringe upon a third party's trademark rights" under Article 52 Section 5 of the Trademark Law.[216] Wang was ordered by the court to not to use its design patent. The courts took the same approach and reached similar conclusions in subsequent similar cases.[217]

216. Case Index: Beijing No. 1 Intermediate People's Court, Yi Zhong Min Chu Zi [2007] No. 4873; Beijing High People's Court, Gao Min Zhong Zi [2008] No. 114.
217. Case Index: Beijing No. 1 Intermediate People's Court, Yi Zhong Min Chu Zi [2008] No. 8046; Beijing High People's Court, Gao Min Zhong Zi [2009] No. 1546.

2. Approach Two – Infringement Recognized, even Though the Court Does Recognize the Outcome of the Infringement Analysis, Would Be Different Depending on Whether or Not the Design Patent Has Been Put to Use.

The subject case, however, adopted a different view from the traditional approach. The court in the subject case believed that the action itself to apply for a design patent registration did not constitute use discussed under the trademark law. Accordingly, the action to apply for a design patent registration would not itself constitute a trademark infringement. However, when considering all relevant factors such as the primary purpose to seek a design patent registration and the possible negative effects after putting the design patent to actual use, the court nevertheless came to the conclusion that the subject design patent had constituted an infringement against the LV Company's senior trademark rights. The court's reasoning is summarized below:

(1) The action to apply for a design patent registration does not constitute use discussed under the Trademark Law.
An infringement act mainly refers to a third party's action when the action constitutes "use" as discussed under the trademark law. "A trademark infringement act refers to an action that constitutes use under the trademark law and the use involves the same or similar trademark. In other words, the defendant's use must either fulfill the use requirements under the trademark law or it involves using the mark at issue as a source identifier. If a third party's use of texts or designs are identical or similar to a senior trademark but the use does not involve using the mark as a source identifier - i.e., not using the mark in trademark sense - the action does not satisfy the use requirement under the trademark law and accordingly, the action would not constitute an infringement towards a third party's trademark rights."[218] Any action involving use of a third party's trademark that does not itself constitute "use" of the trademark as discussed under the trademark law would not be itself a trademark infringement act unless, of course, the action falls under other types of violations discussed under the other types of law. For example, fabricating or manufacturing a third party's registered trademark without authorization, or the selling of fabricated trademarks, are actions involving use of the trademark specimen (but not the "use" as an identifier of a trademark as discussed under the trademark law). The action itself does not identify any specific products or services associated with the trademark, so the action does not constitute "use" of a third party's trademark as discussed under the Law. However, the action is nevertheless still an infringing act because it falls under special discussion of the Trademark Law. In the absence

218. KONG, Xiangjun, *Relationship between the Identification of Trademarks and Trademark Protection – Positive Analysis of the Supreme Court's Judicial Policy and Jurisprudence*, People's Judicature, Vol. 15, 2009 at 44.

of special situations discussed under the Law, one should not expand the infringement definition to actions that do not constitute use of a trademark. An action to seek a design patent registration is an application submitted by the applicant in accordance with Patent Law; the action merely establishes the special relationship between the applicant and the patent examination authorities. The result following the design patent application is twofold: design patent granted or design patent denied. Accordingly, the action itself is not use in trade and accordingly, the act to apply for a design patent should not run afoul with the Trademark Law.

(2) Infringement recognized after considering the applicant's purpose to apply for a design patent registration and the possible consequences in using the design patent.

As discussed above, the action itself of seeking design patent registration, which incorporates the same or similar prominent design of a senior trademark registration in connection with the same or similar products, does not itself constitute business use of a trademark; given such, the application itself does not constitute trademark infringement. Despite the above, it is possible to have different types of IPR coexisting for the same subject[219] and conflicts are therefore possible if these rights do not follow the same principle. To avoid conflicts, despite the fact that the Trademark Law and Patent Law are different types of law, they both follow the same basic principle in recognizing and protecting senior existing rights. For example, Article 32 of the 2013 Trademark Law states, "a trademark application should not negatively impact a third party's senior existing rights and should not seek registration of a third party's trademark which has been put to use and has obtained a certain level of influence through improper means."[220]

Article 2 Section 4 of the 2008 Patent Law states that "a design patent is a novel design regarding the shape and components of the underlying products, or the combined representation of the shape, color, and component ideas of the underlying products and is aesthetic and functional."[221] Given the ultimate goal of the design patent is to use it in an industrial application, and the underlying products embodying the design patent would ultimately enter the markets and the channels of commerce, it would not make sense to assume that one is merely interested in registering the design patent rather than using it in the marketplace. Accordingly, although the act to apply for a design patent does not itself constitute trademark infringement, the court's decision in recognizing trademark infringement is nevertheless appropriate in this case so as to avoid conflicts between different types of law, and especially in

219. LING, Zongliang, *Invalid Design Patent Is Still Protected by Copyright Law*, People's Judicature, Vol. 4, 2010 at 86–89.
220. As the Article 31 of the 2001 Trademark Law.
221. Article 23 of the 2000 Patent Law stipulates that: "Any design for which a patent right is granted shall not be identical with or similar to any design which, before the date of filing, has been publicly disclosed in publications in our country or abroad or has been publicly used in our country, nor shall it be in conflict with the prior lawful right of anyone else."

situations where the owner who has prior trademark rights has specifically challenged the design patent application, and the disputed design patent seeks to incorporate the same or similar designs as the senior trademark and use it in the same or similar products.

24. Damage Determination in a Trademark Infringement Lawsuit

Civil action involving trademark infringement and unfair competition brought by Bayerische Motoren Werke Aktiengesellschaft against Guangzhou Century Bao Chi Clothing Industry Co., Ltd.

- First Instance: Beijing No. 2 Intermediate People's Court (No. 4789; 2011) – Decided on: December 20, 2011
- Second Instance: Beijing High People's Court (No. 918; 2012) – Decided on: November 26, 2012

BACKGROUND

BAYERISCHE MOTOREN WERKE AKTIENGESELLSCHAFT (the "***BMW Company***" or the "***Company***") owns a number of Class 12 registrations covering motor vehicles, motorcycles, and its related parts in China, including but not limited to: Registration Number 282195 for "BMW;" Registration Number 282196 for " "; Registration Number 784348 for "BAO MA" (BMW in traditional Chinese characters); and Registration Number G921605 for "BAO MA" (BMW in simplified Chinese characters). The BMW Company also owns Registration Number G955419 for " " and Registration Number G673219 for " " covering motor vehicles, motorcycles and its related parts in Class 12 and clothing, shoes, and headgear for wear in Class 25. Among these, Registration Number 282195 for "BMW," No. 282196 for " ", and No. 784348 for "BAO MA" (BMW in traditional Chinese characters) were recognized as well-known trademarks.

Guangzhou Century Bao Chi Clothing Industry Co., Ltd. ("***Bao Chi***") was established on November 24, 2009. Bao Chi started to manufacture and sell clothing products bearing infringing marks such as " ", "FENGBAOMAFENG & Design ( )", and "FENGBAOMAFENG in Chinese characters and English Phonetics & Design ( )." Bao Chi also prominently displayed the "FENGBAOMAFENG & Design" mark on its website and stores which included the trade name reference "German Shi Ji Bao Ma Group Limited Company" (in Chinese characters) on its clothing hangtags, websites, and promotional brochures. Bao Chi also actively pursued franchising activities and partners across China. An individual named Li Shuzhi ("***Ms. Li***") was one of Bao Chi's distributors. The local Administration for Industry and Commerce in the Chaoyang district, Beijing City ("***Beijing AIC***"), investigated Ms. Li's store on November 16, 2010, and issued a punishment decision. In its administrative punishment decision, Beijing AIC stated that it had seized and confiscated 63 pieces of products bearing the infringing mark "BLMW and design" and 169 products bearing the infringing mark: "MBWL and design." The Beijing AIC seized a total of 232 products bearing the infringing trademarks from Ms. Li and imposed a fine in the amount of RMB 110,000 (approximately USD 16,424).

The BMW Company brought a civil action asserting trademark infringement and unfair competition against Bao Chi to the Beijing No. 2 Intermediate People's Court (the "***Intermediate Court***"). In its complaint, the BMW Company requested Bao Chi to immediately stop its infringement and to compensate the Company for its economic loss in the amount of RMB 2,000,000 (around USD 300,000). In the meantime, the BMW Company incurred RMB 18,748 (around USD 2,826) in connection with notarization costs, RMB 232,808 (around USD 35,099) for the attorney fees, and RMB 4,481.55 (around USD 675) for copying in connection with the lawsuit.

COURT DECISION

The Intermediate Court reviewed the case and concluded that the logo used by Bao Chi on its clothing products, hangtags, packaging, promotional materials, and websites was confusingly similar to the BMW Company's registered trademark. Bao Chi's use of the logo was prominent. In the normal course of businesses, consumers were unlikely to examine and compare the trademarks in detail and notice the differences between the Bao Chi's logo " " and BMW Company's registered trademark for G955419 " "; in other words, consumers were not likely to notice (or be expected to notice) the differences where one logo was turned upper right while the other was turned upper left. In light of the above, the relevant public was very likely to be misled into believing that the products produced by Bao Chi were associated with or somehow connected with those produced by the BMW Company. Bao Chi had therefore infringed upon the BMW Company's trademark rights over G955419 for " " by using a similar trademark on the same type of products; Bao Chi should bear the corresponding legal responsibilities. Bao Chi's conduct had also constituted unfair competition because it had used the trade name reference, "German Shi Ji Bao Ma Group Limited Company" (in Chinese characters), on its clothing hangtags, websites and promotional brochures and the trade name use was likely to mislead the relevant public into believing that the products offered by Bao Chi were connected with those offered by the BMW Company. The BMW Company failed to provide any concrete support for its economic loss nor any concrete support in connection with Bao Chi's profits as a result of its infringing acts; therefore, the court decided to determine the infringement damage amount by basing their decision on the following factors: the bad faith of Bao Chi, the scope of its infringement, the nature of its infringement, and the fame associated with the BMW Company's registered trademarks. The first level of the court rendered the following decisions:

(1) Bao Chi should immediately stop its infringement and unfair competition acts when the judgment became effective.

(2) Bao Chi should issue an announcement in the *China Industry & Commerce News* regarding its infringement within ten days of the judgment becoming effective so as to eliminate any negative effects caused by its infringements.
(3) Bao Chi should compensate the BMW Company for its economic loss in the amount of RMB 500,000 (approximately USD 75,000) and reasonable litigation costs in the amount of RMB 30,000 (approximately USD 4,500).

Both the BMW Company and Bao Chi appealed the decision to the Beijing High People's Court (the "***High Court***"). The Company believed the damage amount awarded by the Intermediate Court was unreasonably low and had submitted the following evidence during the appeal in the High Court: (1) Bao Chi was active in developing many franchisee stores in the Shan Xi Province; its franchisee stores in Tai-Yuan City, Yun-Cheng City, and Da-Tong City in the Shan Xi Province all carried the Bao Chi logo " ", and the following marks: "Feng Bao Ma Feng in Chinese characters and English phonetics and Logo ( )", "FENGBAOMAFENG and Logo ( )." These franchisee stores also included the references that Bao Chi was the BMW Company's managing distributor in China for clothing and footwear products. The Administration for Industry and Commerce of Shan Xi Province had launched a special action project devoted to the protection of the BMW Company's trademark registrations for its logos and during its investigation, it had seized a large quantity of infringing products, as well as inventory from Bao Chi's various franchisee stores. The value of the seized products in this special action project alone had exceeded RMB 10 million (around USD 1.5 million). The BMW Company also submitted Bao Chi's website information where Bao Chi claimed that "under its leadership, the 'FENG BAO MA FENG' brand (the first and the fourth character 'FENG' means rich in Chinese; and the second and the third characters refer to 'BMW in Chinese characters'." (This coined term, Feng Bao Ma Feng, is a trick of using the same Chinese character immediately before and after the BMW's Chinese brand. Because of the way the term is constructed, it is very likely that the Chinese consumers would misread the brand simply as a BMW Chinese brand). Bao Chi's website further claimed that its brand "has been leading the industry trend and it owns close to 300 endpoint sales centers across China. Bao Chi therefore has an extensive network covering virtually every city in China." Furthermore, one of the business operation conditions to be accepted as one of Bao Chi's franchisees is that the applicant must pay the initial payment of RMB 300,000 (approximately USD 45,230) if the franchisee store is to be set up in a municipality city directly controlled by the central government. The payment is reduced to RMB 200,000 (approximately USD 30,153) if the store is located in a provincial capital city, and RMB 100,000 (approximately USD 15,076) if the store is located in a prefectural-level city in China.

The High Court reviewed the case and believed that the BMW Company failed to provide evidence regarding its actual loss as a result of Bao Chi's infringing activities during the initial trial nor did they provide any evidence showing Bao Chi's profits as a result of its infringing acts.

Accordingly, the amount awarded by the Intermediate Court, based on the submitted evidence, was not inappropriate or lacking legal foundation. However, based on the new evidence submitted by the BMW Company in the High Court appeal process, the evidence was sufficient to prove Bao Chi's clear bad faith in infringing the Company's trademark rights, their long time frame of infringing action, their extensive scope of infringement, and their huge profits as a result of its infringement to the BMW Company's trademark rights. Bao Chi's infringement was therefore serious and was carried out in clear bad faith – its scope of infringement had far exceeded the original awarded damage amount and, in fact, the BMW's requested damage amount – i.e., RMB 2,000,000 (approximately USD 300,000). In addition to the above, the court recognized that the BMW Company's registered trademark for " " under G955419, as well as its other registered trademarks in China, had acquired a high level of fame, and the Company had incurred a substantial amount of attorney fees, notarization fees, and evidence fees which were reasonable litigation costs so as to protect and assert its legal rights in China. With support of the new evidence submitted by the BMW Company during the High Court appeal process, the High Court fully supported the total damage amount requested by the BMW Company. The High Court did this in order to have deterrent effects against infringers and to reduce the trademark owners' costs in protecting its legal rights. Accordingly, the High Court requested Bao Chi to stop its infringing acts, eliminate negative effects by publishing an announcement in the Chinese newspaper, and compensated the BMW Company its economic loss in the amount of RMB 2,000,000 (approximately USD 300,000). Meanwhile, the High Court required Bao Chi to pay the civil penalty in the amount of RMB 100,000 (approximately USD 15,000) regarding its bad-faith infringing acts. Lastly, the High Court issued a judicial recommendation to the SAIC to carry out a full scale raid action against Bao Chi.

ANALYSIS & INSIGHT

Monetary compensation is one of the most important civil reliefs available to the trademark owner during a trademark infringement civil lawsuit. In a civil litigation concerning trademark infringement, it has always been a tricky issue to properly determine the reasonable compensation amount. One of the key issues in the subject case lies in the determination of the damage award. The High Court changed the damage award from the initial RMB 500,000 (approximately USD 75,000) to RMB 2,000,000 (approximately USD 300,000). In other words, the High Court fully supported BMW's arguments and decided to raise the damage amount.

A. Relevant Laws and Rules in Determining the Damage Amount in a Trademark Infringement Lawsuit.

The 1982 Trademark Law did not have specific guidelines on how courts should calculate the damage amount in the trademark infringement litigations. It did, however, have specific guidance noting that the administrative authorities for industry and commerce have rights to request that the infringers compensate the trademark owners' loss – the damage amount should either be the profits acquired by the infringers as a result of its infringing acts during the infringement period or the economic loss suffered by the right holders as a result of the infringement during the infringement period. In 1985, the Supreme Court issued a guidance (No. 53; 1985) ("***Guidance No. 53***") providing further details on how to calculate the damage award in a trademark infringement lawsuit. In Guidance No. 53, the Supreme Court noted that the damage amount could be calculated based on the owner's actual economic loss or the infringer's revenue (i.e., profits after costs and taxes) during the infringement period. In addition, the plaintiff has the right to choose the calculation method between the two. The above approach remained the guiding principle in determining the damage amount in the trademark infringement cases until 2001.

The 2001 Trademark Law offered a more detailed rule on the damage award calculation in a trademark infringement lawsuit. In addition to the two methods discussed above, the plaintiff can also seek compensation for its reasonable costs in seeking to assert its rights in China. In other words, the 2001 Trademark Law specifically allowed the plaintiff to incorporate its reasonable costs as part of its damage award. Furthermore, given the fact that the exact profits or loss cannot be ascertained in most trademark infringement cases, the Law also provided statutory damages. Specifically, in situations where the difficulties to ascertain the defendants' profits or the plaintiffs' losses had been acknowledged by the courts, the civil courts could award a damage amount no greater than the statutory damage amount: RMB 500,000 (approximately USD 75,000). Accordingly, the 2001 Trademark Law had offered three ways to calculate the damage amount in a trademark infringement lawsuit: (1) from the defendants' profits; (2) from the plaintiffs' losses; and (3) from statutory damages. There is, however, a specific order in utilizing these three methods. In other words, option (3) was only available when option (1) and (2) were unavailable. On the other hand, there was no specific order in choosing between option (1) or option (2).

Based on the 2001 Trademark Law, the Interpretation of the Supreme People's Court Concerning the Application of Laws in the Trial of Cases of Civil Disputes Arising from Trademarks (No. 32; 2002) ("***Interpretation No. 32***") offered further details regarding how the courts should calculate the damage amount in a trademark infringement lawsuit:

(1) The defendant's profit amount can be calculated based on the sales volume of the infringing products times the profit per unit. In situations where it is difficult to ascertain the exact profit per product, the information can be calculated based on the profit of the product bearing the registered trademark.
(2) The plaintiff's loss amount can be calculated based on the reduced sales volume or sales volume of the infringing products times the profit per unit of the product bearing the registered trademark.
(3) In situations where the exact amount of the plaintiff's loss or the defendant's profits are difficult to ascertain, the civil courts can determine the proper damage amount after considering the evidence submitted by the plaintiff with

their application or ex officio taking into account Article 56 Section 2 of the Trademark Law. In determining the damage amount, the courts should consider a wide array of factors, such as:

- the nature, duration, and consequence of the infringement,
- the business reputation and fame status associated with the senior marks,
- the licensing fee in connection with use, duration, and scope of the use,
- and reasonable litigation costs.

(4) Reasonable litigation costs, such as notarization fees and on-site investigation fees to obtain infringing evidence, should include costs the plaintiff incurred in order to stop the defendant's infringement. In addition, the court can consider reasonable attorney fees based on the relevant laws in China.

The 2013 Trademark Law had made substantial changes to the way a damage award in a trademark infringement lawsuit could be calculated. The changes are outlined below:

- First, it established the order between the plaintiff's loss and the defendant's profits. The 2013 Trademark Law stated that the damage calculation should first consider the plaintiff's actual economic loss due to the infringement. In the event that the actual economic loss is difficult or impossible to be ascertained, the court can then consider the defendant's profits as a result of its infringement.
- Second, it formally established the licensing fee as a way to calculate the damage amount. Specifically, the 2013 Trademark Law stated that in situations where the plaintiff's loss or the defendant's profits were difficult to ascertain, the court could award the damage amount that would equal several times the amount of the licensing fee. Using the licensing fee as a base to calculate the damage amount was only one of the factors to consider in determining the statutory damage as discussed under the Interpretation of the Supreme People's Court Concerning the Application of Laws in the Trial of Cases of Civil Disputes Arising from Trademarks (No. 32; 2002) ("***Interpretation No. 32***"). However, the 2013 Trademark Law singled it out and formally established it as one of the ways to calculate the damage amount in the trademark infringement litigation.
- Third, it formally established the system to allow a punitive damage award. The 2013 Trademark Law allowed the award of punitive damage, which can be one to three times the award amount based on the above calculation, as long as the infringement is severe or evidence is sufficient to prove that the infringement is motivated by bad faith.
- Fourth, it raised the statutory damage amount limit to RMB 3,000,000 (approximately USD 450,000).
- Fifth, it shifted the burden of proof to the defendants regarding its profits as a result of the infringing activities. In situations where the plaintiff has carried out its obligation in providing evidence, and the accounting materials and

books are mostly controlled (only) by the defendant, the people's courts can require the defendant to provide relevant information as well as accounting materials. Furthermore, in situations where the defendants refuse to provide relevant information or provide false information, the people's court can determine the damage amount based on the information and evidence provided by the plaintiff.

B. Application of the Laws/Rules in Determining the Damage Amount in a Trademark Infringement Lawsuit.

In respect to the actual economic loss suffered by the right holders, most plaintiffs would provide the preinfringement market share and/or revenue information and compare that with the post-infringement market share and/or revenue. Plaintiffs typically utilize the loss of market share or revenue to calculate its actual economic loss. This method of calculation is logical and reasonable, but the information is not commonly accepted by the courts. This is because:

(1) There are multiple factors that would lead to the loss of market share and revenue. Some might be related to the infringement while others might be contributable to other factors, such as the company's poor operation situation, or perhaps the business is losing its competitiveness, or it could be that the business is losing market share simply due to the rise of other legitimate competitors. In other words, the right holders typically have a difficult time establishing the direct causation link between its loss of market share and/or revenue and the defendant's infringing activities.

(2) Most of the market share and revenue information provided by the plaintiff is *not* third-party independent information; rather, it is internal information provided by the plaintiff. Such information is typically challenged by the opposing party and needs to be supported by other independent third-party information. Even assuming the information can be verified and supported by the third-party independent evidence, the information is typically provided to give a snapshot of the right holder's business as a whole. It is therefore difficult to single out the defendant's infringement activities as the reason contributing to the plaintiff's loss of market share or revenue. Such information is therefore, at best, a reference value; it is not entirely reliable as a basis to calculate the damage amount in an infringement lawsuit. In order to resolve this issue, the above-mentioned 2002 judicial interpretation ("***Interpretation No. 32***") states that: "*the plaintiff's economic loss due to the defendant's infringing activities can be calculated based on the profit per unit of the product bearing the registered trademark multiplied by either the loss of sales volume suffered by the plaintiff or the increase of the sales volume of the infringing products for the defendant.*" This interpretation has therefore affirmed that the loss of sales volume of the plaintiff's products is contributable – to some extent – to the defendant's infringing activities. Despite the

> 2002 judicial interpretation, it is still difficult to prove with certainty the profit per unit of the products bearing the registered trademark and the defendant's actual sales volume. Accordingly, in practice, the court rarely calculates the damage amount based entirely on the plaintiff's loss of sales volume.

The damage award in a trademark infringement lawsuit is one type of civil compensation. Accordingly, following the civil principle to make the plaintiff whole, one way to calculate the damage is based simply on the defendant's profits; this is based on the assumption that the defendant's profits are equivalent to the plaintiff's loss. This method of calculation is possible assuming other factors are also present. These other factors may be that the consumers' demand stays constant, and the market has not yet seen any other major players emerging as worthy competitors competing for the plaintiff's market share. This line of reasoning has been taken into consideration in the 2013 Trademark Law in determining the order to calculate the compensation amount between the plaintiff's loss and the defendant's profits. From the perspective to protect rights, there does not exist the need to determine the priority calculation method – the courts can simply pick and choose the most appropriate calculation method based on the facts and evidence submitted in each case to make sure the chosen method affords the maximum protection to the parties. Despite the above, it is objectively more difficult to produce evidence to prove the plaintiff's loss is directly contributable to the defendant's infringing activities. Conversely, the defendant's profits are an objective fact, and it is therefore a more promising way upon which to base the damage calculation. Despite the above, most information and materials supporting the infringer's profits are directly controlled by the defendants. It is therefore difficult for the plaintiff to obtain all the relevant information. In practice, some plaintiffs, in fact, would request evidence preservation with the courts so as to preserve the evidence controlled by the defendants; however, this is not the ideal way to resolve the evidence issue. The issue can be easily complicated by the fact that most infringers do not maintain their books in the appropriate way, or in fact, maintain two sets of books so as to avoid their civil responsibilities as a result of their infringement. Accordingly, in practice, it is still difficult to get a correct and full picture of the defendant's profit situation even though the relevant information has been preserved pursuant to a court order. In light of the practical difficulties, calculating the damage award based solely on the defendant's profits is not a common method either.

In light of the issues discussed above, the courts typically simply use statutory damage in determining the compensation amount in a trademark infringement lawsuit. Statutory damage is the amount determined by the judges after considering all factors relevant to the infringement case and determines the amount within the limit allowed by law. Based on the judicial interpretation, the judge must consider – among other things – the following factors in determining the compensation amount: the nature, duration, and consequence of the infringement; the business reputation and fame status associated with the senior mark; the licensing fee in connection with use, duration and scope of the use; and reasonable litigation costs. In practice, the factors most constantly considered by the courts include:

(1) The nature of infringement, including the type of infringement (i.e., manufacturing infringement or retail infringement) or infringement of the plaintiff's rights as a service provider. Different types of infringement would lead to a different level of loss to the right holder. For example, the loss caused by a manufacturing infringement is usually greater, and the corresponding damage amount would be higher as well.

(2) The scale and duration of the infringement. The bigger the scale - such as when the infringing products have already been available in most cities in China - or the longer the duration of the infringement, the higher the compensation amount (relative to occasional or sporadic infringement).

(3) The commercial reputation, primarily in respect to the use situation and fame status of the registered mark. Trademark infringement is essentially an act to take a free ride on the senior mark in order to obtain unjustified profits. The harm to a famous trademark (such as a well-known trademark) greatly exceeds that to a trademark that has not been put to use and does not have much reputation in the market place. A mark that has not been put to use would not have the corresponding commercial reputation and market share. Accordingly, a use of such a mark by a third party is not an act of seeking to take a free ride on the commercial reputation associated with the senior mark. Despite this, an unauthorized use of a registered trademark that has not been put to use does not mean it would not otherwise cause harm to the trademark owner. Accordingly, even though the senior trademark has not been put to use, a damage award is still possible, although it does need to be adjusted accordingly to reflect the fact that the mark has not been put to use. In other words, the damage amount cannot simply be the defendant's profits. Article 64 of the 2013 Trademark Law states: "*in a trademark infringement situation where the defendant argues that the trademark owner has not put its mark to use, the people's court can request the owner of the registered trademark to provide use materials showing use of the mark in the previous three years. If the trademark owner cannot provide use information reflecting use of the senior mark in the previous three years, nor can it provide information that shows its loss resulted from of the infringement, the defendant does not need to compensate the owner.*" After the law became effective, a trademark owner needs to bear a certain level of burden of proof to show use of its trademark and the loss in an infringement lawsuit if its trademark registration has not been put to use.

(4) The subjective state of the infringer. The court will sometimes take into account the defendant's subjective state when determining the damage amount in an infringement lawsuit. The court would typically require a greater damage award if there was evidence showing the defendant carried out the infringement on purpose, or had already received a punishment decision from the administrative authorities so that the subject infringement was a repeated violation of the law. The higher damage amount would be justified so as to provide a deterrent effect. This practice has already been recognized and formally adopted as a concept of "punitive damage" in the

> 2013 Trademark Law. Conversely, if there were certain backgrounds, histories, objective reasons showing that the infringer did not carry out the infringing acts on purpose, the damage amount can be adjusted downward.

A statutory damage is a damage amount after the court has taken into account various factors involved in the case; however, it does not mean that all damage that has been taken into consideration falls under the category of statutory damage. In situations where the submitted evidence cannot provide the exact amount of the defendant's profits or the plaintiff's loss, but it does amply show that the amount has exceeded the statutory damage and this is a fact that can be verified by the court, the court can award a damage amount that is greater than the maximum amount of statutory damage. In other words, a statutory damage amount is not applicable to such a situation; the court can award the damage amount based on the defendant's profits or the plaintiff's loss so the damage amount is not limited by the statutory amount. Also, in such situations, the court will consider the nature, scale, and duration of the infringement, reputation of the senior mark and the subject state of the infringer when determining the exact damage amount.

The subject case took place before the 2013 Trademark Law was in effect. The plaintiff failed to provide sufficient evidence during the first instance; accordingly, the first level of the court applied statutory damage in accordance with the Trademark Law at that time. Its decision to set the damage amount as RMB 500,000 (approximately USD 75,000) was therefore not inappropriate. During the second level of the court appeal, although it was still insufficient evidence to prove the exact amount of the defendant's profits as a result of its infringement, the plaintiff provided ample evidence in respect to the infringement scale and duration, the defendant's profits as a result of its infringement, and its subjective bad faith. The submitted evidence was sufficient to prove that the defendant's profits had greatly exceeded the statutory damage – RMB 500,000 – in fact, the evidence showed that its profits had greatly exceeded the amount requested by the plaintiff: RMB 2,000,000 (around USD 300,000). Accordingly, the second level of the court fully supported the plaintiff's damage request after it also considered the background fact that the defendant had been involved in an organized large scale infringement for a sustained period of time with great resulting profits. In such a situation, the second level of the court was justified to not continue insisting on a statutory damage; rather, it was appropriate for the court to adjust the damage amount accordingly based on the specific facts of the case. In addition, the second level of the court imposed a civil penalty to the defendant because it had been engaged in an organized bad-faith infringement and it had not been the subject of any administrative punishments. The court also issued a judicial recommendation to the administrative authorities recommending aggressive action against the defendant. The above fully demonstrated the court's determination to combat infringement and was favorably received by the society.

25. Prior Use Defense in a Trademark Infringement Lawsuit

Civil action involving trademark infringement brought by JIANG Yuyou against Nanjing Confucius Temple Diets Co., Ltd. and Nanjing Muslim Qi Fang Ge Caterers Co., Ltd.

- First Instance: Jiang Su Province, Nanjing City Intermediate People's Court (No. 497; 2011) - Decided on: November 15, 2012
- Second Instance: Jiang Su Province, High People's Court (No. 0037; 2013) - Decided on: April 27, 2013

BACKGROUND

JIANG YOU JI is a famous, century-old brand in the Qin-Huai area, Nanjing City in China; the brand is primarily associated with beef fried dumpling and beef broth based soup. The brand was once operated in No. 12 Gong Yuan West Street (the "***Old Address***"). The brand has been recognized as one of Qin-Huai's "Top Eight Must Eat" snacks in Nanjing Confucius Temple (the list provides the top eight tourist attractions in the Qin-Huai area). The brand has enjoyed a long history of fame and popularity in the Jiang Su Province area in China. The brand was originally created by the plaintiff's grandfather (JIANG Yuyou) prior to the Liberation period in China. The brand was inherited and operated by the plaintiff's father, Jiang Qing Qi ("***Jiang Father***") and the store's name is "Qi Ji JIANG YOU JI Beef Store." The store had been operated by both public and private entities and the store name was later changed to "Publicly and Privately Operated JIANG YOU JI Beef and Lamb Store." Jiang Father was the manager of the store. The store was closed during China's Cultural Revolution. Jiang Father retired in 1976 as an employee of a group unit. In 1980, Nanjing Diets Company-Qin Huai District Jiang You Ji Steamed Buns and Dumplings Restaurant, the predecessor of Nanjing Confucius Temple Food & Beverage Co., Ltd. ("***Confucius Temple Food & Beverage Company***"), started to operate the restaurant again under the brand JIANG YOU JI. During the operation, the restaurant name and its address had been changed multiple times and updated accordingly with the local administrative office. The nature of the company had changed from being a collectively owned company to a limited liability company. Despite the changes, the restaurant remained under the operation of Confucius Temple Food & Beverage Company and its predecessor, and Nanjing Muslim Qi Fang Ge Caterers Co., Ltd. (the "***Company***") which was the wholly owned subsidiary of Confucius Temple Food & Beverage Company. The restaurant was in active status during this period.

In 2004, the plaintiff (Jiang Yuyou), and Confucius Temple Food & Beverage Company sought to register the JIANG YOU JI trademark with the China Trademark Office (the "***Trademark Office***"). The Trademark Office decided to determine the trademark applicant through a drawing of lots and Jiang Yuyou was decided by the drawing to be the applicant for the trademark application. The JIANG YOU JI trademark was approved for registration on May 21, 2011 (the "***JIANG Trademark***" or the "***Trademark***").

On August 3, 2011, the store signage at the JIANG YOU JI restaurant located at the Old Address still included the following characters: the "JIANG YOU JI characters" as included in the Jiang Trademark, "century old store" (in Chinese), and "Qing-Zhen" in Chinese characters (meaning "Muslim"). On September 7, 2011, the plaintiff took a series of pictures of a restaurant located at No. 30 Sheng-Zhou Road Nanjing City (the "***New Address***"). The pictures showed that the restaurant's signage was composed of three Chinese characters: Qi Fang Ge (the trade name of the Company). The dishes in the restaurant were imprinted with the characters in the Jiang Trademark as well as Chinese characters meaning "Muslim." During the court trial, the Company admitted that it operated the restaurant located at the New Address - i.e., No. 30 Sheng-Zhou Road Nanjing City where the plaintiff took the pictures.

The plaintiff pointed out that the Company and Confucius Temple Food & Beverage Company continued to use the Jiang Trademark despite its knowledge of the plaintiff's exclusive ownership of the Trademark. Their continued operation of the restaurant bearing the Trademark had caused harm to the commercial reputation of the Trademark and economic loss to his ownership of the Jiang Trademark. The infringement was carried out at two restaurants – one was the JIANG YOU JI restaurant located at the Old Address which was operated jointly by the Confucius Temple Food & Beverage Company and the Company; another was the Qi Fang Ge restaurant operated by the Company located at No. 30 Sheng-Zhou Road Nanjing City. The plaintiff brought a trademark infringement lawsuit to the court, requesting that the Company and Confucius Template Food & Beverage Company immediately stop using the Jiang Trademark, and compensate the plaintiff for his economic loss in the amount of RMB 50,000 (approximately USD 7,600).

During the review of the case, the Nanjing Qin-Huai District Bureau of Commerce provided evidence showing that the Jiang Trademark, under the leadership of the Confucius Template Food & Beverage Company, had been a popular brand embraced and loved by consumers in the area since the 1950s. In the 1980s, the beef broth based soup and beef fried dumpling offered in the restaurant were in fact included as one of Qin-Huai's "Top Eight Must Eat" snacks in the Nanjing area. The food from the restaurant was so great that it was included in the city brochure to promote travel and tourism for the city. According to the Travel Bureau in the Qin-Huai District Nanjing City and the evidence it provided, the JIANG YOU JI restaurant was one of the key welcoming spots to receive foreign guests and visitors. In fact, there had been multiple special reports conducted by the Chinese and foreign media regarding the JIANG YOU JI restaurant. Based on the evidence provided by the Nanjing Confucius Temple Scenery Belt Management Office, Qin Huai's top eight "Must Eat" snacks had been listed as part of the city and area's nonmaterial cultural heritage. The JIANG YOU JI restaurant located at the Old Address had always been an important window to promote culture and city heritage to foreign visitors and guests and it had played a key part in promoting and introducing the city to visitors. Based on the information provided by the Nanjing National Religious Affairs Bureau, the Confucius Temple Food

& Beverage Company restored the operation of the Muslim JIANG YOU JI restaurant and was the recipient of the award – Iconic Brand of Muslim Food Manufacturing and Operation. The Muslim JIANG YOU JI food is a key cousin for the Nanjing city to promote and introduce the city to Muslims in and outside China.

COURT DECISION

Nanjing City Intermediate People's Court reviewed the case and pointed out the following:

(1) The subject mark in the case was a service mark; the plaintiff claimed that it had exclusive ownership over the Jiang Trademark; Confucius Temple Food & Beverage Company countered by pointing out that it had senior use rights over the Jiang Trademark. The Court of First Instance pointed out that the two were in fact conflicting rights as a result of the particular historic backgrounds. Accordingly, the court should adopt a combined approach and consider the relevant historic background and follow the honesty, integrity and market competition principle to protect the senior rights, so as to resolve the dispute in a fair and just way.
China's Trademark Law follows the registration principle which states that only a registered trademark can enjoy legal protection for the exclusive rights associated with the registration. However, the protection of a service trademark did not start until July 1993. There were a number of service marks with use history predating July 1993. Accordingly, if the court simply rigidly followed the registration principle, it meant that the trademark owner would then be able to prevent the senior user of the trademark at issue from using the mark on the same or similar services, and this would have caused unfair consequences to the senior user of the trademark at issue. In order to supplement the deficiencies of the registration system, and balance the conflicting interests between the trademark registrant and senior user, Article 54 of the Implementation Regulation of Trademark Law stated the following: "for a service mark that had been in use until July 1, 1993, and the service mark covers the same or similar services of a registered trademark, the senior user can continue using the service mark. However, for a service mark that had not been in use for more than three years after July 1, 1993, the senior user can no longer use the mark."
In the subject case, the Confucius Temple Food & Beverage Company and its predecessor continued using the JIANG Trademark as an unregistered trademark or company name during a long period of time. Its predecessor restarted the operation of the JIANG YOU JI restaurant at the Old Address in 1980. The restaurant remained in operation despite the fact that the company name and address had been updated on multiple occasions with the local administrative office. In fact, the reason the Jiang Trademark continued to enjoy a high level of fame, popularity and commercial influence in the Qin-Huai area of China

was partly (or in fact primarily) due to the continuous operation by the Confucius Temple Food & Beverage Company and its predecessors.

Since the plaintiff's obtaining of the trademark registration through the drawing of lots in 2011, there had not been any substantial changes regarding the Confucius Temple Food & Beverage Company's scope of use and operation of the Jiang restaurant, as well as its use of characters included in the Jiang Trademark. In fact, the plaintiff did not have any evidence showing that the restaurant was once stopped for operation for more than three years. Accordingly, the Confucius Temple Food & Beverage Company's defense that it enjoyed senior use rights over the JIANG YOU JI characters through its continuous operation of the Jiang restaurant at the Old Address was supported by facts submitted to the court.

As discussed above, the Confucius Temple Food & Beverage Company's use of the Jiang Trademark in its operation of the restaurant at the Old Address had undergone several changes, and its use predated the plaintiff's trademark registration in 2011. Accordingly, its use did not have any subjective bad faith which would result in a violation of the moral principle or a free ride on the plaintiff's registered trademark. In fact, it was through the Confucius Temple Food & Beverage Company's continuous and successful operation that the Jiang Trademark started to enjoy a high level of fame in the Qin-Huai area and a trusted service brand locally. Accordingly, the Confucius Temple Food & Beverage Company's use of the Jiang Trademark for its restaurant at the Old Address was a good-faith use.

Although the plaintiff was the trademark holder of the Jiang Trademark, its exclusive rights should not preclude the Confucius Temple Food & Beverage Company from continuing to enjoy its senior use rights over the Jiang Trademark for its restaurant located at the Old Address. Accordingly, the Confucius Temple Food & Beverage Company enjoyed a senior use right over the JIANG YOU JI characters for its restaurant located at the Old Address as an unregistered trademark.

Despite the above, the protection of senior use rights for service marks is an exception to our country's trademark system. The senior user should not infringe upon the registrant's interests based on its earlier use rights. Another special feature about this case was that the plaintiff and the Confucius Temple Food & Beverage Company in fact applied for the Jiang Trademark on the same date. However, the Confucius Temple Food & Beverage Company failed to provide use evidence showing its use of the JIANG YOU JI characters prior to the application date to the Trademark Office. It therefore failed to exercise its relative rights under the law. This resulted in the Trademark Office choosing the applicant for the Jiang Trademark through the drawing of lots. In light of the above fact, the court should reasonably limit the Confucius Temple Food & Beverage Company's continuous use, scope and manner of the Jiang Trademark. The court of the first level was of the view that in order to maintain the market order, and to protect the plaintiff's exclusive rights over the Trademark, the Confucius Temple Food & Beverage Company could only continue using the Jiang Trademark for its restaurant located at the Old Address. In other words, it was not allowed to change its use of the characters, or expand the scope or operation of its restaurant. Furthermore, in its use of the Jiang Trademark, the Confucius Temple Food & Beverage Company should include further distinctive elements or qualifying languages so as to allow consumers to distinguish its use from the plaintiff's registered trademark.

(2) The plaintiff enjoyed exclusive rights over the Jiang Trademark, and the rights should be protected by the law. Based on the facts in this case which had been verified by the court, the JIANG YOU JI restaurant located at the Old Address was managed and directed by the Confucius Temple Food & Beverage Company after the plaintiff obtained a trademark registration in May 2011. As discussed above, the Confucius Temple Food & Beverage Company enjoyed use rights over the Jiang Trademark for its restaurant located at the Old Address. Accordingly, the court did not support the plaintiff's trademark infringement claim regarding the Confucius Temple Food & Beverage Company's and the Company's use of the Jiang Trademark for its restaurant located at the Old Address.

Despite the above, the Company did not provide any evidence showing that it had senior rights over the Jiang Trademark located at the New Address in response to the plaintiff's trademark infringement claim. By comparing the mark used by the Company with the plaintiff's registered trademark, the two parties' marks were conceptually and phonetically identical; the only difference was that one mark was written in simplified characters while the other was in traditional characters. The similarities were therefore sufficient to cause consumer confusion among the relevant public. The facts showed that the Company continued to use the Jiang Trademark for its restaurant dishes at the New Address after the plaintiff had secured trademark registration for the JIANG YOU JI characters. The Company's use of the Trademark was therefore not supported by the law because it should have known about the plaintiff's exclusive rights over the characters. The Company's use of these characters had thus constituted trademark infringement. The Company should be enjoined from using these characters and bear the associated civil responsibilities.

Based on the above analysis, the first level of the court ruled the following:

- the Company shall immediately stop its use of the Jiang Trademark for its restaurant located at the New Address;
- the Company shall pay the reasonable cost in the amount of RMB 2,000 (approximately USD 300) that the plaintiff had incurred to protect its trademark right within ten days once the judgment had become effective
- the court dismissed the plaintiff's other relief requests.

The plaintiff appealed the decision to the Jiang Su Province High People's Court, requesting the court to enjoin both the Confucius Temple Food & Beverage Company and the Company from using its Jiang Trademark. The

High Court reviewed the case, dismissed the appeal, and maintained the decision rendered by the Court of First Instance.

ANALYSIS & INSIGHT

The Chinese Trademark Law has been following and insisting on the registration principle. Since the introduction of the 1982 Trademark Law, all amendments to the Trademark Law maintain the same principle in that any requests by a natural person, a legal person or any other organization for their exclusive rights of a trademark in connection with its production or business operation must obtain such rights by filing a trademark application with the Trademark Office. Once the trademark application is approved for registration, the trademark owner will then be granted the exclusive rights associated with the trademark. The exclusive rights associated with a registered trademark are limited to those goods or services covered by the trademark. The exclusive rights include rights to exclude others from using the mark in connection with the same or similar goods and/or services without authorization. In practice, a third party may have already started using the mark at issue prior to the trademark owner seeking a trademark application with the Trademark Office. It has always been a key issue in China's Trademark Practice as to whether or not a trademark registrant can stop a senior user from using the trademark once it has been registered, and if the senior user can defend a trademark infringement claim by providing evidence showing its senior use. This is also the key issue that faced the courts in the subject case.

A. The Primary Views in Practice and Approaches.

Prior to the 2013 Trademark Law, there were primarily two views in practice concerning the senior use defense in a trademark infringement lawsuit.

The first view believed that the senior user's defense was not supported by the law and should not be supported by the courts either. This perspective took into account the following:

- First, any defense should have specific legal basis. The Trademark Law at that time did not provide a defense mechanism regarding prior use.
- Second, our country's Trademark Law strictly followed the registration principle. In other words, a trademark must be registered first in order for it to obtain any level of legal protection. Once a mark is registered, the owner would then enjoy exclusive rights including rights to prevent others from using the mark without first obtaining its authorization. The senior user did not seek trademark registration of the mark at issue and accordingly, its rights were not protected by the law. The senior user must then stop using the mark once the mark is registered by a third party. Furthermore, our (China's) trademark law provided two separate systems to address infringement reliefs and its review of the legal effects of a registered trademark. The legal effect of

a registered trademark should be resolved through the administrative procedures. The court reviewing a trademark infringement lawsuit was not in a position to address the rights associated with a registered trademark. Although the Trademark Law did provide a certain level of protection for senior unregistered trademarks that were already in use, such protection was manifested primarily by preventing others from registering the mark through unjust means. If the senior user is interested in opposing or challenging a registered trademark, it should raise an opposition action with the Trademark Office or an invalidation action with the TRAB. The senior user could not be able to raise further defense in a trademark infringement lawsuit if it had failed to first raise a timely opposition or invalidation action to the proper authorities or had lost its actions with the Trademark Office or the Appeal Board. The above was the primary approach especially in the early cases. Many early cases had adopted or at least mentioned the above point of view. For example, in the trademark infringement case brought by Wang Jun against Zhang Ren Cai concerning the trademark "Mr. Du Chicken," the court denied the senior user defense even though there was sufficient evidence to show that the defendant first used the mark prior to the time when the plaintiff was granted trademark registration of the mark at issue. In other words, the court rejected the senior user defense on the basis that China's Trademark Law was to protect the exclusive rights of the trademark owner so as to maintain the market order and accordingly, the defendant's senior good-faith use was not a valid defense in a trademark infringement lawsuit. Furthermore, although the plaintiff and defendant's operation was located in different provinces in China; the plaintiff's trademark registration enjoyed legal effect within China and considering the plaintiff could expand its operation from its original geographic location, the defendant's use of the mark at issue could still lead to consumer confusion. In addition, given the plaintiff and defendant were involved in the same service industry, the defendant's use of the same mark, which covers the same or similar services as those covered in the plaintiff's registered trademark, had constituted trademark infringement. The defendant's senior good-faith use of the mark and the fact that its use was in a different geographic location in China did not take away from the fact that its use had not caused direct economic loss to the plaintiff's business operation. The defendant's senior use, therefore, could be taken into account when considering the damage award.[222]

An opposite view believed that the defendant's senior good-faith use should constitute a valid defense so long as certain criteria were met. The supporters of this view believed that the senior users should be afforded a certain level of recognition and protection for the following reasons. First, the true value of a trademark lies in its business reputation. Although China's trademark system followed the registration principle, it did not mean the system refused to protect senior use of a trademark. For marks that had not been registered, the owner's senior use was nevertheless helpful to

222. Case Index: Hubei Wuhan Jiang'an District People's Court, An Zhi Min Chu Zi [2010] No. 70.

build up the commercial reputation of the marks. Accordingly, such prior use should also be protected by the law. Second, protecting the senior use rights was in fact a basic principle of the Trademark Law. If the senior user already started using the mark prior to the registration date, it should then enjoy senior rights; it would be unfair and unjust to the senior user if it was enjoined from using the mark simply because a third party had obtained a trademark registration. In addition to the above, the Trademark Law had expressly stated that a trademark registration should not negatively impact a third party's senior existing rights; this means that a trademark application should not include a mark that had been put to use by a third party and had enjoyed a certain level of fame through use. This showed that the senior user had rights to prevent later bad-faith trademark registration. Accordingly, a senior user should be entitled to a trademark defense in a trademark infringement lawsuit. Lastly, although the Trademark Law prior to 2013 did not expressly provide a defense mechanism based on senior use as that provided in the Patent Law, it did, in fact, recognize the senior user's rights to continue using the mark as long as certain criteria were met. For example, Article 54 of the 2002 Implementation Regulations of the Trademark Law stated: "for a service mark that had been in use until July 1, 1993, and the service mark covers the same or similar services of a registered trademark, the senior user can continue using the service mark. However, for a service mark that had stopped being used for more than three years after July 1, 1993, the senior user can no longer use the mark." In the subject case, the court utilized the above regulation and found the Confucius Temple Food & Beverage Company's use of the Trademark at the Old Address did not constitute trademark infringement. In addition to the subject case, there are a number of cases showing the courts' support of the senior use defense. In the trademark infringement litigation brought by the Wei-Ta-Long Company against Hui-Er-Kang for example, the court did not support the plaintiff's infringement claim concerning the latter's use of the HUI-ER-KANG trademark. This was because, based on the defense evidence, the defendant had been using the HUI-ER-KANG trademark for a long period of time and the mark had therefore acquired a certain level of fame in the South Eastern part of China. The defendant's use of the unregistered mark had therefore constituted the prior-existing right protectable by the law. Accordingly, the plaintiff did not have the legal basis to challenge the defendant's senior use of the HUI-ER-KANG trademark simply because the plaintiff had obtained exclusive rights of the mark through a trademark registration.[223]

The above two views are both reasonable. The first view follows the legal stipulation principle and the second view focuses more on the substantial justice. The first view strictly follows the registration principle; the second view, on the other hand, emphasizes on the use aspect of a trademark and commercial reputation of a trademark. Overall, the first view was the dominant view in the early times. However, with more understanding of the Trademark Law, through evolvement of society and the overall trademark system, there had been a shift in the dominant principle – the public started to consider the first view as too rigid and absolute. Gradually, the law

223. Case Index: Hunan High People's Court, Xiang Gao Fa Min San Zhong Zi [2005] No. 49.

evolved to allow the defense argument advanced by the senior user and the public started to consider such a defense both logical and just. Despite the above, due to the absence of clear legal support of a senior use defense argument in a trademark lawsuit, the court typically resorts to one of the following two ways to allow such a defense argument:

(1) the fairness principle so as to protect the senior use of the mark at issue; or
(2) the coexistence of the two parties' marks are not likely to lead to consumer confusion which is supported by coexisting use evidence.
The lack of proper legal foundation issue for the courts to accept the senior use defense arguments was finally resolved in the 2013 Trademark Law. Article 59 Section 3 of the 2013 Trademark Law states: "a trademark registrant has no right to enjoin a third party from using a specific trademark in accordance with the way the third party has been using the mark if the third party has been using the mark prior to the application date of the registered trademark, has been using the same or similar mark on the same or similar products as those covered in the registered mark and the use has obtained a certain level of influence. Despite the above, the registrant can request the senior user to incorporate appropriate additional distinctive elements so as to allow consumers to distinguish the two parties' marks."

B. The Defense Concerning the Senior Use.

a. Necessary Elements to Assert the "Prior Use" Defense Argument.

i. The Use Must Be "Senior."

Since it is a defense argument relating to senior use, the defendant must have evidence to prove its use is senior to the trademark application/registration asserted by the plaintiff. The relevant time period is therefore crucial in determining whether or not the use is senior. There were in fact different views regarding the relative time points. The first view was that the use must be prior to the application date of the registered trademark at issue. The second view was that the use must be prior to the registration date of the trademark at issue. In reality, neither view was entirely correct or incorrect. The specific language in Article 59 of the Trademark Law states as follows: "the third party has already put the mark to use prior to the application date of the registered trademark at issue ... ." Based on Section 59, clearly, the use must occur prior to the application date of the subject trademark. Accordingly, using the registration date as the relative time point would clearly violate the registration principle. In addition to the above, Article 59 of the Trademark Law also states: "the third party has already used the mark on the same or similar products prior to the trademark registrant's use ... ." Based on the above, the defendant not only has to use the mark prior to the application date of the registered trademark, but the use must be prior to that of the trademark registrant. In situations where the defendant's use occurs prior to the application date of the registered trademark but is in fact later than the use of the trademark registrant, the defendant's use argument will not be accepted by the court. Conversely, if the trademark registrant does not use the mark prior to application date, then the relevant time point to decide prior use is the application date of the registered trademark.

ii. The Use Must Satisfy the Use Requirement of a Trademark.

First, the use must satisfy the definition of a trademark use – i.e., using the mark on products, product packaging or containers, on documentation relating to goods transaction, or using the mark on promotional materials, brochures, advertising material at exhibits or other commercial activities so that the mark can function as a source identifier allowing consumers to identify the origin of the products and /or services. In other words, any use that can allow consumers to associate the mark as a source identifier pointing to the underlying products or services would be sufficient. For example, a trade name use can also satisfy the use requirement so long as the use can allow consumers to identify the underlying products and /or services.

Second, the use must occur within the "legal geographic boundaries" of China. Trademark is geographic in nature; the same limitation also applies to the senior use defense arguments. In reality, the legal basis to support and allow the senior use defense argument is based on the assumption that the use occurs in China and such a use has obtained a certain level of influence in China; if so, the prior use is justified to be protected as a trademark. If the use does not occur in China, it then lacks the legal foundation and should not be accepted as a valid defense argument. As for the legal geographic boundaries of China, it refers to Mainland China only; any use that occurs in Taiwan, Hong Kong, or Macau would not be recognized as use within the legal geographic boundaries of China.

iii. The Use Must Have Obtained a Certain Level of Influence.

As stated above, the senior use must have obtained a certain level so as to justify the legality and practical necessity for protection – in other words, the use must have obtained a certain level of influence. A prior use defense argument is not acceptable if the senior use is only occasional and has not yet obtained any level of influence. The influence requirement does not mean the mark must be nationally well-known in China; the same standard discussed in Article 32 of the Trademark Law – i.e., "a certain level of influence" – also applies here. According to the Interpretation of the Supreme People's Court on Issuing the Opinions on Several Issues Concerning the Trial of Administrative Cases Involving the Authorization and Determination of Trademark Rights (No. 12; 2010) (the "***Interpretation***"), a prior-existing use would be recognized as having obtained a certain level of fame if there is evidence to support that the senior use has lasted a certain consecutive period of time, in a certain area, with large sales volumes or took place in connection with advertising promotion materials, etc. Similarly, the prior use must have obtained a certain level of influence prior to the application date of the registered trademark, and prior to the trademark registrant's use of the same or similar mark. The senior use defense argument will not be accepted even though the use occurs prior to the application date of the mark at issue if the senior mark has not yet acquired a certain level of fame by the application date of the disputed mark (i.e., the senior use defense would not be supported if the fame associated with the senior mark cannot be established until *after* the application date of the disputed mark).

iv. The Use Must Involve the Same or Similar Marks, in Connection with the Same or Similar Products as that of the Registered Trademark.

According to Article 59 of the Trademark Law, the mark involved in the prior use defense argument must be identical or closely similar to the registered trademark at issue and the products or services that are used in connection with the mark asserted in the prior use argument must be the same or similar as those covered in the registered trademark. This requirement is implied in the senior use defense argument. If the marks involved are neither identical nor similar and the products or services are neither identical nor similar, there would not be such a thing as "senior" use.

b. Legal Consequences.

i. The User Can Continue Using the Mark so long as It Conforms with the Scope of Prior Use.

Based on the Trademark Law, in situations where the prior use defense argument has been supported by the courts, the trademark registrant will not be able to enjoin the senior user from continuing to use the mark so long as the use is consistent with the scope of prior use. This means that the senior use does not constitute trademark infringement. The other implication of this, however, is that an infringement is possible if the use has exceeded the original scope of use and if so, the trademark registrant has rights to request the senior user to stop from continuing to use the mark in a manner that is inconsistent with the original use.

There are different ways to determine whether or not a use has exceeded the original scope. Some make a determination based on the geographic scope of the original use; others consider the way the mark is being used or the categories of the products (or services) being used. Similar to the prior use defense argument discussed regarding Patent Law, the determination of the original use scope should not be too strict or too lax. Instead, the use determination should be based on the manufacturing capabilities. The determination of prior use in the Trademark Law should also follow the same policy principle, and strike a balance between the exclusive rights of a registered trademark, and rights of a prior use. Factors to use to consider the prior use scope should include the exact way the mark is being used, types of products, and scale of operation, etc. In the subject case, although it was decided prior to the effective date of the 2013 Trademark Law, it still made a distinction between use that stayed within the original scope and use that exceeded the original scope. The court also made respective judgments reflecting each use.

In addition, the relevant time period to determine the original scope of use should be prior to the application date of the registered trademark, and before the trademark registrant has started using the mark. Some views believe that the registration date should be the relevant time period; others believe that relevant scope of use should be based on the way the mark is being used when the dispute between the parties arise – none of the above fully reflects the legislative purpose of the Trademark Law.

ii. The Trademark Registrant Has the Right to Request the Senior User to Incorporate Additional Distinctive Elements.

The primary function of a trademark is to operate as a source identifier allowing the relevant public to identify the underlying products or services. Accordingly, confusion is likely among the relevant public if two separate parties are allowed to use the same or similar mark in connection with the same or similar products (or services). To avoid this, the Trademark Law gives trademark registration the right to request the senior user to incorporate additional appropriate distinctive elements if the senior user decides to continue using the mark. Article 1 Section 2 of the Interpretation of the Supreme People's Court on Some Issues Concerning the Application of Law in the Trial of Civil Cases Involving Unfair Competition (the "***Interpretation***") also has similar requirements – "Article 5 Section 2 of the Anti-Unfair Competition Law is not satisfied in situations where use of a mark is similar or identical to the reference, packaging, declaration of a famous mark, the two uses are in different geographic areas, and there is sufficient evidence to prove that the junior use is based on good faith. However, if confusion arises due to the junior user's entry into the same geographic area, the people's court would support the senior user's request for the junior user to incorporate additional distinctive elements in its mark so as to allow the relevant public to distinguish the two parties' marks." Neither the Trademark Law nor the Interpretation provides detailed guidance on how to implement the request so that the relevant public would not be confused. The issue is better left to the disputing parties since they are most familiar with the market condition and the consumers. Common ways to resolve the dispute include incorporating company's trade name, or geographic references so as to allow the public to distinguish the two parties' marks apart.

The subject case fully illustrates the necessary conditions for a senior use defense argument being accepted by the court and the subsequent legal consequences. Based on the facts submitted to the court, it was clear that Confucius Temple Food & Beverage Company had been using the Trademark for a sustained period of time and its use of the mark had obtained a high level of fame. Although Confucius Temple Food & Beverage Company was not listed as the trademark registrant for the Jiang Trademark due to the result of the drawing of lots, the court nevertheless refused to recognize the company's use as trademark infringement and allowed its use of the Jiang Trademark so long as the use was carried out in the same manner, in the same geographic area, as the prior use. Confucius Temple Food & Beverage Company; however, would be required to incorporate distinguishing elements for its continued use of the Jiang Trademark. Meanwhile, the court recognized any use that had exceeded the original scope as infringement and requested the company to bear the corresponding legal responsibilities. Although the subject case was reviewed with the decision rendered prior to the 2013 Trademark Law, the court followed the same principle and criteria as articulated in the 2013 Trademark Law.

26. Fair Use Defense in a Trademark Infringement Lawsuit

Civil trademark infringement action brought by Guan-Nan County Extra-budgetary Funds Administration and Jiangsu Province Tang Gou Liang Xiang He Spirit Industry Co., Ltd. against TAO, Qin

- First Instance: Jiangsu Province, Lian-Yun-Gang City Intermediate People's Court (No. 1; 2006) – Decided on: March 28, 2006
- Second Instance: Jiangsu Province High People's Court (No. 94; 2006) – Decided on: September 8, 2006

BACKGROUND

On January 30, 1987, a spirit factory named "Guan-Nan County, Jiangsu Province, Tang Gou Township spirit factory" located in Tang Gou Town, Guan-Nan County, Jiangsu Province registered a composite trademark inclusive of the English letters "TF" and the Chinese characters for "Tang Gou" and a device; the mark was approved for registration by the China Trademark Office (the "***Trademark Office***") in connection with Class 33 spirit products; its registration number is 276470 (the "***Composite Mark***"). Due to a name change, the Composite Mark was later assigned to "Guan-Nan County, Jiangsu Province, Tang Gou spirit factory," and subsequently, "Jiangsu Province Tang Gou Spirit Industry Co., Ltd." A few years later, the company changed its name to Jiangsu Province Tang Gou Liang Xiang He Spirit Industry Co., Ltd. (the "***Company***") in September, 2004; and the design trademark involving the Tang Gou characters was assigned to Guan-Nan County Extra-Budgetary Funds Administration (the "***Office***"). In January 2005, the Office and the Company entered into a nonexclusive trademark license agreement, allowing the Company to use the Tang Gou design mark with monetary compensation.

In January 2006, the Office and the Company came across some spirit products bearing the brand name "Zhen Tang" (roughly translated to "precious liquor") which was manufactured by Tang Gou Qu spirit factory located in Guan-Nan County (the "***Qu spirit Factory***"); the parties believe the company name for the Qu spirit Factory used the same characters of their registered trademark; furthermore, the Qu spirit Factory's product packaging included the same Tang Gou characters which were written in gold against a red background; the parties believed the Qu spirit Factory's use of the Tang Gou characters infringed their exclusive trademark rights and filed a lawsuit with the people's court in Lian-Yun-Gang City, Jiangsu Province.

The Tang Gou phrase is a location reference; it refers to a town by the name of "Tang Gou." The Tang Gou town is in the Guan-Nan County, Jiangsu Province. The Tang Gou town had been renowned for its white wine production since the end of the Ming dynasty; the Qu spirit Factory was located in the Tang Gou street, Tang Gou town, Guan-Nan County; it was a privately held family owned business started and operated by an individual, Tao Qin. The Qu spirit Factory was registered and approved for business operation on February 24, 2003 by the Administration for Industry and Commerce of Guan-Nan County, Lian-Yun-Gang City.

COURT DECISION

The Intermediate People's Court in Lian-Yun-Gang City (the "***Intermediate Court***") reviewed the case and issued the following decision: "the defendant's registered company name – Jiangsu Province Guan-Nan County Tang Gou Qu Spirit Factory – is distinguishable and clearly different from the plaintiff's registered Composite Mark which includes "TANG GOU in Chinese characters, TG and Design;" accordingly, the defendant's use of its registered trade name is not capable to cause consumer confusion among the relevant public. Furthermore, TANG GOU is a location indicator; it has been a renowned place for white spirit production with a long history and it is therefore more famous than the plaintiff's TANG GOU trademark. Location is a reference term and it belongs to the public domain; a trademark registrant does not have the right to forbid others from properly using the location reference so as to indicate the relationship between the third parties' products and the location, even though the use involves the same or similar products as those covered in the plaintiff's trademark. In this case, the defendant's unique way in using the characters "Tang Gou Qu Spirit Factory" on its own product packaging, and its representation of the Tang Gou characters in gold against the red background were proper use within its legal rights. Furthermore, the defendant's use of its ZHEN TANG trademark also demonstrated that its trademark stylization is clearly different from that of the plaintiffs' trademark which includes both design and character elements. In light of the above, consumer confusion is unlikely." The Intermediate Court dismissed the plaintiffs' requests for relief.

The High People's Court in the Jiangsu Province (the "***High Court***") reviewed the case and noted that the Tang Gou characters in the plaintiff's trademark enjoyed a high level of fame; the defendant's company was approved for registration much later than the plaintiffs' trademark and accordingly, the defendant's use of the same Tang Gou characters on the same products should be more restricted; the defendant's use of these characters should conform with the plaintiffs' prior trademark rights. The defendant's use of these characters should be limited to the need to identify the manufacturing place for its products. The defendant had used the Tang Gou characters in a prominent way on its product packaging (the characters were carefully positioned on its product packaging to attract the consumers' attention and were represented in a bright design); such use was not a proper use of the location reference. The use in fact had demonstrated the defendant's subjective intent to trade on the goodwill associated with the Tang Gou brand; the use is also likely to result in consumer confusion. Although the defendant included its company name – Jiangsu Province Guan-Nan County Tang Gou Qu Spirit Factory – the packaging still prominently displayed the Tang Gou characters in the middle part of its trade name; accordingly, the defendant's use of these characters did not fall under proper use of its trade name either. In light of the above, the High Court believed the defendant's use of the Tang Gou characters had infringed upon the plaintiffs' exclusive rights in its trademark and vacated the

Intermediate Court's Decision. The High Court also required the defendant to immediately stop its infringing acts and compensate the plaintiffs for their economic loss as well as reasonable expenses in bringing the lawsuit.

ANALYSIS & INSIGHT

The subject case involves the discussion relating to the fair use doctrine and the necessary elements to defend a trademark infringement action on the ground of "fair use." The focus of this case is whether or not the defendant's use of the Tang Gou characters on its product packaging is indeed a proper use of the location indicator and is a part of its registered company name.

A. The Difference Between a Trademark Use and a Non-Trademark Use.

The necessary precondition of trademark infringement involves the use of a mark as a trademark; if a third party uses the mark in a way that does not satisfy the use requirements as discussed in the Trademark Law, there would not be any basis to support the use as a trademark infringement. It is therefore important to understand the concept of a trademark use and the necessary requirements to qualify a use as trademark use - this is the key to differentiate trademark use versus non-trademark use.

Trademark use refers to use of a mark or symbol in a way that allows the mark/symbol to function as a source identifier for the underlying products or services in the regular commercial activities. The necessary requirements to satisfy this use are twofold: (1) the use must occur during the regular course of business - in other words, only use that takes place in a business transaction or with the goal to facilitate a business transaction can be recognized as trademark use; (2) the second requirement involves the meaning of the trademark - the use of the trademark must be carried out in a way that allows the relevant public to identify the underlying products or services. The difference between a use involving symbols and a use involving a trademark lies in the fact that the former involves use in connection with its original meaning - the use is carried out with the goal to explain or describe the product name, model, quality or any other features such as manufacturing place or producer information associated with the underlying products or services. Therefore, such use does not allow consumers to identify the origin of the underlying products/services. On the other hand, the use of a trademark involves using a mark in a way that allows the relevant public to identify the origin of the products/services. Accordingly, in a fair use defense discussion, the appropriate subject involves use of a symbol, a mark, rather than use of a trademark.

B. Necessary Elements for a Fair Use Defense.

Although the Trademark Law does not provide clear guidance on what constitutes "fair use," good faith is typically one of the necessary requirements for such use both in theory and in practice.[224] In the trademark infringement decision involving Zhangzhou City Hong Ning Jia Hua Co., Ltd. and Zhangzhou Pien Tze Huang Pharmaceutical Co., Ltd., the Supreme Court pointed out: "the manufacturer's use of a mark or symbol can be recognized as fair use if the use is carried out with the goal to explain or objectively describe the features of the underlying products or services, the use is motivated by good faith, the defendant uses the mark in a necessary way, and the use would not result in consumer confusion among the relevant public. In order to make a determination on good faith and whether or not such a use is necessary, the court can consider commercial customs and related factors in the industry."[225] From the above, it is clear that the Supreme Court allows the determination of good faith to consider factors such as business customs. One of the primary goals of the Trademark Law is to ensure fair competition in the marketplace – "the Trademark Law has traditionally been viewed as part of the Anti-Unfair Competition Law ... the Trademark Law – as a subpart of the Anti-Unfair Competition Law – can only have its place in the Law when there is a possibility of competition."[226] Accordingly, it is appropriate to use the same standard, the "honest business customs," as articulated in the Anti-unfair Competition Law to determine whether or not the underlying use is proper and appropriate. The determination involving "honest business customs" typically takes into account the following factors:

1. Selection of the Symbol/Mark.

The symbol or mark selected for use must belong to or in the public domain; free for use by anyone. Accordingly, if one claims that the use of his or her own name, or the company name falls under fair use defense, the person or company must provide evidence showing that its selection of the name or company name has complied with the honest business customs; the selection is not carried out with the intent to trade off others' commercial reputation and goodwill. None of the following would satisfy the honest business customs – for example, when a use is carried out with the intent to trade on the goodwill and commercial reputation of a third party; a company is seeking to register a third party's trademark as part of its company trade name and is planning on using the company name in connection with the same or similar products as those covered by the registered trademark; or a person changes his or her name so that the new name is identical with a third party's trademark, and is seeking to use the name in the same or similar products as those covered by the senior registered trademark.

In the subject case, the defendant claimed that its use of the TANG GOU characters did not constitute trademark infringement; its use was proper because it was

224. Li Chen, INTELLECTUAL PROPERTY LAW KEYWORD, Law Press, 214 (2006).
225. Case Index: The Supreme People's Court, Min Shen Zi [2009] No. 1310. This decision has taken "whether or not such a use is necessary" into consideration, while this is not a necessary element in the fair use doctrine. This is only required when the use is an indicative use of others' mark. Thus the decision is arguable.
226. Arthur R. Miller, Michael H. Davis, OVERVIEW OF INTELLECTUAL PROPERTY LAW, Translated by ZHOU, Lin, SUN, Jianhong, ZHANG Ying, China Social Sciences Press, 104 (1997).

not only a use of the location indicator, but also a use of its own company name. TANG GOU is a location indicator and is free to be used by either party. Accordingly, the defendant's choice of such characters did not violate the honest business customs standard. As to the defendant's argument that its use of the TANG GOU characters also fell under fair use because it involved the use of its own company name. To substantiate this argument, the defendant must provide evidence showing that its choice of such characters had fully complied with the honest business customs standard. In the subject case where the plaintiff's TANG GOU trademark had enjoyed a high level of fame and the two parties were involved in the same industry in the same location, the defendant should have chosen different characters for its company name. Instead, the defendant chose the same TANG GOU characters; such a choice did not comply with the honesty business customs standard and in fact, it was highly likely the choice was motivated with the intent to trade off the goodwill associated with the plaintiffs' senior and famous trademark. The Intermediate Court was of the view that the defendant's use of the characters was proper because it was part of its company name; accordingly, the Intermediate Court did not support the trademark infringement claim. The High Court on the other hand did not make a clear ruling on this issue – it simply pointed out that the defendant's use of its company name did not comply with the relevant rules. Neither court, in our view, made a proper judgment on this specific issue.

2. Use of the Symbol/Mark.

a. The Use Is Merely to Convey Information Relating to the Underlying Products/ Services.

Non-trademark use of a symbol or mark involves a use which is carried out with the intent to explain or convey product information so as to promote the products and enhance the consumers' understanding of such products. Product information includes the general reference of the products, design, model of such products, quality information, main ingredients, functionality, purpose, weight, and other features, as well as manufacturing place and manufacturer information. Use of a mark or symbol in these instances are not carried out with the purpose to enable consumers to identify the origin of the products; the use, accordingly, would not result in consumer confusion either. None of the above use should be viewed as trademark infringement.

b. The Non-trademark Use of a Mark or Symbol.

In order for a proper defense to be accepted and supported by the courts, the way the mark is being used must comply with the honest business customs – in other words, the use must be carried out in a way to simply convey the product information, as opposed to functioning as a source identifier. A use would not be deemed proper even if the selection of the symbol/mark has fully complied with the relevant business customs, but the way the mark is being used involves prominent use of some parts of the mark which does not conform with the business standards, and the manner in which the mark is being used is sufficient to enable it to function as a source identifier so that there exists a possibility of consumer confusion – if so, even though the initial selection of the mark is proper, the use of the mark would not be considered proper due to the manner in which the mark is being used.

In the present case, if the defendant's intent was merely to convey the manufacturing place information for its products, the use of the Tang Gou characters did comply with the honest business standards. However, in addition to the manufacturing information where it did involve the Tang Gou characters, the defendant's product packaging purposefully left out the characters – Guan Nan County – where it would be helpful to convey the product information, and only included the characters for "TANG GOU QU SPIRIT FACTORY." Based on the way the defendant used these characters, it could be inferred that its goal in using these characters was not only to merely convey the product information, but also to use these characters as a source identifier for its products, which explained why it purposefully "weakened" the representation of its own brand and "strengthened" the representation of the TANG GOU characters in gold coloring with a different contrasting background. The defendant's use of these characters may cause the confusion and have clearly violated the honest business customs. The Intermediate Court's decision of not finding trademark infringement was obviously misled by the defendant's fair use argument. The High Court, on the other hand, had reached a different conclusion on the basis of the defendant's prominent use of the TANG GOU characters which was carried out with the intent to trade on the goodwill and commercial reputation of the plaintiffs' brand; the defendant's use of these characters was not a fair use of its own company name or the location indicator – instead, it used the characters in a way so that it could operate as a source identifier and lead to consumer confusion.

3. Primary Forms of "Fair Use."

The key issues in the subject case involve the determination whether or not the defendant's use of the TANG GOU characters was fair use of the location indicator and its trade name. Based on judicial practice in China, there are four primary ways to use a mark that falls under the fair use doctrine: (1) descriptive use of a public symbol/mark; (2) use of a mark for its primary meaning; (3) indicative use of one's own mark; (4) indicative use of others' trademark.

a. Descriptive Use of a Public Symbol/Mark.

"The policies of free competition and free use of language dictate that trademark law cannot forbid the commercial use of terms in their descriptive sense: *The principle is of great importance because it protects the right of society at large to use words or images in their primary descriptive sense, as against the claims of a trademark owner to exclusivity."*[227] A public symbol means a symbol or a mark that is itself a generic common reference of the product name, shape, or model; or that the mark directly describes the nature, quality, raw materials or manufacturing place of the products; or that the mark is a fixed term used for its original primary meaning. Descriptive use refers to the use of a mark based on its primary meaning so as to explain and promote the underlying products. There are five ways to use a mark based on its primary meaning.

i. Use of a Mark that Is the Generic Product Name, Product Shape or the Model of the Product.

General name, shape, model of the product refers to the name, shape, model that is based on or approved by the country's national standards, industry standards or regulations, or relevant customs. The general name includes a product's full name, abbreviation, short-hand, or nickname. A proper use of such a name includes the inherent generic name, shape, model of the product; it also includes the "acquired" general reference when the product's trademark has been diluted and degenerated to become a common product reference, shape, design, or model of the product. The above use is fully illustrated in the trademark infringement case brought by Beijing Hui-Cheng Spirit Industry Development Company against Beijing Shunxin Agriculture Co., Ltd - Niu Lanshan Brewery concerning the latter's use of the "ZENG LIU" in Chinese character trademark. In the case, the plaintiff was the trademark owner of the ZENG LIU mark under Registration Number 715810; the mark was registered in connection with Class 33 alcohol beverage (except for beer). The defendant was the manufacturer of the white spirit under the brand "Niu LanShan ZENG LIU." In response to the infringement lawsuit, the defendant submitted a publication titled "Beijing City Zhi Gao" (written in 1939; published in 1990); based on this publication, ZENG LIU was a general common reference for one specific type of white spirit; these characters had in fact been a specific reference for the white spirit for a long period of time, particularly in the Beijing and Northern region of China. The court reviewed the case and pointed out that although the plaintiff enjoyed trademark registration rights over the ZENG LIU characters, it did not have the rights to stop others from using the same characters on their products or promotional materials when others simply incorporated these characters as a general reference to indicate the specific white spirit. The defendant's use - e.g., "Beijing Zeng Liu Spirit" and "Niu LanShan Zeng Liu Spirit" - was proper use of these characters because they were included so as to describe the nature and particular features of their white spirit products. The defendant was not using these characters or intending them to function as a trademark. The court dismissed the plaintiff's infringement claim.[228]

227. McCarthy on Trademarks and Unfair Competition §11:45 (4th ed).
228. Case Index: Beijing High People's Court, Gao Min Zhong Zi [2007] No. 39.

ii. Use of a Mark that Is Indicative of the Underlying Product's Quality.

In the petition to the court to confirm noninfringement, Mr. Li Chun Hong ("***Mr. Li***") was the owner of the registered trademark "DP;" the trademark was registered in connection with Class 25 clothing, footwear, and headwear products. The plaintiff was Youngor Group Co., Ltd.; it used the "DP" mark on its "YOUNGOR in English and Chinese" branded cotton non-iron dress shirts which incorporated the company's antiwrinkle fabrics. The plaintiff put the DP mark in the center of its hangtag; the DP mark was represented in a bigger font than that of the plaintiff's trademark – the overall hangtag, however, was smaller than the packaging for the dress shirts. The packaging for the dress shirts, on the other hand, prominently displayed the plaintiff's trademark "YOUNGOR." Mr. Li had sent a cease and desist letter to the plaintiff, Youngor company, prior to the lawsuit regarding the company's trademark infringement; accordingly, Youngor company petitioned to the court to confirm noninfringement. The court reviewed the case and pointed out that the "DP" symbol was in fact a common abbreviation for a particular type of anti-wrinkle technique; the DP abbreviation was widely used in the research field for clothing. In fact, the abbreviation was also used by some companies in the clothing manufacturing industry. The plaintiff chose to use the DP letters on its product hangtags because it was trying to convey to the consumers the quality of its products; the plaintiff also used its own registered trademark on the hangtags. Furthermore, the plaintiff had used its own trademark in a prominent way on its product packaging. In light of the above and the plaintiff's incorporation (and prominent use) of its own trademark, consumer confusion was unlikely. Based on the above, the court decided that the plaintiff's use of the DP letters was proper use because the company used the mark to convey to consumers the quality of its products.[229]

iii. Use of a Mark that Is Indicative of the Raw Materials for the Underlying Products.

This concept is fully illustrated in the trademark infringement lawsuit brought by Li Fengying against Hunan Heng An Paper Industry Company and Shandong Heng An Xin Xiang Yin Paper Manufacturing Company; the lawsuit concerns the LAVENDER in Chinese trademark. The plaintiff was the owner of the "LAVENDER in Chinese and Design" trademark (Registration Number 3334152); the registration covered Class 16 products such as paper handkerchief and table sheet made of paper. In the paper handkerchief and tissue paper products manufactured by the two defendants, these products prominently displayed the defendants' trademark – XIN XIANG YIN in Chinese characters.[230] However, underneath the trademark was the LAVENDER

229. Case Index: Ningbo City Yinzhou District People's Court, Yong Yin Min Chu Zi [2008] No. 2691.
230. Case Index: Trademark Review & Adjudication Board, [2005] No. 4684. In this adjudication No. 1056830 "XIN XIANG YIN in Chinese characters and device" was recognized as well-known trademark. This trademark is owned by the defendant Hunan Heng An Paper Industry's affiliated company Changde Heng, a Paper Industry Company.

Chinese word which was included in a navy oval design. There were also colorful lavender designs right next to the LAVENDER word. Lavender extracts were part of the fragrance incorporated in the manufacturing process for tissue paper. The two defendants' use of the LAVENDER characters was to convey to consumers that their tissue products either included lavender extracts or lavender fragrance or both. Furthermore, the way the defendants were using the lavender word and lavender design would not lead to consumer confusion. Accordingly, the court dismissed the plaintiff's infringement claim.[231]

iv. Use of a Mark that Is Indicative of the Functionality of the Products.

This concept is fully illustrated in the trademark infringement lawsuit brought by Liebherr International German Co., Ltd. against BSH Home Appliances Co., Ltd. concerning the "BIOFRESH" trademark. The plaintiff was the trademark owner of international registration of "BIOFRESH" under G771979; the registration covered Class 11 products such as refrigerating apparatus and machines. In the fresh food compartment in the refrigerators manufactured by the defendant, the compartments were imprinted with the word "BIOFRESH." Furthermore, the term "BIOFRESH" in English along with the following Chinese characters "keeping products fresh" were written in the stickers that were included in the outside side-pocket packaging of the refrigerators – this phrase, however, was not included in the prominent position either on the refrigerator or the packaging box for the refrigerators. In fact, the defendant had included its SIEMENS trademark in bold black letters in the two places referenced above which were singled out by the plaintiff as trademark infringement evidence. In addition to the above, the defendant had included prominent use of its SIEMENS trademark in key positions on the exterior of its refrigerators and packaging. The disputed mark in the case included two words, with BIO refers to biology and FRESH refers to something that is fresh. The combination of these two words can be understood to mean "biological fresh" – the phrase implied that products were kept fresh through biological technology. The defendant used the BIOFRESH term in English, and also included the corresponding translation in Chinese; the purpose to include the phrase was therefore to explain the special function of the defendant's refrigerator products. Furthermore, consumer confusion was unlikely because the plaintiff's registered trademark was stylized differently from that of the defendant's use of the BIOFRESH term, and the defendant had also used its SIEMENS trademark in a prominent way on its products and product packaging. In light of the above, the court ruled that the defendant's use of BIOFRESH was fair use and dismissed the lawsuit.[232]

231. Case Index: Beijing No. 1 Intermediate People's Court, Yi Zhong Min Chu Zi [2006] No. 15269.
232. Case Index: Shanghai High People's Court, Hu Gao Min San Zhi Zhong Zi [2008] No. 61.

v. Use of a Mark that Is Indicative of a Location Indicator.

Use of a mark indicative of a location indicator occurs when such a use merely indicates the manufacturing place or the place where the manufacturer is located; if the use of such a location indicator is sufficient to allow the reference to become a source identifier, consumer confusion is likely and accordingly, it would not be a fair use of the mark. Based on the regular business customs, if a manufacturer wants to convey to consumers the relationship between the products and the manufacturing place, all it needs to do is to include the manufacturing address in appropriate place on the product packaging. Even in situations where the manufacturers want to draw special attention to the manufacturing origin of the products, it can simply include the county or city name. In the subject case, the defendant already included the address for its manufacturing facility in the appropriate spot on the product packaging – Tang Gou County, Guan-Nan City, Jiangsu Province – and such information alone was sufficient to indicate the product origin. Despite this, the defendant used a larger font in the center area of the product packaging for the TANG GOU characters (the COUNTY word was purposefully left out). Also, the defendant used the TANG GOU characters in the same traditional style as that included in the disputed trademark registration. The above was sufficient to show that the defendant's use of the TANG GOU characters had exceeded the necessary boundary to simply indicate the product origin; it was therefore not a proper use of the location indicator.

A location reference can indicate product origin or the location of the users. A trademark inclusive of a location reference is therefore inherently weaker than a coined mark in terms of the overall distinctiveness. In fact, a trademark inclusive of a location reference is likely to result in registrant's monopoly over the location indicator and therefore constitutes unfair competition where other competitors in the same industry also need but are otherwise prevented to use the location indicator. This concept is fully illustrated in the administrative trademark litigation brought by Zhejiang Province Food Company (the "***Food Company***") against the Trademark Office of the SAIC ("***China Trademark Office***"). The Food Company was the trademark owner of the "JIN HUA BRAND JIN HUA HAM & Design" mark (Registration Number 130131); the registration covered Class 29 products such as ham. On September 24, 2003, Zhejiang Provincial Administration for Industry and Commerce ("***Zhejiang AIC*** ") sought guidance from China Trademark Office so as to resolve the trademark infringement dispute between the Food Company and Jin Hua City Jin Hua Ham Manufacturing Company. Specifically, Zhejiang AIC requested China Trademark Office to respond to the issue as to whether or not the use of JIN HUA HAM was a fair use. (Note: JIN HUA is a location indicator in Chinese). In its request, Zhejiang AIC attached seven product packaging for the JIN HUA ham that it sees as fair use and a request concerning the same issue. China Trademark Office issued a response titled "Fair Use regarding JIN HUA HAM" (No. 64; 2004) (the "***Response***").[233] In the Response, China Trademark Office pointed out that the characters "JIN HUA HAM" was in fact a registered

233. The Response is an official instruction of a superior office to a lower authority.

trademark that belonged to the Food Company. Its registration number was 130131; the Food Company's exclusive rights over this trademark were protected by the law in China. Based on the official request from the Zhejiang AIC and the materials included in the request, China Trademark Office believed that the uses in the following three forms "JIN HUA SPECIAL PRODUCT HAM," "[TRADEMARK] JIN HUA HAM," and "JIN HUA [TRADEMARK] HAM" were fair use as discussed under Article 49 of the Trademark Implementation Regulations. Meanwhile, in practice, the use of the above phrases should involve the same font, color, size, character sequence as the rest of the descriptions included on the product packaging; in other words, the above phrases should not be used in any prominent way more so than the rest of the descriptions on product packaging. China Trademark Office instructed Zhejiang AIC to rely on the Response, and instruct other junior administrative authorities for industry and commerce in Zhejiang Province accordingly and conveyed the same message to the Food Company. The Food Company decided to challenge the Response and filed a lawsuit. In the lawsuit, the Food Company's registered trademark was "JIN HUA HAM." The JIN HUA characters in the trademark were in fact a location reference at and above the county level.[234] The trademark, JIN HUA HAM, was therefore indicative of the location origin and meaning. However, the Food Company's trademark was approved for registration prior to the current Trademark Law and it continued to be a valid trademark. In the trademark, JIN HUA was a location indicator, HAM was a generic product reference for the underlying product. Accordingly, any third party can use the term JIN HUA, and HAM. In the court's view, the Response issued by China Trademark Office provided a proper guidance regarding the way to use the Food Company's Trademark; the guidance discussed in the Response was in full compliance with the trademark registration principle as articulated in the Trademark Law. Accordingly, China Trademark Office's decision regarding the three phrases noted in its Response did not violate the law. The court rejected the Food Company's litigation request.

b. Use of a Mark for Its Primary Meaning.

If a trademark is composed of a term and the term has its own meaning, a third party's use of the mark based on its primary meaning should be regarded as fair use. The trademark registrant owns exclusive rights associated with the term as a trademark; however, the registrant does not have monopoly over the term. The above concept is fully illustrated in two trademark infringement lawsuits involving the "MILLENNIUM DRAGON" trademark in Chinese characters.[235] The plaintiff in the two cases was a Chinese company named Xuzhou Han-Du Development Company ("***Han-Du***"); Han-Du owned trademark rights over "MILLENNIUM DRAGON" in Chinese characters

234. In 2002, the AQSIQ (General Administration of Quality Supervision Inspection and Quarantine of PRC) authorized and published the protection to the JIN HUA HAM, for its products from the origin, of fifteen counties, cities or districts; in 2003, AQSIQ published the registration of fifty-five companies' application of using the special mark of the origin sign of the place of JIN HUA HAM, including the Changshan County, Zhejiang Province Ham Company.

235. Case Index: Jiangsu Province High People's Court, Su Min San Zhong Zi [2003] No. 025, and Beijing High People's Court, Gao Zhi Chu Zi [2000] No. 37.

covering Class 9 products such as televisions and cameras. Although Han-Du had invested heavily to promote its MILLENNIUM DRAGON in Chinese character trademark, the promotion did not involve using the mark directly on Class 9 registered products; Han-Du did not manufacture any products bearing the MILLENNIUM DRAGON in Chinese character mark either. The first defendant was a Chinese company called TCL Group Limited Company ("***TCL***"). TCL had started an advertisement campaign titled "MILLENNIUM DRAGON GREAT MOVEMENT" so as to promote its television products. TCL had used extensively the Chinese characters and design associated with its "MILLENNIUM DRAGON" campaign on newspaper, promotional materials and commercial banners between December 18, 1999 and January 30, 2000; despite its extensive use of the "MILLENNIUM DRAGON" characters and the associated design, TCL never used these characters on its television products or product packaging - rather, TCL used its registered trademark "TCL" on its products and product packaging. The second defendant was a Japanese company called "(Japan) Olympus Optics Corporation" ("***Olympus***"). In its WIDE80 series cameras which were manufactured by Olympus, such cameras came with its trademark OLYMPUS and their model, WIDE 80, in the center parts of the front panel of these cameras. However, the cameras also came with the following characters, "MILLENNIUM DRAGON," and the associated design on their left bottom corner which were also shown on the cameras themselves. In addition to the above, the exterior packaging for these cameras were imprinted with the same characters "MILLENNIUM DRAGON" and design as those shown on the cameras themselves. In fact, the same "MILLENNIUM DRAGON" characters were also included in the certificates for these products. Han-Du believed the two companies' use of the "MILLENNIUM DRAGON" characters had infringed its trademark rights and filed separate lawsuits with the courts in Jiangsu and Beijing respectively. There were two key issues in the trademark infringement case. Issue One: whether or not the term - MILLENNIUM DRAGON - had any additional meaning other than that included in the trademark that belonged to Han-Du. The year 2000 was a dragon year in the Chinese culture and it was also a millennium; the year 2000 was therefore a Millennium Dragon year. Issue Two: whether or not the two defendants' use of the MILLENNIUM DRAGON characters were fair use. The way TCL used these characters as included for its MILLENNIUM DRAGON GREAT MOVEMENT campaign involved descriptive use of these characters; it was therefore a fair use of the phrase. Furthermore, TCL did not include these characters on its TV products or product packaging; rather, TCL used its registered trademark - TCL - on its products and packaging. In light of the above, it was unlikely that consumers would perceive the MILLENNIUM DRAGON characters in TCL's advertisement campaign as a trademark; TCL's use of these characters did not involve using them as a trademark. On the other hand, Olympus directly used the MILLENNIUM DRAGON characters on its cameras, boxes for camera and product certificates; although Olympus still included its registered trademark on the above, it was very likely that consumers would be misled into believing that MILLENNIUM DRAGON was one of the subbrands for the company's primary trademark: OLYMPUS. The second defendant's use of these characters had therefore involved using them as a trademark. In light of the above, the court did not believe TCL's use of the characters infringed upon Han-Du's trademark rights; on the other hand, Olympus' use of these characters did infringe upon Han-Du's trademark.[236]

c. Indicative Use of One's Own Mark.

One's own mark includes a natural person's name and a legal entity's trade name. A natural person or a corporate entity has civil rights over its name or trade name; accordingly, it has rights to use such a name under the law without any unlawful interference from others. As for an "indicative use," it refers to the use of one's name or a company's trade name on the products so as to indicate its identity; such use is different from that where a name or company name is being used as a trademark.

i. A Natural Person's Use of Its Own Name.

"Name right" refers to the rights that a natural person has so as to determine, change and use its name. A name includes both the official formal name as reflected on the residence booklet as well as the "unofficial" names such as a person's stage name and pen name. The use right is one of the primary rights in connection with an individual's personal name rights – it involves situations where a natural person has the rights to use his or her name in accordance with the law or allows others to use his or her name. Such rights have two aspects – active use and passive use. Active use of one's name rights involves marking one's own name on physical items so as to indicate the ownership information or wearing the name tag or using one's own name so as to identify him or herself from other members in a group. Passive use of the personal name rights includes the rights to refuse disclosing one's name in certain particular circumstances. In today's society, a person's name especially those of the celebrities has a tremendous amount of commercial value. A person's name is gradually becoming "commercialized;" it can in fact be valued and included as one's personal assets and

236. Jiangsu High People's Court, Su Min San Zhong Zi [2003] No. 025. In this decision, Jiangsu High court rejected the claims of Han-Du. Beijing High People's Court, Gao Zhi Chu Zi [2000] No. 37 ruled: 1. order Olympus to stop infringement acts immediately; 2. order Olympus to make a public apology on People's Daily for its infringement of trademark right to Han-Du in thirty days from the day the ruling becoming effective. (The content of the apology has to be approved by the court. If not to perform, the court will publish the main part of this judgment on the People Daily and the cost will be paid by Olympus.); 3. order Olympus to compensate for the economic loss to Han-Du, of RMB 250,000. The order 1 (to stop infringement) of this judgment is consistent with the Taiwan law for the demand for the stoppage; order 2 (public apology) has a same effect of Taiwan law's credibility of return; order 3 is legal compensation. The court found the act of Olympus did infringe upon Han-Du's trademark; thus, the order 1 (to stop infringement) was in conformity with the law. However, since Han-Du never used the trademark "MILLENNIUM DRAGON" on the cameras, thus the trademarks never acted as a source indicator, nor gained any goodwill, the use of "MILLENNIUM DRAGON" by Olympus would not cause the consumers confusion, with no possibility of taking the goodwill from the Han-Du's trademark. That is, the orders 2 and 3 (public apology and legal compensation) lack the legal ground.

has merchandizing rights associated with it. Accordingly, a natural person has the rights to allow others to be engaged in commercial use of his or her own name. This type of use is therefore based on a person's name rights – such use falls under the category of fair use so long as the use does not involve using the name as a trademark.

The above concept is fully illustrated in the trademark infringement case brought by an individual (Han Chen), against An Hui Old Well Sai-Te Shopping Company ("***Shopping Company***"), Hefei Parkson Xiaoyao Square Co., Ltd. ("***Hefei Parkson***") and Guangzhou Bai-Yun Mountain Sports Clothing Company ("***Clothing Company***") regarding the companies' use of the plaintiff's registered trademark: "OWEN." The plaintiff registered the OWEN trademark in connection with Class 25 clothing products. The plaintiff later discovered that the shopping malls operated by the Shopping Company, and Hefei Parkson were engaged in the retailing activities of clothing products – such clothing products were imprinted with the mark: "OWEn10." These clothing products were manufactured by the Clothing Company. The plaintiff believed these clothing products infringed its trademark rights and brought a trademark infringement case to the court. The court had reviewed the case along with the submitted evidence and noted that the front part of the clothing manufactured by the Clothing Company was imprinted with the following two Chinese characters – YIN BAO. YIN BAO was a registered trademark and it belonged to Wu-Mu-Bu-Luo Company; the back of these clothes at issue did include the term "OWEn10." The number 10 in fact occupied approximately 80% of the entire mark. The court examined the promotional materials for the clothing products and noted that the majority were about pictures and images of an English soccer star Owen and his soccer shirt showing Number Ten. The issue in this case was whether or not the Clothing Company's use of the term "OWEn" was trademark use or personal name use involving the soccer player's name. If the use fell under the category of a trademark use, the Clothing Company would be deemed infringing upon the plaintiff's trademark rights; conversely, if the use involved use of a personal name, it would not be an infringement to the plaintiff's trademark rights. Based on the way the mark "OWEn10" was written on the back of a shirt, it was in fact part of the industry norm for clothes especially sports shirts to show the name of the famous player and their numbers in a team; this was also one of the primary ways to promote clothing products in the sports industry. Although the clothes manufactured by the Clothing Company did include the OWEn mark, most consumers would associate the term with the star soccer player in the UK as opposed to the trademark that belonged to the plaintiff; the use of OWEn term was mainly to promote the clothing products through the achievement and commercial reputation of Owen as a soccer player. In other words, the OWEn use was not intended nor used as a trademark. The primary source identifier on the clothing products in the case were in fact the registered trademark, YIN BAO, as shown in the front of the shirts. As the first level of court pointed out, "the defendant used its licensed mark, a famous brand, and put it on the prominent place of its products. The term at issue in this case was OWEn10 which was composed of both English letters and the number 10. The number 10 had occupied approximately 80% of the entire design and the defendant's promotional materials featured exclusively the English soccer player, Owen. Accordingly, the Clothing Company's use of the term was related to the commercial influence of the soccer player, as opposed to the plaintiff's trademark." Simply put, the defendant's use of the OWEn mark did not fall under the category of a trademark use; the court dismissed the plaintiff's infringement claim.[237]

ii. A Corporation's Use of Its Company Name.

"Trade name right" refers to the rights that a corporate has so as to determine, change, use and assign its company name. A company name should include the following elements (listed in the exact sequence): administrative districts, trade name, industry or special features of its operation, and the corporate structure.[238] Among these elements, the followings are for public/government use and accordingly, they are not capable to function as a source identifier allowing the average consumers to identify the specific corporation: administrative districts, industry or special features of its operation, and the corporate structure. The only element that is capable to allow the public to identify the corporate is therefore its trade name. A trade name refers to each company's name so as to allow average consumers and the public to tell retailers and manufacturers apart. Article 1 Section 1 of the Interpretation of the Supreme People's Court Concerning the Application of Laws in the Trial of Cases of Civil Disputes Arising from Trademarks points out that *"It should be deemed a trademark infringement if a company's trade name includes the same or similar elements of a third party's registered trademark, the trade name is used in connection with the same or similar products as those of the registered trademark, and the company has engaged in prominent use of such a trade name."* In the subject case, although Tao Qin had obtained the trade name registration for "Guan-Nan County Tang Gou Qu Spirit Factory" through the appropriate legal channel, the company name nevertheless included the same TANG GOU characters which were identical to the characters included in the Composite Mark. Furthermore, the products manufactured by Tao Qin were identical to those covered in the two plaintiffs' registered trademark. Under such circumstances, in order to prevent consumer confusion, Tao Qin should have included the full name of its company trade name on the product packaging in a clear way and as required by the law; in other words, Tao Qin should not be engaged in any prominent use of the Tang Gou characters in its trade name. Although Tao Qin already included its company name in

237. Case Index: An Hui Province Hefei Intermediate People's Court, He Min San Chu Zi [2002] No. 94. The plaintiff appealed and in the second instance, the parties settled as: 1. Clothing Company can use the combination trademark "OWEn10" in the legal scope, but not "OWEN" trademark. 2. Clothing Company voluntarily compensate the plaintiff of the reasonable cost of requiring legal remedy, of RMB 25,000. The money should be paid one time fulfilled at the time of the service of the mediation agreements. 3. The court acceptance fee of the first instance: RMB 10,510, and second instance: RMB 12,612 should be borne by the plaintiff. 4. The parties had no other disputes. *See* as settlement: An Hui Province High People's Court, Wan Min San Zhong Zi [2003] No. 27.
238. Article 7 of Provisions on Administration of Enterprise Name Registration. Article 9 of Measures for the Implementation of Administration of Enterprise Name Registration.

the expected place in its product packaging, it purposefully used the same TANG GOU characters in a prominent way when it identified its Tang Gou Qu Spirit Factory in the center part of its product packaging – the defendant's use of the characters exceeded the reasonable use of its company name.

d. Indicative Use of Others' Mark.

"Indicative use" refers to the use of third parties' trademarks which are necessary so as to explain or indicate the nature, functionality or purpose of one's own products. Most of the indicative use appears on advertisements involving products and its parts, products and its associated maintenance services, as well as comparative advertisements. A classic example is the advertisement for cell phone chargers – if such cell phone chargers involve a specific type of cell phone, say Nokia-97, the most effective way for the manufacturers and retailers to inform the consumers the specific type of cell phone their chargers are for is to use the trademark of the specific product and their model – in this case, NOKIA, and Serial No. 97. Another classic example involving indicative use of others' marks is the provision of maintenance services of certain specific products. For example, if a service provider is focused on providing maintenance and repair services for SONY branded televisions; it would result in unfair competition if the owner of the SONY trademark is able to restrict or forbid the service provider to use its trademark in these circumstances.

Although the Trademark Law does not include specific guidance on indicative use of a third party's trademark, such use has long been recognized based on the basic trademark principle – honesty and integrity – as well as the associated commercial customs. The above recognition was reflected in Notification No. 195 issued by the SAIC of the PRC on July 27, 1995. In Notification No. 195 titled "Notification Forbidden Unauthorized Use of Others' Registered Trademarks by Auto Parts Retail Stores, and Automobile Maintenance Stores," it specifically recognized that an unauthorized use of a third party's trademark – such as the use of domestic or international automobile registered trademarks (e.g., "MERCEDES" or "JEEP" in Chinese characters or the registered design marks) on the prominent place in the stores' signage – by the auto part retail stores and automobile maintenance stores and such a use would objectively lead to consumer confusion into believing that the store and the trademark owner is somehow connected should be deemed a trademark infringement. With respect to this type of infringement, Notification No. 195 further pointed out that "an auto part retail store or automobile repair/maintenance store should not be allowed to use or include a third party's registered trademark as their signage ... However, in order to indicate the scope of repair / maintenance services or the type of auto parts the stores provide, the stores are allowed to include a third party's registered trademark in a directly descriptive way such as "our store sells ABC auto parts" or "our store provides repairs and maintenance services for ABC branded cars." The above uses, as discussed in

Notification No. 195, were allowed so long as the use of a third party's trademark was represented in the same font as the rest of the statements, was not presented in any prominent way, and the use did not involve stand-alone use of a third party's registered trademarks (either word marks or design marks).[239]

239. State Administration for Industry and Commerce, Gong Shang Biao Zi [1996] No. 157, "Notification Forbidden Unauthorized Use of Others' Registered Trademarks by Auto Parts Retail Stores, and Automobile Maintenance Stores" expanded the scope of "indicative use" to a "goods sales website and service site," and pointed out "unauthorized use of 'ABC exclusive sales,' 'ABC exclusive business' or 'ABC exclusive repair,' and such a use would objectively lead to consumer confusion into believing that the store and the trademark owner is closely connected and cause a misrecognition of its origin" would damage the trademark exclusive right and should be banned according to the law.

www.ingramcontent.com/pod-product-compliance
Lightning Source LLC
LaVergne TN
LVHW020002031026
849161LV00023B/824
* 9 7 8 9 0 4 1 1 6 8 3 6 8 *